Social Support,
Life Events, and Depression

SOCIAL SUPPORT, LIFE EVENTS, AND DEPRESSION

Edited by

Nan Lin
DEPARTMENT OF SOCIOLOGY
STATE UNIVERSITY OF NEW YORK AT ALBANY
ALBANY, NEW YORK

Alfred Dean
DEPARTMENT OF PSYCHIATRY
ALBANY MEDICAL COLLEGE
ALBANY, NEW YORK

Walter M. Ensel
DEPARTMENT OF PSYCHIATRY
ALBANY MEDICAL COLLEGE
ALBANY, NEW YORK

1986

ACADEMIC PRESS, INC.

Harcourt Brace Jovanovich, Publishers

Orlando   San Diego   New York   Austin
London   Montreal   Sydney   Tokyo   Toronto

ACADEMIC PRESS, INC.
Orlando, Florida 32887

United Kingdom Edition published by
ACADEMIC PRESS INC. (LONDON) LTD.
24–28 Oval Road, London NW1 7DX

LIBRARY OF CONGRESS CATALOGING-IN-PUBLICATION DATA

Main entry under title:

Social support, life events, and depression.

   Includes index.
   1. Depression, Mental—Social aspects.   2. Depression,
Mental—Social aspects—Research.   3. Stress (Psychology)
—Social aspects.   4. Stress (Psychology)—Social
aspects—Research.   5. Mental health—Social aspects.
I. Lin, Nan.   II. Dean, Alfred, Date-   II. Ensel,
Walter M.
RC537.S59   1986   362.2'042   85-11062
ISBN 0-12-450660-7 (alk. paper)
ISBN 0-12-450661-5 (paperback)

PRINTED IN THE UNITED STATES OF AMERICA

86 87 88 89   9 8 7 6 5 4 3 2 1

Contents

3   Study Design and Data

WALTER M. ENSEL

PART II   MEASURING DEPRESSION, LIFE EVENTS, AND PSYCHOLOGICAL RESOURCES

4   Measuring Depression: The CES-D Scale

WALTER M. ENSEL

5   Measuring Life Events

MARK TAUSIG

9 Measuring Community and Network Support

NAN LIN, MARY Y. DUMIN, AND MARY WOELFEL

PART IV CONSTRUCTING AND ESTIMATING BASIC MODELS

10 Modeling the Effects of Social Support

NAN LIN

PART V EXPLORING BASIC MODELS

11 The Age Structure and the Stress Process

NAN LIN, WALTER M. ENSEL, AND ALFRED DEAN

Contributors

Numbers in parentheses indicate the pages on which the authors' contributions begin.

ALFRED DEAN (3, 97, 117, 213), Department of Psychiatry, Albany Medical College, Albany, New York 12208

MARY Y. DUMIN (153, 283), Department of Sociology, State University of New York at Albany, Albany, New York 12222

WALTER M. ENSEL (31, 51, 129, 213, 231, 249), Department of Psychiatry, Albany Medical College, Albany, New York 12208

STEPHEN C. LIGHT (307), Department of Sociology, State University of New York at Albany, Albany, New York 12222

NAN LIN (17, 153, 173, 213, 283, 307, 333), Department of Sociology, State University of New York at Albany, Albany, New York 12222

MARK TAUSIG (71, 117, 267), Department of Sociology, University of Akron, Akron, Ohio 44325

MARY WOELFEL (129, 153, 283, 307), New York State Department of Health, Bureau of Communicable Diseases, AIDS Unit, Albany, New York 12237

Preface

In the spring of 1976, we, along with our colleagues from the Department of Sociology at the State University of New York at Albany and Albany Medical College, met to discuss ways in which the two institutions could cooperate in research and teaching. A series of further meetings made it clear to us that we shared a common interest: the understanding of the social and structural factors involved in the process of maintaining and promoting mental health. We were convinced that it was an important research area and that we should explore it together.

After a thorough survey of the literature, it became clear to us that the one area deserving considerable attention was the way in which social factors operated in the process of distress. An identifiable research area emerged, focusing on such concepts as social integration, social environment, family support, and social support. Yet, little conceptual or empirical work had been conducted. We felt that a concerted and systematic effort in teasing out the various components of social support and how they affected the stress process would be an invaluable contribution to the field.

This volume describes the research experiences and results of a team that we have been working with since 1977 to look into the social process of mental health. This research program has provided an arena for opportunities to explore many topics concerning the relationships among social support, life events, and mental health (primarily depressive symptoms). It further allowed us to train many young medical sociologists and to learn how to work as a team. We feel it has been fruitful on all accounts.

The volume is organized in such a way that a single theme continues throughout the book: How does social support, along with life events, affect depressive symptoms? The organizing theme allows individual authors to explore specific topics in theoretical and methodological terms of their choosing. This resulted from a careful consideration of the alternative: namely, allowing a single theoretical and methodological framework to dictate the volume. We ruled against this alternative because we felt that such a design would not do justice to a field with such rich and diverse conceptual and methodological approaches.

This book is intended primarily for researchers, scientists, professionals, and instructors who are interested in examining both conceptual and methodological issues regarding social factors in mental health. Thus, those working in the area of public health, social and behavioral sciences, and medical professions may find this book useful. Because of the way we have organized the chapters, it is possible for researchers and practitioners alike to select and read chapters pertinent to their specific interests.

Acknowledgments

The research program would not have been possible without the funding support provided by the Center for Epidemiologic Studies of the National Institute of Mental Health, through a series of research grants (MH30301 and MH36962). We are very grateful to Ben Locke, Shirley Margolis, and their staff for their able administrations of the proposals and grants.

It goes without saying that many colleagues have provided valuable information, communication, and challenges throughout our work. We would specially like to mention Jerome Myers, Len Pearlin, Ronald Kessler, Peggi Thoits, Blair Wheaton, Carol Aneshensel, Susan Gore, John Eckenrode, Jay Turner, and Baqar Husaini. They have provided stimulations and responses to our ideas and publications and shared theirs with us. We respected their views—even when we disagreed. However, none of them has seen a significant portion of the manuscript.

Many others have participated in the research program and their contributions were all significant. We are grateful to Ron Simeone, Irene Farrell, Nancy Mason, Barbra Carpenzano, and Delina Bartlett for their able participation and support while on the staff of the program.

Finally, we are deeply indebted to Sandy Johnson, whose technical and administrative skills, persistence, and tolerance have made the completion of the manuscript possible.

Part I ⎯⎯⎯⎯⎯⎯⎯⎯⎯⎯⎯⎯⎯⎯⎯⎯⎯⎯⎯⎯

IDENTIFYING BASIC ISSUES
AND APPROACH

The first part of this book begins, in Chapter 1, with a historical perspective on the key concepts to be dealt with in the book. It traces the development of the concepts and theories of social epidemiology and locates the study in the proper research scheme. The chapter concludes with an introduction to the organization of the chapters in the book. Chapter 2 focuses on the definitional and conceptual issues associated with social support. It reviews alternative views presently available in the literature and offers the definitions and the theoretical framework used in this volume. The third chapter introduces the design of the study and the nature of the data to be analyzed.

The intention of these three chapters is to set the background and scope of the study, which is part of a continuing research program. In so doing, its boundaries and limitations as well as its features are delineated.

1 ————————————————————————————

Social Support in
Epidemiological Perspective

ALFRED DEAN

INTRODUCTION

It has been said that human behavior cannot be adequately understood without an historical and contextual perspective. Such a perspective may deepen the reader's appreciation of the research described in
this monograph. However brief, this chapter provides such a perspective on the present study. The research reported here is based on a two-
stage survey of a representative sample of the population in the Albany
area of upstate New York, an investigation of the effects of social support and life events on the occurrence of depression. This is a study in
psychosocial epidemiology—a field rooted in ancient medicine as well
as in early sociology, one that calls for an alliance between the social
and the psychological approaches and their links to the medical
sciences.

Epidemiology is the study of the occurrence and distribution of diseases in populations, originally directed at mass outbreaks of diseases,
or epidemics. Suitably enough, this interest is traced back to Hippocrates (Brock, 1929). As the classical father of modern medicine, Hippocrates clearly recognized the role of social and other environmental fac-

3

tors in the occurrence of diseases. He noted that the conditions under which diseases occur provide clues as to their origins, and he formulated the principle of multiple causation. Hippocrates, among other Greek physicians, also believed that individuals may be differently predisposed to diseases, due to such factors as constitution and diet. Furthermore, he brought this perspective to the practice of clinical medicine as well as to epidemiology. Yet however ancient such a framework may be, such a comprehensive framework has not typically characterized research on stress and illness. However, this approach may hold distinct promise for a multisystem, multidisciplinary model.

If the study of its social conditions may illuminate the origins of disease, the converse is also true. This principle was clearly at the foundation of Durkheim's study of suicide in 1897 (Durkheim, 1951). In this classic study Durkheim expected suicide rates to reflect his central interest: the nature and functions of various forms of social integration in society. Quite possibly, this study may have been the first work in modern sociological epidemiology and perhaps, as well, one of the theoretical roots of the current conception of social support and related concepts. In any case, Durkheim was the inspiration for several generations of social scientists who have attempted to examine the relationship of social systems to the occurrence of psychiatric disorders. A number of the most influential of these studies involved the collaboration of sociologists and psychiatrists, illustrating Schwab and Schwab's (1978) characterization of social psychiatry: "Social psychiatry is a three-legged creature; it has one foot in psychiatry, one in the social sciences, and one in epidemiology" (p. 7).

Among the classic studies in this tradition are Faris and Dunham's study of the ecology of mental disorders in urban areas (1939); Hollinghsead and Redlich's study of social class and mental illness in New Haven (1958), the Midtown Manhattan studies (Srole et al., 1962; Langner and Michael, 1963; Srole, 1975), and the Stirling County studies by Alexander and Dorothea Leighton and their colleagues (A. H. Leighton, 1959; C. Hughes et al., 1960; D. Leighton, Harding, Macklin, MacMillan, and A. H. Leighton, 1963). Each of these studies indelibly illustrates the basic concepts of social-psychiatric epidemiology and contributes to the evolution of major hypotheses, theories, and empirical findings, as well as to the development of methods, measurements, and techniques in the field. Among them, the concept of social stressors emerged perhaps as most evident and central in the formulations of Langner and Michael (1963).

In particular, the work of a physiologist, Hans Selye (1956), gave impetus to the exploration of environmental stressors and their links to disease. In this work, Selye described his three-stage *general adapta-tion syndrome* as a nonspecific stress model that explained mental and physical reactions to stressors and certain *diseases of adaptation.* He noted that animals exposed to a variety of stressors (e.g., cold, heat, trauma) responded in a characteristic pattern. In physiological terms, he described three stages: an *alarm reaction* that occurs immediately after being stressed, a *stage of resistance* that is a response to repeated exposure to a stressful stimulus, and finally a *stage of exhaustion* in the face of persistent stress. Selye demonstrated that the physiological mechanisms involved neuroendocrine responses, primarily activation of the pituitary–adrenal axis. In general, Selye's work gave great scien-tific credibility to the concept of stress as a biological event and pro-vided a link between environmental stimuli and disease. In a 1982 paper titled "History and Present Status of the Stress Concept," Selye himself aptly describes the impact of his early work:

> My *definition of stress* is the *nonspecific* (that is, common) result of *any* demand upon the body, be the effect mental or somatic. The formulation of this definition, based on objective indicators such as bodily and chemical changes that appear after any demand, has brought the subject (so popular now that it is often referred to as "stressology") up from the level of cocktail party chitchat into the domain of science. (p. 7)

Selye (1982) makes it clear that he regards stressors as psychosocial in nature as well as biochemical, and that stress and disease are thus intimately associated with the issue of human adaptation and adjust-ment. He further states,

> One of the first things to bear in mind about stress is that a variety of dissimilar situations—emotional arousal, effort, fatigue, pain, fear, concentration, hu-miliation, loss of blood, and even great and unexpected success—are capable of producing stress; hence, a single factor can, in itself, be pinpointed as the cause of the reaction as such. To understand this point, it is necessary to consider certain facts about human biology. Medical research has shown that while people may face quite different problems, in some respects their bodies respond in a stereotyped pattern; identical biochemical changes enable us to cope with any type of increased demand on vital activity. . . . In all forms of life, it would seem that there are common pathways that must mediate any attempt to adapt to environmental conditions and sustain life. (pp. 7–8)

There is growing anatomical, physiological, and neurochemical evi-dence that cognitive–affective responses to stress can alter the func-tioning of hypothalamic–pituitary pathways that modulate endocrine, autonomic, and immune processes. Alteration of these systems and of the brain are implicated in the onset of disease (Zegans, 1982). These findings thus challenge social and behavioral scientists as well as clinicians to further identify the nature of potential stressors.

Although it is possible to identify a variety of social stressors, research on personal life changes and illness onset has clearly dominated the field since the mid-1960s. Unquestionably, the hypothesis that stressful life events may be implicated in the etiology of various diseases has earlier historical roots; these include clinical observation, the work of Walter B. Cannon on the relationship of bodily changes to emotions, and the psychobiology of Adolf Meyer. Rabkin and Struening (1976) traced the formal recognition of this area of research to the 1949 Conference on Life Stress and Bodily Disease, sponsored by the Association for Research on Nervous and Mental Diseases.

However, recent research in this area has largely been stimulated and assisted by the development of life-events scales stemming from the work of Holmes, Rahe, and their colleagues (Holmes and Rahe, 1967; Holmes and Masuda, 1974). The current interest in the epidemiological significance of social-support systems stems from the critical appraisal of a decade's research utilizing such scales, on the one hand, and growing evidence of the potential stress-buffering functions of social support, on the other (Rabkin and Struening, 1976; Dean and Lin, 1977; Dohrenwend and Dohrenwend, 1978). The research program on which this monograph is based and the many facets of investigation discussed in its various chapters stem from a critical assessment of the literature done in the mid-1970s; the evolution of our own work; and the remarkable proliferation of inquiries into the nature and functions of social support during the past half dozen years.

Next, we attempt to briefly characterize the major research questions, problems, and methodological considerations that have grown up in this field and that provide the basis for the various activities described in this book.

The kinds of life events and changes typically measured by life-events scales include such items as marriage, divorce, death of a spouse, and loss of a job. In contrast to natural disasters or extreme situations, these types of events are rather frequent experiences in the lives of many people. Indeed, many of these events are inevitably experienced by people if they live long enough. For this reason, some investigators have characterized these events as *personal life changes* (Rabkin and Struening, 1976) or *ordinary events* (Dohrenwend and Dohrenwend, 1978). Because the occurrence of physical and psychiatric disorders is also fairly common in human populations, the extent to which such events may induce stress and/or increase the risk of illness has been a matter of considerable theoretical interest. Holmes and Rahe (1967) considered these events to be social stressors in that they signify or imply changes in an individual's life patterns. Indeed, these investigators regarded such events as stressful to the extent that they required social readjustment (Holmes and Masuda, 1974). A major conclusion that can be drawn from over a decade and a half of epidemiological studies using life-events scales is that life events are associated with a wide variety of physical and psychiatric disorders. Life events are associated with symptoms of undifferentiated psychiatric illness (Gurin, Veroff, and Feld, 1960; Langner and Michael, 1963; D. Leighton et al., 1963; Myers, Lindenthal, and Pepper, 1971, 1975; Myers and Pepper, 1972); depression (Hudgens, 1974; Paykel, 1974; Paykel and Dienelt, 1971; Paykel et al., 1969; Paykel, Prusoff, and Tanner, 1976); and suicide attempts (Paykel, 1974). Life events have also been shown to be associated with the occurrence of heart disease, childhood leukemia (Holmes and Masuda, 1974), and other disorders, illnesses, or symptoms (Dohrenwend and Dohrenwend, 1974a, 1978; Gunderson and Rahe, 1974). These important findings could be fairly drawn from a critical assessment of an extensive literature, but there were serious theoretical, methodological, and empirical limitations in existing studies that, as recently as 1978, led Dohrenwend and Dohrenwend to properly conclude: "We have . . . a body of research results which indicate that life events are associated with a wide range of disorders and distress, but do not provide a clear picture of the nature and strength of this relationship" (p. 9).

Although the evidence indicated that there was a significant correlation between life events and subsequent illnesses, the magnitude of this relationship was generally modest. As Rabkin and Struening (1976) noted, correlation coefficients were typically below .30, indicating that, at best, life events might account for 9% of the variance in illness. In popular terms, these findings were consistent with the view that most people do not get sick from routine life events. In any case, the modest relationship between life events and the occurrence of illness dramatized the overly simplistic character of the life-events–illness model and increased the salience of the question: "What makes individuals differentially *vulnerable* to illness in the face of potential stressors?" The Dohrenwends (1978) therefore emphasized:

> Whether we gain much or little [etiological information from future life stress studies] will depend, we believe, on how well we deal with an important substantive issue that has not been systematically investigated in research to date on the effects of stressful life events. . . . This issue concerns factors that mediate the impact of stressful life events. (p. 12)

In general, it was recognized that individual psychological attributes, constitutional features, social factors, or other contextual variables can affect the impact of life events on the occurrence of illness. In particular, several leading social epidemiologists pointed to the importance of examining the joint effects of life events and social supports in their pioneering studies (Cassel, 1974; Kaplan, 1975; Kaplan, Cassel, and Gore, 1977).

In 1976, we critically reviewed the highly suggestive evidence that social support might buffer stress and reduce the risk of illness (Dean and Lin, 1977). Although we will not again review such studies here, they included studies of psychiatric casualities among combat soldiers (Shils and Janowitz, 1948; Swank, 1949; Titmuss, 1959). A now classic paradigm was illustrated in the work of Nuckolls, Cassel, and Kaplan (1972), who demonstrated the joint effects of stressful life events and "psychosocial assets" on complications of pregnancy, but observed that these variables had no independent effects. We noted that life events, social support, and illness exhibited a variety of complex inter-relationships and sequences that called for longitudinal research in the future. We also declared then that there was need in future studies to utilize large representative samples of community populations, to examine additional approaches to the scaling of life events and measures of illness, to apply multivariate statistical models, and to control for various sociodemographic factors. But the main point is that only 7 years ago social support had been a largely neglected variable in the stressor–illness model.

Thus grounded in suggestive evidence, theoretical relevance, and a conviction of its intuitive validity, the enthusiasm for systematic inclusion of social support in epidemiological modeling became infectious. Interest in this model was further stimulated by a widespread conviction among clinicians, epidemiologists, and behavioral scientists alike that further research in this area could have important practical implications for intervention. Indeed, it was believed that social-support strategies might be especially efficacious, given the problems and limitations in manipulating the constitutional and/or personality factors in illness and its prevention. Actually, the applied importance of social-support systems had already been advanced on the basis of clinical conviction and the work of Caplan and Killilea (1976). Furthermore, the Community Support Systems Task Force of the President's Commission on Mental Health (1978) pointed to the immediate implications of the existing literature for mental-health programs, teaching, and research.

The phenomenal growth of research on social support clearly indi-

cated that this was indeed becoming a central interest in the epidemiological modeling of stress and illness. But such research also
reflected the persistence of a basic issue: the measurement of social
support and the refinements of definition and conceptualization inte-
gral to such an effort. In 1977, we noted:

> Social support is thus considered the most important concept for future study
> and it also presents the most difficult task for instrumentation. A thorough
> search in the social and psychological inventories of scales has failed to un-
> cover any measures of social support with either known and/or acceptable
> properties of reliability and validity. (Dean and Lin, pp. 408–409)

The burgeoning effort to develop social-support models has been
paralleled by a proliferation of proposed scales. By the same token, a
critical literature has emerged addressing basic issues of definition and
measurement. Because these matters are fundamental, complex, and
developmental in nature, they are given considerable attention in this
book.

CONCEPTUALIZATION

One approach to clarifying social support is not only to critique the
various concepts in the literature, but to examine the conceptualizations expressed or implied in various social-support scales that have
been developed. The next chapter takes such an approach and provides
a heuristic classification of social-support elements. It proposes three
elements of social interactions central to the concept of social support:
(1) that these interactions are either actual (objective) or perceived (subjective), (2) that they involve at least three layers of relationships (community, network, and intimate), and (3) that they provide instrumental
and/or expressive functions. The scheme provides a way to compare
and contrast various conceptualizations and definitions in the literature, as well as a frame of reference for the specific scales examined
and/or applied in this study. Although the specific social-support dimensions and scales used in the investigation reported in this book are
necessarily limited, they do fairly represent the various types of social
support discussed in the literature.

Further conceptualization of social support links it to the notion of
social resources. Sociological research has differentiated the utility of
both strong and weak social ties (Granovetter, 1973, 1974). Strong ties
can be characterized as sharings of similar social-psychological characteristics and life styles. Lin (1982) argues that because mental health is

a psychological outcome, resources provided by strong ties are pivotal in the support role. Although more narrowly focused on the source of support, this conceptualization converges with the inner layer of relationship (intimates and confidants) of the aforementioned approach and adds further theoretical richness to the conceptualization of social support.

MEASUREMENTS

After conceptualizing social support (Chapter 2) and briefly introducing our research design and data (Chapter 3), we proceed to our work on measurement, modeling, and specification of social support. Whatever the conceptualization and content of any given social-support measure, a viable scale or measure should be subjected to several basic examinations: (1) it should be subjected to analysis to identify its dimensions, (2) it should be examined for its reliability and validity, and (3) it should be theoretically significant and phenomenologically revealing. These properties should encourage its use in replication or convergent studies, and thereby promote cumulative knowledge. Thus, although several types of social-support scales are explored here, each is extensively examined in terms of its conceptualization, operationalization, and psychometric properties.

The examination of the various social-support scales is guided by our conceptual analysis of social support. Thus, we begin by exploring the support activities provided by the confidants and intimates.

The inner layer of social relations, ego's confidants, we argue, supplies the most significant support. Although this point of view prevails in the literature, it is not clear what aspects of the confidant relationship provide the most effective support. Some have argued that frequency of interactions is a good measure, whereas others consider intensity and intimacy to be more relevant. This dichotomy of quantity and quality is by no means clear-cut, because the two are not independent of one another; nevertheless, it is important to examine separately the various features of confidant support. Our approach to scale development has been first to assess the scale properties of measures that have demonstrated empirically suggestive relationships to depression or other disorders, such as the confidant scale of Lowenthal and Haven (1968) and the family-support scale utilized by Medalie and Goldbourt (1976). Secondly, we have determined the reliability and validity of measures of confidant relationships that have been proposed but not tested (Kaplan, 1975). Third, we have created and tested scales of instrumental and expressive support, based on our own conceptualizations. The nature and implications of these types of social-support scales are discussed in Chapter 7, "Measuring Intimate Support: The Family and Confidant Relationships" (Dean and Tausig), and Chapter 8, "Measuring the Instrumental and Expressive Functions of Social Support" (Ensel and Woelfel).

Structural and contextual effects on individuals have been documented by many investigators, including Leighton's (1963) seminal work on the effect of community characteristics on health and illness and Brenner's (1973) observation that economic changes lead to changes in a variety of health problems. Taking these leads, Lin, Dumin, and Woelfel, examine how well the subject functions within the community, his/her interactions and satisfaction in the neighborhood, and participation in community organizations (Chapter 9).

Social-network analysis represents a relatively distinct approach to the measurement of social support. The network approach attempts to describe how a person is located in the system of actual or potential social relationships. It examines whether an individual has extensive ties to others (range), whether the ties are extensively interconnected among themselves (connectedness), and whether these ties or links provide help in many areas (multiplexity). Broadly stated, network analysis emphasizes social structure and frequently infers the adequacy of social support from the extensiveness, cohesiveness, or strength of social ties. As exemplified in Berkman and Syme's (1979) 9-year follow-up study of social networks, host resistance, and mortality, the social-network approach has often led to provocative findings. Nonetheless, the links between social-network scales and morbidity and mortality, as well as the links between social-network variables and social support, are often unclear. As we have indicated elsewhere (Lin and Dean, 1984), we believe that networks by themselves do not constitute the core of social support, nor do they supersede the social-support concept. However, network approaches may serve to tap the social dimension of social support. Thus networks may provide a framework within which social support can be explicated.

Whereas the preceding discussion indicates that the measurement of social support is of continuing concern in this field, problems of measuring other model variables are also raised by our investigation. In Chapter 5, Tausig, utilizing the data from our study, addresses a number of important questions that have been raised about life-events scales. These issues include the adequacy of the scope of life-event items, the nature and significance of event clusters, and the possible confounding of various life-event items with dependent variables. He also examines the implications of objective versus subjective estimates of readjustment and the effects of desirable versus undesirable events.

As noted earlier, individual psychological factors may also affect the impact of potential stressors on illness. Just as social support may be conceptualized in terms of social resources, individual psychological attributes have been widely conceptualized as personal resources. In Chapter 6, Dean examines the psychometric properties of two scales that have been conceptualized in these terms: the self-esteem scale (Rosenberg, 1965) and the personal-competence scale (Campbell, Converse, Miller, and Stokes, 1960).

Depression, the ultimate dependent variable in the current investigation, is measured here with the 20-item Center for Epidemiologic Studies Depression Scale, or CES-D (Radloff, 1977). This scale essentially measures the magnitude of depressive symptomatology, based on self-reported symptoms occurring during the week preceding the interview. It is applied here as an interval measure of depressive symptomatology. Although the CES-D and other depressive-symptom scales have been widely applied in epidemiologic studies, it is well recognized that they are not simple indicators of the presence, absence, likelihood, or magnitude of depressive disorder. It seems likely that the CES-D scale taps a normal range of depressive symptoms as well as depressive illness (Myers and Weissman, 1980; Roberts and O'Keefe, 1981). Some investigators have used certain CES-D scores as cutoff points to identify the existence of depressive illness (Husaini et al., 1979). However, this approach also has problems and limitations, such as reflecting "false positives" and "false negatives" (Myers and Weissman, 1980). Scales that would further differentiate and classify depressive disorder require the use of some standardized clinical assessment procedure, such as the NIMH Diagnostic Interview Schedule (DIS) (Robins, Helzer, Croughan, and Ratcliff, 1981). The development of the DIS and its application to community surveys is currently a major thrust of the Epidemiologic Catchment Areas Program sponsored by the National Institute of Mental Health (Locke, Eaton, Regier, and Taube, 1981). While recognizing the limitations of the CES-D scale as a measure of clinical depression, we believe that it remains a distinctly useful measure of depressive symptomatology, particularly when developing models of the effects of psychosocial variables.

A growing accumulation of studies utilizing the CES-D scale will enable comparisons of findings, such as the relationships between depressive symptomatology and life events, social support, and a host of sociodemographic factors. There is also something to be said for studying the relationship of these factors to a range of depressive symptoms as well as to major depressive illness. In the final analysis, future studies will serve to clarify the ways in which the predictors of depressive symptomatology and depressive illness differ or overlap. In Chapter 4, Ensel discusses the history of the CES-D scale, its conceptualization, reliability, validity, and usage. As in the other measurement chapters, he also systematically examines the reliability of the scale as reflected in our own data set, preparatory to modeling this variable in subsequent chapters.

CAUSAL MODELING

Although interest has centered on the possible stress-buffering role of social support, it must be emphasized that the model variables may exhibit complex interrelationships and sequences. Thus nine chapters in this monograph deal with various issues, considerations, and aspects of causal modeling. Various attempts to examine the independent compared to joint effects of life events and social support on depression have been characterized by considerable variation in terminology, research design, and statistical approaches. Few studies have incorporated measures of both social support and psychological resources into the life-events—illness model. To my knowledge, only one other study has utilized a latent-structure analysis with multiple indicators of social support (Aneshensel and Frerichs, 1982). In Chapter 10, "Modeling the Effects of Social Support," Lin depicts, defines, and discusses 12 logically exhaustive models of possible relationships among these model variables. He examines these models in the light of our two-wave data using structural models with latent variables. This scheme provides a basis for the modeling in this study but may also serve to clarify the above-noted issues in the general literature. Relatively little is known about the course of depression and the factors that may affect its vicissitudes. Although it is generally believed that most depressions are acute and self-limiting in nature, Brown and Harris (1978) were surprised to find fairly chronic depression in a sample of women. In Chapter 17, Lin and Ensel introduce the construct of *depression mobility* and examine the effects of life events and social support on stability and change in depression.

SPECIFICATIONS AND ELABORATIONS

On the basis of existing evidence or theory, there are additional factors that may be implicated in the modeling of life events, social support, and depression. These include age, gender, marital status, social class or socioeconomic status, and prior history of physical illness. For example, in previous research, we empirically discerned three age groupings (18–24, 25–49, and 50–70) that showed substantial differences in the effects of life events, support, and other model variables (Lin, Dean, Ensel, and Tausig, 1980). These observations suggest that there are significant age, life-stage, or cohort effects.

Because we regard gender, like age, as a social–structural variable, we have investigated its effects. Ensel (1982) found that gender differences and variable rates of depression were associated with age and marital status. Subsequently, we observed that the role of life events, personal competence, and social support, as well as marital status and prior history of physical illness, varied substantially by gender within and across the age categories, and together accounted for a sizable proportion of variance in depressive symptomatology (Dean and Ensel, 1982, 1983). Further study along these lines may substantially increase our understanding of the ways in which these sociodemographic variables are implicated in the stressor–support–illness model.

Thus in Chapter 11, Lin, Ensel, and Dean explore the implications of age.

That marital status is related to physical and psychiatric morbidity as well as mortality is well known. Similarly, the marital-status variable has sometimes been treated as an indicator of social support, social integration, or social stress. In Chapter 12, Ensel examines the relationships of life events and social support to depression in the context of marital status, and discusses their implications for the current literature. Historically, the relationships between social class and psychiatric illness were objects of major thrusts in social-psychiatric epidemiology. In Chapter 13, Ensel explores the implications of social class in terms of the present epidemiological modeling of depression.

Although it is well known that physical illness and psychiatric disorders are frequently associated, measures of physical illness are frequently not incorporated into psychiatric epidemiological surveys. The measurement of prior history of physical illness permits the testing of a number of possible causal relationships among this variable, life events, and subsequent physical illness, as well as life events, social support, and depression. A number of these possible relationships, which are of considerable theoretical and empirical interest, are examined by Tausig in Chapter 14, "Prior History of Illness in the Basic Model."

Although the study of confiding relationships as a form of social support has been a major theme in the literature, few studies have explored the significance of the social characteristics of the confidant.

In Chapter 15, Lin, Woelfel, and Dumin examine the significance of the gender of the confidant. It has often been observed that life-events scaling typically does not reflect the subjective significance of events. Similarly, in many studies, the measurement and modeling of social support does not directly link specific types of social support with specific stressors. In Chapter 16, Lin, Woelfel, and Light do so by examining the effects of supportive responses to "the most important life event."

As can be seen, the topics and issues to be covered in this monograph are varied and complex. It would be naive for us to argue that adequate coverage of any of them is given or even attempted here. Our goals, rather, are to identify as many salient issues as possible and to examine them within the constraints of a particular set of panel data. It is a modest step when viewed in the larger context of psychosocial epidemiology. It is the large context, nevertheless, within which social support assumes meaning and significance.

2

Conceptualizing Social Support

NAN LIN

INTRODUCTION

In order to understand the effect of social support on mental health, three issues must be dealt with: (1) Definitions and concepts; how should social support be defined and conceived of? (2) Operationalizing and measurement; what empirical measures should be designed as indicators of social support? And (3) modeling; how does social support affect mental health both as an independent factor and as a mediating factor between stressors (life events) and mental health (depression)? The conceptualization of social support is addressed in this chapter. Measurement and modeling of social support will be examined in detail in Parts III and IV.

CONCEPTUALIZATIONS OF SOCIAL SUPPORT

Webster's New Collegiate Dictionary defines *support* as an act or process that promotes assists, helps, or holds up something else. Thus, social support denotes forces or factors that sustain human beings. Accordingly, social support can be defined as forces or factors in the social environment that facilitate the survival of human beings. Yet

17

although this definition may be adequate in general discourse, it certainly is not specific enough for research purposes. This meaning could encompass all aspects of social relations and interaction. A definition of social support is needed that specifies those aspects of social relations and interaction distinctively relevant to physical and mental health.

There has been no dearth of attempts to define social support. They range from such parallel concepts as *social integration* (Myers et al., 1975) and *ego strength* (Nuckolls et al., 1972), and surrogate empirical variables (e.g., the use of marital status as an indicator of social support; Berkman and Syme, 1979; Thoits, 1982), to the more elaborate conceptualizations and syntheses in the works of Cobb, Kahn, Caplan, House, Gottlieb, Weiss, Henderson, Brown, Pearlin, and others. Indeed, although definitions continue to display confusion and diversity, clearly converging elements are apparent.

We offer two definitions here. The first represents a synthesis of those offered by researchers during the past 10 years, and the second is derived from the theoretical perspective of social resources. Thus, the synthetic definition is arrived at by induction and the theoretical definition by deduction. We intend to show that these two definitions have shared characteristics as well as distinctive features. The eventual choice between the two definitions or a combination of elements from the two definitions will be the subject of empirical examinations and further conceptual integration in this book.

THE SYNTHETIC DEFINITION OF SOCIAL SUPPORT

Defining social support begins with a dissection of the term itself. Clearly, the concept has two components: *social* and *support*. We argue that the social component should reflect the individual's linkage to the social environment. This can be represented at three distinct levels: (1) the community, (2) the social network, and (3) intimate and confiding relationships. The support component should reflect the essential instrumental and expressive activities. The definition should also reflect the difference between perceptions of as well as actual access to and use of such activities.

Thus, the synthetic definition of social support is *the perceived or actual instrumental and/or expressive provisions supplied by the community, social networks, and confiding partners.* Although an individual, a group of individuals, or a community could be the recipient of support, and therefore constitutes a unit of analysis, for the sake of parsimony in the discussion to follow the unit of analysis will be the individual. Let us now elaborate this definition and determine the extent to which it is consistent with prevailing definitions offered and used by other researchers.

The definition suggested here recognizes that both perceived and actual support are important to the individual. Caplan (1979), for example, called for a distinction between objective and subjective dimensions of support. The objective aspects of support are observable indications of support provisions, about which information can be gathered from others, independently of the individual receiving support. On the other hand, the individual's subjective understanding and evaluation of support reflect reality as the individual sees it. Actual and perceived support may be consistent with each other for some individuals and not for others. In fact the consistency or inconsistency of the two aspects is itself a subject for research. Because of the impact of each aspect on mental health, whether complementary or independent, there is no valid theoretical reason to exclude either from study.

The social aspect of the definition singles out the individual's community, social networks, and confiding partners as sources of support. This is, of course, a simplification of the parts of the social environment, which are much more continuous and enmeshed in one another than these discrete categories suggest. They do, however, represent three different layers of social relations. The outer and most general layer consists of relationships with the larger community, and reflects integration into, or a sense of *belongingness* in, the larger social structure. An individual's participation in voluntary organizations (e.g., church and school, recreation and sports activities, clubs and services, political and civic associations) indicates the extent to which the individual identifies and participates in the social environment at large. Even though such involvement tends to be impersonal, the sense of belonging to and being part of the social environment is significant.

A layer closer to the individual consists of the social networks through which he or she has direct and indirect access to a relatively large number of other individuals. These relations are substantively specific; relations tend to build on such characteristics as kinship, shared working environment, and friendship. These relations provide a sense of *bonding*. A bonding relationship is more substantial than relationships based on a sense of belonging. Bonding relations represent *actual linkages* of the individual with others, even though some of the linkages may be indirect.

Finally, the innermost layer consists of relations among confiding partners. Here, the relationship tends to be *binding* in the sense that reciprocal and mutual exchanges are expected, and responsibility for one another's well-being is understood and shared by the partners.

These social elements, albeit crudely distinguishing categories of the social environment, clearly point to three distinct types of relationships—belonging, bonding, and binding. Each impinges on the other. It can be hypothesized that the closer the layer of relationships to ego, the greater the relations' impact on ego. Thus, it is expected not only that these three types of relationships are significant in providing support, but that the significance of each level differs from the others. Among the three layers of relations, relations with the community, the outermost layer, should have the least effect on the individual's well-being. However, these community relations define the boundaries within which the social network level is constructed. The individual's network is at once restricted by and derived from the community. Network relations represent interpersonal linkages and should, therefore, have a stronger effect on the person's well-being than does the community. In turn, the network provides a morphological structure within which confiding relationships may emerge. These confiding relations, closest to the individual, should be most significantly related to well-being.

Although the social aspect in the definition is conceptualized as having three layers of relationships, the support aspect involves two major dimensions: instrumental and expressive. The instrumental dimension involves the use of the relationship as a means to achieve a goal, such as seeking a job, getting a loan, or finding someone to babysit. The expressive dimension involves the use of the relationship as an end as well as a means. It is the activity of sharing sentiments, ventilating frustrations, reaching understanding on issues and problems, and affirming one's own as well as the other's worth and dignity. Some have called this *emotional* support. We prefer the term *expressive* in order to stress its social (interactive and confiding) rather than its psychological nature. Whereas there are other potential dimensions in relationships, these two are the most clear-cut and identifiable elements.

FURTHER DISCUSSION OF THE SYNTHETIC DEFINITION

There is substantial agreement between this definition of social support and those offered by others. A comparison of this with other definitions appears in Table 2.1. This comparison is not exhaustive, for it does not include many other definitions available in the literature. Rather, it illustrates major (and often contending) views concerning elements that may be central in defining social support. The table lists authors in alphabetical order, with their defining elements. When the element coincides with our proposed element, it is marked with an X. When the element is different from but related to an element of ours, it appears under the appropriate element of our definition.

Cassel (1974) did not explicitly define social support, but he did point out that social support is provided by primary groups most important to the individual. This is consistent with our emphasis on the binding relationships among confiding partners. Indeed, in further elaborating on this view, Kaplan et al., (1977) specifically discussed the confidant relationship. Thoits (1981) in defining social support utilized these binding elements.

Social support is sometimes seen as attachments among individuals or between an individual and a group that serve to (1) promote emotional mastery, (2) offer guidance, and (3) provide feedback about one's identity and performance (Caplan, 1974; Caplan and Killilea, 1976). The first two components are clearly included in our definition (expressive and instrumental supports). The last component suggests a mutual relationship in which both the emotional or expressive (identity) and the instrumental (performance) elements are involved. However, it is the mutual relationship that seems to be the dominant factor in this component, and this reflects our confiding partnership elements.

Cobb (1976) proposed that social support includes emotional support (one is cared for and loved), esteem support (one is valued and esteemed), and network support (one belongs to a network of mutual obligations). Cobb (1979) explicity excluded from consideration instrumental, active (e.g., mothering), and material support. Many other researchers have adopted the positive aspects of this definition as part of their own (e.g., Turner, 1981; House, 1981). Our definition distinguishes instrumental support, and subsumes emotional and esteem provisions under expressive support. Further, network support is one of the three layers of social elements, which we distinguish from the support elements.

In addition, House (1981) suggested that social support be examined in the context of "Who gives what to whom regarding which problems?" He elaborates the forms of social support in terms of a source-by-context matrix. In this matrix, sources of support include spouse/partner, other relatives, friends, neighbors, work supervisor, co-workers, service or care giver, self-help group, and health/welfare professional. Content of supportive acts includes emotional, appraisal, informational, and instrumental support. This effort can be viewed as an elaboration and integration of the works of Cobb, Kahn and Antonucci, Pinneau, and Caplan on the content of support as well as an elaboration

TABLE 2.1
Comparisons of the Elements of the Synthetic Definition and Other Definitions[a]

Researchers	Perceived and/or actual support	Elements of the synthetic definition						Other elements not specified in the definition
		Support elements		Social elements				
		1. Instrumental dimension	2. Expressive dimension	1. The community	2. Social networks	3. Confiding partners		
Berrera (1981)			Support, satisfaction, & needs		Network size			
Bowlby (1969, 1973), Weiss (1973, 1974)						X		
Brown et al. (1975, 1978)						Intimate relations Feedback		
Caplan (1974), Caplan & Killilea (1976)		Guidance	X					
Caplan (1979)	Objective vs. subjective	Tangible	Psychological					
Cassel (1974), Thoits (1981)				X				
Cobb (1976), Turner (1981)			Emotional, esteemed					
Dean & Lin (1977)		X	X			X		
Gottlieb (1978)		Problem-solving environmental action	X			Indirect influence		

Source[a]	Adequacy	Adequacy	Social integration/participation	Availability	Intimate relations	
Gottlieb (1981)				X		
Henderson (1977, 1980, 1981)	X	X	X	X	X	
House (1981)			X	X	X	Appraisal, informational
Kahn & Antonucci (1980)	Aid	Affect, affirmation				
Kaplan, Cassel, & Gore (1977)		X			X	
Lin et al. (1979)			X	X	X	
McKinlay (1973)				X		
Mueller (1980)				X		
Hammer (1981)				X		
Andrews (1978)				X		
Wellman (1981)				X		
Pearlin (1984)				X	Inter-personal	
Pinneau (1975)	Perceived	Tangible				
Sarason et al. (1983)		Satisfaction		Availability		Group Appraisal
Schefer, Coyne, & Lazarus (1981)	Perceived	Tangible		X		Informational

[a] Terms identical to those in the synthetic definition are identified by X. Terms similar or consistent with those in the synthetic definition are given under the appropriate element of our definition.

of the social relations involved. Again, it closely parallels most of our elements, with the exception of appraisal and informational supports, which are difficult to distinguish from other elements.

Several researchers have stressed social attachment and social bonds (Bowlby, 1969, 1973; Weiss, 1973, 1974; Henderson, 1977, 1981; Henderson, Byrne, Jones, Scott, and Adcock, 1980). Bowlby pointed out that individuals are happiest and most capable when they are sure that there will be one or more trusted persons who will come to their aid in time of need. Six positive outcomes of social relationships were further specified by Weiss: attachment, integration, nurturance, reassurance of worth, reliable alliance, and obtaining help and guidance. Henderson identified availability and perceived adequacy of social attachment as the two most important dimensions of social bonds. Again, most of these elements have been incorporated into our definition. Attachment, nurturing, and reassurance of personal worth are aspects of expressive support; reliable alliance characterizes a confiding relation; obtaining help and guidance is instrumental. Weiss defined integration as a network concept, as was Henderson's availability of social attachment. On the other hand, perceived adequacy as defined by Henderson contains both emotional and instrumental elements.

Pinneau (1975) distinguishes tangible, appraisal (information), and emotional support. Tangible and emotional support are contained in our instrumental and expressive dimensions. Appraisal appears to include both expressive and instrumental support. For example, Pinneau spoke of appraisal as passing on information about a job opportunity or explaining a method for solving a problem. These have clear instrumental implications. Information may also provide emotional or expressive appraisal, as when friends tell one another how their faces look. Thus, it is difficult to classify appraisal as an independent element.

G. W. Brown and his associated (Brown, Bhrolchain, and Harris, 1975; Brown and Harris, 1978), in their provocative and ground-breaking analyses of social origins of depression, focused on intimacy, as a major dimension of support. This conceptualization is closely allied with those of Cobb, Cassel, and Weiss as well as to our element of confiding relationships.

Caplan (1979) further differentiated two dimensions: the objective versus subjective, and the tangible versus the psychological. These also corresponded to elements in our definition of social support.

Kahn and Antonucci (1980), on the other hand, defined social support as interpersonal transactions that include one or more of the following key elements: affect, affirmation, and aid. Affect and aid are probably comparable to expression and instrumentation. Affirmation, also referred to as endorsement, probably is a part of expressive support, but whether it deserves a separate heading remains to be seen.

Gottlieb (1978) classified social support using four categories: emotionally sustaining behaviors, problem-solving behaviors, indirect personal influence, and environmental action. The first two elements are incorporated in our definition. The last two elements are difficult to classify. From sampled responses, they seem to represent mutual and trusting relationships ("She's there when I need her" and "He'll do all he can") and instrumental relations ("She helped by talking to the owners and convincing them to wait for the money a while"), respectively.

Later, Gottlieb (1981) summarized a number of contributions and suggested that social support entails three constructs: social integration/participation, interactions in social networks, and access to resources in intimate peer relationships. These loosely parallel the three social elements in our definition.

Another group of researchers have emphasized the importance of network properties as indicators of social support (McKinlay, 1973; Hammer, 1981; Andrews, 1978; Mueller, 1980; and Wellman, 1981). They have argued that networks are more objective and identifiable elements in a person's social environment and therefore should not be confounded with subjective, psychological states.

Barrera (1981) identified network size and support satisfaction and needs as two components in his analysis of social support. The former is embodied in our network element, and the latter in the expressive element.

Pearlin (1984) viewed the network, the (small) group, and interpersonal sources as three elements of social support. He argued that although the network represents the relationships the individual can turn to, it is the smaller group that represents social relationships the individual is most *likely* to turn to for support. The significance of the interpersonal source of support lies in the quality of relationships, such as trust and intimate exchange. Thus, Pearlin's definition of networks coincides with ours, and his *interpersonal sources* closely parallel our element of confiding partners. On the other hand, his group is probably a layer of relationships somewhere between the network and the confiding partners. Further examination is needed to determine whether it is necessary to view the group as a separate category.

Schaefer, Coyne, and Lazarus (1981) focused on perceived, tangible, emotional, and informational support. The first three elements (perception, tangible support, and emotional support) are covered in our definition. The information element is not included as a separate element.

Sarason and his associates (Sarason, Levine, Basham, and Sarason,

1983) emphasized perceived emotional satisfaction and network availability in their measurement of social support. All their elements appear in our definition.

In sum, our synthetic definition seems to have captured the most
salient elements of definitions provided by many researchers. It does
not exhaust all elements that others have proposed. For example, information and appraisal were not included, as they substantially overlap
with other elements. The notion of small groups also needs further
conceptual and operational clarification before it can be considered to
represent a separate layer of relations between social networks and
confiding relations. As in any definition, a compromise is made between specificity and parsimony. How useful this synthetic definition
is depends on its psychometric properties as well as its ability to operate significantly and meaningfully in the models to be studied.

Although the synthetic definition attempts to capture most of the
elements of interest to researchers, it represents an inductive approach
to conceptualizing social support. No single theoretical explanation is
involved or offered. Such a definition may be useful in guiding measurement and empirical work; however, it cannot substitute for a theoretical framework within which to explain the expected effects of
social support on mental health. In the following, one such theoretical
framework is offered.

A THEORY OF SOCIAL RESOURCES AND SOCIAL SUPPORT

It has long been observed that the frequency and intensity of social
interactions among individuals are associated with those individuals
similarities in social characteristics and psychological makeup. Homans (1950), for example, pointed out the significant consequences of
the relationship between sentiment and interaction. Lazarsfeld and
Merton (1964) have called it *the homophily principle,* and Laumann
(1966) named it *the like-me hypothesis.* In these interaction situations,
the relationships are reciprocal in nature. Persons of similar characteristics, attitudes, and lifestyles tend to congregate in similar residential, social, and work environments, which promote interactions and
associations. Similarly, frequency and intensity of interactions promote similar attitudes and lifestyles. This relationship is the fundamental ingredient in the concept of social circles or social networks.
Granovetter (1973) described this phenomenon in terms of the strength
of interpersonal ties. He defined the strength of such ties along four
potential dimensions: amount of time, emotional intensity, intimacy
(mutual confiding), and reciprocal services. He then suggested that

strong ties play significant roles in the ego's sociopsychological activities, whereas weak ties are potential sources for linking the ego to
wider social circles or networks than strong ties are able to provide. His
thesis concerning the importance of weak ties has generated new insights into the process of information flow and social mobility. Much
attention has since been given to the possible bridging functions of
weak ties. (For a recent review of this literature, see Granovetter, 1982).

Extending theory on the strength of social ties, Lin (1982) has proposed that the strength of ties should be evaluated relative to the actions taken by the ego. In general, social actions are taken for either
instrumental or expressive purposes. Instrumental actions are those
taken to achieve specific goals that are distinguishable from their
means. Expressive actions, on the other hand, are actions that have
indistinguishable means and goals. Job-seeking, purchasing, looking
for a stranger, and getting educated are examples of instrumental activities. Sharing emotional problems, exchanging life experiences, and
going out to dinner with someone one likes, are examples of expressive
activities, at least if these by themselves are the ultimate goals of the
participants.

Lin argued that the degree of success for either type of action depends to a large extent on the resources provided by ego's social ties.
Social resources, in contrast to personal resources, are not in the pos-
session of ego. Rather, they represent resources embedded in the ego's
network. Different social resources are needed for different actions. For
successful instrumental actions, access to and use of numerous widely
diverse social resources are desirable. Access to a higher-level job is
more likely to occur through links to high-prestige social resources
(Lin, 1980). The larger and more diverse the social resources that are
accessible, the greater the likelihood that any instrumental action will
be successful. If the homophily principle is true, getting access to resources different from one's own is more likely to occur through weak
ties. Weak ties provide access to a wider range of social resources. We
predict, therefore, that for instrumental actions, the use of weak ties
rather than strong ties leads to diverse social resources that, in turn,
increase the likelihood of successful action.

A series of studies (Lin, Dayton, and Greenwald, 1978; Lin, Vaughn,
and Ensel, 1981; Lin, Ensel and Vaughn, 1981; Ensel and Lin, 1981; Lin
and Dumin, 1982a, 1982b) has shown that the use of weaker ties provides ego with upward links to better social resources (as represented,
for example, by the tie's socioeconomic characteristics), which in turn
increase the likelihood of successful instrumental action (e.g., finding a
good job or finding a stranger).

The social-resources theory further suggests that expressive actions are primarily for the purpose of maintaining rather than of gaining personal resources (Lin, 1982). This purpose is best accomplished by interaction with others who share similar characteristics and lifestyles. If this assumption and the homophily principle are true, then successful expressive actions are more likely to occur through strong ties. Therefore, we predict that in expressive actions, the use of strong ties rather than weak ties leads to similar (homophilous) social resources, which, in turn, increase the likelihood of successful action.

Part of this formulation follows directly from Homans's theory about interaction and sentiment. However, two modifications are made here. First, our theory predicts that such relations hold only in the case of expressive action. Secondly, it stipulates joint effects by the strength of ties and by social resources upon the action taken. The focus is shifted from frequency and intensity of contacts to the nature of the contact (strength of ties—the role relationship between contacts and the patterns of interactions) as well as to the characteristics of the contacts (age, sex, etc.). Thus, our current attention focuses on both form (structure) and content of social ties.

Now we make a very important assumption: mental health represents the psychological and emotional status of a person, and its promotion and maintenance requires expressive action. We agree with the general consensus among researchers and professionals that mental health may be affected by many different types of factors (including genetic, biological, psychological, and social), but that its manifestation is psychological, emotional, and behavioral. From this assumption, the social-resources theory permits certain predictions regarding the process of maintaining mental health: namely, that *access to and use of strong and homophilous ties promotes mental health.* Maintenance of a healthy status, no matter how it is defined, requires sharing and confiding among intimates who can understand and appreciate one another's problems.

Several ramifications of this theoretical proposal must now be discussed. It is clear that *social support can be operationalized as access to and use of strong and homophilous ties.* We believe that this operationalization of social support is consistent with the major conceptual contentions in the literature and can serve to unify our understanding of its meaning. For example, Pearlin, Lieberman, Menaghan, and Mullan (1981) suggest that "being embedded in a network is only the first step toward having access to support. The final step depends on the quality of the relations one is able to find within the networks. . . . They especially critically involve the exchange of intimate communications and the presence of solidarity and trust" (p. 340). They then equate social support with "the mobilization and use of social re-

sources" (p. 341). Henderson's conceptual and research work emphasizes the significance of adequacy of close as well as diffuse relationships (1981). G. W. Brown and his associates (1975) single out the
lack of an intimate, confiding relationship with a husband or a boyfriend as the most powerful mediator between adverse events and psychiatric disturbance for women. In Cobb's formulation (1976), social
support is information that conveys care and love, esteem and mutual
obligation. Similarly, Kahn (1979a; 1979b) views social support as interpersonal transactions that include one or more of three factors: affect, affirmation, and aid. Cassel (1974) suggests that the strongest social support is provided by the primary groups that are of most
importance to the individuals. And from the same perspective, Kaplan
and his associates (1977) define social support as the meeting of a
person's basic needs (approval, esteem, succor, etc.) through the relative presence or absence of psychosocial support resources from significant others. Dean and Lin (1977, p. 407) also single out the significance
of expressive relations with others.

All of these important previous efforts at conceptualizing social support focus on resources provided by strong ties, either as independent
contributors to a person's well-being or as buffers against adverse
events. The theory being proposed solidifies the diverse elements of
social support within a larger theoretical perspective and makes the
testing of propositions possible.

It is clear from this perspective that the central elements of social
support must concern the relations between ego and the sources of
support, the content of the interactions, and the matched characteristics of the interactors.

DISCUSSION

In this chapter, we have addressed the issue of conceptualizing and
defining social support. Two approaches have been used to define social support. The synthetic definition, drawing from the elements discussed in the literature, proposes that social support be considered as
the perceived or actual instrumental and/or expressive provisions supplied by the community, the social network, and the confiding partners. After a review of the definitions offered by other researchers, we
feel this definition captures most of the distinct and salient elements. It
further clarifies the three layers of relations (belonging to the community, the bonding of networks, and the binding together of confiding
partners) as they affect and protect the well-being of the individual.

The second approach, drawing on the theory of social resources, argues that mental health reflects expressive needs that can best be met by access to and use of ties that are close and homophilous (similar) to ego. Such ties tend to be those that are more effective for people's sharing and confiding. Thus, social support can be operationally defined as access to and use of strong and homophilous ties. This seems consistent with many of the discussions in the literature on social support, as they all point to the nature and content of the interactions as well as to the shared characteristics of the interacting parties.

At this early stage of theoretical development, it is wise to leave room for empirical examination of elements identified in the two discussed approaches. The synthetic definition is broader in its cast of elements (social, support, and actual/perceived) and, therefore, should show a greater degree of potential fit with empirical data. However, it is not quite in a propositional form, so that its theoretical structure cannot yet be subjected to rigorous examinations.

On the other hand, the social resources approach is rich with theoretical ideas and makes clear predictions. However, it cannot be expected to fit as well with empirical data as can the synthetic approach.

The two approaches do converge on a single element—the significance of strong binding relationships in the mental-health process. Whatever one uncovers of the process, social support should show its distinctive strength or vulnerability when a person's strong binding relationships are analyzed.

With these conceptual guidelines and precautions in mind, in the remainder of the book we present a set of panel data involving two waves of interviews of a community sample (1) to construct measures for each of the elements identified in these definitions and to test, wherever appropriate, their reliability and validity, and (2) to assess how each of these elements operates as predicted relative to depression. The next chapter describes the study and data to be used for these analyses.

3

Study Design and Data

WALTER M. ENSEL

THE ALBANY AREA HEALTH SURVEY

Area Geographic and Demographic Characteristics

The study was carried out in a tricounty area in upstate New York. The largest of the three contiguous counties is Albany County, with a 1980 population of about 286,000, followed by Rensselaer County (population – 151,966) and Schenectady County (population – 149,946).[1] Albany County, the site of the capital of New York, is the home of a large portion of the New York State government. It also has a wide assortment of light industries. The three counties lie approximately 150 miles north of New York City. They are located mostly in the Hudson River Valley and lie south of the Adirondack Mountains. Two large rivers, Mohawk and the Hudson, with numerous lakes and streams, flow through the area.

The characteristics of residents of the three-county area are, for the most part, representative of the population of New York State (Table 3.1). The proportion of males to females in the three counties is approximately 48 to 52, and the median age is 32. The majority of individuals

[1] Parts of an additional county, Saratoga County, were also covered in the study.

31

Walter M. Ensel

TABLE 3.1
Selected Demographic Characteristics in the Albany–Schenectady–Troy Area and in New York State

	New York State[a]	Albany–Schenectady–Troy SMSA[b]	Albany–Schenectady–Troy		
			Albany County	Schenectady County	Rensselaer County
Sex					
% Male	47.5	48.0	47.3	47.5	48.7
% Female	52.5	52.0	52.7	52.5	51.3
Age					
Median age	32.7	31.2	31.2	33.4	30.1
Race					
% White	79.5	94.0	90.9	95.7	96.2
% Nonwhite	20.5	6.0	9.1	4.3	3.8
Marital status					
% Single	30.6	29.2	33.1	26.2	30.3
% Married	52.2	54.8	50.2	56.8	54.1
% Separated	3.5	2.5	2.8	2.4	2.5
% Widowed	8.7	8.7	8.9	9.4	8.8
% Divorced	4.9	4.7	4.9	5.2	4.4
Education					
% High-school graduate	65.0	70.1	71.7	66.0	71.5
Employment					
% Currently in labor force	60.7	61.2	62.2	59.6	59.2
Income					
Median household income	$16,647	$16,814	$17,006	$15,970	$16,928

[a]Based on 1980 Census of Population: Characteristics of the Population, General Social and Economic Characteristics, U.S. Department of Commerce, Bureau of the Census, PC80-1-C34 (1983).

[b]Based on 1980 Census of Population and Housing: Census Tracts Albany, Schenectady, Troy SMSA, U.S. Department of Commerce, Bureau of the Census, PHC80-2-61 (1983).

are married (55%), 30% are single, just under 5% are currently divorced, and 2.5% are separated. The average individual attends school for 12 years. Sixty-one percent of the population is currently working, with a median household income of approximately $16,000. The percentage of nonwhites residing in the area, however, is lower than that found in New York State as a whole (6% compared to 20%).

The Survey Design

A panel design was the survey method chosen in the current study. The basic strategy entails interviewing the sample group of respondents repeatedly over time. The main advantages of the panel design are twofold: First, it provides for an assessment of change taking place over time. In this sense, it is superior to a cross-sectional design that presents a group of opinions, attitudes, and factual data at a single, frozen point in time. Second, and perhaps more important, it allows a test of causal orderings among the different variables. Given the primary interest in social support and its role in the stress–illness relationship, it was imperative that such a longitudinal design be employed in the current study. Overall, the panel design consisted of three waves of data. Because the third-wave data are currently being processed, we will report in this study on the results of the first two. Wave 1 data were collected in the fall of 1979, and Wave 2 data were collected one year later, in the fall of 1980.

THE PRETEST

Purposes

At the inception of the project (fall 1977), few epidemiological studies of the relationship of stress to illness had been done utilizing a normal community population; we therefore considered it necessary to conduct a pretest. The pretest served three functions: First, it allowed us to field-test our instrument. Given the fact that most of the social-support scales to be used were either new or never before tested, it seemed that a pretest would allow us to assess the reliability and validity of our measures. Second, it presented an opportunity to train our interviewers. Given the length of the interview (some 40 pages) and the amount of time it took to conduct the interview (30–60 minutes), we wanted to be sure our interviewers were able to go through the entire schedule in a manner conducive to interviewer–respondent rapport. Finally, the pretest allowed the research staff to prepare for what lay ahead. Particularly, reviewing the completed questionnaires with each interviewer gave us a sense of the problem areas and the consistency with which our interviewers asked each set of questions.

Characteristics

The pretest was conducted in August of 1978 with a sample of adults aged 18 or older in the Albany–Schenectady–Rensselaer county area of upstate New York. The area was part of a U.S. census Standard Metropolitan Statistical Area (SMSA). In all, 99 respondents were drawn from the area using a modified area probability technique utilizing block statistics for the SMSA area. Two consecutive households were chosen from each sampled block. The sampled blocks were randomly distributed throughout the three-county area.

Assessments

Those interviewed in the pretest were predominantly white (90%), and the majority were women (74%). Respondents were distributed normally across age categories, with the mean age being 42. In testing the instrument, we were able to answer many questions regarding the time frames within which the various questions could adequately be answered. For example, respondents were better able to recall life events from the past 6 months than over the whole last year. On the other hand, respondents were able to recall diagnosed physical illnesses over the past 2 years. In addition, key social-support questions found to be awkward were reworded. Reliability and validity tests were conducted on the various social-support scales as well as on reports of life events and depression. The results proved very positive and encouraging. Preliminary analysis was conducted on the pretest data and published (Lin, Dean, and Ensel, 1981a, 1981b; Dean, Lin, and Ensel, 1981).

The pretest served an equally important function in preparing the interviewers for the main study, as well as in identifying potential problems in contacting respondents. It became apparent that the time of day was crucial in determining the type of respondents that were interviewed. As a result, we emphasized the need to interview at all times of the day (particularly evenings) and, if possible, on weekends. These appeared to be the times most people were at home.

In sum, the pretest allowed us to gain valuable insights into the conduct of our survey, to identify potential problem areas, and to make our main study more valid and reliable.

SAMPLING DESIGN

Drawing the Sample

A modified probability sample of households in the Albany–Schenectady–Rensselaer area of New York State was drawn in 1979. The sampling frame used was the 1970 census block statistics for this SMSA. According to the 1970 census figures, the population of adults

·in the tri-county area was 721,910; this population occupied 240,950 housing units of which 178,693 were in urbanized areas. It was determined that a minimum sample size of 384 respondents was required for a reliability (tolerated error) of ±5% and a 95% confidence level for sample estimates. To allow for subsample (subgroup) analysis and attrition over time (due to deaths, refusals, losses of contact, moves), an initial sample size of 1131 households was selected.

The sample consisted of a set of 377 selected blocks, each of which contained a cluster of three sampled households. The purpose of clustering at the block level was twofold: (1) to contain the cost of the field work, and (2) to ease the burden on the interviewers in finding respondents. Experience in past national surveys, such as the National Opinion Research Center surveys, indicates that a clustering of this magnitude (three households per sampled block) results in minimal and insignificant bias in the estimation of population parameters.

The blocks were selected by a systematic random-sampling procedure. A skip interval was constructed (with a randomly selected starting point) that insured that the households selected were distributed throughout the tricounty area. The specific procedure for this modified probability-sampling technique can be found in Backstrom and Hursch-Cesar (1981) and Lin (1976).

In each selected household, the adult head of household (defined as the person over the age of 18 who provides the major portion of the regular household income) and the spouse of the household head were interviewed alternately. To insure adequate representation of males and females and a normal age distribution, quotas of age and sex were set for each block. The quotas were based on the approximate percentage of males and females (50% each) and the ratio of those aged 18–64 to those aged 65–70 (90:10) found in the population of the area. Respondents over 70 years of age were excluded.

The First Wave

The first wave of interviewing took place in the spring of 1979. In all, 1091 individuals were interviewed. This reflects a response rate of 96.5%. The interviews usually took 45–60 minutes. Seven respondents were over the age of 70 and so were excluded from further analysis.

The Second Wave

The second wave of interviewing took place 1 year after the first wave, in the spring of 1980. Prior to the second wave of interviewing, we attempted to trace and record residential movement of the respondents. (Names were kept confidential and were known only to the project and interviewing staff.) Due to the diligence and perseverance of the staff, we were able to contact and reinterview 80% (871) of the respondents in the original sample. Of those not reinterviewed in the second-wave data collection, 9.8% were not locatable, 8.8% refused to be reinterviewed, and 0.5% had died.

REPRESENTATIVENESS OF THE SAMPLE

Characteristics of the Sample

As mentioned earlier, the first wave of our sample was drawn with a modified probability-sampling technique. The characteristics of the sample corresponded to those of the Albany–Schenectady–Rensselaer population as given by the U.S. census.

The sample contained 51% males and 49% females, compared to 48% and 52%, respectively, in this census area in 1980. Of the sampled respondents, 64% were currently married (compared to 55% of the population), and 68% of those currently married had children. This discrepancy was due, in part, to the fact that census statistics are based on respondents 15 years of age or older, whereas the current study focused only on those respondents 18 to 70 years of age. Of our respondents, 90% were aged 18 to 64, and 10% were between the ages of 65 and 70 (compared to 89% and 11%, respectively, in the population). Likewise, 54% of the sample were currently in the labor force, compared to 61% of the population.

In addition, 75% of the respondents had lived in the county for more than 10 years. About a quarter (26%) of the respondents had less than a high-school education; 34% had a high-school diploma; and almost 40% had at least some college education. The median level of respondents' family income in 1979 was between $10,000 and $14,999.

Comparison of Wave 1 and Wave 2

A large portion of the analysis reported in this book deals with the merged Wave 1–Wave 2 data set (the portion of the sample for which data are available for both time periods). Therefore, it is important to verify that this subset of respondents does not differ significantly from the total sample of 1091. Table 3.2 presents descriptive statistics for respondents on selected survey variables. Four sets of statistics are compared for respondents who participated in the study. These include (1) the Time 1 (T1) characteristics of the entire 1091 respondents interviewed in Wave 1, (2) the T1 characteristics of the 871 respondents

TABLE 3.2
Demographic Characteristics in Albany Area Total Time 1 (T1) Sample and in T1 and Time 2 (T2) Subsamples

| Characteristic | T1 (N = 1091) | | Wave 1 | | | | Wave 2 | |
| | | | T1 (N = 871) | | Lost from T1–T2 (N = 220) | | T2 (N = 871) | |
	% of Respondents	N	% of Respondents	N	% of Respondents	N	% of Respondents	N
Sex								
Male	50.4	546	50.2	434	50.9	112	50.2	434
Female	49.6	538	49.8	430	49.1	108	49.8	430
Race								
White	89.0	963	89.6	773	86.4	190	89.6	767
Nonwhite	11.0	121	10.5	91	12.3	27	10.4	89
Marital status								
Married	64.1	695	67.1	580	52.3	115	65.4	560
Divorced	6.2	67	6.7	58	4.1	9	7.2	62
Separated	4.0	43	3.6	31	5.5	12	5.1	44
Widowed	5.2	45	5.3	46	4.5	19	5.6	48
Never married	20.3	223	17.2	149	33.6	74	16.6	142
Children								
Yes	68.0	735	70.9	611	56.6	124	72.8	622
No	32.0	346	29.1	251	43.4	95	27.2	228
Education								
Less than high school	25.5	276	25.4	219	25.9	57	23.9	204
High school	34.5	374	34.4	297	35.0	77	34.4	294
Some college	19.3	209	19.2	166	19.5	43	20.0	171
College +	20.6	224	21.0	181	19.5	43	21.4	185

(continued)

TABLE 3.2
(Continued)

Characteristic	Wave 1				Lost from T1–T2 (N = 220)		Wave 2	
	T1 (N = 1091)		T1 (N = 871)				T2 (N = 871)	
	% of Respondents	N	% of Respondents	N	% of Respondents	N	% of Respondents	N
Employment status								
Employed	53.8	579	55.0	471	49.5	108	59.9	492
Unemployed	7.9	85	6.7	57	12.8	28	4.8	41
Retired	12.2	131	12.7	109	10.1	22	12.8	109
Keeping house	21.6	232	22.2	190	19.3	42	22.2	189
In school	4.5	48	3.5	30	8.3	18	2.2	19
Occupation								
Prof, tech, and kindred workers	28.4	308	27.8	240	30.9	68	19.0	140
Managers and administrators	6.5	71	6.8	59	5.5	12	11.4	84
Sales workers	3.3	36	3.4	29	3.2	7	4.9	36
Clerical workers	18.7	203	19.	168	15.9	35	20.4	150
Craftsmen and kindred workers	10.4	113	10.9	94	8.6	19	12.4	91
Operatives	10.9	118	11.2	97	9.5	21	10.5	77
Laborers	4.7	51	42	36	6.8	15	5.8	43
Farm workers	.1	1	—	—	.5	1	.1	1
Service workers	16.9	183	16.3	141	19.1	42	15.5	114
Average age	40.7	1084	41.5	684	37.4	220	42.3	856
Average household size	2.3	1084	2.4	863	1.9	220	2.3	856
Median individual income	$7000–$9999		$7000–$9999		$6000–$7999		$8000–$9999	
Median family income	$10,000–$20,000		$10,000–$20,000		$10,000–$14,999		$10,000–$20,000	

in T1 who were later reinterviewed in Time 2 (T2), (3) the T1 characteristics of those 220 respondents interviewed in T1 who were not
reinterviewed in T2, and (4) the T2 characteristics of those 871 respondents interviewed in T1 who were also interviewed again in T2.

Comparing T1 characteristics of the total sample in T1 with the subset that was later reinterviewed in T2 (see Table 3.2), we find no significant differences between them. Moreover, when we compare the T1
data and T2 data for those who were interviewed at both T1 and T2 (N
= 871), we also find no significant differences, except that individual
income was higher in 1980 than in 1979. This is attributable to increases in wages over the 1-year period. In sum, reliability is high for
the distribution of variables; the T2 data set is not significantly different from that obtained in T1. This indicates that over-time analysis of
these data will not be complicated by having to account for differences
in sample background characteristics.

In addition to comparing means, standard deviations, and distributions of the characteristics of our respondents over time, we have also
compared the zero-order correlations between model variables and our
dependent measures for the Wave 2 and Wave 2 samples. Although the
details of these findings will be taken up in more detail in coming
chapters, it should be noted that no significant differences were observed. Thus the behavior of the model variables in separate regression
equations for Wave 1 and Wave 2 would not be expected to show
differences due to any sample bias.

Despite the statistical agreement and the consistency of the T1 (N =
871) and T2 (N = 871) sample characteristics, it should be pointed out
that the portion of the T1 sample that was not reinterviewed at T2 (N =
220) does differ from the reinterviewed cases. As is evidenced in Table
3.2, the 220 cases not reinterviewed may be generally characterized as
younger, making less money, less likely to be married, more likely to be
unemployed, having a slightly greater life-event frequency, and having
less self-esteem. In essence, this represents a very mobile group.

In sum, the data show substantial validity and reliability. The Wave 1
and Wave 2 samples do not differ significantly from each other. However, the panel data (T1 and T2 combined) show a slight tendency to
underrepresent the young unmarried.

THE INTERVIEW SCHEDULES

Types of Variables in the Questionnaire

The interview schedule used in this study consists of a 40-page inter-
viewer-administered questionnaire. Though space restrictions prohibit

us from printing the entire text of the two questionnaires, we have constructed a table to aid the reader in determining the range of information collected (see Table 3.3). The data are organized into seven categories: (1) sociodemographic variables (e.g., sex, race, age, residence, employment and economic information, spouse characteristics, family background, household information), (2) stressful life-event measures (including a composite 118-item modified checklist, subjective evaluation of stress, and nature of most important life event), (3) social-support measures (covering a wide spectrum of information regarding the source of support, its content, demographic characteristics of support givers, measures of reciprocity, the context within which support is given, and numerous other attributes), (4) personal resources (self-esteem and personal competence), (5) physical/psychological health measures (including a variety of subjective and objective measures, such as the CES-D scale, Hopkins Symptom Checklist, Gurin Symptom Scale, Cornell Medical Index of Diagnosed Illness, and others), (6) health-behavior measures (including information on doctor/hospital visits, professional help, smoking, alcohol- and drug-taking, weight gain), and finally (7) the attitude of the respondent toward the interview and the questions.

Additions and Deletions to the Second-Wave Questionnaire

In the 1-year interval between the first and second wave of interviewing, substantial analysis of our T1 data led us to add a number of items and scales to our instrument and to delete others. The decision to drop variables from the T2 interview schedule was based on four criteria: (1) the unreliability of the items/scales, (2) the lack of a significant relationship between the items/scales and model variables or their failure to provide information that supplemented the root questions, (3) judgment problems (on the part of the respondents) in the wording or scope of questions, or (4) the assumption that information gathered in T1 would not change in T2 or would change in an expected pattern and direction. In particular, criteria 1 and 2 were the basis for omitting certain social-support scales from the T2 questionnaire. Criteria 4 was used when dealing with such questions as age, religion, or ethnicity.

New scales were added to the T2 instrument in response to three needs: (1) to explore serendipitous findings arising from analysis of the T1 data, (2) to further extend the scope and nature of social-support measures, or (3) to incorporate measures of social support utilized by other investigators. The content of the items added to or deleted from the questionnaire can be found in Table 3.3.

TABLE 3.3
The Nature of Data Obtained in Wave 1 and Wave 2 of the Albany Area Health Survey

	Wave 1	Wave 2
Sociodemographics		
Sex	X	X
Race	X	X
Age	X	—
County of residence	X	X
Length of time in county	X	X
Length of time at present address	X	X
Current marital status	X	X
Marital history	X	—
Length of time married (if married)	X	—
Has marital status changed in last year	—	X
Household composition	X	X
Presence of children	X	X
Number of children	X	X
Number of children living with respondent	X	X
Number of children living with respondent under 18 years	X	X
Number of children living with respondent under 6 years		
Religious preference	X	X
Husband's/wife's religious preference (if married)	X	—
Ethnic group identification	X	—
Education	X	—
First full-time job	X	X
Employment status	X	X
Current occupation	X	X
Wife/husband's education	X	X
Wife/husband's employment status	X	X
Wife/husband's current occupation	X	X
Father's education	X	X
Father's occupation	X	—
Mother's education	X	—
Mother's occupation	X	—
Individual income	X	—
Family income	X	X
Subjective class identification	X	X
Subjective rating of importance of job	X	X
Own or rent house/apartment	X	X
Type of dwelling unit respondent lives in	X	X
State of repair of respondent's residence	X	X
State of repair of residences on respondent's street	X	X
Stressful life events	X	X
118-Item checklist (presence or absence of event in last 6 months)	X	X
Importance of the event (118 items)		
Desirability of the event (118 items)	X	—

(continued)

TABLE 3.3 (Continued)

	Wave 1	Wave 2
Most important life event	X	X
Subjective evaluation of stress (respondent, in last 6 months)	X	X
Weight of the most important life event	—	X
Weight of the most valued event	—	X
Social support	—	X
Community neighborhood support	—	X
• Satisfaction with neighborhood		
• Interaction with people in neighborhood	X	X
• Satisfaction with community	X	X
• Interaction with people in neighborhood	X	X
SES support	X	X
• Satisfaction with work		
• Satisfaction with employer	X	X
• Satisfaction with earnings	X	X
• Satisfaction with financial situation	X	X
Voluntary group membership	X	X
• Number belong to		
• Attendance	X	X
• Contribution	X	X
• Committee membership	X	X
• Office	X	X
Marital support (Medalie–Goldbourt scale)	X	X
• Present family conflicts		
• Past family conflicts	X	X
• Spouse/children don't listen	X	X
• Spouse shows love	X	X
Instrumental Expressive Social Support Scale (items in last 6	X	X
months; 27 items)	X	X
Perceived social support (10 items)		
• Someone to help	X	—
• Relationship of person to respondent	X	—
Anyone to trust and talk to (in last 6 months)	X	X
Number of people able to trust and talk to (in last 6 months)	X	X
Network of three most likely confidants (5 items)	X	X
Characteristics of three confidants—relationship, age, sex,	—	X
occupation, education		
Characteristics of most important confidant (Kaplan scale; 7	X	X
items)		
Most important confidant to help with social-support problems	X	—
(10 items)		
Most important person to help with most important life event	X	—
Sociodemographic Characteristics of Most Important Person—	X	X
relationship, age, sex, education, occupation		
Presence of someone to help if respondent had job problems	X	—
Characteristics of person helping if respondent had job	X	—
problems (7 items)		

(continued)

TABLE 3.3 (*Continued*)

	Wave 1	Wave 2
Job-problems helper to help with other social-support problems (10 items)	X	—
Job-problem helper to help with most important life event	X	
Sociodemographic characteristics of job-problem helper (5 items)—relationship, age, sex, education, occupation	X	
Organizational support for particular problem (9 items)	X	X
• In contact with social-service agencies, self-help groups, service organizations, family and children services, financial and credit groups	X	X
• Satisfaction with same agencies or groups	—	X
Need help with most important life event	—	X
Get help with most important life event	—	X
Relationship to person who helped with most important life event	—	X
Length of time respondent has known person who helped with most important life event	—	X
Characteristics of person who helped with most important life event (Kaplan scale; 7 items)	—	X
How much did person help during most important life event	—	X
Characteristics of person who helped with most important life event	—	X
• Age, sex, occupation, education	—	X
Ability to talk over N problem areas with any of seven types of persons		
• Problem areas—money, health, job, household, legal, responsibilities, love relations, loneliness, personal problems, problems communication, lack of freedom		
• People —spouse/lover, other family member, friend, neighbor, co-worker, other acquaintance, helping professional		
Personality/psychological support	X	X
Campbell Personal Competence Scale (8 items)	X	X
Rosenberg Self-Esteem Scale (10 items)		
Subjective health rating	X	X
Center for Epidemiologic Studies Depression (CES-D) Scale (in last week; 20 items)	X	X
Hopkins Symptom Checklist (in last week; 26 items)	X	X
Gurin Symptom Scale (in last month; 19 items)	X	X
Abbreviated Cornell Medical Index of Physical Symptoms (in last month; 45 items)	X	X
Modified Cornell Medical Index of Diagnosed Illness (ever and in last two years; 39 items)	X	—
Modified Cornell Medical Index of Diagnosed Illness (in last 6 months; 39 items)	—	X
Hospitalized for major physical illness (in last 2 years)	X	X
Infections (in last 6 months)	X	X

(continued)

TABLE 3.3 (*Continued*)

	Wave 1	Wave 2
Health Behavior		
Number of visits to doctor, outpatient clinic, or emergency room (in last 6 months)	X	X
Professional help with nervous or emotional problems (no. of visits in last 6 months)	X	X
Number of hospitalizations for nervous or emotional problem (in last 6 months)	X	X
Smoking behavior	X	X
Change in smoking behavior (in last 6 months)	X	X
Drug-taking behavior	X	X
Change in drug-taking behavior (in last 6 months)	X	X
Weight gain (in last 6 months)	X	X
Miscellaneous		
Part of interview respondent liked most	X	X
Part of interview respondent disliked most	X	X
Respondent's attitude toward interview	X	X
Respondent's understanding of questions	X	X
Respondent's cooperation	X	X

Respondent Attitudes toward the Interview

In addition to the study-related items in the questionnaire, we also included questions to be answered by our interviewers about the respondents' attitudes toward the interview, their understanding of the questions, and their cooperation with the interviewer. Respondents were asked which part of the interview they liked the most and which part they most disliked. Table 3.4 reports the distribution of responses to these questions.

As can be seen, the large majority of respondents were rated by interviewers as friendly and interested. In fact, only 2% in Wave 1 and 3% in Wave 2 were considered impatient and restless in the interviewing situation. More than 90% of the respondents were considered to have a good understanding of the questions and to be very cooperative with the interviewer. Although allowing for the fact that these ratings are subjective, the pattern nevertheless is indicative of high respondent–interviewer rapport and an interest on the part of residents in our health study.

When asked what part of the interview they disliked, most respondents reported that they did not dislike any of it. In fact, less than 10% reported that they disliked a particular question or a particular set of

TABLE 3.4
Interviewer Ratings of Respondent Attitudes and Reactions to the Albany
Area Health Survey

Respondent profile	Wave 1 %	Wave 2 %
Respondent's attitude toward interview		
Friendly and interested	83.2	82.8
Cooperative but not particularly interested	14.7	14.5
Impatient and restless	2.1	2.8
	100.0	100.1
Respondent's Understanding of Questions		
Good	90.7	90.8
Fair	8.1	8.5
Poor	1.2	.7
	100.0	100.0
Respondent's Cooperation		
Very cooperative	92.7	91.7
Somewhat cooperative	6.3	7.1
Somewhat uncooperative	1.0	1.0
Very uncooperative	—	.1
	100.0	99.9

questions. These responses were unpatterned and did not indicate that
any particular item or set of items were annoying or obtrusive to any
significant category of respondents.

TIME FRAMES FOR QUESTIONS

As we mentioned earlier, the first two waves of our panel study were
conducted a year apart, in 1979 and 1980. In each questionnaire we
specified time frames to which certain questions applied (the specific
time frames for all variables can be found in Table 3.3). It is worth
emphasizing the time frames used for the major variables under study,
such as life events, social support, and depressive symptoms (CES-D).

Figure 3.1 presents a schematic time table for the model variables. As
can be seen, life events and social support are measured for the 6
months preceding Wave 1 (1979) and preceding Wave 2 (1980) of the
study. Depression, on the other hand, is measured for the week preceding the interview. It should be noted that the use of these time frames
for the questions results in a gap of 6 months between the two periods
covered by data collection, for which no information is collected on life

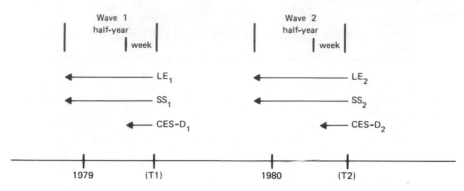

Figure 3.1 Time frame for reports of life events, social support, and depression in the Albany Area Health Survey.

events or social support. For depression, the gap is even greater, almost a year (51 weeks).

The alternative strategy of organizing the time frames so that the entire period between them was covered was abandoned to insure that our respondents were not pushed beyond their ability of recall, undermining the reliability of their responses. In the pretest (fall of 1978), we asked for information from respondents on life events in two time periods, the first and the second 6 months in the previous year. Analysis of the pretest data, coupled with the interviewers' reports indicated that although respondents had no trouble recalling significant life events in the 6 months preceding the interview, many did have trouble recalling events that occurred 6 to 12 months before the interview. This recall problem led to our decision to limit the time frame to the most recent 6 months so as to maximize the reliability of the responses. Myers and Pepper (1972) also addressed the problem of recall of life events in periods covering 1 year or more and concluded that reliability of recall was approximately 6 to 12 months.

The same rationale was applied to a series of questions we asked about levels of social support experienced by our respondents. Specifically, these questions dealt with social-support problems and the number of people the respondents felt they could talk to when they had problems. (It should be noted that many social-support questions did not have the 6-month limit. Again, see Table 3.3.)

Finally, a 1-week interval was utilized in measuring depression, primarily because that is the accepted time period about which the questions comprising the scale are traditionally asked (Radloff, 1975). (Chapter 4 deals with this issue in more detail.)

THE INTERVIEWING STAFF

The interviewing staff used in the Albany Area Health Survey consisted of an initial group of 20 females, the majority of whom had prior experience in census interviewing, public-opinion polling, academic surveys, and marketing-research polls. This group of interviewers had been utilized by members of the project in other studies over the past 5 years. Based on prior experience with these interviewers, as well as on extensive training and debriefing sessions, we concluded that we had a highly competent, personable, and professional interviewing staff.

Of the 20 interviewers utilized in Wave 1 of the study, 14 were brought back in 1980 for Wave 2 of the study. Ten of these 14 interviewers were responsible for completing more than 90% of both the Wave 1 and the Wave 2 interviews.

Although tight controls were placed on the training sessions, debriefing sessions were equally rigorous. At least one staff member went over each returned interview schedule with the interviewer. This insured that all questions were answered and that any uncertainties or incomplete sections were clarified. It also provided us with a sense of the respondents' understanding of the questions and the nature of the specific interviewing situation. As a result of this review, less than 1% of the returned interview schedules contained errors or incomplete information that ultimately resulted in their exclusion from analysis.

SUMMARY

This chapter has presented the background and process of the Albany Area Health Survey. It has outlined briefly the geographic and sociodemographic characteristics of the three-county area in upstate New York that was the site of the study. It has presented the survey design employed, as well as information on the pretest, the sampling design, and the representativeness of the sample. The types of questions in the survey as well as information on the interviewing staff and the community residents who agreed to participate in the study have been given.

The study was designed and carried out in a rigorous and meticulous scientific manner. We wished not only to insure the reliability and validity of the data, but to provide a structured and standardized set of questions that would lend themselves to replication by other researchers. Such scientific rigor and standardization, we feel, should be a part of any epidemiological study.

We have high confidence in the integrity of our data. However, there must be certain caveats. First, the panel data show a slight underrepresentation of young unmarried adults. In addition, caution is also called for in drawing inferences from our regional data to the state or the nation as a whole. Wherever appropriate, our results are compared with studies by other researchers in other regions or societies. Only such comparisons can make possible meaningful generalizations beyond the study site.

Part II

MEASURING DEPRESSION, LIFE EVENTS, AND PSYCHOLOGICAL RESOURCES

These three chapters and Part III describe the measurements of the key concepts studied. Part II focuses on the dependent variable (depression), one of the two independent variables (life events), and the key control variable (psychological resources). The major independent variable, social support, will be dealt with in Part III.

The selection of particular measures is guided by conceptual as well as practical considerations. We strive to obtain or construct measures that seem to be appropriate indicators for the variables. Also, we must take into account the prevailing usage and availability of certain measures generally associated with the variables. The measures ultimately constructed or used reflect these considerations and, at times, also reflect compromises between precision and convention. Wherever possible, multiple indicators and alternative forms of measurement are examined in determining what particular measures will be used in later analyses.

In these measurement sections as in subsequent analysis sections, we present much detail regarding the conceptual and analytic procedures used. We report failures as well as successes. In so doing, we hope to reduce the amount of trial and error in future efforts and to sharpen the focus on the problems and promises of various measures we have incorporated.

4 ———————————————————————————————

Measuring Depression:
The CES-D Scale

WALTER M. ENSEL

INTRODUCTION

This chapter introduces the measure of depression, which is used as the main dependent variable in the study. It begins with the introduction of the measure, the Center for Epidemiologic Studies Depression Scale (known as the CES-D scale), and clarifies that it is a measure of symptoms and mood rather than of illness or disorder. Data from the study are then used to examine the reliability and validity of the scale as a whole. Further analysis is conducted to identify the factors, or dimensions, of the measure. The results are compared with findings from previous works. Also examined is the notion of a cutoff point on the scale, used to establish two dichotomous categories of people, those likely to be in a depressed state and those who are not. The utility and limitations of such a dichotomy are discussed.

We harbor no illusion that this is the optimal measure of distress or even of depressive mood. Nevertheless, from the initiation of the study until the present time, the CES-D scale has remained a desirable measure of distress with many desirable psychometric properties. The fact that other more diagnostically oriented criteria and instruments have

51

recently become available does not diminish its utility, especially as a continuous measure of the degree of depressive symptomatology in large-scale community surveys.

MEASURING DEPRESSION: MOOD, SYMPTOM, OR SYNDROME?

There is some current confusion about the meaning of four concepts frequently used to describe states of mental health: mood symptom, syndrome, and illness. A mood is a conscious state of mind or a predominant emotion or feeling. A symptom, on the other hand, can be defined as subjective evidence of disease or disturbance. A syndrome is a group of symptoms that occur together and can characterize a particular abnormality. Psychiatric illness can be said to exist when we have evidence of an unhealthy condition of mind. Most self-reported symptom scales in epidemiology today treat mental illness as a single condition that may vary in intensity or severity but is undistinguishable with regard to syndromes.

In using self-reported depressed-mood or symptom scales, we are not measuring diagnosed psychiatric illness. Rather, we are attempting to measure depression as a group of symptoms. It is actually the prevalence of depressive symptoms that we are measuring in a population. The inferential leap from depressive symptoms to depression is, as yet, unmeasured. With some exceptions (Myers and Weissman, 1980; Schoenbach et al., 1981; Boyd, Weissman, Thompson, and Myers, 1982; and Roberts and Vernon, 1983), little has been published on the relationship between self-reported symptom-rating scales and the clinical diagnosis of depression in normal community populations.

However, with the advent of the National Institute of Mental Health Diagnostic Interview Schedule, which is currently being fielded nationally, we look forward to an increasing ability to study diagnostically specific psychiatric disorders in a community population (Locke et al., 1981; Robins et al., 1981; Robins et al., 1980). Ideally, the use of a reliable and valid diagnostically specific depression scale with a self-reported symptom scale would give us the opportunity to compare the two measures. Specifications as to how the two instruments relate would give us the information necessary to infer from depressive symptoms to a psychiatric illness syndrome (i.e., depression).

At present, however, we must be content with studying depressive symptomatology in a community population. Since the inception of our work, we have been concerned with examining the relationships of stressful life events and social support to psychiatric disorders. We chose the Center for Epidemiologic Studies Depression (CES-D) Scale based on the judgment that it was the most feasible measure of depression available at the time. The scale is a self-reported measure designed to tap the prevalence of depressive symptoms in a given population during the week prior to the actual interview.

THE CENTER FOR EPIDEMIOLOGICAL STUDIES DEPRESSION (CES-D) SCALE: HISTORY OF DEVELOPMENT

Usage

In the present study, depression is measured using the Center for Epidemiological Studies Depression (CES-D) Scale. The scale was designed for use in the measurement of current depressive symptomatology. The 20 items comprising the scale were chosen from 5 previously utilized depression scales: the Zung Depression Scale (Zung, 1965), the Beck depression scale (Beck, Ward, Mendelson, Mock, and Erbaugh, 1961), portions of the Minnesota Multiphasic Personality Inventory (Dohlstrom and Welsh, 1960), the Raskin self-reported depression scale (Raskin, Chulterbrandt, Reating, and McKeon, 1970), and the Gardner symptom checklist (Gardner, 1968). These items are assumed to represent all of the major components of depressive symptomatology. According to Radloff (1975), these include: (1) depressed mood, (2) feelings of guilt and worthlessness, (3) feelings of helplessness and hopelessness, (4) loss of appetite, (5) sleep disturbance, and (6) psychomotor retardation.

The CES-D scale was first tested in the early 1970s using a community sample and a psychiatric patient sample (Weissman, Prusoff, and Newberry, 1975; Weissman, Scholomskes, Pollenger, Prusoff, and Locke, 1977). It was found to have high internal consistency (Radloff, 1977) and test–retest reliability. It has been documented to be highly related to other standardized depression scales (Weissman and Locke, 1975; Weissman et al., 1977). Some researchers have looked at its sociodemographic correlates (Comstock and Helsing, 1976; Craig and Van Natta, 1979; Markush and Favero, 1973; Radloff, 1975), whereas others have controlled for socioeconomic factors (Frerichs, Aneshensel, Clark, and Yôkopenic, 1981). The findings point to subgroup differences in amount of depression experienced as well as to economic strain as an important determinant of higher rates of depression.

TABLE 4.1
The Center for Epidemiological Studies Depression (CES-D) Scale

Please indicate how often you have felt this way during the last week.
  3. Most or all of the time (5–7 days a week)
  2. Occasionally or a moderate amount of time (3–4 days a week)
  1. Some or a little of the time (1–2 days a week)
  0. Rarely or none of the time (less than once a week)

1. I was bothered by things that usually don't bother me.
2. I felt that everything I did was an effort.
3. I felt I was just as good as other people.
4. I had trouble keeping my mind on what I was doing.
5. I felt sad.
6. I felt fearful.
7. I felt lonely.
8. I had crying spells.
9. I talked less than usual.
10. My sleep was restless.
11. I enjoyed life.
12. I felt that I could not shake off the blues even with the help of my family/friends.
13. I thought my life had been a failure.
14. I was happy.
15. I could not get "going."
16. I felt hopeful about the future.
17. People were unfriendly.
18. I did not feel like eating; my appetite was poor.
19. I felt depressed.
20. I felt that people disliked me.

Reliability

The CES-D scale consists of 20 symptoms (see Table 4.1). Sixteen of the symptoms are worded negatively, whereas the other four are worded positively. This was done to avoid the possibility of patterned responses. Respondents are asked how often they experienced each of the 20 symptoms during the past week. Responses are rated on a four-point scale: (0) *rarely or none of the time (less than once a week)*, (1) *some or a little of the time* (1–2 days a week), (2) *occasionally or a moderate amount of time* (3–4 days a week), or (3) *most or all of the time* (5–7 days a week). The responses to the four positive items (numbers 3, 11, 14, and 16) are then scored in reverse (0 becomes 3, 1 becomes 2, etc.). A total sum of the responses constitutes the scale score for the respondent. The item–item and item–total scale correlations are generally high in both patient populations and community samples. The alpha coefficients range from .84 to .90 (Radloff, 1977), thus evidencing high internal consistency.

It should be pointed out that the scale was designed to measure only current symptomatology. It is likely that symptomatology may vary over time. Indeed, as Radloff noted, the correlations between reports of depressive symptomatology decreased, on the average, over time. That is to say, the shorter the period of time between the initial test and the subsequent retest, the higher the correlations of symptoms in the two time periods. However, all the correlations were in the range of .45 to .70. Furthermore, these correlations are consistent with those found previously for the SCL-90 Depression Scale (Radloff, 1977).

Validity

Radloff has also tested the validity of the CES-D scale. Because the scale was based on depressive symptoms identified in clinical cases (Radloff, 1975), it seemed likely that the scale would discriminate between clinical groups and general community groups. This was found to be true. In fact, the correlation of the CES-D scale with Hamilton Clinician's Rating Scale scores increased substantially after a 1-month treatment period.

Correlations between the CES-D scale and other scales (such as the Lubin Scale and the Bradburn Negative Affect Scale) range from .50 to .70. This could be taken as evidence of its discriminant validity. An attempt at discerning its construct validity was made by examining the average CES-D scores of respondents who reported presence or absence of certain life events for a 1-year period preceding the interview. The absence of events was related to a decrease in this mean depression score both over events and over time. In addition, the more negative the event, the higher the CES-D score. Assuming that stressful life events bring about a depressive mood state, these results appear to indicate the sensitivity of the CES-D scale to mood determiners.

TYPES OF DEPRESSIVE SYMPTOMATOLOGY

As noted earlier, the CES-D scale was constructed by choosing components of symptomatology from depression scales that were popular at the time. Subjecting the 20 items comprising the scale to a factor analysis, Radloff found that the items clustered in four dimensions:

1. depressed affect, which included items like "having the blues," "feeling lonely," "crying," "feeling sad";
2. positive affect, including the four positively worded items ("feel good," "hopeful," "happy," and "enjoy life");
3. somatic and retarded activity (trouble sleeping, decrease in appetite); and
4. interpersonal ("feel people are unfriendly" and "disliked the person").

When replicated with other samples (Ensel, 1982; Ross and Mirowsky, 1984), the factor structure remained consistent. More important, the factors were similar to the components of depression that the scale was intended to tap. Thus the scale is empirically sensitive to dimensions of depressive symptomatology. However, because they are all dimensions of depression, Radloff recommends use of a total scale score.

In contrast, measuring the prevalence of depression in a population (as has been undertaken by Comstock and Helsing, 1976; Craig and Van Natta, 1976, 1979; Frerichs et al., 1981; Myers and Weissman, 1980; Radloff, 1975, 1977; Weissman and Myers, 1978), Dohrenwend and Crandell (1975) have suggested an alternative approach to the study of depression. Specifically, they make the case that we should concern ourselves with the persistence, or duration, of symptoms.

The work of Craig and Van Natta (1976, 1979) has proceeded in this vein. These researchers have found that the persistence of symptoms over the 1-week period preceding the interview better discriminates community respondents and nondepressed inpatients from their depressed counterparts than does prevalence. They further found that demographic factors differentially affect prevalence and persistence of depressive symptoms (Craig and Van Natta, 1979). They claim that any depression scale combining prevalence and persistence (i.e., affect and syndrome) will confound the measure if a total summated score is used. This will pose a particular problem in cases in which we are interested in identifying *mood swings* in individuals over time.

Given the current and rapid accumulation of work using the CES-D scale with regard to these issues, two questions need to be addressed: (1) To what extent can we replicate in the current study the validity and reliability of the CES-D scale, and (2) to what extent do our results replicate or fail to confirm others' findings? We will now proceed to address these issues.

RELIABILITY AND VALIDITY OF THE CES-D SCALE IN THE CURRENT STUDY: A COMPARISON WITH PREVIOUS WORK

The Reliability and Validity of the CES-D as an Interval Scale

As mentioned earlier, we utilized the same procedure in operationalizing the CES-D as has been used in earlier studies. Because we are dealing with two waves of data, the reliability of the scale was calculated for both time frames. As can be seen in Table 4.2, the alpha was consistently high in both Time 1 (T1) and Time 2 (T2) (α = .89 and .90, respectively). The correlations of the individual scale items with the total scale (with each respective item deleted from the total when calculating item–total correlations) was relatively consistent. With the exception of one of the positive-affect items ("I felt I was just as good as other people"), the item–total correlations ranged from .32 to .73 in T1 and from .31 to .76 in T2. To further insure that no single item within the scale was significantly reducing the reliability of the total scale, alpha coefficients were recalculated with each item removed. The result was that no single item significantly reduced the internal consistency of the scale. The alphas ranged from .88 to .91. In short, the scale not only proved to be reliable in the two waves of the current study, but the magnitude of the reliability coefficient proved to be consistent with those found by Radloff and her associates.

The validity of the CES-D scale was next addressed by an examination of the correlations of the 20 individual items and the total scale with a variable that, together with a measure of depression, forms the basis of one of the most enduring epidemiologic models currently in existence, the stressor–illness model. This variable is commonly referred to as the life-events measure.

Findings from numerous studies on the relationship of stressful life events to depression over the past 20 years show that an increase in the experience of life events is related to an increase in the level of various measures of illness (depression, psychophysiological symptomatology, etc.). The magnitude of this zero-order relationship ranges from .10 to .30 (Dohrenwend and Dohrenwend, 1974b, 1978; Ensel and Tausig, 1982; Gurin et al., 1960; Holmes and Rahe, 1967; Myers, Weissman, and Thompson, 1979; Rabkin and Struening, 1977; Radloff, 1975; Tausig, 1982; Williams, Ware, and Donald, 1981).

Utilizing the summated score on the life-events schedule (see Chapter 5 for details on the scoring procedure), we find that the correlation

TABLE 4.2
Reliability and Validity of the CES-D Scale in Albany Area Total Time 1 (T1) Sample and in T1 and Time 2 (T2) Subsamples

Scale items	Sample T1 (N = 1091)			Subsample T1 (N = 871)			Subsample T2 (N = 871)		
	Item-total correlation[a]	Alpha if item deleted	Item-SLE[b] correlation	Item-total correlation[a]	Alpha if item deleted	Item-SLE[b] correlation	Item-total correlation[a]	Alpha if item deleted	Item-SLE[b] correlation
Bothered	.54	.89	.22	.52	.89	.21	.58	.90	.17
Poor appetite	.43	.89	.13	.39	.89	.13	.53	.90	.13
Blues	.67	.88	.15	.66	.88	.15	.72	.89	.16
Felt as good as others	.27	.90	.04	.27	.89	.06	.15	.91	−.06
Hard to concentrate	.50	.89	.24	.49	.89	.23	.58	.90	.21
Depressed	.74	.88	.22	.73	.88	.18	.76	.89	.20
Everything an effort	.59	.89	.21	.59	.88	.18	.61	.90	.18
Hopeful	.41	.89	.05	.41	.89	.05	.31	.90	.06
Failure	.45	.89	.10	.47	.89	.10	.58	.90	.10
Fearful	.60	.89	.21	.60	.88	.21	.62	.90	.23
Restless sleep	.49	.89	.15	.47	.89	.15	.56	.90	.19
Happy	.55	.89	.14	.54	.89	.14	.62	.90	.19
Talked less	.44	.89	.18	.43	.89	.18	.50	.90	.16
Lonely	.62	.89	.23	.62	.88	.22	.66	.90	.20
People unfriendly	.34	.89	.16	.32	.89	.14	.38	.90	.11
Enjoyed life	.52	.89	.06	.51	.89	.08	.49	.90	.12
Crying spells	.51	.89	.12	.50	.89	.14	.51	.90	.15
Sad	.68	.88	.24	.69	.88	.23	.71	.90	.23

	T1 (1091)			T1 (871)			T2 (871)		
People disliked me	.49	.89	.20	.48	.89	.18	.50	.90	.11
Couldn't get going	.58	.89	.24	.59	.88	.24	.60	.90	.22
Total scale			.29			.26			.26
Total scale mean	8.60			8.44			8.70		
Total scale standard deviation	9.27			9.12			9.53		
Average item means	.43			.42			.43		
Standard deviation of item means	.21			.16			.17		
Min/max item means	.15/.67			.14/.66			.13/.66		
X inter-item correlation	.30			.30			.33		
Standard deviation of inter-item correlation	.11			.11			.14		
Min/max inter-item correlation	.09/.66			.08/.67			.01/.68		
Alpha-total scale	.89			.89			.90		

[a] Corrected.
[b] Stressful life events.

of life events (LE) to depression (CES-D) in T1 is .28. The same correlation in T2 is .26. The range of the individual CES-D items' correlations to LE in T1 is .06 to .24, and in T2 it is .06 to .23. Thus, this test of the external validity of the CES-D scale produces results consistent with those found in the literature.

Comparison of Means and Standard Deviations across Subgroups

A further test of the reliability and the validity of the CES-D scale was conducted in this study for various subgroups of the sample. Given the importance of the CES-D scale as the ultimate dependent variable in our study, we considered it necessary to test rigorously the representativeness and consistency of this scale.

Table 4.3 compares the means and standard deviations of the CES-D scale in our Albany Area Health Survey to those reported by Radloff in the Kansas City and Washington County studies. As can be seen, the mean scores on the CES-D scale are consistent across the three studies ($\bar{X}$ CES-D Kansas City = 9.9; $\bar{X}$ CES-D Washington County = 9.1; $\bar{X}$ CES-D Albany area = 8.6). Furthermore, the CES-D proves to be consistent across the three studies when we control for such key demographic factors as gender, marital status, employment status, age, education, and income. (It should be noted that the greater discrepancy in income is due, in part, to the use of different income categories in the studies. The income categories in the Albany Area Health Survey had to be redistributed proportionally to conform to those in the Washington County and Kansas City studies, and thus should be treated as only approximations of these categories.)

Comparison of Factor Analyses

As we mentioned earlier, attempts have been made to subdivide the CES-D scale into specific subtypes of depression. The most commonly used method has been to conduct a factor analysis of the scale (Radloff, 1977). Given the precedents and our interest in types of depression, in this study we conducted a factor analysis (orthogonal factors with varimax rotation 0 and eigenvalues greater than 1) of the CES-D scale. Table 4.4 shows the results of this analysis.

As can be seen, four separate factors are distinguishable as a result of this analysis. Interestingly, with the exception of one item in the T1 data and two items in the T2 data, we replicate the factor structure found by Radloff in her study. That is, we find four factors: (1) Somatic-

TABLE 4.3

Average CES-D Scores for Whites in Kansas City, Washington County, and Albany Area for Selected Demographic Categories

Demographic categories	CES-D field-test sites[a]								
	Kansas City			Washington County			Albany area		
	N	X̄	SD	N	X̄	SD	N	X̄	SD
Total (whites only)	1173	9.92	9.32	1672	9.13	8.27	1091	8.60	9.27
Gender									
White males	335	8.18	8.24	679	7.85	7.13	468	7.83	8.27
White females	541	10.32	9.48	959	10.03	8.95	470	9.54	10.33
Marital Status									
Married	568	8.88	—	1142	8.35	—	620	7.31	8.28
Divorced/separated	86	11.17	—	126	12.39	—	86	13.05	12.44
Widowed	105	10.94	—	210	10.56	—	48	12.21	12.44
Never married	111	9.84	—	159	10.13	—	184	10.35	9.32
Unemployed	122	11.84	10.16	77	11.34	8.95	41	11.11	12.59

Demographic categories	Combined field-test sites			Albany area		
	N	X̄	SD	N	X̄	SD
Age (for married whites only)						
<25	171	11.34	—	39	10.49	11.21
25–64	1358	8.41	—	520	7.32	8.14
65+	180	6.75	—	61	5.20	6.56
Education (for married whites only)						
Less than high school	636	9.42	—	129	7.47	9.30
High-school graduate	614	8.86	—	231	7.62	8.77
Some college	262	6.98	—	122	7.68	7.60
College graduate	197	6.73	—	137	6.32	6.91
Income (for married whites only)						
<$4000	152	10.28	—	96	8.03	9.24
$4000–11,999	740	9.00	—	207	7.46	8.52
$12,000+	704	7.69	—	317	7.00	7.80

[a] Radloff (1975, 1977)

TABLE 4.4
Factor Analysis of CES-D Scale in Albany Area Study (Wave 1)[a]

	Factor loadings on CES-D scale				
CES-D scale items	Factor 1	Factor 2	Factor 3	Factor 4	
Bothered	.538	.259	.123	.112	
Poor appetite	.453	.165	.120	.088	
Everything an effort	.553	.203	.222	.214	
Restless sleep	.518	.122	.171	.087	Somatic-Retarded
Couldn't get going	.500	.269	.201	.182	Activity
Hard to concentrate	.523	.173	.129	.124	
Blues	.511	.462	.189	.165	
Depressed	.480	.580	.285	.135	
Lonely	.319	.486	.253	.241	
Crying spells	.217	.525	.160	.160	Depressed Affect
Sad	.367	.687	.212	.123	
Fearful	.344	.462	.214	.210	
Felt as good as others	.074	.047	.422	.082	
Hopeful	.167	.127	.518	.092	Positive Affect
Happy	.243	.260	.653	.061	
Enjoyed life	.173	.265	.658	.037	
People unfriendly	.207	.112	.092	.425	Interpersonal
People disliked me	.191	.258	.096	.782	Relations
Failure	.141	.381	.205	.259	
Talked less	.384	.194	.074	.231	

Alphas for factors
  Factor 1 = .80
  Factor 2 = .83
  Factor 3 = .70
  Factor 4 = .60

[a]Range of factor r's: .25–.71. N = 1091.

retarded Activity, (2) Depressed Affect, (3) Positive Affect, and (4) Interpersonal Relations. The Positive Affect and the Interpersonal Relations factors contain the same items as did Radloff's comparable factors. With regard to the T1 data, there was a crossover of one item from Radloff's Depressed Affect factor to the Somatic-Retarded Activity factor (the inability of the respondent to "shake off the blues"). With this and two minor exceptions in the T2 factor analysis, the Somatic-Retarded Activity factor and the Depressed Affect factor hold up quite well. In fact, the alpha coefficients for the four factors in the two time periods are not only high ($\alpha = .60 - .83$), they are consistent in magnitude with those reported elsewhere. (See Table 4.5 for details.)

Although the interpretation of these factors is beyond the scope of the current chapter, we can nevertheless conclude that the internal structure of the CES-D scale can be consistently and reliably factored into a set of exclusive depressive categories.

RELATIONSHIP OF THE CES-D SCALE OVER TIME

At this juncture, it would be appropriate to examine the stability of the CES-D over time. Although a case for the test–retest reliability of the scale could probably be made from the results presented thus far, we feel this would not be a proper test. It must be recalled that the scale is designed to detect depressed mood during the week prior to the interview, and that the likelihood of change occurring during the 1-year interval between the two measurements is highly probable. Furthermore, the changes that may have taken place during this period more than likely have been affected by the occurrence of certain life events or other social conditions. An examination of these conditions and their effects will be postponed until Chapter 17. What we will examine here is the magnitude of the relationship of depression measured in T1 to depression measured 1 year later.

The range of the over-time correlations for items in the scale is from .15 to .37. The relationship of each factor to itself 1 year later ranges from .26 to .39. It is interesting to note here that two of the four factors are more highly related to each other over time than other factors. These factors are the Somatic-Retarded Activity factor and the Depressed Affect factor (over-time r's — .39 and .38, respectively). It may be that internal symptoms such as trouble sleeping, poor appetite, not being able to shake off the blues, and feeling sad and fearful are more enduring than are symptoms reflecting a more external nature (people being unfriendly, feeling disliked by others). Again, we must caution that it is difficult to separate change over time that is due to the unreliability of the measure from change that is caused by particular events. It is equally possible that the person's state of psychological well-being has changed many times over the 1-year period and that our measurements have picked up only two separate mood states.

Finally, the overall scale shows an over-time correlation of .41. Although the reader should be alert to the caveats already mentioned, a correlation of such magnitude over a 1-year period would appear to be indicative, at least in part, of some stability in mood state over time. In Chapter 17, we deal with this issue in more detail.

TABLE 4.5
Reliability and Validity of the Factor Structure in Albany Area Total Time 1 (T1) Sample and in T1 and Time 2 (T2) Subsamples

CES-D item/factor	Total sample T1 (N = 1091)				Subsample T1 (N = 871)				Subsample T2 (N = 871)			
	Item-factor correlation	Alpha	Alpha if item deleted	Factor-SLE[a] correlation	Item-factor correlation	Alpha	Alpha if item deleted	Factor-SLE[a] correlation	Item-factor correlation	Alpha	Alpha if item deleted	Factor-SLE[a] correlation
Somatic/ retarded activity		.80		.28		.79		.28		.83		.26
Bothered	.52		.77		.52		.76		.57		.81	
Poor appetite	.44		.79		.41		.78		.54		.82	
Everything an effort	.60		.76		.59		.75		.65		.80	
Restless sleep	.51		.78		.49		.77		.58		.81	
Hard to get going	.58		.76		.57		.75		.61		.80	
Hard to concentrate	.51		.78		.50		.77		.56		.81	

Blues	.55		.77		.56		.76		.57		.81	
Depressed affect		.83		.26		.83		.26		.85		.25
Depressed	.70		.78		.70		.78		.70		.81	
Lonely	.57		.81		.57		.81		.63		.82	
Crying spells	.62		.80		.61		.80		.66		.82	
Sad	.55		.82		.54		.82		.59		.84	
Fearful	.74		.77		.74		.76		.75		.79	
Positive affect		.70		.11		.70		.11		.66		.10
Felt as good as others	.37		.70		.36		.71		.30		.69	
Hopeful	.47		.65		.49		.63		.44		.59	
Happy	.55		.59		.55		.60		.51		.55	
Enjoyed life	.55		.59		.55		.59		.54		.52	
Interpersonal		.60		.18		.61		.18		.67		.13
People unfriendly	.43		—		.44		—		.51		—	
People disliked me	.43		—		.44		—		.51		—	

[a]Stressful life events.

THE CES-D AND CLINICAL CASENESS

Origin of Clinical Caseness Cutoff Points

There have recently been some attempts to estimate the prevalence of possible clinical depression in a community by using various cutoff points on the CES-D scale. From this has been developed what has come to be referred to as the *clinical caseness* cutoff point (Comstock and Helsing, 1976; Eaton and Kessler, 1981; Myers and Weissman, 1980; Radloff, 1975).

Myers and Weissman (1980) have pointed out that little is known about the relationship between symptom-rating scales and clinical diagnosis of depression in a community, based on the Schedule for Affective Disorders and Schizophrenia–Research Diagnostic Criteria (RDC). This is due, they feel, to the fact that diagnostic instruments appropriate for a large-scale community study have not been available. The results of their study show that a self-report symptom scale (CES-D) can be used to identify the degree of possible clinical caseness for research and screening purposes, with a major depression cutoff point of 21 or above producing a false positive rate (percentage of cases missed) of only 4.1% but a false negative rate (percentage of cases incorrectly classified as positive) of 45.5%, based on a comparison with the RDC, a clinical scale. Using the traditional CES-D cutoff point of 16 and above for probably caseness produced a false positive rate of 6.1% and a false negative rate of 36.4%. Other researchers (Husaini, Neff, and Harrington, 1979), using a cutoff point of 17 and above for *probable caseness*, found similar false negative rates. Myers and Weissman (1980) concluded that the cutoff points on the CES-D scale are not as efficient in identifying cases of depression as other clinical instruments. Therefore, for present purposes, the cutoff points will be used only as rough indicators of clinical depression in the community.

In the current study, we have constructed a dichotomous variable to indicate the degree of possible clinical caseness in the community. A score of 0–15 reflects noncaseness, and a score of 16 or above reflects possible caseness.

Differences across Subgroups with Regard to the Percentage of Possible Clinically Depressed

Table 4.6 presents a comparison of the percentage of the population in our Albany Area Health Survey that scored above the cutoff point for clinical caseness with those found in three other studies utilizing the

TABLE 4.6
Proportions of CES-D Possible-Clinical-Depression Scores in National, Kansas City, Washington County, and Albany Area Samples for Selected Demographic Categories[a]

Demographic categories	Hanes national (1975) ($N = 2867$)	Kansas City (1973) ($N = 1154$)	Washington County (1974) ($N = 859$)	Albany area (1979) (Time 1 Subsample) ($N = 871$)
Total	16.4%	21.5%	17.0%	16.90%
Gender				
Male	10.8	17.5	11.9	13.6
Female	20.8	24.1	20.7	20.2
Age				
18–24	—	30.6	29.0	19.5
25–44	15.9	22.0	17.4	16.7
45–64	16.4	17.3	14.7	17.0
65+	14.8	19.6	12.3	14.3
Marital Status				
Single	17.1	27.3	20.4	18.1
Married	14.5	17.7	14.7	13.6
Widowed	23.4	26.4	19.4	34.8
Divorced/separated	28.2	29.4	30.1	27.0
Years of education				
0–7	25.3	22.4	25.2	19.6
8–11	24.6	27.8	18.8	
12	15.6	21.6	16.9	17.2
13+	8.8	15.3	11.7	15.0
Employment				
Working	13.1	18.6	14.4	12.7
Housework	20.6	22.5	21.3	22.1
Retired/student	14.8	23.7	16.8	18.0
Unemployed	28.1	32.8	28.1	31.6
Race				
White	15.3	19.8	17.0	16.8
Black	28.5	26.4	—	17.6

[a] The data reported under the Hanes national study came from augmented collection period of 1975 and can be found in Eaton and Kessler, 1981. The data reported for the Kansas City and Washington County studies is a composite of information presented in an article by Comstock and Helsing, 1976. It should be noted that although the Kansas City sample contained both blacks and whites, the data reported for Washington County applies to whites only.

20-item CES-D scale: the Hanes Augmented National Study (Eaton and Kessler, 1981), the Kansas City Study and the Washington County Study (Comstock and Helsing, 1976; Radloff, 1975, 1977). In addition, percentages are presented for various subgroups in the population.

As can be seen, 17% of the sample in the Albany Area Health Survey were at or above the cutoff score for possible clinical depression. This is comparable to the percentages found in the Hanes national study (16.4%) and in the Washington County study (17.0%). The Kansas City sample was somewhat higher (21.5%). Controlling for various sociodemographic factors within the samples reveals two general findings: (1) The percentages for the Albany area are generally more consistent with those in the national Washington County sample than they are with those in the Kansas City sample. (2) The percentage of individuals possibly clinically depressed is generally higher across the various categories in the Kansas City sample than in the other three studies. This is due, in part, to the larger percentage of blacks in the Kansas City sample (26%) than in the national sample (8%), the Albany area sample (8%), or the Washington County sample (0%). With the exception of married individuals, the blacks in the Kansas City sample are significantly more depressed than their white counterparts. This, coupled with the larger proportion of blacks in the sample, tends to inflate the percentage of individuals possibly clinically depressed in the total Kansas City sample and in its subgroups.

Of particular interest here are the categories of the population that have a greater risk of being clinically depressed: females; young adults; the widowed, the divorced, and particularly the separated; and those with less than a high-school education, those out of work, and housewives. Although it is tempting to speculate as to what factors may affect this differential susceptibility to depression, we will defer this discussion to Part V. It is enough to say at this point that the comparability of the Albany Area Health Survey findings to those of the Washington County study and, more significantly, the national study, strengthens our faith in the inferential capabilities of this research. However, although the Albany area data compare closely to the national data, it must be pointed out that there is a 5-year gap between the data-collection periods for the two studies.

SUMMARY

In the current study, depression is measured using the Center for Epidemiological Studies Depression Scale (CES-D). This is a 20-item self-report scale designed to measure depressive symptoms during the week prior to the interview. This chapter had detailed the history and use of the scale. The reliability and validity of the scale proved to be strong across both waves of data collection in the current study. It also compared quite favorably and consistently with findings reported in other studies in which its psychometric properties have been evaluated. A factor analysis of the scale resulted in a set of four factors (Somatic-Retarded Activity, Depressed Affect, Positive Affect, and Interpersonal Relations), which were identical to those empirically uncovered in another study (Radloff, 1975). Future work should be conducted to determine whether it would be preferable to use these four components of depressed mood or a total score. A test of the degree to which these factors are consistent across subgroups (i.e., men–women, married–not married, young–old), as well as an examination of their correlates, remains to be conducted. Although there was a 1-year gap between our measurements of depression, the CES-D showed a rather strong over-time correlation ($r = .41$). Although we pointed out caveats regarding this rather long time period, we believe there is consistency and stability of depressive symptomatology over the 1-year period between measurements.

Work has been done utilizing a cutoff point for clinical caseness on the CES-D scale. Using this cutoff point, our results showed that 17% of our community sample could be considered to have been possibly clinically depressed. Our results in comparing percentages of possible clinical depression across various demographic categories of respondents in our sample compared favorably to those found in other studies employing the CES-D.

However, there are three issues that still remain: (1) What, if any, alternative diagnostic measures of depression exist? (2) To what extent can we use the CES-D as a true measure of clinical depression? And (3) what are the limitations in using the CES-D as a clinically diagnostic tool in evaluating the level of clinical depression in a general community?

These three issues are all related to each other. The ideal method of evaluating the degree to which the CES-D scale is a true barometer of depressive symptomatology in a community, for use as a diagnostic tool, would be to employ a large staff of trained clinicians to utilize a standardized technique for making psychiatric diagnoses in a community, for purposes of comparison. In addition, it would be well advised to have a control group consisting of a patient population. In this way, a precise comparison of the CES-D scale with such a diagnostically specific instrument administered by professionals could be conducted. An exact count of what Myers and Weissman (1980) term *false positives* and *false negatives* on the scale (in short, errors in accuracy) could be reached. Errors due to variance in depression criteria, subject fatigue, external events, and other potential confounding factors could be evaluated. Unfortunately, such data do not exist for the first two waves of our panel study.

However, with recent advances in the development of instruments applicable to large-scale surveys, and with increasing capability of diagnosing specific psychiatric disorders (Locke et al., 1981; Robins, Helzer, Croughan, and Ratcliff, 1980; Weissman, Myers, and Harding, 1978), we have added an additional scale to the third wave of our panel study. Specifically, in our third wave we have incorporated a segment of the third version of the NIMH Diagnostic Interview Schedule (DIS) pertaining to depression, as an additional measure of depression (Robins et al., 1980). This we feel will provide for a systematic comparison of results for the CES-D and the DIS depression measures. Specification of the relationship between the two measures will allow more confidence in any inferences about levels of possible or probable clinical depression in a community population. The degree of potential variations obtained with the two measures can also be evaluated. This would, at a minimum, serve to further clarify the implications of our own study, as well as other studies that have used the CES-D. Issues of accurately measuring depressive symptomatology and its prevalence and persistence, and of determining levels of clinical depression, could be more readily assessed and illuminated. Furthermore, when the diagnostic capabilities of the two measures are understood, the brevity and ease of administration of the CES-D scale might remain an attractive research instrument for epidemiological investigators whose concern lies mainly with the pervasiveness of symptoms and the causal process affecting the symptoms. We hope to report our findings on these issues in subsequent publications.

For the present, the reliability, validity, and consistency of the CES-D measure in the current study has proven quite strong.

5

Measuring Life Events

MARK TAUSIG

INTRODUCTION

This chapter describes our measure of life events and explores its properties. In the process we review some of the theoretical issues that have attended the use of the life-events construct and use our data to empirically evaluate them. We also indicate some of the alternate ways in which the life-events scale may be employed in which it is used within this volume.

THE STRESS(OR) CONSTRUCT

Stress has several related meanings that are embedded in the use of the stressor construct by social epidemiologists. Stress can be defined in terms of physical pressure exerted by either one thing on another (strain), the importance or significance attached to a thing (emphasis), an internal response to external forces (reaction or resistance), or a stimulus that disturbs or interferes with the normal physiological equilibrium of an organism (disruption).

Social epidemiologists focus on a class of stimuli that has its origin in the course of social life (Dohrenwend and Dohrenwend, 1974a). There is, however, variation in *which* component of the definition of stress is intended by researchers who study these social stimuli. For instance, those working from a biogenic perspective view life events as strains (noxious stimuli) that are equivalent to disruption. From a psychogenic perspective, the emphasis (i.e. desirability) of an event predicts disruptive effects.

Efforts by social epidemiologists to describe the stress process offer, we believe, a more comprehensive perspective (Pearlin et al., 1981; McFarlane, Norman, Streiner, and Roy, 1983). The outline of the stress process not only embodies the different meanings of the stress conduct but can be employed to clarify some of the ambiguities of previous research on the relationship between stress and illness.

In essence, the components of the definition of stress comprise a model of the stress process that contains an explicit causal sequence and a clarification of the role of each component in the sequence (Pearlin et al., 1981). This sequence suggests that the occurrence of a life event, per se, does not directly lead to disruption, but that the life event's effect is mediated by the emphasis placed on the event and by the nature of the reaction or resistance generated to the life event.

Most importantly for this chapter, this model of the relationship between components of the definition of stress can also be employed to specify the nature and meaning of our measure of life events and the types of analytic inquiries we should make. The interest here is to evaluate our measure as an indicator of either strain or emphasis—the sources of stress.

ANALYTIC TASKS

The assessment of our measure of life events has three major goals: (1) to establish the reliability of the measure, (2) to examine the utility of using our measure as an indicator of strain (frequency of events) and/or as a measure of emphasis (desirability), and (3) to assure that the measure is not confounded with our principal outcome measure, depressive symptoms. In the process we clarify the construct meaning of the indicator as used in this study, and set the stage for its use in general models of life events, social support, and depression.

Accordingly, the remainder of this chapter addresses the following subjects: the origin and description of the life-events measure, the assessment of its psychometric properties, its use as an indicator of strain and/or emphasis, and its relationship to CES-D depression scores.

Life Event Schedules and Their Variations

The measurement of significant and stressful life events is beset by a peculiar contradiction. A single instrument (Holmes and Rahe, 1967) has largely served as the operational model for measuring life events for the past 20 years, while it has been simultaneously subject to severe criticism both as a measurement tool and as an operational equivalent of the stress(or) construct.

The original 43-item Holmes and Rahe Social Readjustment Rating Scale (1967) was designed to assess the relative readjustment required in an individual's life resulting from a variety of life events. According to Holmes and Rahe, adjustment to life events, regardless of the desirability of the events, can be taken as an indicator of stress induced by the need to respond to a given event or series of events. The Holmes and Rahe scale fits a biogenic model of illness onset, developed by Meyer (Lief, 1948) and Selye (1956), in which the greater the magnitude of expected adjustment to events (life change units), the more likely that subsequent illness will be observed. The scale combines the strain and emphasis components by its use of weights to estimate the emphasis given to particular events. The preliminary application of this scale in a variety of contexts indicated that the assessment of life-change units could be used to account for subsequent illness (Holmes and Masuda, 1974; Masuda and Holmes, 1967; Pugh, Erickson, Rubin, Gunderson, and Rahe, 1971; Rahe, Pugh, Erickson, Gunderson, and Rubin, 1971).

Other researchers have added to the basic list of events, and some have prepared lists of types of events important for special populations (Dohrenwend, Krasnoff, Ashebasy, and Dohrenwend, 1978; Meyers et al., 1972; Rahe, 1975). The basic structure of the instrument has remained the same, however.

Life Events as Emphasis: Desirability of Events

Perhaps the most persistent criticism of the Holmes and Rahe scale revolves around the definitional assertion that events are related to the onset of illness regardless of their desirability. We have already mentioned that Holmes and Rahe developed the scale with a biogenic model of stress and illness in mind. Both sociogenic and psychogenic interpretations of this relationship tend to emphasize the critical importance of the desirability of events as an explanation of this relationship.

Most authors who have empirically investigated this question find that undesirable events are better predictors of illness than are desirable events (Myers and Pepper, 1971; Paykel, 1974; Gersten, Langner, Eisenberg, and Orzek, 1974; Vinokur and Selzer, 1975; Ross and Mirowsky, 1979). Still, Tausig (1982) has shown that the measure of total events and of undesirable events alone are related to depression to a similar degree.

Construct Validity: Confounding with Depression

Several researchers have noted a theoretical overlap between particular life events in the scale and frequently used outcome measures (Morrison, Hudgens, and Barcha, 1968; Hudgens, Robins, and Delong, 1970; Ilfeld, 1976; Mueller, Edwards, and Yarris, 1977; Dohrenwend and Dohrenwend, 1978; Thoits, 1981). Indeed, many of the events in the life-events scale are either physiological or psychological in nature, and might therefore be reflected in measures of illness used as outcomes. Relationships between the independent variable of life-events scores and the dependent measures of illness would be incorrectly discovered to be higher because we would be measuring the same thing in both cases. Hudgens et al. (1970) estimated that 29 of the original 43 items in the Holmes and Rahe scale were themselves indicators of psychological distress. Thoits (1981) has suggested that scale items concerned with physical health will confound the observed relationship of the scale with outcome measures of physiological distress, although Ensel and Tausig (1982) did not find evidence of an overlap.

In their review article, Rabkin and Streuning (1976) point out that life-events researchers (many using the Holmes and Rahe measures) have generally reported correlation coefficients of .30 or less between life-events measures and various types of illness. This implies that, at best, life events may explain 9% of the variance related to illness outcomes. Life-events measures appear to be weak predictors of illness even though on the face of it the construct would seem to have high validity.

OUR MEASUREMENT OF LIFE EVENTS

The measure of life events used in this study is based on the Schedule of Recent Events (SRE), developed by Holmes and Rahe (1967) and the Recent Life Change Questionnaire (RLCQ) developed by Rahe

(1975). It includes additional and modified items from Myers et al. (1975) and Dohrenwend et al. (1978). The entire scale consists of 118 items (see Table 5.1). The expansion of the number of items from the 43 in the SRE and the 55 in the RLCQ was designed both to extend the scope of events tapped and to differentiate perceived desirable and undesirable events. The same list of events was used in both time periods.

Time Span

The respondents in the survey were asked to indicate whether any of the events listed had occurred during the previous 6 months. Several authors (Jenkins, Hurst, and Roser, 1979) have demonstrated that recall of life events diminishes over time. The recall of events appears to drop off at the approximate rate of 5% per month following the event. Therefore, 6 months was deemed to be a reasonable time frame. Theoretically, then, there should be no overlap among the cited events from Time 1 (T1) to Time 2 (T2), because the time between surveys was 1 year.

Desirability and Importance of Events

Respondents were asked to describe the desirability of each event that had occurred to them. A 3-point scale (good, uncertain, or bad) was used.

Respondents were also asked to assess the relative importance of each event. A 4-point scale ranging from very important to not important at all was provided. Our analysis of this dimension of life events indicated that respondents viewed every event as either important or very important. Therefore, we concluded that this aspect of life-events experience was not well measured. Importance was not measured in the T2 survey.

Scale Computation

We suggest that simple unweighted life events when counted up adequately represent the strain component of the stress definition. Weighting schemes applied to lists of life events seem to represent attempts to assess the relative emphasis (stressfulness) of different events. Whether it is strain or emphasis that is measured by a life-events list, a number of research studies report extremely high correlations between weighted and unweighted scoring of life-events inventories (Vinokur and Selzer, 1975; Mueller et al., 1977; Grant, Sweetwook, Gerst, and Yager, 1978; Ross and Mirowsky, 1979; Lei and Skinner, 1980). Empirically, then, weighting schemes do not appear to distinguish strain from emphasis. In our study we have used an unweighted, summated scale of life events that we have interpreted as an index of stressor frequency (strain), and a summated scale based on subjective reports of desirability/undesirability as an index of the emphasis placed on different events reported.

STATISTICAL DESCRIPTION OF LIFE-EVENTS SCALES

Table 5.1 contains a list of life events used in the study, together with the number of reported occurrences of each event for each of our samples. Examination of these data form the basis of all our subsequent analyses. The data from the total original sample (N = 1091) and the panel (N = 871 at T1 T2) are analyzed separately.

Despite the fact that we examine the data outlined in this table from a variety of additional perspectives in subsequent sections, the information provided in the table warrants some preliminary comments.

No scale for covering all events that might occur in people's lives can ever be considered exhaustive, because the list of possible events is theoretically infinite. Nevertheless, a satisfactory measure must include enough of their variety to provide a general picture of the frequency of significant events. Moreover, if many respondents' reported events are exceedingly infrequent, then no variations in the scale scores will be observed and measures of statistical association will demonstrate few relationships. Our use of 118 events, then, represents an attempt to capture a sufficient range of events.

Table 5.1 indicates that respondents in all three samples reported an average of almost $4\frac{1}{2}$ events in each previous 6-month period (4.47, 4.32, and 4.32, respectively). The relative frequency with which each event was reported in the two time periods is very similar. Therefore we can speak with some confidence of the relative frequency of events. For instance, serious physical illness are more frequent than are serious injuries or accidents. Only between 15% and 16% of respondents reported none of the listed events; 6 of 7 respondents reported at least 1 event.

These consistent patterns seem to indicate that event categories continued to be interpreted the same way by our panel of respondents and that the face validity of the items is reasonably good.

TABLE 5.1
Frequency of Life Events Reported for Previous 6 Months for All Samples

		Number of events		
	Total sample		Panel sample	
Life event	Time 1 (N = 1091)	Time 1 (N = 871)	Time 2 (N = 871)	
School				
[a]1. Started school	77	59	73	
[a]2. Graduated from school	53	39	29	
[a]3. Failed school	2	2	0	
[a]4. Ceased attending school	15	14	11	
[a]5. Changed schools	3	3	6	
[a]6. Problems in school	23	15	5	
Subscale total	173	132	124	
Home				
[a]7. Moved within same town	83	49	48	
[a]8. Moved to a different town	50	29	26	
[a]9. Moved to same type of neighborhood	60	33	24	
[a]10. Moved to a better neighborhood	43	26	34	
[a]11. Moved to a worse neighborhood	20	11	10	
[a]12. Built a new house	10	6	6	
[a]13. Remodeled house	92	82	91	
[a]14. Changed living conditions	64	51	56	
Subscale total	422	287	295	
Love and marriage				
[b]15. Began serious relationship	54	36	46	
[b]16. Ceased steady dating	42	28	22	
[b]17. Increased arguments with partner	28	21	16	
[b]18. Engaged	14	9	9	
19. Broke engagement	2	2	2	

(continued)

TABLE 5.1 (Continued)

| | Total sample | Panel sample | |
	Time 1 (N = 1091)	Time 1 (N = 871)	Time 2 (N = 871)
Life event		Number of events	
[a]20. Married	18	12	8
21. Child married with approval	6	5	7
22. Child married without approval	3	2	2
23. Divorced	3	2	7
[a]24. Marital separation	14	9	21
[b]25. Separated from spouse (tour, business, vacation)	53	44	43
26. Began extramarital affair	9	5	4
[a]27. Increased arguments with spouse	22	18	26
[a]28. Improved relations with spouse	28	25	19
[a]29. Trouble with in-laws	31	25	18
[a]30. Marital reconciliation	9	7	7
Subscale total	336	250	257
Family			
[a]31. Birth of first child	17	11	6
[a]32. Birth of other child	22	18	17
[a]33. Adoption of first child	0	0	0
[a]34. Adoption of other child	1	1	1
[a]35. New person moved into household	39	28	34
[a]36. Child left home—married	7	6	9
[a]37. Child left home—college	9	6	8
[a]38. Child left home—other reason	17	14	14
39. Family member entered armed forces	9	9	6
[a]40. Other family member left home	15	10	24
[a]41. Change in number of family get-togethers	80	57	42
[b]42. Birth of grandchild	36	28	28
Subscale total	252	188	189

Health			
[a]43. Serious physical illness	94	74	100
[a]44. Serious injury or accident	33	26	24
[a]45. Death of child	1	1	0
[a]46. Death of brother or sister	11	6	8
[a]47. Death of parent	21	14	9
[a]48. Death of other close family member	91	71	82
[a]49. Death of close friend	37	30	47
[a]50. Death of spouse	5	4	3
[b]51. Divorce of parents	4	2	3
[b]52. Remarriage of parent	2	2	2
[a]53. Change in health of family member	134	111	96
[a]54. Wanted pregnancy	40	28	27
[a]55. Unwanted pregnancy	3	2	1
56. Menopause	25	23	13
[b]57. Miscarriage	4	3	2
58. Stillbirth	0	0	0
59. Frequent minor illness	67	47	36
[b]60. Major dental work	64	54	36
61. Mental illness	7	7	4
62. Death of pet	49	40	32
[b]63. Abortion	5	3	4
64. Sexual difficulties	29	24	17
Subscale total	726	572	546
Personal change			
[a]65. Change in personal habits	66	51	61
[a]66. Change in amount/type of recreation	158	129	143
[a]67. Change in church activities	34	27	39
[a]68. Change in sleeping habits	95	69	64
[a]69. Change in eating habits	87	66	100
[a]70. Change in social activities	78	56	66
[b]71. Change in religious beliefs	13	11	16
[b]72. Change in political beliefs	16	14	27
Subscale total	547	423	516

(continued)

TABLE 5.1 (Continued)

Life event	Total sample Time 1 (N = 1091)	Panel sample Time 1 (N = 871)	Time 2 (N = 871)
Number of events			
Work and finance			
[a]73. Spouse started/ended work	49	47	39
74. Started to work first time	13	12	8
75. Started to work other than first time	42	30	38
76. Change to same type of job	30	28	29
[a]77. Change to different type of work	49	33	45
[a]78. More responsibilities at work	99	83	86
[a]79. Fewer responsibilities at work	15	13	17
[a]80. Promotion	26	24	36
[a]81. Demotion	4	3	2
[a]82. Transfer	9	9	9
[b]83. Laid off (temporarily)	39	28	26
[a]84. Expanded business	34	30	25
[a]85. Business failing	7	6	6
[a]86. Troubles with boss	53	42	32
[b]87. Troubles with co-workers	27	19	20
[b]88. Troubles with persons under your supervision	20	16	9
[b]89. Other work troubles	25	17	25
[a]90. Change in work hours or conditions	85	74	74
91. Out of work over a month	81	55	52
92. Out of work less than a month	44	29	17
[a]93. Fired	10	8	5
94. Reorganization at work	54	46	38
[a]95. Retirement	19	18	9
96. Significant success at work	100	89	101
[b]97. Home study to improve you in your work	33	28	20

[a]98. Major improvement in financial status	73	62	68
[a]99. Financial status a lot worse than usual	95	68	67
[a]100. Foreclosure of mortgage or loan	7	5	5
[a]101. Outstanding personal achievement	71	59	44
[b]102. Credit rating difficulties	25	2'	17
[a]103. Moderate purchase	185	142	141
[a]104. Major purchase or mortgage	45	38	41
Subscale total	1468	1181	1152
Legal			
[a]105. In court	51	40	36
[a]106. In jail	2	1	2
107. Arrested	8	3	5
[a]108. Law suit or legal action	31	22	28
109. Loss of driver's license	7	4	4
[a]110. Minor violations of the law	42	34	18
[b]111. Loss, robbery, or damage of personal property	53	36	30
Subscale total	194	140	123
Other			
112. Serious argument with neighbor, friend, relative	33	23	34
113. Improve relations with neighbor, friend, relative	49	36	30
114. Separation from significant person N.E.C.	75	50	33
[a]115. Vacation	194	164	189
[b]116. Accident	52	45	34
[b]117. Major decision regarding the future	238	184	144
118. Community crisis (fire, crime, etc.)	84	61	72
Subscale total	725	563	536
Total number of events	4,843	3,736	3,738
Number of respondents	1,084	864	864
Mean events per respondent	4.47	4.32	4.32
Percentage of respondents reporting no events	16.1	15.7	14.5

[a]Holmes and Rahe item (SRE, 1967) The original Holmes and Rahe instrument (1967) contained 42 items (excluding Christmas), which implicitly or explicitly contained subquestions (e.g., "Major Change in Responsibilities at Work— e.g., promotion, demotion, lateral transfer"). Each of these implied items was asked individually in this study; therefore, the number of items is greater than 42.

[b]Rahe (RLCQ, 1975 Revision).

Scale Properties: Psychometrics

The internal properties of the life-events scale can be approached from a psychometric perspective by examining the internal statistical properties of the scale. It can be argued that the experience of any given event is independent of the experience of any other event in the scale. Thus, no internal evaluation of items, such as a factor analysis or inter-item correlation matrices, would be expected to reveal any internal structure. The scale, then, would consist of a collection of items assumed to be statistically unrelated.

On the other hand, there is in fact evidence that the items in the scale do have an internal structure (Pugh et al., 1971; Rahe et al., 1971; Ruch and Holmes, 1971; Ruch, 1977; Skinner and Lei, 1980). These analyses suggest that not all events have an independent likelihood of occurrence. Others have divided the scale into categories based on conceptual classifications, for instance, school-related events, work-related events, and so on (Myers et al., 1971; Paykel et al., 1969; Paykel 1974). Although not based on statistically derived criteria, this latter approach also imposes a structure on the scale.

The scale has also been subdivided in other ways, including events consisting of entry or exit from the social field (Myers and Pepper, 1972), anticipated or unanticipated events (Pearlin and Lieberman, 1979), ego-controlled or uncontrolled stressors (Fairbank and Hough, 1979; Paykel, 1974), and chronic or acute stressors (Marshall, Funch, and Feather, 1982). Each of these attempts to specify some dimensions of the scale represents a different conceptual approach to interpreting the meaning of the scale.

The various attempts to do factor or cluster analysis on the life-event scale (Pugh et al., 1971; Rahe et al., 1971; Ruch and Holmes, 1971; Ruch, 1977; Skinner and Lei, 1980) have shown similar but relatively unenlightening results. These studies generally find that a principal factor consists of items assessing changes in such personal life activities as eating and sleeping habits or social activity. Additional factors are both statistically weak and conceptually inconsistent. Our own factor analysis of the (T1) sample largely agreed with previous results (Tausig, 1982).

Part of the difficulty in performing these sorts of analyses on life-events measures comes from the great differences in the total frequency of different events and part from the fact that the events in the lists are intended to be independent of one another.

The weight of the evidence suggests that the scale does not possess regular internal statistical properties; that is, empirically the scale does not seem to have a statistical structure. Theoretically, however, the scale may be divided in many ways into a priori categories. These categories, in turn, may be examined for their selective impact on a dependent variable and among themselves.

The most frequently applied categorization of events classifies them according to life-activity areas (Myers et al., 1971; Rahe, 1975; Tausig, 1982). Our list of events were grouped according to this logic into nine life-activity areas: school, home, love and marriage, family, health, personal change, work and finances, and miscellaneous events. The mean number of events of each type and their correlations with depression (CES-D) were computed. The results are summarized in Table 5.2.

Subscale Differences

If we compare the actual means for each subscale's events frequency with its expected mean computed by multiplying the proportion of all items that are in the subscale by the total sample's observed mean frequency of all events on the total scale, we can see that some subsets' types of events are observed more than expected, and others less than expected. The differences are small, however. Events in the subscales for love and marriage, health, personal change, and legal events occur less frequently than expected, whereas events in the subscales for family and for work and finances occur more frequently. Nevertheless, it does not appear that events in any one subscale are particularly over-represented.

The situation is somewhat different when we examine the correlation of each subscale event occurrence with depression scores (CES-D). Occurrence of personal change, health-related events, and events concerning love and marriage are consistently more highly correlated with depression scores than are the other subscales. In only one case (personal-change events in T2), however, does a subscale correlation exceed the correlation of the total scale with depression, and this difference is not significant.

Thus although the observed frequency of events does not always differ from expected frequencies, the relationship with our dependent variable does vary by subscale. However, although this is true, the absence of any significantly greater correlations with depression compared to the total scale suggests that no particular life-activity areas are uniquely responsible for the overall observed relationship with depression. That is, no single life-activity area is especially critical to the development of depressive symptoms. School-related events are not

TABLE 5.2
Life-Events Subscales: Number of Items, Means, and Correlations with Depression Scores (CES-D) for All Samples

Life-events subscale	Number of items	Expected mean[a]	Actual Mean			Correlation with Depression (CES-D)		
			Total sample	Panel sample		Total sample	Panel sample	
			Time 1 (N = 1091)	Time 1 (N = 871)	Time 2 (N = 871)	Time 1 (N = 1091)	Time 1 (N = 871)	Time 2 (N = 871)
School	6	.23	.24	.21	.20	.07	.05*	.02*
Home	8	.30	.36	.32	.34	.10	.08	.09
Love and marriage	16	.60	.27	.26	.25	.19	.19	.20
Family	12	.45	.30	.29	.33	.20	.18	.13
Health	22	.83	.64	.64	.59	.24	.25	.24
Personal change	8	.30	.49	.49	.57	.25	.27	.28
Work and finances	32	1.20	1.35	1.36	1.33	.18	.17	.13
Legal	7	.26	.16	.14	.14	.14	.08	.13
Other	7	.26	.64	.64	.58	.17	.15	.06
Total life-events scale	118	—	4.47	4.32	4.32	.29	.28	.26

*Correlation is not significant at the .05 probability level.

[a] Expected mean = 118 $\dfrac{\text{N(Subscale items)}}{\text{N (total items)}}$ × 4.47 (mean total events).

significantly correlated with depression in either of the 871-case panel data sets.

Reliability and Validity of Subscales

The event frequency means for each subscale are essentially constant across our three sets of panel data. The subscales, then, are all reliably measured. Of course, this outcome is related to our previous observation that the three panels' means for the total scale are equivalent; however, we now know that this is also true for the different subscale components of the total scale (see Table 5.2.)

We have seen that the zero-order correlations of the subscales with depression scores (CES-D) are also consistent, although there are some variations. Our correlations of the total life-events scale with depression scores is within the usually reported range of .10 to .30 (Rabkin and Struening, 1976). The consistency of means across the three data sets and two time periods indicates that the reliability of measurement is good. The consistency of the relationship between these measures and depression also suggests that the scale is valid.

Another way of assessing the reliability of the subscales is to examine the intercorrelations among the subscales in each of the three sample data sets. If the content of each subscale is being reliably measured, we would expect that the correlations among the subscale frequencies for each sample would be stable over time.

The range of subscale correlations with the total score is largely constant from T1 to T2. Table 5.3 indicates that this is true for all subscales

TABLE 5.3
Summary of Life-Events Subscale Intercorrelation Matrices for All Samples

Life-events subscale	Total sample	Panel sample	
	Time 1 ($N = 1091$)	Time 1 ($N = 871$)	Time 2 ($N = 871$)
Correlations of subscales with total scales			
School	.44	.44	.31
Home	.51	.52	.52
Love and marriage	.48	.49	.48
Family	.45	.42	.46
Health	.61	.61	.59
Personal change	.68	.69	.63
Work and finances	.81	.82	.78
Legal	.47	.46	.43
Range	.44–.81	.42–.82	.31–.78
Range of intersubscale correlations	.07–.43	.06–.44	−.01–.39

except for the correlations with the school-events subscale. However, this subscale is not significantly related to depression scores. If we exclude the school-events subscale, the range of variation is more stable and indeed shows a high degree of consistency.

Intersubscale correlations across the three panels also vary widely but consistently (again, except for the school-events subscale), as presented at the bottom of Table 5.3 The generally low magnitude of these correlations indicates that events subscales do not overlap extensively. That is, the subscales measure essentially distinct life-activity areas. This observation suggests the validity of the a priori subscales. It also tends to support the assertion that the events should be considered as having independent likelihoods of occurring.

Distribution of Events by Desirability

The biological model of the stress–illness relationship does not differentiate among emotional or interpretative states resulting from the experience of different sorts of events. Sociologically, however, some events are more highly valued than others, and psychologically some events have more positive effects. Some events are joyous or exciting, and others are disappointing and psychologically painful. If we take such perspectives into account, then it becomes reasonable to hypothesize that reactions to events will be affected by the subjective reactions of those persons experiencing the events.

As we noted earlier, most investigators report undesirable events to be more important than desirable ones for predicting illness. Desirability can be scored in two basic ways: according to objective values or subjectively, according to each respondent's evaluation. Although these two methods of scoring differ in the number of responses assigned to each category, Tausig (1982) has shown that objective and subjective scoring procedures yield approximately equivalent results. We will use subjective estimates of desirability to examine this issue.

Our measured life events are listed by degree of subjective desirability in Table 5.4. It should be noted that although only T1 results are reported, the findings are similar for T2. Those items unanimously or nearly unanimously perceived to be positive are listed first, and items universally or nearly universally perceived to be negative are listed last. These rankings could be converted into objective ratings by applying the subjective rankings in this table to other studies. The result would be similar to procedures used by others to establish objective desirability weights or scores using test panels (Holmes and Rahe, 1967; Dohrenwend et al., 1978). Although the relative positions of

TABLE 5.4
Percentage Distribution of Subjective Desirability of
Life Events (Total Sample, Time 1)

Events that 90–100% of respondents rated as desirable
  Started school
  Graduated from school
  Moved within town
  Moved to new town
  Moved to same type of neighborhood
  Moved to better neighborhood
  Built new house
  Remodeled house
  Began relationship
  Engaged
  Married
  Improved relations with spouse
  Birth of first child
  Birth of other child
  Adoption of other child
  Child left home—college
  Other family member left home
  Birth of grandchild
  Wanted pregnancy
  Change in religious beliefs
  Started to work first time
  Changed to same type of job
  Promotion
  Expanded business
  Significant success at work
  Home study
  Major improvement in finance
  Outstanding personal achievement
  Moderate purchase
  Major purchase
  Improved relations with neighbor, friend
  Vacation
  Major decision regarding future
Events that 80–89% of respondents rated as desirable
  Changed living conditions
  Child married with approval
  Began extramarital affair
  Marital reconciliation
  New person entered household
  Child left home—other reasons
  Family member entered armed forces
  Major dental work
  Started to work other than first time
  Change to different work

(continued)

TABLE 5.4 (Continued)

More responsibilities at work
Transfer
Retirement
Events that 70–79% of respondents rated as desirable
   Ceased attending school
   Ceased steady dating
   Marital separation
   Change in personal habits
   Change in church activities
   Spouse started/ended work
   Reorganization at work
Events that 60–69% of respondents rated as desirable
   Changed schools
   Separated from spouse (tour, business, vacation)
   Menopause
   Change in amount/type of recreation
   Change in eating habits
   Change in social activities
   Law suit or legal action
Events that 50–59% of respondents rated as desirable
   Moved to a worse neighborhood
   Child married without approval
   Child left home—married
   Change in family get-togethers
   Change in political beliefs
   Demotion
   Change in work hours/conditions
   Fired
   Foreclosure of mortgage of loan
   In court
Events that 40–49% of respondents rated as desirable
   Increased arguments with fiancee or steady date
   Business failing
Events that 30–39% of respondents rated as desirable
   Problems in school
   Divorced
   Serious physical illness
   Divorce of parents
   Change in sleeping habits
   Out or work less than a month
   Serious argument with friend, neighbor, relative
   Separation from significant person N.E.C.
   Accident
Events that 20–29% of respondents rated as desirable
   Increased arguements with spouse
   Trouble with in-laws
   Serious injury or accident
   Death of parent

(continued)

TABLE 5.4 (Continued)

Troubles with persons under supervision
Out or work over a month
Events that 10–19% of respondents rated as desirable
    Death of other close family member
    Death of close friend
    Change in health of family member
    Mental illness
    Death of pet
    Sexual difficulties
    Fewer responsibilities at work
    Laid off
    Troubles with boss
    Troubles with co-workers
    Arrested
    Loss of driver's license
    Loss, robbery, or damage of property
    Community crisis
    Abortion
Events that 0–9% of respondents rated as desirable
    Failed school
    Broke engagement
    Death of child
    Death of brother or sister
    Death of spouse
    Unwanted pregnancy
    Miscarriage
    Frequent minor illness
    Other work troubles
    Financial status worse
    Credit rating difficulties
    In jail
    Minor violations of the law

---

events in terms of desirability are generally consistent with expectations, there are some counterintuitive findings. For instance, divorce
and serious illness are ranked as desirable by 30% to 39% of our respondents. Although these situations may be described by many as
undesirable, they are not universally described as such. If researchers
wish to prepare lists of undesirable events, it would seem most reasonable to use events that are perceived as undesirable by at least 80% of
respondents (e.g., 0–19% desirable).

An illustration of the distribution of subjective desirability scores for
life-events subscales is provided in Table 5.5. The proportions of desirable and undesirable ratings for the total scale were used as the expected proportions for each subscale.

TABLE 5.5
Percentages and Correlations of Desirability Ratings with Depression (by Subscale)

	Time 1 (N = 1091)		Time 1 (N = 871)		Time 2 (N = 871)	
	Desirable	Undesirable	Desirable	Undesirable	Desirable	Undesirable
Percentages						
Total scale	57	31	58	30	57	32
School	79	8	86	10	90	5
Home	83	6	84	3	82	9
Love and marriage	59	30	58	31	52	32
Family	57	30	59	31	55	33
Health	30	58	30	56	25	63
Personal change	55	35	55	33	53	35
Work and finances	60	28	60	27	63	25
Legal	25	63	21	64	21	71
Correlations with CES-D						
Total scale	.16	.33	.16	.33	.04	.41
School	.03	.09	.02	.08	.01	.08
Home	.07	.06	.06	.03	.04	.12
Love and marriage	.10	.19	.10	.20	.06	.26
Family	.12	.14	.10	.14	.03	.16
Health	.09	.23	.13	.24	.07	.24
Personal change	.13	.23	.14	.24	.03	.39
Work and finances	.10	.19	.09	.20	.01	.24
Legal	.08	.12	.07	.09	.06	.11

The distributions clearly indicate that the scale does not present equal proportions of desirable and undesirable events within each subscale, nor similar proportions among the subscales. For instance, more desirable events are found in the school and home-events subscales; more undesirable events are found in the health and legal-events subscales. These findings were similar in both T1 (871) and T2 (871).

As we have observed earlier, certain subscale events are more frequently experienced than others. The distributions by desirability indicate that events within the subscales differ in degree of desirability as well.

Correlation with Depression Scores

Although distributions of events by desirability vary by subscale, the more important question is how desirability scores are related to depression. The second half of Table 5.5 indicates the zero-order correlations of desirable, undesirable, and total subscale scores with the depression measure. Overall, undesirable events are more highly correlated with depression than are desirable life events. For home-related, family, or legal events, there is little difference in correlations by desirability or undesirability. The most pronounced differences are seen in the categories of love and marriage, health, personal change, and work and finance—in which events perceived as undesirable are more highly correlated with depression than are desirable events.

When we compare correlations with depression for undesirable events with total events, however, the correlations are equivalent. That is, both total event counts and the count of those events regarded as undesirable have approximately the same correlations with depression. Thus, in terms of our use of the life-events scales in models predicting illness, either total events or undesirable events alone will behave in the same manner (Ensel and Tausig, 1982).

Our results are not at variance with those of other investigators (Vinokur and Selzer, 1975; Ross and Mirowsky, 1979; Mueller et al., 1977). These researchers have compared desirable and undesirable total scores and reported the differences in correlation patterns. We have considered the problem from a different perspective, however, which contrasts total events (regardless of desirability) with undesirable events only. This, we feel, is a better test of the alternative theoretical perspectives (strain or emphasis) represented in the literature. The choice of which perspective to adopt is clearly a function of theoretical orientation rather than of empirical results.

If we look back at Table 5.2 for a moment, we note that individual subscales are differently correlated with depression scores (CES-D). For example, the health and personal-change event subscales are notably more highly correlated with depression than are school, home, or legal events. We need to know whether the higher correlation coefficients for health and personal events are a result of the overlap of the personal-events items and the depression items.

Such confounding of variables is clearly present when two measures contain exactly the same items. When similar ideas are represented in two different scales, the problem of overlap is more difficult to judge on a theoretical basis.

The easy and obvious way to test for confounding is to compute the responses to two versions of the scales for the independent variables, one with the suspect items included and one without these items. The relationship of these scales to the scale of the dependent variable can then be examined. If a significant difference appears between the two relationships, then the independent-variable scale with the closer relationship to the dependent variable is the one more likely to be confounded with the dependent variable if the overlapping items are not removed.

Thoits (1981) has argued that health-related events are likely to be related to health-related outcomes. This issue has been dealt with elsewhere (Ensel and Tausig, 1982). A similar argument can be made for a relationship between personal-change events and psychological outcomes. Depression is diagnosed, in part, by reports of change in eating and sleeping habits and in social activities. Because these events are categorized as *personal* events, we must consider the possibility that some operational confounding has occurred between these life events, as part of our independent variable, and our measure of depression, the dependent variable.

Our investigation of this issue is summarized in Table 5.6. Life-events scores were computed for the total scale, for the total scale minus health-related events, the total scale minus personal-change events, and the total scale minus health and personal-change events. Correlations with depression were then computed for the three data sets for each of these four versions of the total scale. (See Tables 5.7 and 5.8 for additional statistics upon which these correlations are based.)

The results indicate that confounding is not present to a meaningful degree between our life-events scale and our depression scale. Although correlations are smaller when either health and/or personal-change events are subtracted, they are not significantly lower. In other words, health-related and personal-change events are not contributing to an artificially enhanced relationship of life events to depression. We

TABLE 5.6
Correlations of Total Events and Unconfounded-Events Subtotals with Depression
Scores (CES-D) for All Samples

	Total sample	Panel sample	
Life-events scale	Time 1 (N = 1091)	Time 1 (N = 871)	Time 2 (N = 871)
All events	.29	.28.	.26
All events minus health events	.27	.26	.22
All events minus personal-change events	.27	.26	.23
All events minus health & personal-change events	.23	.23	.18

find, therefore, no significant evidence of confounding between our
measure of life events and our measure of depression.

CONCLUSIONS

The purpose of this chapter has been to describe the nature of our
study measure of life events. In the process of modeling any set of
relationships it is important to understand the identity of the constructs employed and to be assured that operationalization of these
constructs is adequate.

TABLE 5.7
Means, Standard Deviations, and Percentage of Respondents Reporting for Total Life-
Events Scale, with and without Health Events and Personal-Change Events

	Total sample			Panel sample					
	Time 1 (N = 1091)			Time 1 (N = 871)			Time 2 (N = 871)		
Life-event scale	$\bar{X}$	SD	%	$\bar{X}$	SD	%	$\bar{X}$	SD	%
Total	4.47	4.81	83.9	4.32	4.74	84.3	4.32	4.41	85.5
Total minus personal-change events	3.95	4.22	83.2	3.84	4.14	83.6	3.75	3.82	84.6
Total minus health events	3.80	4.30	79.5	3.69	4.23	79.9	3.74	3.95	81.6

TABLE 5.8
Correlations of Subscales with Total Life-Events Scales with and without Personal-Change Events and Health Events

Scale or subscale	Total life-events scale			Total minus personal-change events			Total minus health events		
	T1 (N = 1091)	T1 (N = 871)	T2 (N = 871)	T1 (N = 1091)	T1 (N = 871)	T2 (N = 871)	T1 (N = 1091)	T1 (N = 871)	T2 (N = 871)
Life-events subscale									
School	.44	.44	.31	.46	.45	.35	.46	.46	.33
Home	.51	.52	.52	.53	.53	.53	.53	.54	.54
Love and marriage	.48	.49	.48	.48	.49	.48	.49	.50	.50
Family	.45	.42	.46	.45	.42	.44	.44	.40	.45
Health	.61	.61	.59	.61	.61	.57	.47	.46	.44
Personal change	.68	.69	.63	.54	.56	.45	.67	.68	.62
Work and finances	.81	.82	.78	.83	.84	.82	.83	.84	.79
Legal	.47	.46	.43	.48	.47	.43	.48	.48	.43
Total	—	—	.98	.99	.99	.98	.99	.98	.96
Total minus personal-change events	.99	.99	.98	—	—	—	.97	.97	.96
Total minus health events	.99	.98	.98	.97	.97	.96	—	—	—

The life-events construct can have various meanings vis-à-vis stress. In our study it will stand for two of these meanings. The frequency of events is interpreted as strain, and the summated desirability of events indicates the emphasis (stressfulness) of experienced events. Depending on the way in which our life-events scale is constructed, it can reliably represent either meaning.

The life-events construct model must also be conceptually and operationally distinct from other constructs in the model. To this end we have demonstrated that the zero-order relationship of life events with depression is not confounded. That is, the relationship is factual and not artifactual. Whether life events are taken to indicate strain or emphasis, they are theoretically related to depression in the same manner (albeit with different strengths).

As we have treated them, life events represent sources of stress that impinge upon one's social life, and it is our hypothesis that such stress is related to illness outcomes. However, the substantial literature on psychosocial epidemiology makes it quite clear that this bivariate relationship is far from the complete story. Both social and psychological resources must clearly be introduced for consideration, and attention must be given to their causal relationships with both stress and illness. Not only do we need to examine how social and psychological resources mediate the relationship between stress and illness; we also need to know whether social and psychological resources affect the frequency or stressfulness of subsequent events.

Now that we have an understanding of the meaning and empirical characteristics of our life-events scale, we can continue to examine these relationships.

6 _____

Measuring Psychological Resources

ALFRED DEAN

INTRODUCTION

The search for factors that might explain the differential vulnerability of individuals to illness in the face of potential stressors has typically recognized two broad classes of variables: external coping resources such as social support and individuals' internal characteristics such as personality traits (Rabkin and Struening, 1976; Dohrenwend and Dohrenwend, 1978). We are concerned in this chapter with this second class of *predispositional factors* (Dohrenwend and Dohrenwend, 1981). Because this latter category may also include constitutional, or biological, factors (Kobasa, Maddi, and Coddington, 1981), we should note that our concern here is exclusively with psychological variables, which we shall broadly conceptualize as *psychological resources*. Although such variables may be of considerable importance intuitively or theoretically, research in this area has been quite limited, particularly when contrasted to recent research on social support. The basic concept, assumption, or hypothesis underlying this line of research is that personality factors may influence the individual's reactions to events through such mechanisms as the meaning of the event, the perceived ability to cope, actual coping ability, coping

97

SOCIAL SUPPORT,
LIFE EVENTS, AND DEPRESSION

behavior, and/or the effectiveness of coping (Kohn, 1972, 1977). The bulk of the research in this area has focused upon various *sense-of-control* scales and has most typically conceptualized them under the rubric of *personal resources* (Pearlin and Schooler, 1978; Wheaton, 1983b).

The conceptualization of personality factors, the selection of appropriate scales, and their incorporation into epidemiological studies raises a number of issues that will be only briefly considered. First, it should be noted that there are numerous definitions of personality, because it is a complex construct. Essential to the construct, however, is the idea that its attributes are relatively fixed, stable, and enduring (Wheaton, Muthin, Alwin, and Summers, 1977). Secondly, there are numerous theoretically relevant personality attributes that might be explored. Third, it should be noted that there is conflicting evidence about the feasibility of predicting actual behavior on the basis of personality factors (Folkman and Lazarus, 1980; Kohn and Schooler, 1978; Sarason, Smith, and Diener, 1975; Schweder, 1975). Without question, there is a further need to specify and demonstrate the links between personality measures and the various aspects of coping (Wheaton, 1983b).

Recognizing these issues—and with a commitment to incorporate individual psychological variables into an extended model of the relationships among stressors, social support, and illness—we chose the following desiderata for selecting specific scales by which to measure these constructs: (1) The scales should have demonstrated validity and reliability; (2) the scales should be capable of being integrated into the time and circumstances of large-scale surveys; (3) the scales should be theoretically significant in terms of expected relationships to the other basic model variables; (4) the scales ideally should lend themselves to testing major formulations in the literature; and (5) the scales should be able to be compared to other research findings in the field. In the final analysis, we chose to to apply two scales: personal competence (Campbell et al., 1960) and self-esteem (Rosenberg, 1965). These scales are discussed extensively in subsequent sections in terms of the criteria listed above. But we must first consider briefly the objectives for examining these scales in this chapter and in this monograph.

PRESENT OBJECTIVES

Broadly stated, our examination of these two scales is aimed at examining their relevance to the present investigation and to the literature. In this chapter, we consider the constructs behind these scales, their operationalization, existing evidence for their reliability and validity, and their relationships to other scales. A major purpose of this chapter is also to provide an independent conceptual and psychometric evaluation of the scales before describing their application to the model presented in this monograph. We thus provide detailed information about the internal consistency and predictive validity of these two scales. Finally, summarize the implications of using one or both of these scales in our modeling efforts, and discuss some issues for further investigation of these and related scales.

THE CONCEPT OF PERSONAL COMPETENCE

Basically the concept of personal competence refers to the attitude that one has control over events that occur in one's environment in contrast to the feeling that one is the victim of fate or chance occurrences. As Robinson and Shaver (1975) note, the essential referent of the concept of personal competence is the feeling of mastery over oneself and one's environment. In other words, this is a concept of *personal efficacy*. Campbell and associates suggest that: "The person lacking such a sense of mastery may either be tense and anxious about the course of his personal life, or may be resigned in a fatalistic way to a succession of events with which he does not feel that he can cope adequately" (1960, p. 517). The authors further state:

> The efficacy of ego functioning bears directly on the way in which an individual can or must allocate his energies in dealing with the environment. Where such functioning is chaotic, more energy is drained off in the maintenance of the psychological economy and less remains to initiate and create beyond the immediate emotional necessities. Where the ego is strong, however, the individual can maintain a higher level of involvement in these secondary areas of behavior. (1960, pp. 518–519)

Theoretically, personal competence appears to be convergent with other concepts of personal control (Seeman and Seeman, 1983). Husaini and Neff (1981) have suggested that personal competence is analogous to Rotter's (1966) construct of *locus-of-control orientation*. Rotter suggested that individuals differ in the extent to which they perceive *environmental reinforcers* as being under their control. *Internals* perceive these events as being under their control, and *externals* perceive reinforcers as being the result of fate, luck, chance, or powerful others. Thus, as Johnson and Sarason (1978) note, the locus-of-control construct appears to reflect the extent to which individuals believe themselves capable of exerting personal control over environmental events.

The construct of personal competence is also similar to Pearlin and Schooler's (1978) *concept of mastery*, "which concerns the extent to which one regards one's life chances as being under one's own control in contrast to being fatalistically ruled" (p. 5). Similarly, Wheaton (1983b) has drawn on Rotter's I–E items to construct a *fatalism* scale. As Wheaton notes, we thus may see a basic thematic similarity in a number of related concepts, including also *personal mastery* (deCharms, 1968), *helplessness* (Seligman, 1975), and *powerlessness* (Dohrenwend and Dohrenwend, 1970; Fried, 1975). In summary, we agree with Seeman and Seeman (1983) that despite variations in terms, these concepts refer generically to a person's *sense of control* (i.e., degree of personal control as opposed to fate). A growing body of literature emphasizes the positive health effects of increased personal control over life events. Whatever name given to the sense of low control, the evidence indicates that feelings of low control are associated with a variety of predictable outcomes (Phares, 1976; Seeman and Seeman, 1983).

As might be expected, the operationalizations of these various constructs also reflect their basic similarities. However, caution must be exercised in considering these scales as convergent, because variations in operationalization can lead to significantly different results. To our knowledge, there has been little systematic comparison of the various scales or scale items. Furthermore, there has been limited application of such scales to epidemiological studies (Johnson and Sarason, 1978; Kobasa, 1979; Lefcourt, 1981; Wheaton, 1983b).

Measuring Personal Competence

Several versions of the personal-competence scale (Campbell et al., 1960) have been applied in various political surveys (see Robinson, Rusk, and Head, 1968). The items were apparently developed as an extension of the Political Advocacy Scale by Douvan and Walker (1956). These authors observed that people who scored low on competence consistently gave answers to projective questions (Thematic Apperception Test pictures) "which reflected a posture of an oppressive, uncontrollable external reality." In general, measures of personal competence have shown acceptable internal consistency and good construct validity.

The measure of personal competence applied by our group consists of eight items (see Table 6.1) to each of which four responses are possible: (1) *strongly agree*, (2) *agree*, (3) *disagree*, and (4) *strongly disagree*. The responses for all the items are totaled to produce a measure of the degree of personal competence. A high score indicates a high sense of

TABLE 6.1
Reliability and Validity of Personal-Competence Scale in Albany Area Time 1 (T1) Total Sample and T1 and Time 2 (T2) Subsamples

| | Total sample | | | Subsample | | | | | |
| | T1 (N = 1091) | | | T1 (N = 871) | | | T2 (N = 871) | | |
Personal-competence items	Item–total r	Alpha if item deleted	Item–CES-D r	Item–total r	Alpha if item deleted	Item–CES-D r	Item–total r	Alpha if item deleted	Item–CES-D r
Rather decide things when they come up	.35	.59	−.08	.37	.57	−.11	.45	.64	−.12
Pretty sure lie will turn out as expected	.50	.52	−.17	.46	.53	−.18	.54	.60	−.25
More bad luck than good luck	.55	.51	−.24	.53	.50	−.22	.58	.59	−.33
No trouble making up mind	.44	.55	−.16	.44	.54	−.16	.51	.62	−.20
More will power than most	.55	.51	−.11	.56	.50	−.12	.56	.60	−.20
No use planning ahead	.56	.50	−.19	.57	.49	−.18	.55	.60	−.27
Always feel pretty sure of self	.47	.52	−.11	.49	.51	−.09	.51	.60	−.16
No use trying to get anywhere	.55	.50	−.18	.53	.50	−.18	.57	.59	−.27
Total scale mean	21.96			22 04			22.21		
Total scale SD	2.75			2 70			2.96		
Average item means	2.74			2 75			2.78		
SD of item means	.26			26			.28		
Min/max items means	2.37/3.21			2.39/3.24			2.38/3.28		
X̄ inter-item correlations	.14			14			.18		
SD of inter-item correlations	.24			12			.13		
Min/max inter-item correlations	−.10/.38			−.13/.38			.02/.22		
Alpha—total scale	.56			56			.64		
Scale r with CES-D	−.31			− .33			−.41		

personal competence; a low score indicates a low sense of personal competence. Table 6.1 describes the scale properties of this measure in each of the three samples.

It can be seen that the various indicators of internal consistency are relatively stable. Item–total correlations range from .35 to .58. The alpha coefficients range from .56 to .64, thus indicating acceptable, although not strong, internal consistency. It may be noted that other personal-control scales (Husaini and Neff, 1981; Wheaton, 1983b) have demonstrated discriminating relationships with comparable internal consistency. Further factor analyses possibly could improve these results. It should be noted that the scale as applied here exhibits rather consistent and strong relationships to depression, with correlations ranging from $-.31$ to $-.41$. In sum, the scale possesses sufficient strength—in terms of reliability and validity, convergence with other personal-control constructs, and theoretical relevance to the stressor–illness model—to warrant its application in the present study.

THE CONCEPT OF SELF-ESTEEM

Self-esteem, among other self constructs, has been a subject of considerable interest across the broad spectrum of clinical disciplines and behavioral sciences, at least since the stimulating work of William James (1890), Charles Horton Cooley (1902), and George Herbert Mead (1934). Self-esteem was certainly a matter of significance for such leading clinical theorists as Adler (1917), Sullivan (1947), Erickson (1959), Maslow (1954), and C. R. Rogers (1961). Similarly, in the field of academic psychology, self-esteem figured in the distinguished work of Murphy (1947) and Allport (1955). Extensive empirical studies of self-esteem and other self constructs have emerged largely in the last two decades (McGuire and Padawer-Singer, 1976; Ostrow, 1982).

Because personality factors have been incorporated only recently and in a limited way into epidemiological models (Dohrenwend and Dohrenwend, 1981; Rabkin and Struening, 1976; Wheaton, 1983b), it is not surprising that this construct has not had much attention. But because positive self-esteem has come to be regarded as such an important part of healthy personality development and structure, and poor self-esteem is considered a feature of neurotic personality and other personality disorders, the continued neglect of this variable is hard to understand. Of course, low self-esteem is often regarded as a symptom of psychiatric disturbances, particularly of the depressive disorders (*Diagnostic and Statistical Manual of Mental Disorders, 3rd Edition*,

1980). Thus some indicators of low esteem are included in the Beck Depression Scale (Beck, 1967), the PERI (Psychiatric Epidemiology Research Interview) (Dohrenwend, Shrout, Egri, and Mendelsohn, 1980), and the CES-D (Radloff, 1977).

Therefore low self-esteem can and should be distinguished as a feature of personality and/or depression (Pearlin and Schooler, 1978; Rosenberg, 1965). Self-esteem clearly may be regarded as a feature of personality that represents a coping resource (Pearlin and Schooler, 1978); a dispositional or predispositional factor (Dohrenwend and Dohrenwend, 1981; Wheaton, 1983); a dimension of ego strength (Barron, 1953); and/or a predictor of coping style or coping behavior (Dohrenwend and Dohrenwend, 1981; Husaini and Neff, 1981; Wheaton, 1983b).

Measuring Self-Esteem

The measure of self-esteem applied in this study was developed by Rosenberg (1965) and has been widely used in various studies. The reader is referred to this original source for a full discussion of the author's construct of self-esteem. However, the following excerpts should serve to describe the essential features of Rosenberg's construct:

> Thus far we have used the term "self-esteem" rather loosely, implying that its meaning was self-evident. Self-esteem, as noted, is a positive or negative attitude toward a particular object, namely, the self . . .
>
> When we speak of high self-esteem, then, we shall simply mean that the individual respects himself, considers himself worthy; he does not necessarily consider himself better than others, but he definitely does not consider himself worse; he does not feel that he is the ultimate in perfection, but on the contrary, recognizes his limitations and expects to grow and improve.
>
> Low self-esteem, on the other hand, implies self-rejection, self-dissatisfaction, self-contempt. The individual lacks respect for the self he observes. The self picture is disagreeable, and he wishes it were otherwise. (pp. 30–31)

Rosenberg operationalized this construct with 10 statements to which respondents were asked to strongly agree, agree, disagree, or strongly disagree. The items (see Table 6.2) include: "On the whole, I am satisfied with myself" and "At times I think I am no good at all." Rosenberg found that responses to all the items yielded a Guttman scale. Reproducibility of this scale is 92%, and its scalability is 72% (pp. 16–17). Rosenberg also found good evidence for the validity of the scale in terms of its relationship to measures of social status and subjective and objective reputation. As predicted, self-esteem scores were also significantly correlated with symptoms of depression, anxiety, and

TABLE 6.2
Reliability and Validity of Self-Esteem Scale in Albany Area Time 1 (T1) Total Sample and T1 and Time 2 (T2) Subsamples[a]

| | Total sample | | | Subsample | | | | | |
| | T1 (N = 1091) | | | T1 (N = 871) | | | T2 (N = 871) | | |
Self-esteem items	Item–total r	Alpha if item deleted	Item–CES-D r	Item–total r	Alpha if item deleted	Item–CES-D r	Item–total r	Alpha if item deleted	Item–CES-D r
Feel a person of worth	.64	.85	-.06	.67	.84	-.08	.69	.87	-.17
Possess good qualities	.69	.84	-.08	.72	.84	-.07	.76	.87	-.15
Feel a failure	.71	.84	-.11	.71	.84	-.10	.74	.87	-.24
Do things as well as others	.64	.85	-.10	.64	.85	-.08	.68	.87	-.15
Not much to be proud of	.66	.85	-.09	.64	.85	-.05	.73	.87	-.16
Positive attitude toward self	.73	.84	-.22	.72	.84	-.21	.78	.87	-.30
Satisfied with self	.71	.84	-.25	.70	.84	-.23	.71	.87	-.33
Wish more self-respect	.63	.85	-.24	.62	.85	-.24	.57	.89	-.32
Feel useless at times	.63	.85	-.28	.63	.85	-.30	.69	.88	-.44
Think I am no good at all	.65	.85	-.30	.65	.85	-.29	.75	.87	-.32
Total scale mean		31.84			31.97			32.29	
Total scale SD		4.04			4.04			4.26	
Average item means		3.18			3.20			3.23	
SD of item means		.20			.20			.19	
Min/max item means		2.78/3.43			2.79/3.45			2.87/3.47	
X̄ inter-item correlations		.39			.39			.45	
SD of inter-item correlations		.10			.11			.11	
Min/max inter-item correlations		.22/.65			.22/.70			.26/.70	
Alpha—total scale		.86			.86			.89	
Scale r with CES-D		-.26			-.25			-.37	

[a] r between competence and esteem (T1 1091 = .53; T1 871 = .51).

psychosomatic disturbances. For example, 80% of those with the lowest self-esteem were highly depressed, compared to 4% of those with the highest self-esteem (r = .30). Similarly, self-esteem was inversely related to a psychophysiological measure of anxiety (r = .48).

Our independent examination of the properties of the Rosenberg self-esteem scale is presented in Table 6.2. It may be seen that the scale shows excellent stability and internal consistency in the three samples. Every indicator of internal consistency is strong. The alphas range from .86 to .89. The scale also shows good predictive validity: Correlations between self-esteem and depression are inverse and range from − .25 to − .37. In summary, there are strong conceptual, theoretical, and methodological grounds for applying the Rosenberg self-esteem scale in studies of this kind. However, several points should be noted regarding the use of the self-esteem and personal-competence scales.

First, although we can distinguish between personal efficacy and self-esteem conceptually and operationally, we may well expect these two variables to be closely related to each other and to be similarly related to other variables. In this regard, it may be observed that personal competence and self-esteem display similar relationships to sociodemographic variables and to the model variables (see Table 6.3). Neither of these two measures shows an association with age, gender, or marital status. Both variables are related to education, particularly personal-competence, although neither are strongly related. It is noteworthy that neither personal competence nor self-esteem is associated with life events, although both show moderate relationships to strong-tie support.

TABLE 6.3

Demographic and Epidemiologic Correlates of Esteem and Competence in Albany Area Time 1 (T1) and Time 2 (T2) Subsamples

	Demographic correlates				Epidemiological correlates		
	Age	Gender	Marital status	Education	Life events	Strong-tie support	CES-D
Personal competence							
T1 (N = 871)	−.065	−.146	.047	.264	.039	.207	−.33
T2 (N = 871)	.003	−.088	.094	.218	−.052	.283	−.41
Self-esteem							
T1 (N = 871)	−.076	−.092	.064	.157	.025	.140	−.25
T2 (N = 871)	−.052	.023	.037	.143	−.015	.261	−.37

TABLE 6.4

Over-Time Correlations of Self-Esteem and Personal Competence Between Albany Area Time 1 (T1) and Time 2 (T2) Subsamples

	Self-esteem T1	Self-esteem T2	Personal competence T1	Personal competence T2
Self-esteem T1	1.000	.441	.513	.379
Self-esteem T2	.441	1.000	.309	.586
Personal competence T1	.513	.309	1.000	.478
Personal competence T2	.379	.586	.478	1.000

OVER-TIME CORRELATIONS

Table 6.4 presents the over-time correlations of the self-esteem and personal-competence scales we used. These data bear on two issues: the stability of self-esteem and personal competence over time, and their interrelationships. It may be seen that the correlation between self-esteem in Time 1 (T1) and self-esteem in Time 2 (T2) is .441, compared to a correlation of .478 between personal competence in T1 and personal competence in T2. The magnitude of these correlations appears to be sufficient to warrant the incorporation of both scales into the model. Nonetheless, the fact that these over-time correlations are not extremely high raises the question as to the extent to which they have state and/or trait properties. Although further examination of this issue is beyond the scope of this chapter, it would be of interest in further investigations to examine how sociodemographic or other psychosocial variables might influence differences in self-esteem and feelings of personal competence. Table 6.4 also provides additional indications that self-esteem and personal competence are fairly strong related to each other. For example, the correlation between personal competence and self-esteem in T1 is .513. As expected, the correlations are stronger when measured in the same time frame, but the relationships of these two variables to each other over time remain relatively high. Overall, these observations indicate that any effort to incorporate personal competence and self-esteem simultaneously into a causal model will pose difficult problems of multicollinearity.

TESTING THE PROXY ISSUE

The reader may well have wondered about the extent to which the measures of personal competence and/or self-esteem may overlap or be redundant with depression (CES-D). This question may reasonably be raised, particularly when both these measures are based on subjective self-reports and are administered during the same session. Some investigators have suggested that virtually any subjective characterizations by respondents may be rendered unusable by being confounded with depression and other illness measures (Dohrenwend and Dohrenwend, 1981). This central question has also been raised as a criticism of subjective social-support scales to the degree that some critics would reject them ipso facto. For this reason, the superiority of social-network scales as objective measures has been proposed by some investigators.

Methodologically and theoretically, this is a complex issue that cannot be considered here extensively. However, we will explore the overlap among personal competence, self-esteem, and depression by comparing the results of their regression on the same set of sociodemographic and model variables (Table 6.5). Essentially, redundancy is claimed whenever two scales are used that measure the same thing, in this case, depression. If this is so, one scale may be taken as a proxy for the other. Similarly, if this is the case, we would expect a common set of predictor variables to bear the same relationship to both measures. Thus the comparative regression technique has been applied as one test of this question (Lin, Ensel, and Vaughn, 1981).

Differences in the magnitude of beta coefficients, their rank-ordering, as well as total R^2s may be noted. A notable example is life events, which are the second most important predictor of depression but which do not predict self-esteem or personal competence. Education is a much more important predictor of psychological resources, particu-

TABLE 6.5
Albany Area Test of Self-Esteem and Personal Competence as Proxy Measures in Predicting Depression

Factor	Self-esteem		Personal competence		CES-D	
	B	Beta	B	Beta	B	Beta
Age	−.008	−.029	.007	.040	−.004	−.007
Gender	.317	.037	−.431	−.073*	1.38	.073*
Marital status	−.184	−.021	.093	.015	−.616	−.031
Education	.219	.143*	.253	.239*	−.296	−.087*
Life events	.008	.008	−.017	−.026	.389	.181*
Strong-tie support	.975	.275*	.675	.275*	−3.19	−.404*
R^2	.094		.139		.244	
Constant	22.44		14.59		32.48	
Error of estimate	4.07		2.76		8.29	

*Significant at .01 level.

larly personal competence, than of CES-D. Interestingly, gender is a significant predictor of personal competence and CES-D, but not of self-esteem. In addition, there is a marked overlap between personal competence and self-esteem. But in general, Table 6.5 indicates that although there is some overlap between personal competence, self-esteem, and CES-D, as would be expected, these scales appear to be significantly independent.

FACTOR ANALYSES OF PERSONAL COMPETENCE AND SELF-ESTEEM

The question as to whether the personal competence and self-esteem scales we used would yield subscales when subjected to a factor analysis is a matter of psychometric interest. We are unaware of any such examination of the personal-competence scale in the literature. However, Pearlin and Schooler (1978) have subjected the Rosenberg self-esteem scale to a factor analysis, the results of which they termed self-denigration and self-esteem (p. 20). We thus conducted a factor analysis (varimax rotation, orthogonal solution) and applied a cutoff point of .50. The results of this analysis are indicated in Table 6.6.

It may be seen that the personal-competence scale yielded two distinct sets of factors, each consisting of three items. The first appears to characterize pessimism or external control. It includes the items "more bad luck than good," "no use planning ahead," and "no use trying to get anywhere." The second more clearly appears to reflect a sense of

TABLE 6.6
Individual Factor Analysis of Personal Competence in Time 2 Data[a]

Personal competence	Pessimism: factor 1	Personal efficacy: factor 2
Decide things when they come up	.371	.003
Sure life will turn out as expected	.341	.312
More bad luck than good luck	.622[b]	.129
No trouble making up mind	.017	.572
More will power than most	.063	.706
No use planning ahead	.599	.009
Always feel pretty sure of self	.089	.559
No use trying to get anywhere	.594	.119

[a]Numbers are factor loadings.
[b]Representative items for each factor are underlined.

TABLE 6.7
Individual Factor Analysis of Self-Esteem in Time 2 Data[a]

Self-esteem	Self-esteem: factor 1	Self-denigration: factor 2
Feel a person of worth	.706[b]	.240
Possess good qualities	.851	.230
Feel a failure	.650	.360
Do things as well as others	.524	.383
Not much to be proud of	.634	.357
Take a positive attitude toward self	.510	.579
Satisifed with self	.381	.585
Wish more self-respect	.202	.465
Feel useless at times	.162	.766
Think I am no good at all	.390	.610

[a]Numbers are factor loadings.
[b]Representative items for each factor are underlined.

personal efficacy or competence. It consists of the items "no trouble making up my mind," "more will power than most," and "always feel pretty sure of myself." Thus, although the previous examination of the personal-competence scale justifies the use of the overall scale, these findings also provide indications for the separate examination of these two subscales, which we will term *Pessimism* (Factor 1) and *Personal Efficacy* (Factor 2). In general, it is of basic interest to explore whether these two subscales have different functions in the model. Illustrative questions to be explored in future investigations include: Are these measures differentially stable over time? Are they differentially related to depression-proneness? Do they have different sociodemographic or other predictors?

As presented in Table 6.7, the factor analysis of self-esteem also yielded two separate factors. The first consists of five items. In general, the results of our findings are fairly consistent with those of Pearlin and Schooler. In particular, our first factor was quite similar to the scale that Pearlin and Schooler called *self-esteem*. Four of the five items that loaded on our Factor 1 also loaded on their scale. These items are, "feel a person of worth," "have a number of good qualities," "feel I am a failure," and "do things as well as others." A fifth item that loaded on their scale, "take a positive attitude towards self," loaded .510 on our self-esteem factor, but loaded even more strongly on our second factor.

Regarding our second factor, two of our items, "feel useless at times" and "think I am no good at all," also loaded on Pearlin and Schooler's four-item scale of "self-denigration." Had we not used a stricter factor-loading criterion than they did, a third item, "wish I had more respect for self," would also be shared by their and our self-denigration factors. These subscales are thus clearly convergent, but not as strongly as for the first factor.

Conceptually, and consistent with the terminology of Pearlin and Schooler, Factors 1 and 2 appear to tap the dimensions of *Self-Esteem* versus *Self-Denigration*. We thus apply these terms to our two sub-scales.

The implications of these two discernibly distinct self-esteem sub-scales are, in principle, the same as noted for the two subscales of personal competence. In essence, their possible variations in our model call for further exploration. Other questions include: To what extent is self-esteem versus self-denigration influenced by life events and social support? How do scores on these subscales differ in normal versus depressed samples? How do they change as individuals move from depressed to nondepressed states?

SUMMARY

This chapter has examined the construct of psychological resources as a variable in the life-event–illness model. The properties of two scales, self-esteem and personal competence, have been subjected to independent examination of their psychometric properties. Each of the scales exhibit acceptable properties of reliability and validity. Several different kinds of data have been compiled that indicate that the scales are distinguishable and have somewhat different correlates. However, the scales are also significantly interrelated, which poses problems of multicollinearity if they are to be used simultaneously in our model. The overlap of these two measures with depression was also examined. A test of this proxy issue found that personal competence, self-esteem, and depression have discernable variations in their predictors, despite some similarities. We were led to conclude that, although there is some overlap between these variables, they are significantly independent of each other. Factor analyses of the two scales indicate that personal competence yielded two subscales: one termed *Pessimism*, the other *Personal Efficacy*. Similarly, the self-esteem yielded two subscales: *Self-Esteem* and *Self-Denigration*. Overall, these findings indicate that it is justifiable and of interest to use in our model the overall personal-competence and self-esteem scales as well as their various subscales. One virtue of using the overall scales is that it would permit more direct comparison to findings based on previous research. Some of the types of questions that should be explored with the four subscales were indicated. The use of the overall scales as well as of the specific subscales is further motivated by other specific kinds of research questions, hypotheses, or purposes for which the results may prove illuminating.

There are arguments and evidence in the literature that the modeling of psychological resources may need to take into consideration the type of potential stressors as well as the social supports that might be involved. Such an elaborate examination of these measures of psychological resources is beyond the scope of this chapter and indeed of this monograph. Thus, in subsequent chapters the modeling of psychological resources will apply the original scale of either self-esteem or personal competence as a single indicator of the construct of personal resources. It is clear that the construct of psychological resources is central in current theoretical perspectives on potential stressors, the occurrence of stress, and the incidence of illness.

This chapter has provided a foundation for the examination of psychological resources in this study as well as indicating some lines of inquiry for further research.

Part III

MEASURING SOCIAL SUPPORT

In this section, three chapters describe our efforts to measure social support. As discussed in Chapter 2, the major elements of social support identified in the literature include: (1) three types of social relations—community and neighborhood relations (the sense of belongingness), network relations (the sense of bonding), and intimate relations (the sense of binding)—and (2) two types of support (instrumental and expressive). Further theoretical considerations have made plausible the measurement of social support as access to and use of strong and homophilous ties. It has also been noted that social support might be measured with objective instruments (observations independent of ego) or subjective instruments (observations elicited from ego).

In this study, none of the measures can be claimed to be objective. Although some measures may tap "objective," or behavioral, aspects (frequency of contact, relations with supportive persons, etc.), data were generated from each respondent, and within the cognitive realm of ego. Therefore, the measures developed are to varying degrees all subjective.

Efforts were made, however, to tap the different elements of social support conceptualized. Several considerations compromised the abil-

ity to develop measures that would be isomorphic (a one-to-one correspondence) with each element of social support. First, there was a need
to incorporate measures proposed or examined by other researchers in
previous studies. Historically, it is essential to carry forward these
measures so that comparative analyses can be made and cumulative
knowledge about these measures can be documented. It became problematic to classify each of these measures as strictly indicative of a
single element of social support as originally conceived. These previous measures were designed by others with different conceptualizations in mind or, in some cases, on an ad hoc basis. We decided to
evaluate each of the measures adapted from previous studies with
regard to the primary element of social support involved. This evaluation was a judgment on our part. As long as the measures are intact, we
argue, refinement of their conceptualization can be done as research
proceeds. Thus, these measures are presented in chapters where we
consider them appropriate, with the recognition that such fitting is
tentative at best.

As the study progressed, our own experiences as well as the contributions of many other researchers modified and expanded the ways in
which social support could be defined. Measures conceived of at one
time as adequate indicators of social support with clean-cut or desirable properties were subsequently found to contain a mixture of elements. A case in point is the Instrumental–Expressive Social-Support
Scale we developed in our pretest and have continued to use throughout our study. The scale, containing items tapping both instrumental
and expressive elements of support, showed good reliability (test–retest consistency, and cross-group consistency), desirable properties
(clean factor structures), and validity (satisfactory differentiation from
life events and depression while at the same time being predictors of
depression). Yet subsequent evaluation suggested that the items contained varying degrees of social relations as well. Thus, it became
difficult to tease out the social elements from the support elements
inherent in the scale. An effort was made to isolate the items that
clearly indicate support from strong ties (companions and close
friends). Nevertheless, the entire scale remains a reasonable indicator
of instrumental–expressive support (Chapter 8), in which the subscale
of strong-tie support is also discussed. Other measures developed for
the study also faced similar evaluations and reassessments. They are
presented in chapters that we feel are reflective of their primary operational objectives.

A third consideration was the problem with areas of social support
for which clear-cut measures were lacking, and our efforts to develop

such measures met with mixed results. Network support is one such area. Past research showed little success in developing measures predictive of mental health. Mere indicators of network forms or structures have been shown to have little causal influence on mental health. For example, frequency of interaction with network members, size and density of networks, and multiplicity of relations (the extent to which a given relationship serves multiple functions) have shown little effects on mental-health measures. Yet, given their compelling conceptual appeal, the potential contributions of network support cannot be ignored. Our attempts at examining these effects and at developing additional measures of network support have not been as satisfactory as we had anticipated. In general, these measures (as well as newly developed measures) have shown little effect on depression. Nevertheless, we decided to present these efforts at measuring various elements of social support, even though they were not psychometrically strong. The documentation of these attempts and measures may help future researchers in the selection and refinement of their operationalizations. In certain areas, such as network support, where conceptualization and measurement are so complex, such information, it seems to us, is particularly useful.

With these considerations in mind, we present the social-support measures in three chapters. Chapter 7 focuses on measures by which we attempted to operationalize intimate and confidant support (the binding relations). Chapter 8 presents measures on instrumental–expressive supports, as well as the derived measure of strong tie support. Chapter 9 reviews our measures of community and network support (the belonging and bonding relations). Table III.1 is provided to guide the reader through all the measures used as well as the elements of social support tapped by each (either as a primary or secondary measure).

TABLE III.1

Chart of Social-Support Measures Examined in Part III[a]

Measure(s)	Chapter	Intimate and confiding	Strong or homophilus ties	Instrumental– expressive	Network	Community
					Type of support	
Family-support (Medalie–Goldbourt scale)	7	P	S	S	—	—
Presence of confidant(s) (Lowenthal-Haven item)	7	P	S	S	S	—
Relations between ego and confidant (Kaplan items)	7	P	S	S	—	—
Confidant's help with most important life event	7	P	S	S	—	—
Homophily of characteristics between confidant and ego	7	S	P	P	—	—
Instrumental–expressive functions	8	S	S	S	—	—
Strong-tie support	8	S	P	S	—	—
Community–neighborhood support (interaction and satisfaction)	9	—	—	—	—	P
Participation in voluntary organizations	9	—	—	—	S	P
Use of organized services	9	—	—	—	—	P
Role (multiplexity) support for problems	9	S	S	S	P	—
Confidant network characteristics	9	S	S	S	P	—
Help following an important life event	9	S	S	S	P	—

[a] P = Primary classification of measure; S = Secondary classification of measure.

7

Measuring Intimate Support: The Family and Confidant Relationships

ALFRED DEAN

MARK TAUSIG

INTRODUCTION

In this chapter we examine several measures of family and confidant relationships. In part, we are specifically interested in their applicability as measures of family and confidant support. This involves consideration of their conceptual, operational, and psychometric properties. However, we are also basically interested in examining these measures as distinct approaches to tapping intimate support systems—relationships that have been characterized in Chapter 2 as *binding* and *at the inner layer*. These measures may thus be compared and contrasted to measures of community and network support as well as to other measures of intimate support.

There can be little doubt that intimacy was implied by early formulations of social support, although the referents of this term still require substantial specification. In our review of the existing literature (Dean and Lin, 1977), we suggested how primary relationships may be implicated in stress reduction and induction and how primary-group theory

117

could shape and sharpen the conceptualization and measurement of social support. Certainly, the family requires study in this perspective being, in theory at least, the prototype of the primary group. Such groups are characterized by: emphasis on mutual responsibility, caring, and concern; strong mutual identifications, emphasis on the uniqueness of group members; face-to-face interaction and communication; norms of intimacy; close associations and bonds; and the provision of affection, security, and response.

Several important and influential studies have explored the stress-buffering role of certain family relationships, most notably the respondent's relationship to spouse and/or other family members. For example, Nuckolls et al. (1972) found some evidence that the relationships of pregnant women to their husbands and other family members influenced their risk of pregnancy complications. Similarly, Gore (1978) observed that among men who were laid off due to a plant closing, the occurrence of physical symptoms and affective changes were influenced by the relationships they had with their wives. Beyond theory, such evidence demonstrated the importance of further investigation of the family as a support system. In general, studies of the family as a support system have been limited and require further conceptualization and operationalization. We may well expect that the family is normatively defined as having distinct supportive responsibilities. In essense, family members have a mutual obligation to provide emotional and material support, on a day-to-day basis as well as in times of critical events. It may be noted that many of the life events associated with depression and other disorders represent losses, changes, or disturbances in family relationships (G. W. Brown and Harris, 1978; Myers and Pepper, 1972; Myers et al., 1975; Paykel et al., 1969). Furthermore, the family may serve to communicate three types of support functions identified by Cobb (1976): affection and caring, self-esteem, and group solidarity. We thus felt it necessary to incorporate and develop some meaningful measures of the family as a support system.

A review of inventories of scales failed to yield measures that had face validity and/or that had acceptable properties of reliability and validity. We were particularly interested in several measures that had shown predictive validity, among which were the measures applied in the previously cited studies of Nuckolls et al. (1972) and Gore (1978). However, descriptions of these measures indicated that they are comprised of diverse items, apparently tapping psychological, interpersonal, and situational factors. To our knowledge, the scale or subscale properties of these instruments had not been reported. On the other hand, Medalie and Goldbourt (1976) applied a more homogeneous set of items focusing on relationships within the conjugal family. In a study of cardiovascular disorders in 10,000 men, they found that those who reported favorable relationships with their wives were significantly less likely to develop symptoms of angina pectoris, even in the presence of biological risk factors. We thus decided to examine the scale properties of the Medalie–Goldbourt instrument and its relationship to depression in a community population.

ANALYSIS OF THE MEDALIE–GOLDBOURT SCALE OF FAMILY RELATIONSHIPS

The scale consists of four items that apparently attempt to tap the quality of the relationships of the respondent to his/her spouse and other members of the conjugal family. Essentially, these items focus on family problems: (1) problems in the past, (2) problems at present, (3) effects of spouse/children not listening or opposing, (4) whether the spouse shows his/her love. The responses to the four questions are measured on a four point scale. A low score reflects fewer problems and a more favorable expression of love by the spouse. The assumption is that the fewer the problems, the better the relationship.

It seems reasonable to expect family conflicts and problems to reflect the quality of family relationships, including family support. Because the nature of the problems are unspecified in three of the items, these items may be conceived of as indirect measures of social support. By contrast, the love item specifically measures a theoretical attribute, element, or form of social support. Overall, this measure would appear to tap expressive disturbances. However, because the family problems are undifferentiated, instrumental problems may also be implicated.

The Medalie–Goldbourt Scale of Family Relationships shows acceptable internal consistency, with alpha coefficients ranging from .62 in Time 1 (T1) to .69 in Time 2 (T2) (see Table 7.1). Item–total correlations range from .26 to .61. The means and standard deviations are stable across the three samples. The fourth item in the scale, "Does your spouse show you his/her love?", is not well correlated with the other scale items, but its removal does not increase the alpha coefficients.

The scale shows, as presented in Table 7.1, significant and consistent predictive validity; correlations with depression range from .26 to .34. Thus, the poorer the family relationships (low support), the higher the depression. It is noteworthy that family relationships are also signifi-

TABLE 7.1
Reliability and Validity of Confidant-Support Scales

Confidant scale	No. of items	Mean	Standard deviation	Range of inter-item (r's)	Range of item-total (r's)	Range of alphas when each item is deleted	Alpha, total scale	Total scale with CESD (r)	Total scale with LE (r)
Time 1 (T1) (N = 1091)									
Medalie–Goldbourt family-support scale	4	6.65	1.83	.16–.60	.26–.55	.46–.64	.62	.26	.28
Lowenthal–Haven presence-of-a-confidant item	1	1.06	.24	—	—	—	—	.07	−.07
Kaplan confidant-relationship scale	6	7.66	2.47	.10–.64	.35–.67	.66–.75	.75	.12	.14
Confidant help with most important life event	1	1.88	1.20	—	—	—	—	−.03	−.02
Durability	1	25.50	24.92	—	—	—	—	.03	−.22
Confidant–respondent difference in:									
age	1	7.61	10.00	—	—	—	—	.03	−.08
Sex	1	.54	.50	—	—	—	—	−.05	−.08
Occupational status	1	16.03	16.43	—	—	—	—	.05	.05
Education	1	1.52	2.10	—	—	—	—	.02	−.08
T1 (N = 871)									
Medalie–Goldbourt family-support scale	4	6.66	1.86	.15–.59	.27–.54	.43–.64	.62	.27	.29
Lowenthal–Haven presence-of-a-confidant item	1	1.05	.23	—	—	—	—	.04	−.05

Kaplan confidant-relationship scale	6	7.62	2.47	.10–.64	.36–.68	.66–.75	.75	.12	.14
Confidant help with most important life event	1	1.93	1.21	—	—	—	—	.00	-.03
Durability	1	25.56	24.03	—	—	—	—	-.01	.17
Confidant–respondent difference in:									
Age	1	7.36	9.69	—	—	—	—	-.08	-.07
Sex	1	.54	.50	—	—	—	—	-.05	-.08
Occupational status	1	11.32	15.89	—	—	—	—	.04	.01
Education	1	1.54	2.20	—	—	—	—	.07	-.07
Time 2 (N = 871)									
Medalie–Goldbourt family-support scale	4	7.01	2.04	.20–.63	.36–.61	.53–.70	.69	.34	.27
Lowenthal–Haven presence-of-a-confidant scale	1	1.32	.47	—	—	—	—	-.13	-.31
Kaplan confidant-relationship scale	6	7.36	2.42	.32–.68	.48–.70	.75–.80	.81	.23	.07
Confidant help with most important life event	1	1.43	.50	—	—	—	—	-.15	-.24
Durability	1	—	—	—	—	—	—	—	—
Confidant–respondent difference in:									
Age	1	6.75	8.72	—	—	—	—	.01	-.03
Sex	1	—	—	—	—	—	—	—	—
Occupational status	1	18.51	19.67	—	—	—	—	.04	-.06
Education	1	1.36	1.80	—	—	—	—	.11	.02

cantly and consistently related to life events, with zero-order correlations ranging from .27 to .29. An increase in life events is associated with lower family support.

One important limitation of this scale is that it is applicable only to married persons. Furthermore, with the exception of the love item, no explicit support attribute is directly measured. However, the scale was an attempt to develop and apply a relatively simple and easily administered, if rough, measure of support.

Coupled with acceptable internal consistency, the significant correlations of this scale with depression and life events suggests that it merits further application in epidemiologic studies of stress and illness. It would also be useful to discern the relationship of this scale to other measures of family relationships and support functions.

CONFIDANT SUPPORT: CONCEPTUALIZATION AND MEASUREMENT

The concept of confiding relationships as supportive relationships are traceable to the work of Lowenthal and Haven (1968). They conceived of the need to study confidant relationships as part of a larger need to study various forms of intimacy. Similarly, they hypothesized that the availability of intimate relationships might serve as a crucial factor in adapting to the problems of aging and thus influence the risk of depression. They defined a *confidant* as someone with whom the elderly person could talk to intimately about themselves or their problems. Using this operational definition, they found some evidence that the presence of a confidant reduced the risk of depression associated with role losses, widowhood, and other problems of aging. Subsequently, Brown and Harris (1978), in an attempt to discern factors that might explain the differential susceptibility of women to depression under conditions of stressful life events, found some evidence that the presence or absence of a confiding relationship with their husband, boyfriend, or other male was a significant factor. The work of Lowenthal and Haven has stimulated further attention to confidant relationships as support systems in terms of conceptualizing and operationalizing them and examining their epidemiologic significance.

As operationalized by Lowenthal and Haven, the construct of confidant relationships carries a strong suggestion of reactive support. More specifically, it makes reference to the ability to talk about one's problems, and these problems are assumed to be associated with the stressors of aging. Thus, their measure of the confidant relationship generally taps the presence or absence of a trusting relationship in which sensitive matters can be discussed. The ways in which confiding relationships may reduce stress is not explicit in this formulation. We have attempted to extend our knowledge of the nature and functions of confidant support in several ways that need to be further specified.

We attempted to examine several operationalizations of confidant relationships, given a number of conceptual, operational, and empirical considerations. In T1 we defined a confidant relationship as the presence of someone the respondent felt he/she could trust and talk to. This definition was made deliberately broad and did not include specific reference to problems or to oneself. We felt that this might be a more comprehensive definition of an intimate relationship and one that need not imply the contingency of having a problem or a stressful experience. However, we were also interested in more complex measures of confidant relationships. For example, whereas Lowenthal and Haven emphasizes the importance of the presence or absence of confidant relationships, we were interested in operationalizing a number of features of confidant relationships that Berton H. Kaplan (1975) had proposed as theoretically significant. These include:

1. *Durability*: Number of years respondent has known the confidant
2. *Frequency*: Frequency of contact with the confidant
3. *Density*: How often the respondent has talked over problems with the confidant
4. *Directedness*: How often the confidant has talked over problems with the respondent
5. *Reachability*: How easy it has been for the respondent to get hold of the confidant
6. *Content*: How freely the respondent has been able to talk about things with the confidant
7. *Intensity*: How important the confidant is to the respondent

Thus, we had a special interest in the question of whether these attributes formed a unidimensional scale.

The relationship between the confidant and the respondent can also be assessed according to the similarities or differences of their sociodemographic characteristics. The concept of homophily or heterophily has been discussed by sociologists as a construct to measure social distance. It can be argued that a homophilous confidant represents a strong tie in that the social distance between the confidant and the respondent is short and communication is facilitated. Thus, se-

lected sociodemographic characteristics about the confidant can be obtained and used to assess the homophily between the confidant and the
respondent.

We were also interested in the question of whether the confidant
actually provided help to the respondent with regard to life events. We
thus had a one-item scale tapping perceived help with the most important life event.

Scale Analysis

In T1, the availability of a confidant was tapped by the question,
"During the past six months, have you had anyone that you could trust
and talk to?" This question called for a response of yes (scored 1) or no
(scored 2). All other confidant scales were built on this broad definition
of a confidant in T1.

The next question asked, "How many people have you been able to
trust and talk to?" Each respondent could name up to three such confidants. We assessed the most important confidant from among the respondent's three-person confidant group by asking, "Of those (persons
mentioned above) you have thought about, think about one you are
most likely to trust and talk to about your problems." Respondents
were then asked a series of questions about the relationships between
them and the confidant: how many years they had known this person
(durability), the frequency of contact (frequency), how often they talked
to the contact about their problems (density), and how often they confided in the most important confidant about their problems (directedness), how easy it had been for the respondent to contact of the confidant (reachability), how freely the respondent had been able to talk
about things with the confidant (content), and how important the confidant was to the respondent (intensity).

Durability was later found not to be significantly related to the remaining six items. It was analyzed as a separate item. Each of the
remaining Kaplan items were scored on a 4-point scale as follows: (1)
most or all of the time, (2) *occasionally or a moderate amount of time*,
(3) *some or a little of the time*, and (4) *rarely or none of the time*. Thus,
on the six items, possible summated scores ranged from 6 (strong relationship) to 24 (weak relationship).

With regard to confidant help with the most important life event, as
well as the confidant relationship attributes (Kaplan), the respondent
was asked to consider the person he/she was "most likely to trust and
talk to." The respondent was then asked, "How much did this person

help you with [the life event designated previously as most important]?" The responses were *very much, much, some,* or *not very much* and were scored from 1 to 4.

Finally, each respondent was asked to specify certain sociodemographic characteristics of the confidant: role relationship, age, sex, occupation (subsequently converted to the Duncan Socioeconomic Index score), and education. The role relationship was specified with the following categories: spouse/lover, son/daughter, mother/father, brother/sister, in-law, other relative, close friend, other acquaintance, neighbor, co-worker, boss or supervisor, helping professional, and other. To construct the heterophily scores, we calculated the absolute difference of each sociodemographic characteristic (age, sex, occupational status, and education) between the confidant and the respondent.

Initial analyses of the relationship between the T1 confidant-support scales (Lowenthal–Haven and Kaplan items) to depression indicated weak or nonsignificant relationships (Table 7.1). This came as something of a surprise, because we felt initially that we had broadened, but not essentially changed, the Lowenthal–Haven scale. However, we decided that reverting to the original Lowenthal–Haven wording of the question was indicated for future waves of the study. Thus at T2 the availability of a confidant was identified by the question: "During the past six months, has there been anyone in particular you confided in, or talked to, about yourself or your problems?" All of the T2 confidant scales are based on this operationalization of the confidant relationship. Thus, the reader should keep in mind that the T1 and T2 confidant scales reported in Table 7.1 are not strictly comparable. Variations in T1 and T2 statistics on the reliability and correlates of the scales may well reflect these differences in wording.

The T1 Kaplan scale shows good internal consistency and stability with alpha coefficients of .75 in both samples. However, with this operationalization of confidant support, none of the confidant scales show significant correlations with depression (Table 7.1). Defining a confidant as a person one can talk to about oneself or one's problems, as operationalized in T2, clearly makes a difference (Table 7.1). It may be seen that the Kaplan scale exhibits strong internal consistency (alpha = .81). Furthermore, it is significantly correlated with depression (r = .23).

The other confidant scales used in T2 exhibit significant correlations with depression and/or life events. The presence of a confidant is associated with life events (r = .31) in the expected direction. Also, the presence of a confidant shows a slight inverse relationship with depression ($r = .13$). Comparable relationships are exhibited for confidant help with the most important life event.

Similarly, confidant help with the most important life event was correlated with depression and life events in T2 but not in T1. Again, we suspect that the wording of the confidant question might have induced a more focused response in T2. Durability of the relationship between the respondent and the confidant did not correlate with either depression or life events.

Homophily of characteristics between the respondent and the confidant did not correlate with depression or life events. There was a slight correlation between educational differences and CES-D at T2, but all other correlations were low and insignificant. We suspect that the use of the spouse as a confidant may have confounded the expected effect of the homophily principle. The spouse is of the opposite sex and perhaps also different in age, occupational status, and education to varying degrees. In Chapter 15, we examine more closely the issue of the gender of the confidant.

In summary, the internal consistency of both versions of the Kaplan scale suggests that both may be regarded as tapping the strength of confidant relationships. The correlation between the T1 and T2 scales is .31. However, the preceding observations indicate that the T2 scales have stronger internal consistency and predictive validity. For these reasons, we believe that the definition of a confidant as a person whom one can talk to about oneself or one's problems holds more promise for future research.

DISCUSSION

This chapter briefly discussed attempts at measuring confidant relationships. Scales were constructed and examined for family support (the Medalie–Goldbourt four-item scale), presence of confidant(s) (Lowenthal–Haven item), relationships between ego and confidant (Kaplan items), confidant's help with the most important life event, and homophily of characteristics between the confidant and the respondent. The family-support scale and the Kaplan items showed consistent and valid results for both T1 and T2. The other items showed more varied results. Because of a wording change in the leading question (focusing on the confidant's value as someone with whom to talk about oneself and one's problems), T2 results for these items had higher cross-sectional correlations with the CES-D.

Our recommendations are, therefore: (1) that the Medalie–Goldbourt family-support scale should be used for married individuals, (2) that the Kaplan items should be selectively used, and (3) that further evaluations are necessary before researchers can confidently use the Lowenthal–Haven items concerning the confidant's help with the most important life event as well as items regarding homophily.

SUMMARY AND CONCLUSIONS

In this chapter we briefly discussed family relationships and confiding relationships as primary relationships and intimate forms of social support. The conceptual and psychometric properties of several candidate measures were examined. The Medalie–Goldbourt scale appears to tap the quality of conjugal family relationships (ego's relationship to spouse and children). The scale demonstrates acceptable internal consistency and stability and exhibits significant correlations with depression. In these terms, the scale warrants further application in this and similar studies. This measure has both the value and limitations of a subjective measure of family support. An important limitation of this scale is that with the exception of the spousal-love item, the items do not clearly identify supportive elements. Further instrumentation efforts should be made to incorporate such attributes.

The ability to confide in one's spouse should be a defining feature of conjugal support. This point also illustrates that the examination of confiding relationships and familial relationships need not and should not be examined entirely separately. This leads us to note that other social-support scales discussed subsequently sometimes overlap with the constructs and measures discussed here—as well as complement or extend them. For example, in Chapter 15 we examine the implications of the spouse serving or failing to serve as a confidant, and this is an important predictor of depression. Furthermore, Chapter 9 also deals with confidant networks, in contrast to the most-important confidant discussed here.

It should also be noted that the Medalie–Goldbourt scale can only be applied to married individuals. This also illustrates the important difference between scales that attempt to measure the *availability* of support from specific support groups, such as the family, and scales designed to measure the general *adequacy* of support functions. The latter approach is exemplified by the instrumental–expressive scales discussed in Chapter 8. Furthermore, the network approach sometimes usefully combines the examination of social categories with support functions.

Two different definitions of a confidant were applied in T1 and T2 and led to different findings. The original Lowenthal–Haven definition shows the strongest relationship to depression. As a result, we believe that this measure deserves further application and examination. Our findings also indicate that with the exception of durability, the attributes of a confiding relationship proposed by Kaplan form a unidimensional scale with high internal consistency and may tap the strength of the confidant relationship. In T2 this measure shows a significant relationship with depression. In the T2 version, confidant help with the most important life event shows a significant though modest correlation with risk of depression (in the expected direction). Homophily of the confidant does not generally demonstrate significance. This may be obscured and confounded by the gender of the spouse and thus is further explored elsewhere. Beyond describing the nature and significance of these specific measures, the findings in this chapter and those to be presented in Chapters 8 and 9 increasingly point to the importance of intimate, binding forms of social support.

8

Measuring the Instrumental and Expressive Functions of Social Support

WALTER M. ENSEL

MARY WOELFEL

SCALE DEVELOPMENT

In the early stages of our work (1977–1978), as mentioned earlier, there were few measures of social support available in the literature. With the exception of the early work of Lowenthal and Havens (1968), Kaplan (1975), Medalie and Goldbourt (1976), and a few others, there were few measures available that differentiated types of social support. However, it was clear from the existing literature (see Chapters 1 and 2) that social-support systems seemed to serve both instrumental and expressive functions. For example, research on the effects of job loss (Gore, 1978) and "exits from the social field" (Paykel et al., 1969) suggested that these life events may reflect problems in either expressive or instrumental functioning. Given these findings, and the growing interest at that time in the potential buffering functions of expressive support, an attempt was made to operationalize a set of 26 items that we felt would reflect the instrumental and expressive support available to individuals (Lin, Dean, and Ensel, 1981a).

129

Our objective in constructing these items was to allow for a description of types of support that were not strictly a function of sociodemographic differences (e.g., employment status, marital status, family arrangements). The items cut across a number of roles and statuses inherent in a community population. The original (pretest) set of 26 items (later expanded to 28 with 3 new items added and 1 item dropped-see Table 8.2), were prefaced by a brief introduction ("Could you tell me how often you have been bothered by the following problems over the past six months?").

The items covered a wide variety of subjects, including financial problems, time and effort demands, presence or lack of adequate companionship, and communication, dependency, familial, and household-related problems. The exact wordings of the original 26 support items appear in Table 8.1.

TOTAL SCALE RELIABILITY AND VALIDITY

The reliability and validity of the Instrumental–Expressive Support Scale for the Time 1 (T1) and Time 2 (T2) panel data is presented in Table 8.2. With the exception of the item "Feeling too dependent on others," all items in the T1 data set had a high level of internal consistency (range of r's = .3 to .7). In addition, the total alpha for the scale indicates consistently high reliability in both the T1 and T2 data (.89 to .93). Validity can be determined by examining the correlations of both the individual items and the total-scale score with depression. As can be seen, the items' range of correlations varies from − .15 to − ,43, whereas the total-scale correlation remains consistent over time (− .58 in T1 and − .59 in T2). For the most part, the items were consistently related to depression over time (see columns 3 and 6 in Table 8.2). In short, the total scale remains relatively stable over time. However, given the large number of items comprising the scale, an attempt is made to further examine the various types of instrumental and expressive support.

DETERMINING DIMENSIONS OF THE INSTRUMENTAL AND EXPRESSIVE ITEMS

In this chapter, we describe further work that we have done with the instrumental–expressive scale. Briefly, this has consisted of two approaches. The first was to examine the extent to which the scale could

TABLE 8.1
The Instrumental–Expressive Social-Support Scale

The following is a list of problems that people sometimes have. Would you tell me how often you have been bothered by these problems over the past 6 months.

    1. Most or all of the time
    2. Occcasionally or a moderate amount of the time
    3. Some or a little of the time
    4. Rarely
    5. Never

  1. Having problems managing money . . . . _____
  2. Not having a close companion . . . . _____
  3. Having too many responsibilities. . . . . _____
  4. Not having people you can depend on. . . . . _____
  5. Too many demands on your time . . . . _____
  6. Not having a satisfactory sex life . . . . _____
  7. Having problems communicating with others . . . . _____
  8. Not seeing enough of people you feel close to. . . . . _____
  9. Deciding on how to spend money . . . . _____
10. Not having enough responsibilities. . . . . _____
11. Having too little leisure time . . . . _____
12. Not having enough money to do the things you want . . . . . . _____
13. Problems with children . . . . _____
14. Not having a satisfying job . . . . _____
15. Feeling too controlled by others . . . . _____
16. Not enough money to get by on. . . . . _____
17. Dissatisfied with your marital status (single, married). . . . . . _____
18. Not having enough close friends . . . . _____
19. Problems with spouse/ex-spouse . . . . _____
20. Not having someone who shows you love and affection. . . . _____
21. Feeling too dependent on others . . . . _____
22. Not having children . . . . _____
23. Problems with in-laws/relatives. . . . . _____
24. Not having someone who understands your problems . . . . . _____
25. Having too much time on your hands . . . . _____
26. Conflicts with people who are close to you . . . . _____
Are there any other problems that I have not mentioned that really bother you?

TABLE 8.2
Reliability and Validity of the Instrumental–Expressive Social-Support Scale[1] in Time 1 (T1) and Time 2 (T2) Subsamples[2]

Instrumental–expressive items	T1 (N = 871)			T2 (N = 871)		
	Item–total correlation	Alpha if item deleted	Item–CES-D correlation	Item–total correlation	Alpha if item deleted	Item–CES-D correlation
1. Having problems managing money	.47	.89	−.25	.57	.92	−.31
2. Not having a close companion	.53	.89	−.39	.56	.92	−.38
3. Having too many responsibilities	.59	.89	−.36	.60	.92	−.36
4. Not having people you can depend on	.53	.89	−.34	.64	.92	−.36
5. Too many demands on your time	.52	.89	−.27	.55	.92	−.30
6. Not having a satisfactory sex life	.49	.89	−.31	.60	.92	−.36
7. Having problems communicating with others	.63	.89	−.33	.65	.92	−.41
8. Not seeing enough of people you feel close to	.58	.89	−.35	.59	.92	−.34
9. Deciding on how to spend money	.48	.89	−.23	.55	.92	−.29
10. Not having enough responsibilities	.28	.89	−.19	.31	.93	−.22
11. Not having someone who shows concern for your problems[1]	.46	.89	−.23	.66	.92	−.36
12. Having too little leisure time	.50	.89	−.28	.45	.92	−.20
13. Not having enough money to do the things you want	.47	.89	−.32	.54	.92	−.25
14. Problems with children	.40	.89	−.27	.49	.92	−.29
15. Not having a satisfying job	.59	.89	−.36	.28	.93	−.28
16. Feeling too controlled by others	.43	.89	−.25	.63	.92	−.40
17. Not having enough money to get by on	.37	.89	−.21	.48	.92	−.26
18. Dissatisfied with your marital status (single, married)	.51	.89	−.35	.53	.92	−.35

19. Not having enough close friends	28	.89	−.18	.57	.92	−.39
20. Problems with spouse/ex-spouse	49	.89	−.32	.53	.92	−.35
21. Not having someone who shows you love and affection	42	.89	−.37	.61	.92	−.43
22. Feeling too dependent on others	17	.89	−.15	.58	.92	−.43
23. Other people interfere with things you want to do[1]	42	.89	−.24	.62	.92	−.35
24. Problems with in-laws/relatives	63	.89	−.40	.43	.92	−.26
25. Not having someone who understands your problems	23	.89	−.25	.68	.92	−.43
26. Having too much time on your hands	60	.89	−.35	.28	.	−.24
27. Conflicts with people who are close to you	47	.89	−.32	.66	.92	−.42
28. Not being able to get somewhere because of lack of transportation[1]	—	—	—	.45	92	−.23
Total Scale			−.58			−.59
Total scale mean	97.63			99.56		
Total scale SD	10.55			12.81		
Average item means	3.62			3.56		
SD of item means	.25			.24		
Min/max item means	1.75/3.94			2.78/3.87		
X inter-item correlation	.24			.32		
SD of inter-item r	.12			.12		
Min/max inter-item r	−.03/.60			−.03/.72		
Alpha—total scale	.89			.93		

[1] It should be noted that items 11 and 23 were added between the pretest and T1 survey and that item 22 in Table 8.1 was dropped. In the T2 survey, item 28 was added to the instrumental-expressive scale.

[2] Because the total T1 sample ($N = 1091$) results are virtually identical to the T1 subsample ($N = 871$) results, only the latter statistics are presented here.

be broken down into subgroups or factors that more explicitly describe the instrumental and/or expressive functions of social support. To do this, we relied on factor analysis. Our rationale for using this technique is presented below. After reviewing what we consider an acceptable factor structure, the reliability and validity of the factors are discussed. An attempt is made to confirm this factor structure with both the T1 and T2 data sets.

The second approach was a two-level approach in which we initially selected a subgroup of the instrumental and expressive items based on certain theoretical and conceptual exceptions. This subgroup of items was subsequently subjected to a series of rigorous empirical tests to arrive at a set of items that would tap elements of the theoretical scheme underlying the initial operationalization. The relationships of the factors to each other over time, as well as their reliability and validity, are examined below. Critical questions regarding the scale are addressed, and a rationale is presented for the use of the scale in this study.

FACTOR ANALYSIS

One of the most important functions of factor analysis is to serve as a data-reduction technique. That is, it allows us to reduce a large set of variables to a smaller set of factors. The variables within each factor are more highly related to each other than they are to items in other factors. In this chapter, we utilize factor analysis as an exploratory technique— that is, as a method of uncovering potential types of instrumental and expressive social support. Once these different types of support are uncovered, we can create factor indices that may then be treated as new variables in any further analysis.

Subjecting our items to a factor analysis (orthogonal solution, varimax rotation, with a limiting eigenvalue of 1 or more), we came up with an initial set of six factors in the total T1 sample data set. If an item's factor loading (correlation with the other items) was .5 or greater, it was retained in the factor. Together, the six factors accounted for 62% of the variance in the 28 items. As shown in Table 8.3, Column 1, the six factors were: (1) *Demands*, consisting of three items ("too many responsibilities," "too many demands," and "too little leisure time"); (2) *Money*, consisting of three items ("problems managing money," "not enough money to get by on," and "not enough money to do the things you want"); (3) *Companionship*, consisting of three items ("not enough close friends," "no close companions," and "no one who understands your problems"); (4) *Marital,* consisting of three items ("no one who shows love/affection," "dissatisfied with marital status," and "problems with spouse"); (5) *Conflict,* consisting of two items ("problems with in-laws/relatives," and "conflict with people who are close to you"); and finally, (6) *Communication,* consisting of two items ("problems communicating with others" and "too controlled by others").

Before testing for the validity of these factors, a major concern of ours was the extent to which the factors would hang together over time. With the exception of some preliminary work in our pretest, this was the first time our Instrumental–Expressive Social-Support Scale had been tested with a representative community sample. We therefore conducted factor analyses of two additional sources of data: (1) the responses of the 871 respondents who completed the second, T2 interviews and (2) the same 871 subjects' interview responses from our first wave of data collection. Table 8.3 presents the results of all three analyses. As can be seen, the factor structures of the three analyses (total T1 sample and the subsamples from T1 and T2) differ from each other. In fact, with the exception of the first two factors, none of the other factors hold together with strict consistency over the three separate analyses. However, although some of the items found in some factors cross over into other factors over time (that is, between T1 and T2), there is still some consistency over time within certain factors. For example, three of the five items that loaded in the Companionship factor for the factor analysis of the T1 subsample ("dissatisfied with marital status," "no one shows love/affection," and "no one understands problems") load on the same factor in the analysis of the T2 subsample.

It should be pointed out that a very likely source of the inconsistencies in factor structures over time may be the nature of inter-item correlations among the variables. For example, if for three variables X, Y, Z, the $X-Y$ pair and $X-Z$ pair are moderately correlated (one slightly higher than the other), but the $Y-Z$ pair is not, a factor analysis of the three variables can show that Y and Z load on separate factors. Variable X, on the other hand, can load on both, but its magnitudes (loadings) may exceed a given point on one and not the other. Because measurement in the social sciences is not perfect, minor fluctuations in the magnitude of correlations is very likely to result when doing over-time analysis. These minor fluctuations may have major consequences in the factor-loading structure, especially if an arbitrary cutoff point is used to select "representative" items for each factor.

Compounding the above situation with 25 more variables considered simultaneously, one can imagine a case in which items loading strongly on one factor in one time period might switch over to other factors in

TABLE 8.3
Factor Analyses of Instrumental and Expressive Items for Total Time 1 (T1) Sample and Time 1 and Time 2 (T2) Subsamples

Total T1 sample (N = 1091)

Factor and items	Loading	Alpha	Alpha if item deleted
Factor 1			
Too many responsibilities	.57	.70	.63
Too many demands	.75		.52
Too little leisure	.50		.67
Factor 2			
Problems managing money	.63	.78	.77
Not enough money to do things	.71		.67
Not enough money to get by	.78		.66

T1 subsample (N = 871)

Factor and items	Loading	Alpha	Alpha if item deleted
Factor 1			
Too many responsibilities	.59	.80	.77
No one to depend on	.45		.79
Too many demands	.76		.77
Problems communicating	.40		.79
Not seeing enough of people	.41		.78
Too little leisure	.54		.79
Too controlled by others	.43		.78
Factor 2			
Problems managing money	.63	.78	.77
Not enough money to do things	.69		.68
Not enough money to get by	.78		.65

T2 (N = 871)

Factor and items	Loading	Alpha	Alpha if item deleted
Factor 1			
Too many responsibilities	.66	.86	.84
No one to depend on	.42		.85
Too many demands	.79		.84
Problems communicating	.43		.85
Not seeing enough of people	.43		.85
Too little leisure	.54		.86
Too controlled by others	.59		.84
Conflicts with people close	.59		.64
Others interfere	.59		.84
Factor 2			
Problems managing money	.67	.82	.76
Not enough money to do things	.80		.83
Not enough money	.79		.74
Deciding how to spend	.47		.76

Factor 3

Item			
Not enough close friends	.45	.75	.74
No close companion	.61		.67
No one understands problems	.44		.67

Factor 4

Item			
Dissatisfied with marital status	.58	.66	.55
Problems with spouse	.50		.47
No one shows love and affection	.59		.64

Factor 5

Item			
Conflict with people close	.57	.62	.99
Problems with in-laws/relatives	.45		.99

Factor 6

Item			
Problems communicating	.41	.60	.99
Too controlled by others	.41		.99

Factor 3

Item			
No close companion	.60	.67	.56
Unsatisfactory sex life	.45		.75
Dissatisfied with marital status	.54		.66
No one shows love and affection	.81		.55
No one understands problems	.40		.59

Factor 4

Item			
Problems communicating	.42	.58	.45
Not seeing enough of people	.42		.48
Not enough responsibility	.39		.54
Unsatisfying job	.57		.56
Too much time on hands	.43		.58

Factor 5

Item			
Problems with in-laws/relatives	.48	.70	.64
No one understands problems	.54		.62

Factor 3

Item			
Dissatisfied with marital status	.67	.83	.80
Problems with spouse	.65		.80
No one shows love and affection	.70		.77
No one understands problems	.48		.79
Conflict with people close	.50		.80

Factor 4

Item			
Not enough responsibility	.57	.64	.58
Not enough close friends	.49		.56
Too dependent on others	.45		.56
Too much time on hands	.55		.60

Factor 5

Item		
No one shows concern	.51	

TABLE 8.4
Composite Factor Structure of the
Instrumental–Expressive Social-Support
Scale

Factor 1: Excess of Responsibliities/Demands
  • Too many responsibilities
  • No one to depend on
  • Too many demands
  • Problems communicating
  • Not seeing enough of people
  • Too little leisure
  • Too controlled by others
Factor 2: Lack of Money
  • Problems managing money
  • Not enough money to get by on
  • Not enough money to do things
Factor 3: Unsatisfactory Intimate Relations
  • Dissatisfied with marital status
  • No one shows love and affection
  • No one understands problems
  • No close companion
Factor 4: Lack of Involvement
  • Not enough responsibilities
  • Too much time on hands
Factor 5: Family Problems
  • Problems with in-laws/relatives

---

a subsequent period. Indeed, an examination of the results of the factor analyses under discussion shows this to be the case.

To deal with this multicollinearity-type effect, we devised a strategy for simplifying the examination of factor-structure similarities across time periods and data sets. If an item loaded on the same factor in two out of three of the separate samples' factor analyses, it was considered to be a stable element of that factor. Table 8.4 shows the results of implementing this procedure.

The Composite Factor Strcture

As can be seen, the data-reduction technique used here resulted in a composite factor structure consisting of five factors that utilize 17 of the 28 items in the total scale. The factors are (1) Excess of Responsibilities/Demands, (2) Lack of Money, (3) Unsatisfactory Intimate Relations, (4) Lack of Involvement, and (5) Family Problems. It should be noted that the labeling of these factors is somewhat arbitrary and by no means definitive. That is to say, the labels do not necessarily represent all of the items within each factor. For example, under the factor Excess of Responsibilities/Demands, the fifth and sixth items ("not seeing enough of people" and "too little leisure time") are more than likely brought about by the excessive burden of too many responsibilities or demands rather than being indicators of them. For the most part, however, the labels appear to convey the essence of the items comprising the factor. It is clear that an excess of responsibilities and demands, lack of money, and lack of involvement are instrumental problems. On the other hand, expressive difficulties are reflected in unsatisfactory intimate relations and family problems. When we had determined the composite factor structure, the next step was to evaluate the reliability and validity of these factors in T1 and T2 data sets.

Reliability and Validity of the Factors in Time 1 and Time 2 Samples

Table 8.5 presents the reliability and validity of the composite factor structure in the two waves of data. An examination of the correlation of each item in a factor with the factor itself (with that item deleted) indicates that the internal consistency of the factors is for the most part rather high (range of r's = .60 to .89). In addition, all of the alphas for the first three factors are high and consistent with each other over the T1 and T2 data sets (range of alphas is .74 to .83). The one exception to this high reliability is the fourth factor (Lack of Involvement), where the alpha for T1 is approximately .31 and the alpha for T2 is .52. Given the fact that the alpha coefficient is affected by the number of items comprising the subscale or factor and that the item correlation for the two variables is relatively high, we defer judgment on the reliability of this factor until a later point in this chapter. We were unable to calculate an alpha coefficient for the fifth factor, because it consisted of only one item. Therefore, for the time being, we felt confident about the reliability and consistency of the first three factors in the composite factor structure.

The next step was to examine the validity of the factor structures. This was done in two steps: (1) by examining the correlation of the individual items in the factor with a key dependent variable (in this case the Center for Epidemiologic Studies Depression Scale) and (2) by examining the correlation of the factors themselves with the dependent variable (CES-D). The results show that the range of the individual items' correlation with depression is − .17 to − .43. The pattern shows that the more frequently a particular set of social-support problems was

TABLE 8.5
Reliability and Validity of Composite Factor Structure

Factor and items	Total time 1 sample (N = 1091)					Time 1 subsample (N = 871)					Time 2 subsample (N = 871)				
	Item–factor correlation	Alpha	Alpha if item deleted	Item–CESD correlation	Factor–CESD correlation	Item–factor correlation	Alpha	Alpha if item deleted	Item–CESD correlation	Factor–CESD correlation	Item–factor correlation	Alpha	Alpha if item deleted	Item–CESD correlation	Factor–CESD correlation
Excess of Responsibilities/Demands		.79			−.43		.81			−.46		.83			−.47
Too many responsibilities	.70		.76	−.35		.71		.78	−.36		.70		.79	−.36	
No one to depend on	.63		.77	−.32		.64		.79	−.34		.60		.81	−.36	
Too many demands	.73		.75	−.24		.75		.77	−.27		.75		.78	−.30	
Problems communicating	.64		.77	−.31		.65		.79	−.33		.61		.81	−.41	
Not seeing enough people	.67		.77	−.34		.69		.79	−.35		.65		.82	−.34	
Too little leisure	.65		.78	−.20		.67		.79	−.23		.62		.81	−.20	
Too controlled by others	.66		.77	−.34		.67		.79	−.36		.65		.80	−.40	
Lack of Money		.79			−.31		.78			−.33		.83			−.33
Problems managing money	.82		.78	−.24		.81		.77	−.25		.82		.83	−.31	
Not enough money to get by on	.88		.68	−.23		.82		.67	−.25		.91		.70	−.25	
Not enough money to do things	.89		.67	−.26		.89		.66	−.28		.87		.73	−.26	
Unsatisfactory Intimate Relations		.74			−.42		.75			−.42		.79			−.46
Dissatisfied with marital status	.71		.74	−.20		.71		.75	−.21		.68		.74	−.35	
No one shows love and affection	.82		.61	−.30		.82		.61	−.32		.73		.70	−.43	
No one understands problems	.71		.70	−.40		.68		.72	−.40		.65		.75	−.43	
No close companion	.75		.68	−.39		.77		.66	−.39		.67		.78	−.38	
Lack of Involvement		.31			−.26		.32			−.28		.52			−.28
Not enough responsibilities	.67		.99	−.17		.67		.99	−.19		.67		.99	−.22	
Too much time on hands	.85		.99	−.23		.85		.99	−.25		.80		.99	−.24	
Family Problems					−.24					−.24					−.29
Problems with in-laws/relatives	1.00					1.00					1.00				

experienced, the higher the recorded depression score. Although the individual factors prove to be consistent over time, and the magnitude of the correlations ($-$ .24 to $-$ .47) is consistent with those found by other investigators of the social-support–depression relationship (i.e., Pearlin et al., 1981; Turner, 1981; Williams et al., 1981), there also appear to be significant differences across factors. In particular, two of the support factors (Excess of Responsibilities/Demands and Unsatisfactory Intimate Relations) reflect significantly higher correlations with depression than do any of the other factors.

In sum, therefore, the instrumental and expressive social-support factors presented here appear to be consistent across data sets. In addition, three of the five factors show high internal reliability and validity. We are satisfied with the manner in which the scale stood up to rigorous testing.

Confirming the Composite Factor Structure: A Latent-Variable Approach

Based on these findings, the three-factor solution appears to be more reliable and valid. Because the reliability of the fourth factor is somewhat questionable, a factor-analytic technique based on maximum-likelihood estimation procedures was employed to assess whether a three- or four-factor model best fit the data. This technique can be described as a general approach by which it is possible to specify exactly which social support items load on which factors, how strong the relationships among the factors must be, and how many factors best fit the data. In other words, expected or known values of parameters can be fixed and/or constrained to be equal, with the remaining parameters free to be estimated (see Joroskog and Sorbom, 1981).

Given the above discussion, we would expect our 14-item, 3-factor oblique model to provide a better fit with the observed sample data than would our 16-item, 4-factor model. Put another way, we expect the 3-factor solution to conform more to the observed 14-item correlation matrix than the 4-factor solution will conform to the 16-item observed correlation matrix. Although prior knowledge is used to specify which items load on which factors, the analysis is treated as an exploratory exercise to assist in identifying the number of factors needed to represent the observed matrix.

Due to the sensitivity of the chi-square test statistic to sample size, the ratio of chi-square to degrees of freedom (χ^2/df) is used as a measure of overall goodness of fit between the proposed model and the sample correlation matrix. Wheaton and associates (1977) suggest that a ratio of

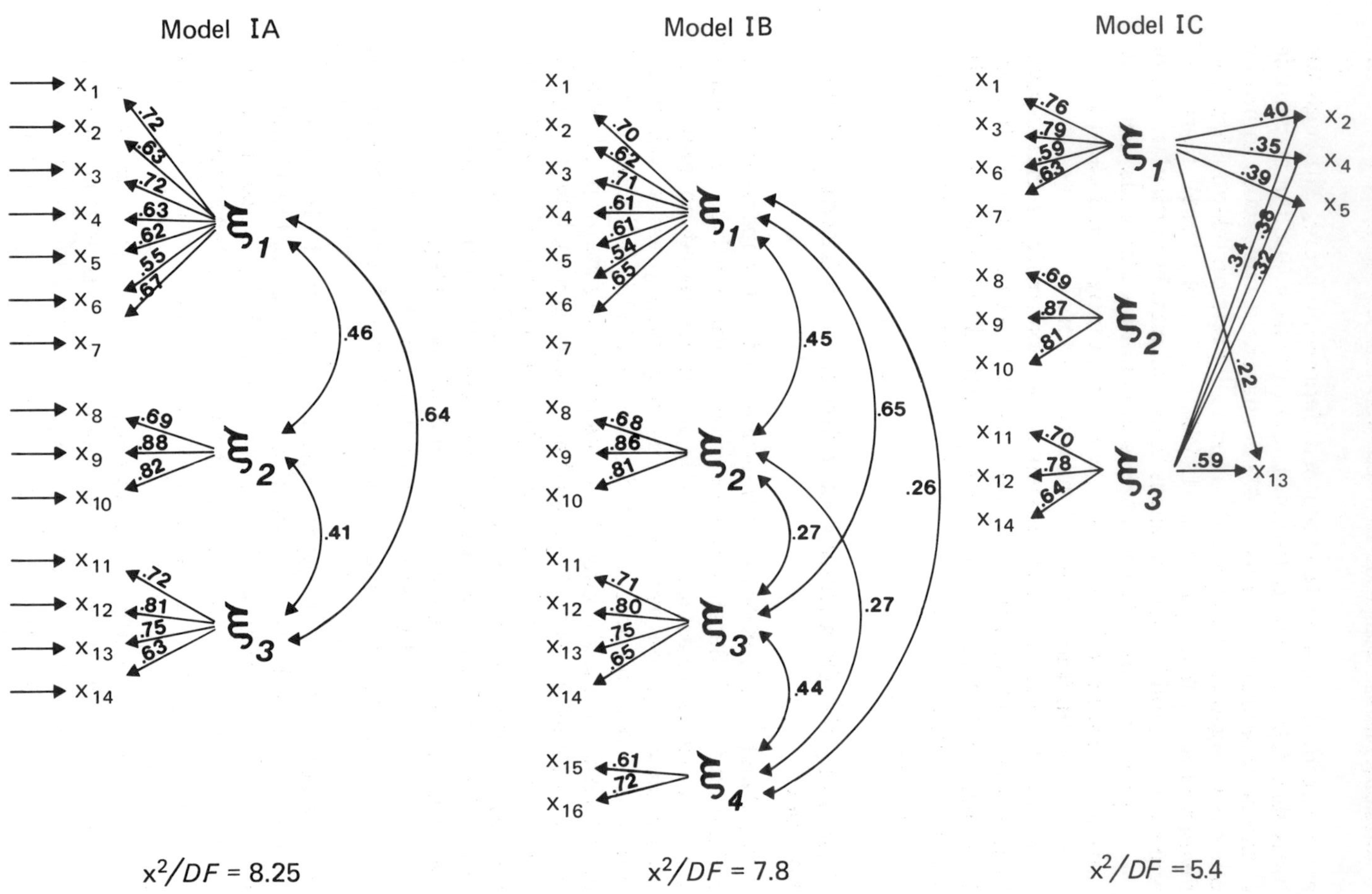

Model IA

Model IB

Model IC

$x^2/DF = 8.25$

$x^2/DF = 7.8$

$x^2/DF = 5.4$

Figure 8.1

5 to 1 or less begins to resemble an acceptable fit. Because we are interested here in comparing two alternative models, we examine the difference in χ^2 values, divided by the difference in degrees of freedom, between the two models; the resulting statistic itself is distributed as a chi-square.

In Figure 8.1 and Table 8.6, we present solutions for both these models, along with a solution for a refined model. All solutions here are estimated with the LISREL program (Joreskog and Sorbom, 1981).[1] The relative chi-square test for Model 1B ($\chi^2/df = 733/94 = 7.8$) indicates a better fit between the four-factor model and the data than for Model 1A, whose three-factor model fits the data less well ($\chi^2/df = 586/71 = 8.25$). The difference in fit between the two models, however, is not statistically significant. Because the four-factor solution does not constitute a statistically significant improvement over the three-factor solution, and because neither model provides a clearly acceptable fit (i.e., a $\chi^2/df \leq 5$), we attempted to improve both models by examining the first-order derivatives in conjunction with the residual matrix for each model (formed by subtracting the correlation matrix produced by the model from the sample correlation matrix). Because several attempts to improve the four-factor model resulted in severe multicollinearity problems, we confined our attention to the three-factor oblique solution. The less restricted oblique three-factor solution presented in Model 1C of Figure 8.1 shows a considerable improvement over the more restricted initial three-factor solution, which fails mainly because

---

[1]In a more technical sense, inconsistencies in loading structure over time may be due to the failure of the particular factor-analytic technique chosen to perform procrustean rotation. This procedure rotates one set of dimensions onto another set of dimensions using the criteria of minimizing the sum of squared distances between every point and every other point, whereas the varimax-rotation routine most commonly used (and used here) looks for simple structure within each group investigated, which consequently may be different for each data set, particularly when a different number of factors is being rotated across groups (Hunter, 1981).

Figure 8.1 Comparison of three potential social-support models. Items:

X_1 = Too many responsibilities	X_{11} = Dissatisfied with marital status
X_2 = No one to depend on	X_{12} = No one shows love and affection
X_3 = Too many demands	X_{13} = No one understand problems
X_4 = Problems communicating	X_{14} = No close companion
X_5 = Not seeing enough people	X_{15} = Not enough responsibilities
X_6 = Too little leisure	X_{16} = Too much time on hands
X_7 = Too controlled by others	ξ_1 = Excess of Responsibilities/Demands
X_8 = Problems managing money	ξ_2 = Lack of Money
X_9 = Not enough money to do things	ξ_3 = Unsatisfactory Intimate Relations
X_{10} = Not enough money to get by on	ξ_4 = Lack of Involvement

TABLE 8.6
Factor-Analytic Results for Various Unrestricted Models

Factor loading items	3-Factor oblique			4-Factor oblique				3-factor oblique refined		
	1	2	3	1	2	3	4			
1. Too many responsibilities	72	00	00	70	00	00	00	76	00	00
2. No one to depend on	63	00	00	62	00	00	00	40	00	34
3. Too many demands	72	00	00	71	00	00	00	79	00	00
4. Problems communicating	63	00	00	61	00	00	00	35	00	38
5. Not seeing enough people	62	00	00	61	00	00	00	39	00	32
6. Too little leisure	55	00	00	54	00	00	00	59	00	00
7. Too controlled by others	67	00	00	65	00	00	00	63	00	00
8. Problems managing money	00	69	00	00	68	00	00	00	69	00
9. Not enough money to do things	00	88	00	00	86	00	00	00	87	00
10. Not enough money to get by on	00	82	00	00	81	00	00	00	81	00
11. Dissatisfied with marital status	00	00	72	00	00	71	00	00	00	70
12. No one shows love and affection	00	00	81	00	00	80	00	00	00	78
13. No one understands problems	00	00	75	00	00	75	00	22	00	59
14. No close companion	00	00	63	00	00	65	00	00	00	64
15. Not enough responsiblities	00	00	00	00	00	00	61	00	00	00
16. Too much time on hands	00	00	00	00	00	00	72	00	00	00
Factor correlations	1			1				1		
	46	1		45	1			42	1	
	64	41	1	65	42	1		44	42	1
χ^2/df	8.25			7.8				5.4		

the items "no one to depend on," "problems communicating," "no one understands problems," and "not seeing enough people" appear to be related to more than one construct.

In conclusion, it appears that the restricted 14-item, 3-factor oblique solution offers reasonable, reliable, and valid social-support dimensions that appear to hold up over time. However, it is also clear that the variance in several of the items cannot be explained by a single construct. That is to say, some of the items in some of the factors are related to other factors. But, as pointed out by Alwin and Jackson (1980), rarely in the social sciences are indicators of constructs so pure that their variation is solely determined by one construct.

FURTHER DEVELOPMENT: STRONG-TIE SUPPORT

In Chapter 2, a classification scheme is presented in which many of the conceptualizations of social support developed by other researchers, as well as our own, are discussed. A substantial portion of the present work considers social support as a network concept. However, a modified version of this approach (Lin, Dean, and Ensel, 1981b; Lin and Ensel, 1982) suggests that although the study of networks does shed light on the context within which social supports exist, it is important to look at the functions and the emotional context of the relations imbedded in the network. In this sense, social support can be defined as the access to and use of social resources for the preservation of one's well-being. (The reader is referred to Chapter 2 and to Lin (1982) for further explication of the theory of social resources and social support).

One of the key elements of this definition is that it differentiates between strong and weak social ties. In our 28-item Instrumental–Expressive Social-Support Scale, social ties and social relations are implicated in varying degrees. In some of these items, social relations are implied (e.g., "feeling too dependent on others," "too many demands," "problems communicating with others," "unsatisfying jobs"), whereas in others the relation of an individual is more explicitly identified (e.g., "no close companion," "no one who shows love and affection," "no one who understands problems").

Therefore, in accordance with the definition of social support presented here, the instrumental and expressive items that explicitly identify relationships were selected from the total scale. In all, there are 12 items:

1. Problems with in-laws/relatives
2. No one who understands problems

3. Conflicts with people who are close
4. No close companion
5. Not seeing enough of people close to you
6. Not enough close friends
7. Dissatisfied with marital status
8. No one who shows love and affection
9. No one to depend on
10. Problems with children
11. Problems with spouse/ex-spouse
12. Not having children

These items were then subjected to a factor analysis. Table 8.7 presents the results of this factor analysis. As can be seen, the first factor seems to tap problems and conflicts with others (e.g., in-laws, relatives, people close to the respondent). The second factor taps a lack of support from close companions and people close to oneself. These types of relationships are considered strong ties. The third factor taps unsatisfactory intimate relations or lack of affectionate support (e.g., dissatisfaction with current marital status, not having anyone who shows love and affection.)

In short, this conceptually derived scheme yielded a set of factors that seem to tap the functioning (or lack thereof) and emotional content of the social relations that are embedded in the social-support network. Rather than describing the characteristics of the network, they seem to

TABLE 8.7
Factor Analysis of Explicitly Defined Social-Relational Instrumental–Expressive Items

Social-support item	Loading on		
	Factor 1	Factor 2	Factor 3
Problems with in-laws/relatives	.51[a]	.16	.05
No one who understands problems	.54	.40	.23
Conflicts with people who are close	.68	.29	.11
No close companion	.18	.68	.21
Not seeing enough of people close to you	.28	.45	.10
Not enough close friends	.31	.55	.05
Dissatisfied with marital status	.04	.23	.77
No one who shows love and affection	.24	.44	.52
No one to depend on	.42	.33	.13
Problems with children	.42	.12	.13
Problems with spouse/ex-spouse	.35	.04	.43
Not having children	.08	.27	.13

[a]Representative items for each factor are underlined.

indicate the extent of problems with, or an imbalance in, a particular type of social relation. Intuitively, the second factor, which we will hereafter refer to as Strong-Tie Support, seems to carry the most weight in that it measures the extent to which certain social resources (i.e., strong ties) are deemed adequate by the individual.

RELIABILITY AND VALIDITY OF STRONG-TIE SUPPORT

We next examined the reliability and validity of the Strong-Tie Support measure across our data sets. The results of this analysis indicated that the reliability of this factor was acceptable (alpha = .65 in T1, .66 in T2) and that its validity (as measured by the correlation of the factor with depression) was in the range of the expected value, ($r = .47$). In addition, the correlations with depression of the individual items comprising the factor were consistent both in T1 and in T2. Whereas the other two factors had relatively high alphas (.73 for Factor 1 and .70 for Factor 3), these two factors were less related to depression ($r = .4$ and .3, respectively). Therefore, the decision was made to focus on only one of the three factors, the Strong-Tie Support factor.

CRITICISMS OF THE INSTRUMENTAL AND EXPRESSIVE SUPPORTIVE SCALES: AN EMPIRICAL TEST

It has been argued elsewhere (Dohrenwend, Dohrenwend, Dodson, and Shrout, 1984; Huessy, 1981; Williams et al., 1981; Wolfe, 1981) that the strong relationship between social-support items and depression may be caused by an overlap between the scales for the two constructs. That is to say, the social-support scales have been criticized as being measures of depression more than of social support. The issue here is a proxy issue. We need to determine, therefore, whether the instrumental and expressive factors presented here could be proxies for the criterion dependent variable (depression) in the study. That is, do the instrumental and expressive factors merely reflect the level of depression experienced by an individual, or do they cause it?

If the instrumental and expressive factors are simply proxies for depression, we should observe two empirical phenomena: (1) The distribution of the two variables among the subjects of the study should be approximately the same; and (2) the two measures should show similar causal patterns in terms of their relationships to a given set of independent variables. These independent variables, incidently, should consist of variables that have been documented in the literature as being related to the criterion proxy variable, depression in this case.

Now, as has been pointed out elsewhere (Lin, Ensel, and Vaughn, 1981), the failure to find support for the first empirical test does not, by itself, reject the proxy hypothesis. It may very well be the case that the proxy variable measures a different type of criterion and may subsequently be subject to different kinds of variation or a different amount of error. However, the pattern of relationships between the dependent variable (in this case depression) and a set of independent variables should be similar in magnitude and rank-ordering to those between the proxy variable (instrumental–expressive support) and the same set of independent variables.

We found with regard to the first criterion that distributions of the instrumental and expressive factors are not similar to the distribution of the dependent measure, depression. Although the instrumental–expressive factors are skewed to the right, indicating a rather high level of support, depression is much more evenly distributed across the entire range of the scale. Table 8.8 presents the results of the more critical test of the proxy hypothesis, the regression of the two dependent measures on a set of independent variables (gender, age, marital status, work satisfaction, prior illness, personal competence, and life events). If depression and instrumental–expressive support were measures of the same concept, we would expect the predictors of these two factors to be equivalent in magnitude and ranking for both factors. As can be seen, this is not the case. In fact, the set of explanatory factors predicts instrumental–expressive support and depression quite differently. For example, although life events are the strongest predictors of social support, personal competence has the greatest effect on depression. Prior history of illness makes a significant contribution to explaining depression, yet it has virtually no impact on social support. In addition, the magnitude and rank-ordering of gender, age, and marital status are different for social support than they are for depression. These findings would support the conclusion that the two measures are substantially distinct.

Dohrenwend et al. (1984) have raised questions regarding various items in the instrumental–expressive scale and their conceptual and operational distinction from adverse health changes (i.e., depression). Utilizing a sample of clinical psychologists as judges, Dohrenwend et al. had the instrumental–expressive items rated with regard to their likelihood of being symptoms of psychological disorder. Using 5 anchor items from the 20-item Langner (1962) scale as "clear" indicators of symptoms and 5 anchor items from Barrera et al.'s (1981) Inventory of Socially Supportive Behaviors (ISSB) as indicators least likely to

TABLE 8.8
A Test of the Proxy Issue Using Regression Analysis

| | Instrumental–expressive support factors[a] | | | | | | Depression | |
| | Factor 1 | | Factor 2 | | Factor 3 | | (CES-D) | |
	B[b]	Beta[c]	B	Beta	B	Beta	B	Beta
Gender	−.25	−.03	−.14	.03	−.38	−.09	1.32	.07
	(.27)[d]		(.19)		(.14)		(.62)	
Age	.03	.13	.03	.20	−.01	−.05	−.03	−.05
	(.01)		(.01)		(.01)		(.02)	
Marital status	−.31	−.04	.42	.07	1.20	.27	−2.51	−.13
	(.29)		(.20)		(215)		(.66)	
Work satisfaction	−.63	−.12	−.52	−.15	−.21	−.08	1.90	.16
	(.17)		(.12)		(.09)		(.40)	
Prior illness	−.16	−.07	−.10	−.06	−.09	−.07	.92	.17
	(.08)		(.06)		(.05)		(.19)	
Personal competence	.20	.13	.22	.23	.11	.14	−.96	−.28
	(.05)		(.04)		(.03)		(.11)	
Life events	−.37	−.44	−.10	−.17	−.13	−.30	.39	.21
	(.03)		(.02)		(.02)		(.07)	
Constant	22.01		3.75		13.60		24.70	
Error of estimate	3.41		2.38		1.82		7.80	
R^2	.30		.21		.24		.28	

[a]Factor 1 = Excess of Responsibilities/Demands.
  Factor 2 = Lack of Money.
  Factor 3 = Unsatisfactory Intimate Relationships.
[b]Unstandardized beta.
[c]Standardized beta.
[d]Standard error.

represent a symptom of psychological disorder, the 26-item instrumental–expressive scale was rated on a 5-point scale (1 = very *likely*, 5 = not *very likely*) as to the degree to which each item was likely to be a psychological symptom. From the results (Dohrenwend's judges gave our items average ratings of between 2.0 and 3.6), Dohrenwend concluded that items in the Instrumental–Expressive Social-Support Scale were closer to the symptom scale than to the nonsymptom scale.

Although we have reservations about the anchor items used in this test (and will return to this issue shortly), we nonetheless decided to re-examine our scales based on Dohrenwend's findings. We chose two of the instrumental–expressive factors (Excess of Responsibilities/Demands and Lack of Money) for the test. Items in these factors that were rated lower than the midpoint (3.0) by Dohrenwend's clinical judges (indicating by their criteria that the items were likely or almost certainly a symptom of psychological disorder) were dropped from the factors. The new subscales were then correlated with our dependent measure (CES-D) using both T1 and T2 data. If confounding was taking place, we expected to find correlations lower than those where the confounding items were included in the factor. This was true of the Excess of Responsibilities/Demands factor, where the original seven-item scale correlated $-.46$ and $-.47$ with CES-D in T1 and T2, respectively, compared to $-.36$ and $-.34$ with the revised, three-item Excess of Responsibilities/Demands factor. However, this was not the case with the Lack of Money factor ($r = -.31$ and $-.30$ with depression in T1 and T2 for the original three-item factor, compared to $-.29$ and $-.28$ with CES-D in T1 and T2 for the revised two-item factor). In both cases, the revised factor still maintained large and significant correlations with depression.

It should be noted that the items in the expressive factors (Unsatisfactory Intimate Relations and Family Problems) all had items that rated lower than the midpoint, thus leaving no unbiased items remaining in the subscales. This brings us back to the items used by Dohrenwend et al. to anchor the nonsymptomlike criteria. It must be pointed out that four of the five anchor items (someone who "loaned or gave you something," "loaned you under $25," "gave you information," and "provided you with some transportation") are instrumental in nature. Only one ("someone who talked with you recently about some interests of yours") could be considered expressive in nature. Thus, with the lack of an adequate representation of expressive supports in the anchor scale, it is logical to assume that a clinician would rate an expressive support item (e.g., "not enough close friends," "lacked a close companion") as being close to the symptomlike anchor items, which are totally expressive in nature. A true test of the confounding issue would thus require a nonsymptom anchor scale that contained expressive as well as instrumental items. Until such a test is conducted, our findings, supplemented by our proxy tests, lead us to conclude that the instrumental–expressive items are conceptually and empirically distinct from our measure of symptoms.

SUMMARY AND IMPLICATIONS

In this chapter, we have attempted to further refine and specify dimensions of our Instrumental–Expressive Social-Support Scale. We initially derived a composite factor structure consisting of three instrumental factors (Excess of Responsibilities/Demands, Lack of Money, and Lack of Involvement) and two expressive factors (Unsatisfactory Intimate Relations and Family Problems). After conducting tests for the reliability of these factors and submitting them to a confirmatory factor analysis, we concluded that three of the five factors show strong internal consistency, over-time stability, and validity. Two of these factors were instrumental in nature (Excess of Responsibilities/Demands and Lack of Money) and one was expressive (Unsatisfactory Intimate Relations).

An alternative approach to the further explication of the instrumental–expressive scale resulted in the development of what we have termed Strong-Tie Support. This is a measure that initially consisted of three items ("no close companion," "not seeing enough of people close to you," and "not enough close friends") but was subsequently reduced to a two-item measure ("no close companion" and "not enough close friends"). This measure carries a strong intuitive appeal and was derived from the theory of social-support resources presented in Chapter 2.

Rather than making a decision at this point as to the superiority of the factors derived from these two approaches, we decided to retain both the instrumental–expressive factors and the Strong-Tie Support measure in our analysis. There may be conditions under which the instrumental factor may shed the most light on the content in which social support is functioning. For example, it may be the case that the instrumental factor Lack of Money may have much more serious consequences for depression for lower-class or blue-collar individuals than for white-collar individuals. By the same token, Unsatisfactory Intimate Relations, an expressive measure, might function differently for married individuals than for single, divorced, separated, or widowed individuals. On the other hand, it may be Strong-Tie Support items that most readily distinguish different degrees of depressive response to stressful life events.

Therefore, in retaining these measures, as well as the total instrumental–expressive scale measure, we are providing an opportunity for the measures to show one of two things: (1) consistent and unchanging relationships to other key model variables (most notably life events and depression) given different social conditions (i.e., being married versus not being married, being male versus being female, belonging to the blue-collar class versus belonging to the white-collar class, being young versus being old, etc.), or (2) significantly different patterns of relationships that are contingent upon certain sociodemographic criteria.

Finally, analysis was conducted in response to criticisms of the instrumental–expressive support scales found in the current literature. Specifically, it has been suggested by others that the strong relationship we find between support and depression may be a result of an overlap between the scales used to tap the respective constructs. Utilizing an empirical test of this proxy issue, we conclude that the items comprising our instrumental–expressive scale are conceptually and empirically distinct from our measure of symptoms (the CES-D scale).

Based on our findings, we feel confident that the measures derived here are reliable and valid measures of social support. By the same token, they are not the only measures of social support available. The reader should be aware that the measures of support discussed in Chapter 2 and those presented in Chapters 7 and 9, along with those analyzed here, are not exhaustive, nor are they intended to be. They may be found to be measures that function only under certain conditions or in certain situations. We document such findings in later chapters. In the next chapter, we turn to an alternative set of social-support measures that attempt to tap various concepts found under the rubric of community and network support.

9

Measuring Community and Network Support

NAN LIN

MARY Y. DUMIN

MARY WOELFEL

INTRODUCTION

This chapter is concerned with the broader levels of social relations as measures of social support, and examines the community and net work involvement of the individual. The measurement task is massive and complicated. Some of the measures we employed are adaptations of existing or proposed measures, whereas others were constructed for this study. Therefore, some measures are more exploratory than others. As a consequence, the measurements, judged by reliability and validity tests, have shown varying degrees of success. We have decided to pre- sent the measuring efforts in detail, even though some of the work is exploratory and the results less than fully satisfactory. At a minimum, they can provide insight and reference points for future research.

There is an ongoing debate on the utility and proper interpretation of cognitive versus behavioral network data (Bernard, Killworth, and Sail- er, 1980; Bernard, Killworth, and Sailer, 1981; Burt and Bittner, 1981). Our position is that both approaches are methodologically meaningful

153

and conceptually interpretable, and should both be utilized whenever possible to explain the effects of social environment (i.e., social structure, social networks, and interpersonal interactions) on the individual. Their ultimate usefulness depends on their ability to explain system activities and individual behaviors as well as their accessibility for statistical manipulation. However, because of the nature of our survey, the instruments we used measure perceived, or cognitive, realities rather than observed behaviors. That is, no data were obtained from external observers.

Our study employs a variety of measures for community and network support. They can be roughly grouped into two types of support indicators. First, we explore participation and satisfaction in the community and neighborhood as indicators of *community support*. For example, we attempt to measure each respondent's interaction and satisfaction with the neighborhood and with the community. We also attempt to measure the extent to which the respondent participates in voluntary organizations and utilizes organized social services.

Secondly, we examine relationships between the respondents and their partners as possible indicators of *network support*. Three situations are explored. In one, respondents are given hypothetical problems (money, love relations) and asked with whom (spouse, relative, friend, etc.) they might talk over the problem. This problem-help-by-role matrix allows us to test the multiplexity issue (one type of relationship is helpful for multiple problems) and the possible effects that roles might have on instrumental or expressive problems.

Although the first situation presents the respondents with hypothetical problems and examines their reports of potential support, the second situation is more concrete. We pursue the question of respondents' confidants (Chapter 7) and attempt to map their networks of multiple confidants. Identification of confidants allows us to assess the characteristics of such a network (e.g., size, density, centrality), as well as the strength of ties and the similarity of characteristics (the homophily principle) between respondents and their confidants, as indicators of network support. In this situation, although no hypothetical problems are given to the respondents to consider, the relationships are more focused. Indepth measures are used.

The third situation, still more concrete, explores actual support received by respondents as help after an important life event. The approach traces an actual event experienced by the respondent in the past 6 months and tracks down the one person who actually provided help. In this manner, it becomes possible to study the characteristics of the helper, as well as the nature of the relationship between the helper and the respondent, as possible indicators of network support.

In this chapter, we describe each of the measures used and, whenever appropriate, their univariate characteristics (means and standard deviations). If a measure involves more than one item, we assess inter-item correlations and their reliability (alpha) coefficients. To check validity, we report the zero-order correlation between each measure and the dependent variable, the CES-D scale score. Not all measures were incorporated in both Time 1 (T1) and Time 2 (T2), and we identify the measures accordingly. (Some measures also underwent wording changes from T1 to T2.) Although the changes in measures improved the reliability and validity of the measures, they also created inconsistencies between T1 and T2, and we point out these changes as we proceed.

COMMUNITY SUPPORT

The community represents the outermost layer of social relations within the social environment exerting an impact on an individual. In order to capture integration into the larger social structure—a sense of belongingness—three measures that tap community support are used: (1) community–neighborhood interaction and satisfaction, (2) participation in voluntary organizations, and (3) use of organized services.

Community–Neighborhood Interaction and Satisfaction

One approach to measuring social support is to measure social interaction. Social interaction is a precondition for the provision of social support. Thus, social-interaction scales may be regarded as indirect indicators of social support. Studies using such measures have demonstrated clear inverse effects of social support on the occurrence of psychiatric symptoms (Lin, Simeone, Ensel, and Kuo, 1979) and other measures of morbidity and mortality (Berkman and Syme, 1979). An alternative argument is that social interaction is in fact itself a form of social support. Based on the discussion in Chapter 2, the measurement of community interaction is an attempt to discern various social spheres of support or attachments. Communities may be viewed along a continuum of relationships, beginning with the conjugal family and moving toward the most secondary of relationships.

The first measure of community support, the Community–Neighborhood Interaction and Satisfaction Scale, was adapted by Lin et al. (1979) in a study of Chinese–Americans in Washington, D.C. This scale consists of four items that tap interaction in the neighborhood, interaction in the community, satisfaction with the neighborhood, and satisfaction with the community. The scale shows acceptable internal consistency and stability in three samples. As shown in Table 9.1, alpha coefficients were high for both T1 and T2 measures. Means, standard deviations, and inter-item correlations were also consistent across samples. The Community–Neighborhood Interaction and Satisfaction Scale shows a significant and consistent relationship with the CES-D scale in the samples, (Table 9.1), with zero-order correlations ranging from .19 (T1) to .25 (T2).

TABLE 9.1
Community Support Measures

	No. of items	Mean SD	Range of inter-item r's	Alpha	Correlation with CES-D
Community support: Time 1 (all respondents, N = 1091)					
Community neighborhood interaction and satisfaction	4	7.53 (2.69)	.14–.59	.63	.20
Participation in voluntary associations	5	1.83 (1.90)	.38–.87	.88	−.10
Uses of organized services	9	35.40 (1.45)	.01–.34	.46	−.19
Community support: Time 1 (panel sample N = 871)					
Community neighborhood interaction and satisfaction	4	7.40 (2.68)	.20–.59	.64	.19
Participation in voluntary associations	5	1.96 (1.92)	.38–.86	.88	−.10
Uses of organized services	9	35.44 (1.35)	.00–.35	.42	.24
Community support: Time 2 (panel sample, N = 871)					
Community neighborhood interaction and satisfaction	4	7.15 (2.63)	.12–.64	.63	.25
Participation in voluntary associations	5	3.22 (1.29)	.13–.57	.64	−.08
Uses of organized services	11	43.30 (1.69)	.00–.41	.52	.22

We next examined the reliability and validity of two interaction items and of the two items separately. For the two interaction items, the inter-item correlations were .43 at T1 and .49 at T2. Their summed scores correlated .17 and .20, respectively, with CES-D at T1 and T2. For the two satisfaction items, the inter-item correlations were .59 and .64 at T1 and T2, and their summed scores had correlations with CES-D of .13 and .22. All of these correlations were significant. Thus, there is evidence that community–neighborhood satisfaction was the more significant dimension. Nevertheless, the total scale (based on the four items) showed a reasonable reliability and a relationship with CES-D almost as strong as that shown by the two satisfaction items. Thus, we recommend the use of a four-item scale.

Participation in Voluntary Organizations

Another measure of social support at the outermost layer of social interaction is the individual's participation in voluntary organizations. Membership in formal organizations reflects integration into the larger social environment. Although these associations are organized around specific purposes, they also present opportunities for interpersonal interaction and the formation of primary relationships. In this sense, therefore, they may provide active social support. Similarly, they may represent a resource of contacts or relationships that could be utilized if necessary. Put differently, the social relations formed within formal organizations might reflect the availability of expressive and/or instrumental support.

The scale utilized here consists of five yes or no items tapping increasing degrees of participation in voluntary organizations. The respondent is first asked if he/she is a member of any voluntary organizations or associations, such as church and school groups; labor unions; or social, civic, and fraternal groups. For each group the respondent belongs to, four additional questions are asked to determine if the respondent attends meetings regularly, contributes financially, serves on any committee, or holds any office. Yes responses were scored 1 and no responses were scored 0. Possible scores ranged from 0 (low participation support) to 5 (high participation support).

This scale shows very high internal consistency at T1, with alphas of .88 for both samples. Inter-item and item–total correlations are also consistently high (Table 9.1). However, this measure shows a negligible correlation with depression and therefore has no predictive significance. In T2, however, the alpha coefficient drops to .64. The scale mean and inter-item correlations also show considerable differences between T1 and T2. Because of this, the reliability of this scale is questionable.

Use of Organized Services

The final community-support measure taps help from organized services. Agencies, organizations, and professional services are community resources available to assist individuals. These organizations may provide a variety of instrumental and expressive supports and as such are hypothesized to be associated with lower levels of depression.

We constructed an inventory of nine types of organizations in the T1 survey. They included social-service agencies, self-help groups, service organizations, family and children's services, counseling centers, Veterans' Administration, and religious, community, and financial aid and credit groups. This list was expanded in T2 to also include social-service agencies, drug and alcohol counseling centers, job counseling, training programs, rehabilitation services, mental-health clinics (counseling, parents without partners, therapy groups), church or synagogue, clergy-sponsored help groups, hotlines, legal aid and lawyers, and senior citizens centers.

In both waves, respondents were asked how often they had been in touch with any of the listed agencies for some particular problem during the past 6 months. Frequency of contact was scored on a four-point scale: 1, *weekly*; 2, *monthly*; 3, *every few months*; 4, *never*. At both T1 and T2 for the panel sample, the alpha coefficients were .42 and .52, respectively (Table 9.1). Admittedly, these scores are below what is generally considered acceptable, yet the organizations listed are varied, and there is no conceptual or theoretical reason to expect that an individual using one type will also use another. In fact, the mean scores on individual items (3.79 to 3.97) were skewed in the direction of no organizational contact. The scale can, however, still be tested for its validity. The correlations with depression were .24 and .22 in T1 and T2, respectively, for the two panel samples.

NETWORK SUPPORT

Moving closer to the individual, measures that tap various dimensions and properties of support within an individual's social network were constructed and analyzed. Before discussing them, however, a brief discussion of network analysis and its relevance to social support is needed.

Network analysis has a long research tradition in the social sciences. In 1934, Moreno developed a technique to tap interpersonal relationships by mapping individuals as nodes and their relationships as lines linking the nodes. The sociometric map was then subjected to certain matrix manipulations (Festinger, 1949) in order to explicate both the direct and indirect relationships among the individuals. With the advent of sophisticated computer technology in the late 1960s, in terms of both speed and memory, it became feasible to collect sociometric data from much larger groups of individuals (Coleman and MacRae, 1960) and to perform more complex analytic manipulations of the relational matrix (see recent reviews by Burt, 1981; Wellman, 1981). In addition, during the late 1950s and early 1960s, a number of British social anthropologists (Bott, 1957; Mitchell, 1969) began to apply the network approach to rural and urban communities in both developed and developing countries. In recent years, significant advances have been made in the theory, method, and research connected with network analysis (see examples in Leinhardt, 1977; Holland and Leinhardt, 1979; Fischer, 1982; E. M. Rogers and Kincaid, 1981; Berkowitz, 1982; Burt, 1982; Burt and Minor, 1982; Marsden and Lin, 1982).

A number of researchers have stated specifically that network analysis should either be the central focus of the concept of social support or should serve as a substitute for that concept (Wellman, 1981). Hammer (1981), for example, suggests that researchers concentrate mainly on social networks, with social support as just one possible function of a network. Mueller (1980) similarly contends that the social network concept may provide the unifying framework within which diverse findings on the relationship of social factors to levels and types of distress may be integrated. McKinlay (1973) also notes that the network concept is highly underused, and attempts to uncover some of the ways in which researchers might use the concept in understanding help-seeking behavior.

We contend that to understand distress, major emphasis should not be placed on the network properties per se—that is, on its form—but rather on the substance of interaction and the role relations a person maintains with network members—the content of the network. Nevertheless, we constructed measures for both the form and the content of networks. Network support is evaluated within three distinct conceptual themes: (1) role support for problems, (2) confidant network, and (3) help following an important life event. Following a brief introduction to the underlying theoretical issues, we present the measurements in detail, along with the reliability and validity tests of these measures. Because analyses of the two T1 samples ($N = 1091$ and 871) have shown consistent results, the remainder of this chapter reports on the 871 respondents interviewed in both time periods.

Role Support for Problems

We attempted to assess whether the respondent perceived help as being available in potential problem situations. The problems were selected from two sources: (1) problems identified in the instrumental–expressive support situations (see Chapter 8), and (2) theoretical expectations as to those problem areas that might constitute sources of need for support. We further distinguished between instrumental and expressive problems. The instrumental problem areas investigated included money, health, job, household or child care, legal issues, and responsibilities. The expressive problems included love relations/marital problems, loneliness, personal and communication problems, and lack of freedom. However, the T1 questionnaire did not include legal problems but had transportation as a problem area; the T2 sample did not ask about transportation but about legal problems. Only two of the expressive problem areas were included in the T1 questionnaire: problems over love relationships and loneliness. The roles of helpful persons included spouse or lover, other family member, friend, neighbor, coworker, other acquaintance, and helping professional. These roles are categorized in terms of the strength of their tie to the respondent. Spouse, for example, is classified as a strong tie, and acquaintance as a weak tie.

It is within this role-by-problem matrix that we examine *multiplexity*. Multiplexity refers to multiple bases for interaction in a dyad (Verbrugge, 1979). The basic proposition is that as a dyad has more bases for interaction, it promotes the strength of the relationships and has positive consequences for the well-being of the participants. Our concept of multiplexity is consistent with that of Kapferer (1969), who looks at multiplexity as the overlap of different activities or exchanges in a dyadic relationship. Multiplexity in this sense is treated as a structural feature of a dyad. The dyad here consists of the respondent and the role type whom the respondent perceives as available for talking over problems. When the respondent is involved with a particular role type in three or more problem areas, the relationship is considered multiplex (Kapferer, 1969; Fischer, et al. 1977, 1982). A relationship with a spouse/lover, for example, is multiplex if the respondent feels able to talk to the spouse/lover about problems in three or more areas. Presumably, when a tie is multiplex, the two people share a greater proportion of their time and activities. It is in this sense that Fischer et al. (1977) argues that multiplex (what he refers to as *multistranded*) relations provide more social support. Granovetter (1973) also suggests that multiplex relations are more emotionally supportive, whereas uniplex relations are more instrumentally supportive. Thus, according to the multiplexity argument, a multiplicity of relations is healthier than uniplex relations.

The respondent was presented with the instrumental and expressive problem areas listed above and asked: "When you have any of these problems, do you feel you can talk it over with any of these persons?" At this point each role type (e.g., spouse) was mentioned, to which respondents answered yes or no. Because information on only two expressive problems (love relations and loneliness) was gathered in T1, and because measures of multiplexity require a minimum of at least three problem areas, we focused our attention on our T2 data. The presence or absence of a multiplex relationship was determined for each of the seven role types. That is, a continuous variable of *total multiplexity* was created that reflects the number of role types providing multiplex support. The scores, therefore, range from 0 to 7. Analysis indicates a *positive* relationship between our dependent variable, depression (CES-D), and the total multiplexity score. Hence, the number of role types with whom one has a multiplex relationship does not appear to alleviate distress.

Social-resources theory suggests that access to and use of strong ties is associated with lower levels of distress. Thus, it is important to ascertain whether a healthy mental state is promoted by using strong ties for the resolution of various problems. Combining network and social-resources theory suggests that multiplex relationships with strong ties are associated with low levels of depression. We established validity by first examining the correlation of each of the multiplex role types with depression as measured by CES-D. The results show that level of distress (CES-D) is *negatively* associated with multiplex relations with strong ties; that is, the stronger the multiplex tie, the lower the CES-D score (see Table 9.2). Having a multiplex relationship with one's spouse (a strong tie) is associated with *lower* levels of CES-D. However, having a multiplex relationship with another family member or a close friend (weaker ties) is related to higher levels of depression. The reader whould bear in mind that we use the term *weak tie* in this instance to indicate all relationships other than those with a spouse or lover. A friend is a weaker tie only relative to the strong tie one has with a spouse or lover. Therefore, dependence on weaker ties for three or

TABLE 9.2
Correlation Matrix of Role Support for Problem Variables with Depression (CES-D),
Time 2 Sample

| | CES-D |
Multiplex relationship (three or more problems discussed)	(N = 871)
Spouse/lover	− .18**
Other family member	.07**
Close friend	.11**
Acquaintance	.09
Neighbor	.04
Co-worker	.04
Helping professional	.00
Total multiplexity	.05**

**Significant at less than .01 level.

more specific types of problems is associated with higher levels of CESD.

To determine if multiplex relations with strong ties were more effective for dealing with expressive problems than with instrumental ones, we analyzed the expressive and instrumental problems separately. For each group of problem areas, we assessed the effects of the multiplex relations with strong ties and with weak ties on depression (CES-D). There was no significant difference between stronger multiplex ties and the weaker ones on depression for either expressive or instrumental problems. Because of the mixed results, we conclude that there is insufficient evidence on the relationship between role multiplexity and depression. Nor were significant relationships found between multiplex role relations with other still weaker ties (acquaintances, neighbors, co-workers, or helping professionals) and depression. The *total* number of multiplex role relations in fact showed a slight relationship with more depression (see Table 9.2).

These results are difficult to interpret. Although it was anticipated that multiplex role relations with strong ties (e.g., spouse) should be negatively associated with depressed mood, it was not anticipated that multiplex relations with some weaker ties (other family member, close friend) would be linked directly to the presence of depression. The expectation was that multiplex role relations with somewhat weaker ties would be less associated with absence of depression, but not positively associated with more depression. Further, the fact that multiplex role relations with other still weaker ties (acquaintance, neigh-

bor, co-worker, helping professional) and total multiplexity had insignificant or even small positive relationships with depression makes
any *post hoc* explanation hazardous.

Confidant Network

In this section we explore the nature and function of the respondent's
network of confidants. Attention is focused on the patterns in whom
the respondent confides. Past research has tended to focus on a single,
most important confidant. Lowenthal and Haven (1968) argued that the
maintenance of a stable intimate relationship is closely associated with
good mental health and high morale. They found that the presence of a
confidant reduced the risk of depression among elderly individuals
who had suffered role losses, widowhood, and other problems associated with aging. This hypothesis is examined and partially supported
in Chapter 7. It has been argued that the number of confidants ego has
may also affect mental health. Moriwaki (1973) found that the number
of confidants reported by individuals was correlated with emotional
well-being.

The presence of multiple confidants provides a possible network of
confidants that has characteristics beyond their mere number. For example, the relationships between these confidants may tap the strength
of ties between them and ego. The closeness of the relationships among
the confidants—that is, whether the confidants knew each other—reflects the density of the network. Furthermore, whether the confidants
know each other because of ego may indicate the centrality of ego in
this network. Also, social-resources theory suggests that homophilic
similarity of characteristics between the confidants and ego may play a
role in ego's state of mental health. We use these properties of the
confidant network as indicators of social support.

Before we proceed, it should again be noted that wording changes
regarding confidants in T1 and T2 produced different results. In T1, the
presence or absence of a confidant was ascertained by asking the respondent, "During the past six months, have you had anyone that you
could trust and talk to?" In T2, the availability of a confidant was
identified by the question, "During the past six months, has there been
anyone in particular you confided in or talked to about yourself or your
problems?" In T2, if respondents answered "yes," they were asked,
"How many people have you been able to confide in or talk to about
yourself or your problems?" The change in T2 to a more specific definition and operationalization of a confiding relationship from the very

general and broad definition that had been used in T1 renders the confidant items not strictly comparable. (See Chapter 7 for further discussion.) The T2 questions appear to produce more significant and valid results than did the T1 operationalization of this concept.

Size, Density, and Centrality of the Confidant Network

Respondents were then asked to think about and keep in mind up to three persons whom they were most likely to confide in or talk to. General confidant support measures were generated using information about these three most important persons in ego's network of confidants.

We begin with the size, density, and centrality measures of the respondent's confidant network. Size refers simply to the number of confidants (up to three) in the respondent's network. Density refers to the extent of interconnectedness among the three confidants. Each respondent was asked if the people in the three-person group knew each other. We used the formula $a/n(n-1)/2$ as our density measure, where a is the number of linkages, and n is the network size (limited here to 1, 2, or 3). Scores range from 0 to 1. For example, for those respondents who had no or one confidant, the density score equals 0. For those respondents having two confidants, the number of possible linkages is 1, producing a score of 1 on the density scale. The formula tells us the number of dyadic relationships (linkages between each pair of confidants) in the network in proportion to the number of linkages possible given the network size (up to 3 persons). Density was only measured in T2.

Centrality was constructed for both T1 and T2 and consisted of asking whether ego's network members knew each other because of ego. Scores for this measure may range from 0 to 3. Because these measures showed significant correlations with depression (CES-D) in T2 but reveal no consistent pattern over time, we conclude that the changes in wording from T1 to T2 have improved our measures but do not allow over-time comparisons.

About two thirds (68%) of the respondents named one or more confidants; on the average, each respondent named 1.8 confidants. Simple zero-order correlations of these measures with CES-D were inconsistent with expectations (see Table 9.3). Size and density of the confidant network (T2 measures) were both related to positive CES-D; that is, a larger or more dense confidant network is related to higher distress. We do not know of any theory that would predict these results.

TABLE 9.3
Correlations of Network of Confidant Variables with Depression (CES-D)

	CES-D	
Measure	Time 1 N	Time 2 N
Size of confidant network (0 to 3)	− .01 (790)	.14** (849)
Centrality of ego in confidant network	− .07* (845)	.05 (853)
Density of confidant network	—	.10** (853)
Ego-confidant relations		
Spouse	—	− .14** (381)
Relatives	—	.00 (583)
Friends	—	.08* (583)
Acquaintances	—	.01 (583)
Helping professionals	—	.19** (503)
Strength of tie with confidant		
1st Confidant (weak tie)	—	.18** (572)
2nd Confidant	—	.07 (419)
3rd Confidant	—	.17** (257)
Homophily with Confidant		
Gender		
1st Confidant	—	.08* (569)
2nd Confidant	—	− .04 (416)
3rd Confidant	—	− .16 (253)
Education		
1st Confidant	—	− .13** (552)
2nd Confidant	—	.02 (402)
3rd Confidant	—	− .08 (239)

*Significant at less than .05 level.
**Significant at less than .01 level.

Strength of Ties and Similarity of Characteristics between Ego and Confidants

The homophily principle (Chapter 2) assumes that frequency and intensity of social interactions are associated with similarity of social characteristics and psychological make-up. It is hypothesized that successful expressive action is more likely to occur through strong and homophilous ties. In T2, we included measures to examine these confiding relationships and the similarity of characteristics between ego and each member of ego's confiding network.

Role relationships between each respondent and each of the three (confidants) were classified into 12 preselected categories: (1) spouse/

lover, (2) son/daughter, (3) mother/father, (4) brother/sister, (5) in-law, (6) other relative, (7) close friend, (8) other acquaintance, (9) neighbor, (10) co-worker, (11) boss/supervisor, and (12) helping professional. Validity was assessed for two measures. A role-relation measure indicated the frequency with which each role relation was mentioned for all three confidants; scores therefore ranged from 0 to 3. Strength of tie with each confidant was constructed as a continuous variable ranging from *strong tie* to *weak tie*. Role types were used as proxies for tie strength, with spouse given a value of 1; other family member, a value of 2; friend, 3; neighbor, 4; co-worker, 5; other acquaintance, 6; and helping professional, 7.

Having identified through the questionnaire the respondent's relationship to each person in the confidant network, there followed a series of questions about the demographic characteristics of each member in the confidant network. These items include age, gender, education, and occupation (Siegel, 1971); they formed the basis for indices of homophily. First, the absolute difference score was computed for each of these items between ego and each of the three confidants. The score was then reversed so that the higher the score, the greater the similarity (homophily) between ego and each confidant.

The validity of these confidant network variables was determined by correlating the variables with CES-D (see Table 9.3). Results show naming spouse as a confidant is related to negative CES-D and naming helping professionals is related to positive CES-D. There was a slight but significant positive correlation between CES-D and naming friends. These correlations seem consistent with the social-resources theory: The stronger the tie, the less distressed ego is. The same patterns are observed for two of the three strength-of-tie variables.

Comparisons of the characteristics between ego and confidants show that having a same-sex, first-chosen confidant was associated with depression, primarily due to the negative associations between not naming a spouse and CES-D. The effect of having an opposite-sex confidant on CES-D will be further analyzed in Chapter 15. The respondent's similarity of educational level with the first confidant was negatively related to CES-D, a confirmation of the homophily principle.

There was no relationship between homophily in occupational prestige and depression. This may be due, in part, to the fact that many named spouses were housewives without occupations and, therefore, excluded from the analysis.

In summary, the effort to measure confidant network support met with mixed results. Several factors seem to account for the problems. The wording change from T1 ("anyone you could trust and talk to") and T2 ("anyone in particular you confided in or talked to about yourself or your problems") showed that the more general and speculative nature of the T1 wording generated much less reliable and valid information compared to the more concrete wording in T2. Secondly, computation of various measures based on a set of up to only three confidants created limited variations of the responses, generating less reliable and valid results. This problem would probably not be resolved simply by asking about more confidants, because most respondents volunteered less than three confidants. Thirdly, the measures are rather crude, in part reflecting the general problems of generating network samples and measures in large-scale surveys. Much conceptual and methodological refinements are needed before definitive measures can be developed to tap characteristics of confidant networks.

Help Following an Important Life Event

Another approach to conceptualizing network support centers on specific help following a particular life event of importance to ego. This conceptualization is central to studies directed at assessing the buffering hypothesis. In essence, the buffering thesis maintains that social support mitigates the potential negative effects of significant life events on depression. A full examination of the buffering hypothesis will appear in Chapters 10 and 16. Here, we only develop measures to indicate whether and to what extent a helper's characteristics (strength of tie with ego and similarity of characteristics) are related to perceived support following the experience of an important event. We expect individuals receiving support from strong and homophilous ties following a most important life event to exhibit fewer signs of distress than do those receiving support from weak ties. Strong and homophilous ties should result in greater health benefits than no ties or weak and heterophilous ones.

In T2 the respondents were presented with a list of 118 life events (see Chapter 5) and asked to identify all those events that had happened to them during the previous 6 months. Each respondent was then asked: "Of all these events occurring to you, which one would you say was the most important?" That is, which one, for better or worse, changed or affected your life the most?" After the most important event was identified, the respondents were asked whether they needed help with the event, and whether anyone did help during or after the event.

If help was received, we examined the characteristics of the helper as well as the strength of the tie between the helper and the respondent. The strength of tie with the helper was assessed in two ways: In one measure, its strength was indicated by the role relationship between ego and helper. That is, the helpers were grouped into the following categories: (1) spouse or lover, (2) other relatives, (3) close friends, and (4) weak ties, which included other acquaintances, neighbors, co-workers, boss or superior, and helping professionals. We assume that these roles form an ordinal scale, spouse/lover representing the strongest of ties and helping professional, the weakest.

A second way to measure the strength of tie with the helper was to estimate the various dimensions of interaction between ego and helper (Kaplan, 1975, and Chapter 7). Respondents were asked the number of years each of them had known the helper (durability), the frequency of contact during the previous 6 months (frequency), the frequency with which the respondent talked about problems with this person (density), and how often this person had talked to the respondent about problems (directedness). Responses were categorized as: (1) *most or all of the time*, (2) *occasionally or a moderate amount of the time*, (3) *some or a little of the time*, and (4) *rarely or none of the time*. Next, respondents were asked how easy it was to get in touch with the helper (reachability), and how freely they could talk to the helper about any topic (content). Response categories were: (1) *very freely*, (2) *freely*, (3) *somewhat freely*, and (4) *not very freely*. Finally, respondents were asked how important the person was to them (importance). Response categories consisted of: (1) *very important*, (2) *important*, (3) *somewhat important*, and (4) *not very important*. Reliability for dimensions of interactions is based on item-to-total correlations as well as Cronbach's alpha. (The results are shown in Table 9.4.)

All of the alphas (with the given item itself deleted) are high, ranging from .81 to .85. The alpha coefficient is highest with the importance item deleted. The overall scale reliability alpha coefficient is .85. Therefore, apart from the importance item, we conclude that the reliability for this scale is very high.

To examine the validity of these items, we correlated each item with CES-D. The correlations ranged from $-.18$ to $-.04$ (see Table 9.4). Although all dimensions of interactions are negatively related to CES-D, they are not all statistically significant. The validity of this set of measures, we conclude, is not consistent across its items.

Measurement of homophily between the respondent and helper was based on the demographic characteristics of age, gender, education, and occupation. Occupational prestige was measured by the Siegel SES Scale (1971). For homophily, the absolute scores of difference between respondent and helper were constructed for each of the demographic characteristics. The absolute difference was then reversed so that the

TABLE 9.4

Correlations between Depression (CES-D) and Characteristics of Helper after the Most Important Life Event

Helper characteristics	Alpha (with item deleted)	CES-D (Time 2)
Dimensions of interaction (Kaplan items)		
Durability	.83	− .04
Frequency	.81	− .12*
Density	.81	− .06
Directedness	.83	− .16**
Reachability	.83	− .18**
Content	.82	− .04
Importance	.85	.10*
Homophily		
Age		− .03
Sex		.12*
Education		− .04
Occupational status		− .14*

*Significant at less than .05 level.
**Significant at less than .01 level.

higher the score, the more the similarity (homophily) between the respondent and the helper in terms of that specific characteristic. The gender difference variable was constructed as a dummy variable, with 0 representing opposite sex and 1 representing same-sex helper.

Due to the fact that our operationalization of the homophily variable is a rather crude measure involving few items measured only at one point in time (T2), we are unable at this time to assess its reliability. The validity of these measures, however, is determined by correlating each indicator of homophily with depression (see Table 6.4). Only two of the four correlations are significant. Gender similarity between the respondent and the helper is positively associated with CES-D, whereas occupational homophily contributed to a lower depression score. There were no significant relations between age or educational similarities and depression. That gender similarity contributed to depression was in part due to the effects of opposite-sex confidants (including spouses) in reducing depression. Chapter 15 explores this effect in detail.

In sum, examining support received following an important event shows some potential promise. Role relations with the helper, interaction patterns, and homophily measures seem to provide merely suggestive but nevertheless interpretable validity. We recommend following and expanding this line of research.

CONCLUDING REMARKS

This chapter presents our efforts at measuring community and network support. Many measures were constructed and examined, not all of them with the same success. On the positive side, we have found that respondents' interaction and satisfaction with neighborhood and community, participation in voluntary organizations, and use of organized services are reasonably reliable and valid measures of social support. Role relations and interactions with the confidants also seem acceptable as measures of network support. Support provided by certain strong and homophilous helpers following an important life event also seems to be a promising indicator.

On the other hand, we were unable to draw conclusions about the reliability and validity of role multiplexity (the extent to which a role relation serves multiple functions), as well as a number of characteristics (size, centrality, and density) of the confidant network. Also, homophily of characteristics with interactive partners must be assessed in conjunction with marital status, as less depressed married respondents tend to name spouses (who are opposite-sex persons) as confidants.

Much work needs to be done in improving measures of network support. Our less successful measurement of such support does not indicate that network characteristics are insignificant for mental health. Clearly, however, network content (interaction patterns, role relations, and homophily of characteristics) deserves further research attention. These network characteristics, along with community and neighborhood support, constitute the measures we shall use in subsequent analytic chapters.

Part IV

Constructing and Estimating Basic Models

Chapter 10 delineates a series of causal time-lagged models describing the relationship among social support, life events, and depression. A review of the literature clearly shows a lack of systematic examination and verification of these models. Data are then used to estimate these models. The objective is to identify the most plausible causal relationships among the key variables. To confirm these relations, psychological (coping) resources are incorporated as a control variable. This chapter, therefore, brings data to bear on the conceptual and measurement issues discussed thus far. It also sets the stage for subsequent elaboration of the models in Part V, where other related variables are incorporated into the analyses.

10

Modeling the Effects of Social Support

NAN LIN

INTRODUCTION

Having identified the fundamental concepts and measures in this study, we can now discuss how social support and mental health are related. This chapter quantifies the effects of social support on depressive symptoms in two ways: (1) by estimating various causal models linking social support and depressive symptoms, while taking into account undesirable life events and psychological resources, and (2) by estimating the significance of various social support elements in these models. The first task involves constructing causal models that can logically link social support and depressive symptoms, estimating the magnitude of their relationship while other significant factors are taken into account. The second task entails verification of the measurement significance of various social-support elements. As will be seen, both tasks are performed in a singular analytic approach. Nevertheless, the discussion begins with the construction of causal models.

Basically, there are two views regarding this relationship. One view holds that social support, as an indication of the individual integration into the social environment, should exert a direct and positive influence on mental health. That is, if an individual is embedded in a sup-

173

portive environment, he or she should be mentally healthier than someone who is not. Furthermore, this direct influence should not diminish even when other factors are taken into account. This direct and independent effect of social support on mental health should operate, for example, regardless of the person's socioeconomic background, sex, psychological resources, age, or marital status. It should remain true when a person is confronted with a significant life event. This view does not deny that these other factors will also influence mental health. But it argues that even when these factors in mental health have been taken into account, the degree of social support should remain a direct influence on predicting and explaining the variations in mental health among individuals.

The second view, a more dominant one in the literature, posits that social support mediates possible effects of life events on mental health. It argues that all life events are potentially stressful and if unbuffered will have detrimental effects on mental health. As a general principle, an individual experiencing a significant life event will show a lower degree of mental health than someone who is not. There are factors that can buffer the stressing effects of life events, and social support may be an important one. It is argued that if an individual experiencing a significant life event is able to mobilize a strong social-support system, then such potential detrimental effects can be reduced. This view, of course, espouses the buffering hypotheses regarding the effect of social support in reducing the potentially harmful impacts of life events on mental health.

Thus, there is much discussion among researchers as to the role social support plays relative to mental health. It is an independent factor with a direct positive effect or a mediating factor with a buffering effect?

There is also much confusion. Many different terms are used, and research findings are therefore difficult to compare. For example, what is the difference between an *independent* effect and a *direct* effect? Or consider the many terms used for mediating effects, among them *intervening, buffering, exacerbating, moderating, counteracting, alternating,* and *interactive.*

Adding to the conceptual confusion is the confusion about what kinds of data and analytical techniques are called for in examining each type of effect. Are cross-sectional data collected at one point in time adequate for examining mediating effects? If not, what kinds of techniques are required to examine panel data?

Rather than treating each of these issues as a discrete problem, in the following section we (1) specify a number of causal models and briefly describe the nature of each of them, (2) discuss the implications of these models for understanding the effects of social support, and (3) bring our data to bear on these models to identify the more plausible ones.

MODELING THE EFFECTS OF SOCIAL SUPPORT

In this chapter, only life events (as stressors), social support, psychological resources, and depression are discussed, not only because of the centrality of these variables, but also to simplify the discussion. Life events are not meaningful in all situations, but they are included so as to retain consistency in the interpretation of the models. Furthermore, the visual presentations we make are easier to follow when the same variables appear in every model. In all these models, depression, of course, is the dependent variable. Elaboration of the model then incorporates psychological resources (personal coping resources) as an additional independent variable.

There are other important factors that deserve consideration. We are aware of the relevance of many other factors, such as sociodemographic characteristics and prior health and illness history. But our purpose here is to outline a series of models in their simplest forms. Extension and expansion of the models are deferred to Part V ("Exploring Basic Models"). In modeling the effects of social support, our primary focus is on its relationships with other variables. Therefore each model will be labeled according to the substantive *significance of social support* in the model.

Based on the varying causal sequence of life events and social support, three classes of the variables' temporal sequence are identified. These models appear in Figure 10.1. The first class of models assumes that social support precedes significant life events in leading to depression. These models appear in the left-hand column (Class A) of Figure 10.1. In this class, four such models can be identified. The first of these suggests that the absence of social support preceding and in conjunction with subsequent life stressors will increase the probability of depression. This is one type of interaction effects in which lack of social support provides the condition within which the occurrence of significant life events will crystalize an effect on depression. We call this the *conditioning effect*. The second model in this class suggests that social support has effects on both life events and depression. It reduces the likelihood of both stressful life events and of depression. Social support has a *suppressant effect* on the likelihood of occurrences of life

Class A

The Effect of Social Support (SS)
Preceding Life Events (LE)

1. The conditioning effect

2. The suppressant effect

3. The vulnerability effect

4. The independent effect

Class B

The Contemporaneous Effects of
SS and LE

1. The contemporaneous interactive effect

2. The contemporaneous mediating effect

3. The contemporaneous counteractive effect

4. The contemporaneous independent effect

Class C

The Effect of Social Support
Subsequent to Life Events

1. The interactive/exacerbating effect

2. The mediating effect

3. The counteractive effect

4. The independent compensating effect

+ = positive effect
- = negative effect

events. The third model suggests, on the other hand, that social support induces the likelihood of stressful life events, and their positive causal relationship with depression. It indicates, therefore, that the presence of social support provides a *vulnerable context* for the occurrence of life events. Finally, the fourth model suggests that social support does not affect the likelihood of subsequent life events one way or another and that life events and social support affect depression in opposite directions. This is identified as the *independent effect* of social support.

A second class of models can be identified when social support and life events occur contemporaneously, both preceding depression. These are illustrated in the middle column (Class B) of Figure 10.1. The first of these models again depicts an *interactive effect* of social support and life events on depression. The second model assumes that social support and life events are negatively correlated with each other and suggests that each affects depression in the opposite direction. This represents a *contemporaneous mediating effect* of social support, because it is negatively correlated with life events. The third model assumes that social support and life events are positively correlated with each other and again suggests that they affect depression in opposite directions. This reflects a *contemporaneous counteractive effect* on the part of social support, as far as its relationship with life events is concerned. The fourth model assumes that there is no consistent correlation between social support and life stress, and that they have opposite effects on depression.

The third class of models, probably most familiar to researchers, examines the relationship among the three variables when social support follows life events. As shown in the third column (Class C) of Figure 10.1, the first model proposes that depression increases as a consequence of the presence of prior stressful life events in conjunction with subsequent lack of social support, reflecting the *interactive* or *exacerbating effect* of social support. The second model states that life events reduce the strength of social support and that each affects depression in the opposite direction. This represents the *mediating effect* of social support. The third model suggests that stressful life events increase social support and that both affect depression, but in opposite directions. Social support in this model is said to have a *counteractive effect* on the impact of life events on depression. Finally, in the fourth model, life events exert no influence on subsequent social support, and

Figure 10.1   Twelve causal models relating social support to the effect of life events on depression.

each affects depression in the opposite direction. Because of the opposite effects, the effect of social support is said to have an *independent* or *compensating effect* on life events.

In summary, three classes of models (A, B, and C) have been identified in terms of temporal sequences between social support and life events. Further, for each temporal sequence, there are three plausible additive models (2, 3, 4) and one plausible interactive model (1). An additive model is one in which each and every independent variable is assumed to make a significant contribution to the explanation of the dependent variable, whereas an interactive model proposes that two or more independent variables jointly create conditions that contribute to the explanation of the dependent variable. Obviously, these models are not exhaustive of all relevant modeling possibilities. We choose to focus only on those that seem logically or theoretically grounded. Most of the models have been discussed and examined by the research community. However, a systematic presentation and discussion of these models allows us to clarify a number of modeling issues currently under debate.

PROPERTIES AND IMPLICATIONS OF THE MODELS

Further clarification of these models is useful. First, we discuss the intraclass relationships among the models. Within each class, model 1 can jointly exist with any of the remaining models. That is, an interactive or conditioning effect can theoretically exist regardless of the manner and degree to which its component variables are related to one another. Secondly, models 2, 3, and 4 are mutually exclusive models. That is, one model precludes the other two models in any one class. This is self-evident, because a specific causal relationship between social support and life events is incompatible with a contrary relationship within a class of models.

Interclass models can generally all coexist in theory. However, the probability of coexistence varies due to empirical likelihoods. It is highly unlikely, for example, that the suppressant effect (A2) and the counteractive effect (C3) will both take place at the same time, though it is conceivable when different time periods are involved (e.g., SS_1 negatively affects LE_2, which in turn thereafter positively affect SS_3). Nevertheless, these theoretical possibilities cannot be ruled out.

Certain models may be contingent upon the presence of a particular condition. For example, it has been argued that social support may counteract an adverse effect of life events only if the prior state of social support is relatively strong (Models B3 and C3) (Lin et al., 1979).

Let us now examine the ramifications of these models for the problems of modeling presented in the beginning of this chapter.

1. A direct effect of social support is said to occur when there is a direct path leading from social support to depression. Thus Models 2, 3, and 4 in each class all show the *direct effect* of social support on depression. The presence of a direct effect of social support is not contingent upon whether or not social support also serves as an intervening variable for life events. An *independent effect* of social support occurs, on the other hand, only when it is *not* related at all to life events except through their respective paths to depression. Thus Model 4 in each class shows an independent effect of social support.

2. Social support intervenes between life events and depression only when social support temporally coexists or follows life events and when there is a significant additive or interactive relationship between social support and life events. Thus, Models 1, 2, and 3 in Classes B and C are *intervening models*. Strictly speaking, if we rule out the potential causal relationship between contemporaneous social support and life events (in the models of Class B), only the models in Class C (C1, C2, and C3) are intervening models. However, at this point, we wish to somewhat relax this restriction, as long as depression is measured subsequent to both social support and life events.

What is the buffering effect, then? Following *Webster's, to buffer* may be defined as the lessening of the shock of something—the cushioning or separating of two things. Thus, the buffering variable must come between two other variables and must lessen or neutralize the potential effect of one on the other. Yet three interpretations of the buffering effect have been given by researchers. In the most restrictive interpretation, the buffering effect is equated with the interaction effect. Social support is seen to exert an effect only in conjunction with an adverse condition. This is probably the most popular interpretation, and the buffering effect is represented by Model C1.

A second integration argues that social support buffers not only because of its interaction with life events, but perhaps also when it counteracts life events. Social support becomes mobilized as a result of the occurrence of an adverse condition (e.g., occurrences of life events induce stronger social support) (Lin et al., 1979; Wheaton, 1983). This interpretation, therefore, would include Models C1 and C3 as representing buffering effects of social support. In this interpretation, the net effect of life events on depression is said to be reduced because of the mobilization of social support.

The third and perhaps most liberal interpretation states that if the direct effect of life events on depression is reduced because of the presence of social support, then social support serves as a buffer. In other words, buffering occurs when the presence, absence, or degree of social support affects the direct relationship between life events and depression (Lin and Dean, 1984; Kessler and McLeod, 1984b). In this interpretation, Models C1 and C2 represent buffering effects.

Because of the different interpretations, there is substantial confusion about what constitutes the appropriate models and, therefore, about what constitutes evidence for the buffering effect of social support. To avoid any misinterpretation, we will address each specific model rather than a buffering effect. However, if we were to take a position, our present preference is to take a more liberal interpretation. At the minimum, Models C1 and C3 are buffering models. If a mediating effect is also considered a buffering effect, then Model C2 can also be included.

3. The temporal or causal sequence of the variables is made explicit in the models. It is clear that in order to test these models, we need at least three waves of panel data. Obviously, realistic compromises may have to be made, as there are not many three-wave panel data sets. For Class B models, only two waves are absolutely required, for example. However, we must place the empirical evidence in its proper place among the models. The question of whether time frames for the variables (life events during the past 6 to 12 months, social support in the past 6 months, and depression in the past week) reconstructed at a given point in time are reasonable surrogates for an actual sequence of tests over time is an empirical question and requires careful scrutiny.

The reader should keep in mind that the above discussions focus on the role of social support in the models. If one wishes instead to address the role of life events, for example, and to identify their direct, independent, moderating, counteracting, intervening, and buffering effects relative to social support, one could accordingly discuss the models identified in Figure 10.1 from that approach.

EVIDENCE FROM OTHER STUDIES

Having presented the 12 basic causal models that are logically or theoretically plausible, we will now examine evidence provided by other studies as to which of the models are empirically more credible. Although numerous studies pertain to social support and mental health, we impose two criteria for excluding studies from this review. First, we exclude studies that do not clearly specify any stressors as a condition or as an independent variable. Thus, much strong evidence about the effects of social support on mental health will not be examined here. This restriction is necessary to insure that the stressor–social-support–mental health models remain the focal point for validation. It is argued that only when stressors are present, either as a condition or as an independent variable, can the independent, direct, indirect, and interactive nature of social support be assessed.

Secondly, studies that employ marital status as the only or primary measure of social support will be excluded. Although we recognize the significance of marital conditions for health and illness, we argue that it should be treated as a concept distinct from, although related to, social support. A later chapter (Chapter 12) examines the basic model in terms of the gender and marital status of the respondents. To use marital status as a surrogate indicator of social support is to equate social support or its absence with being married or not being married, an unacceptable assumption.

On the other hand, we will examine studies that are less than ideal for the purpose of validating one or more of the models. It is clear that only an extremely limited number of studies fulfill the requirements for the rigorous testing of any of the models. Namely, the data must be longitudinal, the measurements should be reliable and valid, and samples need to be representative of meaningful and normative populations. As will become clear, it is debatable as to whether any existing study fulfills these requirements. Thus, we decided to include studies that have the following imperfections or problems. First, we will mention several studies in which all the subjects were in the same stressful condition. For example, several studies examine the unemployed (Cobb, 1974; Gore, 1978), the institutionalized (Turner, 1981), or mothers with pregnancy complications (Nuckolls et al., 1972). Because there is no nonstressor group, it is difficult to classify the results as testing the interactive or the compensating effect of social support. Nevertheless, they are included because several are well known and much cited as evidence linking social support to the stressor–illness models; although interpretation is difficult, the evidence clearly demonstrates the potentially interactive effect of social support. We are also including several studies in which it is unclear as to whether there was a life stress condition or not. However, the research designs and the description of findings gave clues that such stressors indeed were present but not reported. We classify these studies as evidence for or against independent or compensating effects (Models A4, B4, or C4), because the lack of reporting a relationship between stressors and social support is taken to indicate no relationship between the two or an insignificant one.

Secondly, cross-sectional data will also be examined. Although all the models presented in Figure 10.1 specify causal sequences among the variables, to impose the necessary temporal requirements would eliminate all but one or two studies in the literature. Several studies, for example, had data from a two-wave or a multiwave survey but only examined measures from a single wave (Williams et al., 1981; Pearlin et al., 1981). Thus, for the time being, we will include cross-sectional data and rely on the researchers' own judgments on causal and temporal sequences among the variables they examined.

Thirdly, many studies included both stressors and social support as independent variables, but did not report the relationship between them. The focus has tended to be solely on their independent and joint contributions to mental health. The relationship between stressors and social support was not reported. Thus, it is impossible to determine whether they provided evidence for Models 2, 3, or 4. We will include them as evidence for or against Model 4. Future analyses by these and other researchers of those data sets may clarify their proper causal classification.

Finally, there are studies that present mixed or problematic results, some of which seem to confirm a model whereas others do not. For example, one group of researchers tested a large number of interactions between measures of stress and social support (LaRocco, House, and French, 1980). A certain portion of the interactions turned out to be statistically significant, whereas the remaining were not. To what extent these correlations can reasonably be accepted as beyond statistically random chance is problematic. Similarly, another study failed to find a significant relationship when a multiplicative interaction between stressors and social support was used (Turner, 1981). But when the respondents were split into (high, medium, and low) levels of stress, social support had a much stronger effect on depression for the high-stress group as compared to the medium- and low-stress groups. Whether the data support discrete functions of stressors or are artifacts of abritrary groupings presents interpretative difficulties. Nevertheless, these data at least present partial confirmation of the interactive model and will, therefore, be included in our review. Other findings may be due to statistical or measurement problems. For example, one study showed a positive relationship between contemporaneous stressors and social support (Aneshensel and Frerichs, 1982). Further studies and evidence are needed to rule out potential multicollinearity effects due to the relatively higher correlations among the independent variables compared to their correlations with the dependent variable (depression).

Because of these relaxed criteria for inclusion, we give all evidence the benefit of the doubt and thus offer our models maximum opportunity to be confirmed. Whatever confirming evidence there is probably represents the upper limit of empirical validity. We point out wherever appropriate the problematic nature of the data sets involved.

Further allowances in this evaluation of data become necessary when it is recognized that there is not a sufficient number of studies for the three causal sequence classes of the models. Most of the studies present cross-sectional data, preventing examination of the temporal sequence among the variables. Thus, in relating the relevant literature to our causal models, we concentrate only on the four submodels rather than on the three classes. However, we point out whether or not a particular study is appropriate for a model with a particular temporal sequence.

It is not our intention to relate all studies that have been done to our model. Rather, the studies are representative of the types of evidence available in the literature. The results are presented in Table 10.1.

TABLE 10.1
Empirical Evidence for Each of the Four Submodels of Models 1, 2, and 3
(in Figure 10.1)

Model tested	Author	Data (cross-sectional/ panel)	Test result
1 Conditioning/ interactive Effect (A1, B1, or C1)	Andrews et al. (1978)	Cross-sectional	Not confirmed
	Aneshensel and Stone (1982)	Cross-sectional	Not confirmed
	Barrera (1981)	Cross-sectional	Not confirmed
	Bell et al. (1982)	Cross-sectional	Not confirmed
	Brown et al. (1975)	Cross-sectional[a]	Partially confirmed
	Caplan et al. (1975); Pinneau (1975, 1976); LaRocco et al. (1980)	Cross-sectional	Partially confirmed
	Henderson (1977)	Cross-sectional	Not confirmed
	House and Wells (1978)	Cross-sectional	Partially confirmed
	Husaini and Neff (1982)	Cross-sectional	Not confirmed[c]
	Lin et al. (1979, 1982)	Cross-sectional	Not confirmed

(continued)

TABLE 10.1 (*Continued*)

Model tested	Author	Data (cross-sectional/ panel)	Test result
	Nuckolls et al. (1972)	Cross-sectional[a]	Confirmed
	Thoits (1982)	Cross-sectional	Not confirmed
	Turner (1981)	Cross-sectional	Partially confirmed
B1 Contemporaneous/ interactive effect	Cobb (1974)	Panel	Confirmed
	Gore (1978); Cobb and Kasl (1977)	Panel[b]	Confirmed
	Henderson et al. (1981)	Panel	Not confirmed?
	Pearlin et al. (1981)	Panel[d]	Not confirmed
	Schaefer et al. (1981)	Panel	Not confirmed
	Turner (1981)	Panel	Partially confirmed
	Williams et al. (1981)	Panel[d]	Not confirmed?
2 Suppresant/ mediating effect	R. A. Bell et al. (1982)	Cross-sectional	Confirmed
	Lin et al. (1982)	Cross-sectional	Confirmed
	R. A. Bell et al. (1982)	Panel	Not confirmed
3 Vulnerability/ counteractive effect	Lin et al. (1979)	Cross-sectional	Not confirmed
	Aneshensel and Frerichs (1982)	Panel	Confirmed[e]
4 Independent/ compensating effect	Andrews et al. (1978)	Cross-sectional[f]	Confirmed
	Aneshensel and Frerichs (1982)	Cross-sectional	Confirmed
	Aneshensel and Stone (1982)	Cross-sectional	Confirmed
	Barrera (1981)	Cross-sectional[f]	Partially confirmed
	R. A. Bell et al. (1982)	Cross-sectional	Confirmed
	Carveth and Gottlieb (1979)	Cross-sectional[f]	Partially confirmed
	Husaini and Neff (1982)	Cross-sectional	Confirmed (females only)
	Lin et al. (1979)	Cross-sectional	Confirmed

(*continued*)

TABLE 10.1 (Continued)

Submodel Tested	Author	Data (cross-sectional/ panel)	Test result
	Schaefer et al. (1981)	Cross-sectional and panel	Confirmed
	Turner (1981)	Cross-sectional[f]	Confirmed
	Warheit et al. (1982)	Cross-sectional	Confirmed
	Wilcox (1981b)	Cross-sectional[f]	Partially confirmed
	Berkman and Syme (1979)	Panel[b,f]	Partially confirmed
	G. W. Brown and Harris (1978)	Panel[f]	Confirmed
	Medalie and Goldbourt (1976)	Panel[b,f]	Partially confirmed
	Pearlin et al. (1981)	Panel[d,f]	Not confirmed
	Turner (1981)	Panel[f]	Confirmed
	Williams et al. (1981)	Panel[d,f]	Confirmed
	Sarason et al. (1983)	Small group (40 students)	Confirmed

[a]Only stress conditions.
[b]Stress conditions uncertain.
[c]An interactive effect reported for the female sample; however, the regression coefficient only −08.
[d]Variables all measured at T2, although panel data collected.
[e]One of two coefficients examined show such effect.
[f]Relationship between stressors and social support not reported and not applied.

As can be seen, most of the studies bear on Models 1 and 4 (the conditioning or interactive and independent or compensating effects). For the conditioning/interactive model, the cross-sectional data provide mixed results. Some confirm the expected relationship and some do not. If we exclude the data sets that only have those stressor conditions, then the evidence leans against the conditioning/interactive model. Similarly mixed results are apparent among the panel studies, with the majority failing to confirm the interactive effect. Furthermore, observations confirming the relationship tend to come from studies of special or captive populations (factory workers, hospitalized persons, pregnant mothers using certain health services), and nonconfirming data tend to come from general or community samples (Lin et al., 1979;

Andrews, Tennant, Hewson, and Valliant, 1978; Henderson, 1981; Pearlin et al., 1981; Williams et al., 1981; Aneshensel and Stone, 1982; R. A. Bell, Leroy, and Stephenson, 1982; Thoits, 1982; Husaini and Neff, 1982). Thus, the conditioning/interactive effect has, at best, a tenuous credibility.

Two studies confirm Model 2, the suppressant/mediating effect. One is a cross-sectional study and the other a panel study. However, as we mentioned above, many of the studies classified under Model 4 may in fact have unreported information confirming the negative relationship between stressors and social support. Thus, there may be stronger evidence for Model 2. However, as it stands in the literature, confirmation for Model 2 is, at best, tentative.

Two groups of researchers have explicitly examined Model 3, the vulnerability/counteractive effect of social support. A cross-sectional study (Lin et al., 1979) did not confirm it, whereas a panel study (Aneshensel and Frerichs, 1982) suggested confirmation. However, the later study only found a contemporaneous rather than a time-lagged positive relationship between stressors and social support, and in only one of the two time periods when such measures were assessed. We must conclude that so far there is no clear evidence in support of the vulnerability/counteractive models.

Model 4, the independent or compensating effect of social support, has received the strongest confirmation by far. Only 2 of the 16 studies reviewed completely failed to confirm the model. However, although most of the studies did not report an analysis of the relationship between stressors and social support, many of them, if fully reported, might conceivably lend confirmation to Model 2 or 3, instead. Nevertheless, we must conclude that there is sufficient evidence for the independent or compensating effect.

In summary, the empirical evidence points to confirmation of the independent or compensating effect of social support, and to probable confirmation of the suppressant/mediating effect as well. There is some tentative confirmation for the interactive/conditioning effect, but the evidence is not as convincing. There is no evidence that social support acts to trigger life events that lead to vulnerability and depression or that stressors increase social support (Model 3). Because most of these researchers used cross-sectional data, the specific temporal causal sequences in models of the three classes simply could not be examined. The only genuine panel data were provided by Turner (1981) in a study of mothers following births and by Henderson and his associates in a study of a community sample in Australia (Henderson, Byrne, and Duncan–Jones, 1981). Turner's data were gathered in three waves within 12 months after the mothers gave birth, but only the first two waves of data (immediately after birth and 6 months after birth) were used in the analysis. It confirmed the mediating or independent effect of social support (Model B2 or Model B4), depending on the (unreported) relationship between stressors and social support; and it also partially confirmed the interactive effect (Model B1), depending on the method of analysis used (the trichotomizing of the stressors versus using them as a continuous variable). The Henderson study involved data from a community sample with 4-month intervals between four waves. Its longitudinal analysis of two waves of the data did not confirm a mediating effect from social support, although the cross-sectional data did. It did report a significant but very modest interactive effect. In short, then, the evidence confirming any specific model, beyond the cross-sectional data, is very thin indeed. Much of this lack of evidence is due to the fact that study designs have lacked the required samples, measures, and temporal sequences. However, if cross-sectional data fail to confirm a specific model, there is even less likelihood that it can be confirmed in panel studies, because time lags tend to reduce rather than increase the effect of one variable on another. We now present our own two-wave data to test the various models.

DATA AND THE ANALYTIC TECHNIQUE

The data used to examine the models consists of indicators of the three critical variables: life events, social support, and depression. Because two waves of data are available, all the models to be examined involve cross-time (time-lagged) designs. In testing for Class A models, indicators of degree of social support are from the Time 1 (T1) data; indicators of life events and of depression are from the Time 2 (T2) data. For testing Class B models, indicators of both life events and social support come from the T1 data, and the indicator of depression (CE-SD) comes from the T2 data. For Class C models, the indicator of life events is from the T1 data, and the indicators of social support and depression are from the T2 data.

The sum total undesirable life events as precipitated by respondents is used as the indicator of stressful life events. As discussed in Chapter 5, perceived undesirable life events seem to be efficient predictors of depression. Their use maximizes the potential contribution of life events to the explanation of the dependent variable, depression, in the models. Our interest is in assessing the effect of social support on depression, but fair assessment can only be made if psychological resources (personal coping resources, Chapter 6) are also examined. Other potential factors, such as age, sex, marital status, and illness history, are also taken into account in subsequent chapters.

As our indicator of depression, the full score of the CES-D scale is used. We considered using merely the factors in the CES-d scale (see Chapter 4), but for reasons of comparability, because most studies in the literature utilize the CES-D, the decision was made to use the entire scale score. Debate regarding the interrelationships among the factors as well as regarding the elimination of positive affect from the scale (Craig and VanNatta, 1979) is beyond the scope of this book but should be examined more fully in future studies.

For social support, we decided to use indicators that reflect the theoretical components outlined in Chapter 2 and that show reasonable reliability and validity (Chapters 7, 8, and 9). These components and indicators are listed in Table 10.2.

These social-support indicators were selected not only because they are indicators of the components discussed in Chapter 2, but also because of their significant zero-order correlations with CES-D (as shown in Chapters 7, 8, and 9). As a result, most of the measures of network support were eliminated. We group under network support the number of confidants and the frequency of interactions with the most important confidant to differentiate between these quantitative measures of network support and the more qualitative aspects of confidant support (intensity, intimacy, etc.). These are not rigid classifications for the various social support components. Rather, they are shown here as illustrations of the types of indicators used to measure social support.

It should be noted that three measures (Comnei, Frequency, and Fam) are in the negative direction. A high score reflects a lack of such support. We retain these measures and response categories as they were originally used by the proposing authors, so that strict comparisons can be made with other studies using these measures. Thus, they are expected to show *negative* associations when paired with other social-support measures.

After the indicators had been selected, the structural equation modeling technique was used to test the models. This technique is well suited for a model that incorporates many indicators and time-lagged variables. The computer program as LISREL (Linear Structural Relations), Version VI), written by Joreskog and Sorbum (1979); it utilizes the maximum-likelihood solution to evaluate whether each particular causal model proposed to explain the possible relationships among the indicators and the *latent variables*—the concepts—is consistent with the actual patterns found among the empirical variables (indicators) in

TABLE 10.2
Social-Support Components and Indicators

Component	Indicator	Measurement chapter	Abbreviation to be used[a]
Community support	Lack of community–neighborhood interaction and satisfaction	9	$Comnei_1/Comnei_2$
	Participation in organizations	9	$Parti_1/Parti_2$
Network support	Number of confidants	9	$Range_1/Range_2$
	(Infrequent) interaction with confidant	9	$Frequency_1/Frequency_2$
Confidant support	Role relationship with confidant	7	$Role_1/Role_2$
	Kaplan items on relations with confidant	7	$Kaplan_1/Kaplan_2$
	Medalie–Goldbourt items on lack of family support	7	Fam_1/Fam_2
	Strong-tie support	8	STS_1/STS_2
Instrumental–expressive support	Factor 3: Expressive	8	Exp_1/Exp_2
	Factor 1: Responsibility	8	$Resp_1/Resp_2$
	Factor 2: Money	8	$Mony_1/Mony_2$

[a]The subscript 1 refers to measures at Time 1; the subscript 2 is used for measures at Time 2 in the text.

the data. The technique, therefore, does not state firmly which models are the "right" ones. Rather, it determines which of them are reasonable and consistent with the data.

When a model does not fit the data, modifications are made by relaxing certain of the *fixed* (assumed) relationships in the model. These shifts are guided by a modification index, by the residual coefficients between the empirical and the model-derived relationships among the indicators, and by the first-order derivatives of the fitting function, all provided by the computer program (LISREL VI. Caution was exercised in the selection of the relationships, which were relaxed one at a time, so that theoretical interpretations could be made.

To test the models in each class, we first examined the additive models (Models 2, 3, and 4). Because these are exclusive models (any one of them precludes the two others), one test should identify the reasonable models among them. We then examined Model 1 where an interaction term is constructed for undesirable life events and social support indicators. These two tests, combined, inform us as to which of the 12 models are reasonable for assessing the contributions of undesirable life events and of social support to the explanation of depression.

THE ADDITIVE MODELS (MODELS 2, 3, and 4)

Our examination of the additive models began with an evaluation as to whether multiple latent variables (factors) should be constructed for measuring social support. The question is whether there are components or factors in social support sufficiently independent of each other that they should be identified as though they were subconcepts. These factors, for example, may be consistent with the identified components of social support, such as community support, network support, confidant support, and so on. On the other hand, because these components are all part of the concept of social support, they should be related to each other and may not be seen as distinct factors. These two approaches are presented in Figure 10.2 for Class A Models 2, 3, and 4, where social support temporally precedes undesirable life events.

The test, using the LISREL program, showed that multiple latent variables for social support (Figure 10.2) does not fit the data, as many indicators have substantial relationships with more than one of the latent social-support variables. In contrast, the models in which a single inclusive latent social-support variable is used (Figure 10.3) show good fit with the data. This result holds true for all three classes (A, B, and C) of additive models. Thus, in presenting the results for the additive models, only discuss models in which a single latent variable for social support appears.

CLASS A MODELS

The initial structural model, similar to the one in Figure 10.3, where social support precedes undesirable life events, was examined for its fit with the relevant T1 and T2 data. After taking into account several correlations among the error terms (residuals) for the indicators of social support (SS_1), the model presented in Figure 10.4 had a goodness-of-fit index of .97, suggesting that it is a reasonable model, as far as the T1–T2 data were concerned.[1]

[1]The chi-square value for 59 degrees of freedom was 176.35. As mentioned before, because the sample size is relatively large, it would be difficult to achieve a low chi-square value.

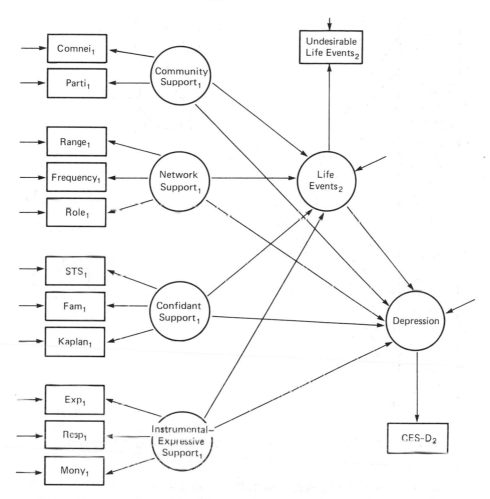

Figure 10.2 Class A model with components of social support as separate latent variables.

Focusing on the relationships among the three structural variables (social support, SS_1; life events, LE_2; and depression, Dep_2), the data indicate that Model A2, showing the suppressant effect of social sup- port, is a credible model. In the test of this model, both SS_1 and LE_2 have direct effects on depression (having path coefficients of $-.17$ and $.37$, respectively). More significantly, SS_1 has a negative effect on LE_2 ($-.18$), an indication that prior level of social support may reduce the occurrence of undesirable life events.

The data also show which of the indicators are stronger as far as measuring SS_1 is concerned. As expected (see Table 10.2), $Comnei_1$,

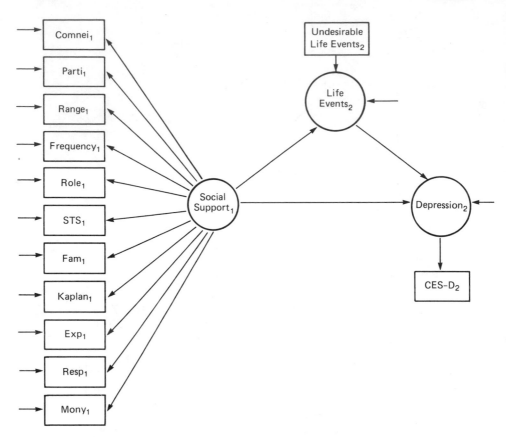

Figure 10.3 Class A model with social support as a single latent variable.

Frequency$_1$, and Fam$_1$ show significant *negative* relationships with SS$_1$, because these measures were scored *negatively* (the higher the score, the greater the lack of such support). The support indicator based on strong ties (STS) had a fixed (predetermined) regression coefficient of 1.0 and SS$_1$. This assumption fits the data model, so no modification of the model was needed in this respect. Other strong indicators included the three instrumental–expressive supports (Exp$_1$, Resp$_1$, and Mony$_1$) and the Medalie–Goldbourt family support scale (Fam$_1$). Kaplan's confidant support items (Kaplan$_1$), community–neighborhood support (Comnei$_1$), and frequency of interaction with confidant (frequency$_1$) also showed reasonable relationships with SS$_1$. On the other hand, participation in organizations (Parti$_1$), range of confidants (Range$_1$), and role relationship with confidant (Role$_1$) were not good

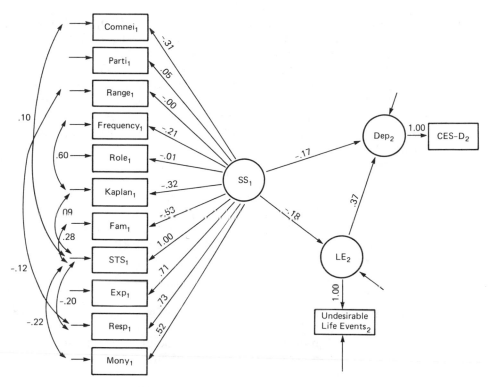

Figure 10.4 Class A final structural model of Time 1 social-support effects on life events and depression at Time 2; $df = 59$, $\chi^2 = 176.35$, and Goodness-of-fit index = .97.

indicators of social support given their low correlations. These results support our theoretical expectation (see Chapter 2) that confidant, instrumental, and expressive support should be more effective than community and network supports.

However, certain community and network support indicators (Comnei$_1$, Range$_1$, and especially Frequency$_1$) shared commonality with certain confidant, strong-tie, and instrumental–expressive indicators (Kaplan$_1$, STS$_1$, and Resp$_1$), as indicated by the curved double-arrowed lines on the left-hand side of Figure 10.4. These lines, showing correlations among the *error terms* of the indicators, in fact reflected some interdependent relations among the indicators. We checked the zero-order correlations among them and found that the coefficients ranged from moderate (.12) to strong (.66). Therefore, they suggest that although community and network supports may not directly and strongly figure in the relations between social support and undesirable life events and depression, they may indeed, as argued in Chapter 2, provide the context within which significant confidant and instrumental–expressive supports are formed.

Further, because one of the two items that tap Strong-Tie Support (close companion) was also incorporated in the five-item Expressive-Support scale (Exp_1), a question might be raised as to whether this overlap unduly inflated the relationships of SS_1 with LE_2 and Dep_2. This is doubtful, because they were all indicators of a single variable, SS_1. Nevertheless, a revised model was constructed in which the expressive factor, Exp_1 was eliminated as an indicator of SS_1. The resulting coefficients showed that SS_1 and LE_2 maintained their magnitudes of relations with Dep_2, whereas negative relationships between SS_1 and LE_2 were even slightly increased (from $-.18$ to $-.30$), reaffirming the suppressing effect of social support on undesirable life events. Among indicators of social support, instrumental support (Responsibility, $Resp_1$) was the most important, having the highest possible value, .73.

CLASS B MODELS

In this class, contemporaneous effects of social support and life events (SS_1 and LE_1) are assessed. After modifications, the final fitted model appears in Figure 10.5.

The data confirm Model B_2, the contemporaneous mediating effect of social support. SS_1 shows a strong direct negative effect on Dep_2, whereas LE_1 does not show much effect at all. There is a strong negative correlation between LE_1 and SS_1. Thus, part of the effect of undesirable life events is moderated by the presence of social support. The goodness-of-fit index for the final model is .98.

In this model, the assumed fixed correspondence of 1.0 between SS_1 and Strong-Tie Support (STS_1) had to be relaxed, because of strong relationships between the instrumental–expressive factors and SS_1 (notably the contribution of instrumental and expressive support factors $Resp_1$ and $Mony_1$). The general pattern of relationship between the indicators and SS_1 again confirmed the importance of confidant support ($Kaplan_1$, Fam_1, and STS_1) and instrumental–expressive supports rather than community ($Comnei_1$, $Parti_1$) and network supports ($Range_1$ and $Frequency_1$). One network support indicator, $Range_1$, had a shared variation with one instrumental support factor, $Resp_1$ (see double-arrowed curved line in Figure 10.5), suggesting that network support has an indirect effect through other, more significant social support.

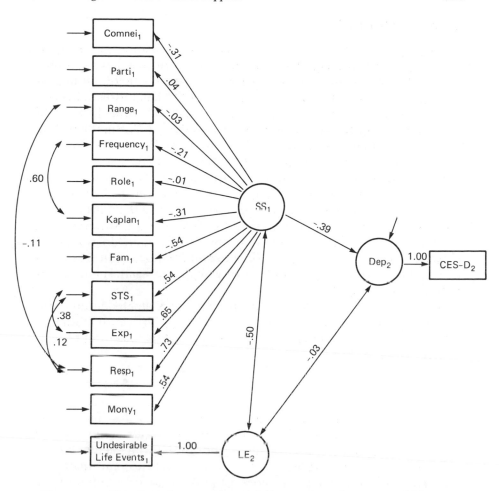

Figure 10.5 Class B final structural model of Time 1 social-support and life-events effects on depression at Time 2; $df = 61$, $\chi^2 = 126$, and Goodness-of-fit index = .98.

Eliminating the Expressive Support factor (Exp_1) as an indicator of SS_1 brought a slight decrease in the path coefficient from SS_1 to Dep_2 (from $-.39$ to $-.26$), but the magnitude remained statistically significant. Relationships between SS_1 and LE_1 and between LE_1 and Dep_2 remained unchanged. The instrumental support factor of Responsibility ($Resp_1$) became the most important indicator of social support, followed by the other instrumental support factor of $Mony_1$, Strong-Tie Support (STS_1), and the Medalie–Goldbourt family support scale (M–G).

CLASS C MODELS

In Class C models, the effects of life events preceding social support are assessed. The final model, appearing in Figure 10.6, has a goodness-of-fit index of .90 with the data. This model shows that both undesirable life events at T1 and social support at T2 have direct effects on depression at T_2, with SS_2 having a stronger relationship than LE_1 (path coefficients being $-.44$ and $.11$, respectively). Furthermore, there is a significant negative path $(-.27)$ from LE_1 to SS_2. Thus, SS_2 mediates the effect of LE_1 on Dep_2, confirming Model C2.

Again, this model accepts the assumption of perfect correspondence between strong-tie support (STS) and SS_2, and the rest of the relationships between indicators and SS_2 are similar to the ones found for the Class A model (see Figure 10.4). Confidant and instrumental–expressive supports have greater relevance to SS than do community (Comnei) and network supports (Range and Frequency) in this model. One of the network support indicators, Frequency, again share variance with the Kaplan scale.

When the Expressive Support factor, Exp_2 was deleted as an indicator of SS_2, the mediating effect of social support was increased, as reflected in the path from LE_1 to SS_2 (from $-.27$ to $-.34$) and from SS_2 to Dep_2 (from $-.44$ to $-.55$).

Summary

The data show that social support strongly mediates the effects of preceding or contemporaneous undesirable life events, and it also suppresses the likelihood of subsequent undesirable life events. Furthermore, confidant support (especially) with strong ties) and instrumental–expressive elements are more important than community and network supports as indicators of social support. Community and network relations, nevertheless, provide the context within which the confidant and instrumental–expressive supports are formed or obtained. Now, we turn our attention to the interactive models, A_1, B_1, and C_1).

THE INTERACTIVE MODELS

To test interactive effects between undesirable life events and social support, each of the indicators of social support was multiplied by the summed score of undesirable life events. However, in anticipation of multiple high correlations between these product terms and their com-

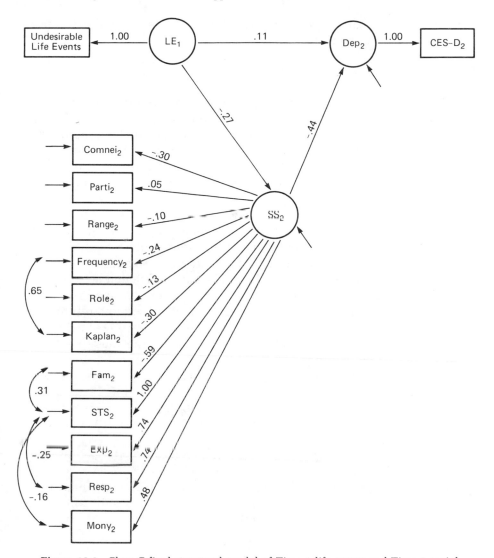

Figure 10.6 Class C final structural model of Time 1 life events and Time 2 social-support effects on depression at Time 2; $df = 62$, $\chi^2 = 510$, and Goodness-of-fit index $= .90$.

ponent terms when the joint effects of additive and interactive variables were assessed, we used the score for deviation from the mean for each indicator in the product term (see discussion of this method in Smith and Sasaki, 1979). For example, the interaction term between community–neighborhood support at T1 and undesirable life events at T2 was constructed as follows:

$$(\text{Comnei}_1 - \overline{\text{Comnei}_1}) * (\text{LE}_2 - \overline{\text{LE}_2})$$

This product term does not bias the estimate of the interaction effect, because only constants (the means) of the component variables are subtracted from them. The regression coefficient of such an interaction term with a dependent variable (such as depression) reflects any contribution of the interaction terms, independent of and in addition to the contributions of the component terms themselves (e.g., Comnei_1 and LE_2).

Three interactive patterns were examined, for the Class A, B, and C models, respectively. In the Class A interactive model, the product terms between social-support T1 indicators and undesirable life events at T2 were computed and analyzed for their effect on depression at T2. (The results are shown in Figure 10.7) The path coefficient between $\text{SS}_1 \times \text{LE}_2$ was .22 and significant beyond the .05 level. The goodness-of-fit index was high, at .85. Again, we then eliminated Exp_1 and refitted the model. The results (shown in parentheses in Figure 10.7) showed improved fit (goodness-of-fit index at .95) between the model patterns and the observed patterns.

Similar computations were carried out for the interaction terms of $\text{SS}_1 \times \text{LE}_1$ and $\text{LE}_1 \times \text{SS}_2$. (The results are presented in Figures 10.8 and 10.9, respectively.) The overall effects of these interactive terms on depression were lower than that of $\text{SS}_1 \times \text{LE}_2$, but were still significant at the .05 level.

Thus, the three types of interaction (when SS occurred before, contemporaneously with, or subsequent to undesirable life events) were all significant when considered *individually*. The next step, then, is to examine whether any of these interactions remain significant when jointly considered with additive effects.

MODELS OF JOINT ADDITIVE AND INTERACTIVE EFFECTS

The ideal model for testing additive and interactive effects combines all three classes of models that we have so far considered individually. Such a model would incorporate measures of social support, of life events, of the interactive terms of SS and LE, and of depression at both T1 and T2. Further, it should also incorporate measures of personal resources (self-esteem and personal competence) at T1 and T2 as con-

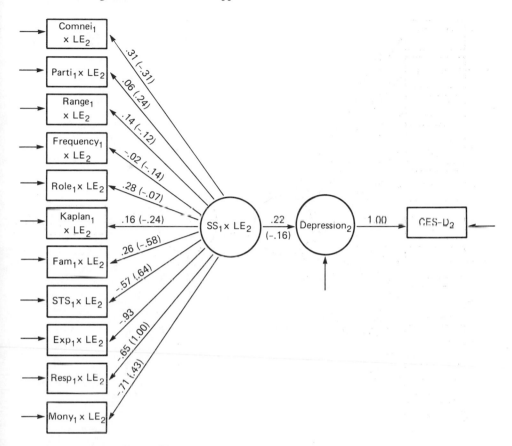

Figure 10.7   Effects of interactions of social support at Time 1 and life events at Time 2 (Model A1). (Figures in parentheses are estimates for a model with 10 indicators of SS_1 × LE_2 by elimination of Exp_1 × LE_2.) Sign reversals are due to assigning 1.00 to the relationship between SS_1 × LE_2 and $Resp_1$ × LE_2. df = 49 (35), χ^2 = 830 (253.20), and Goodness-of-fit index = .85 (.95).

trol variables. Such a model, however, would involve many variables with high intercorrelations (e.g., between SS_1 and SS_2 measures), resulting in multicollinearity problems creating biased estimates of their relationships with depression. One alternative approach would be to construct a change score for a variable between its T2 and T1 measures (e.g., STS_2 − STS_1) and to use this in place of its T2 measure in the model. Kessler and Greenberg (1981) have shown that conversion between a change score and its original measure is straightforward and meaningful. The only thing one needs to keep in mind is that, due to

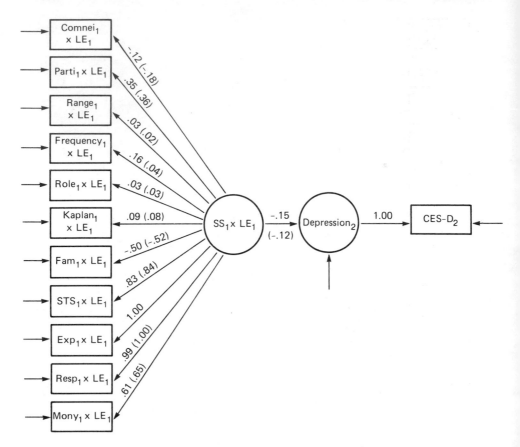

Figure 10.8 Effects of interactions of life events and social support at Time 1 on depression at Time 2 (Model B1). (Figures in parentheses are estimates for a model with 10 indicators of $SS_1 \times LE_1$ by elimination of $Exp_1 \times LE_1$.) $df = 49$ (34), $\chi^2 = 93$ (98), and Goodness-of-fit index = .93 (.95).

the regression toward the mean between T1 and T2 data, the correlation between the T1 measure and the change score will be in an inverse (negative) direction. The model proposed here, however, tends to eliminate the multicolinearity problems mentioned above.

Because a change score is computed for each indicator over time, the model would contain a great number of indicators, especially with the addition of the control variables (personal resources). Thus, we made three decisions to make the modeling more manageable:

1. Only four indicators of social support will be retained. These are: Strong-Tie Confidant Support (STS), the instrumental Responsibil-

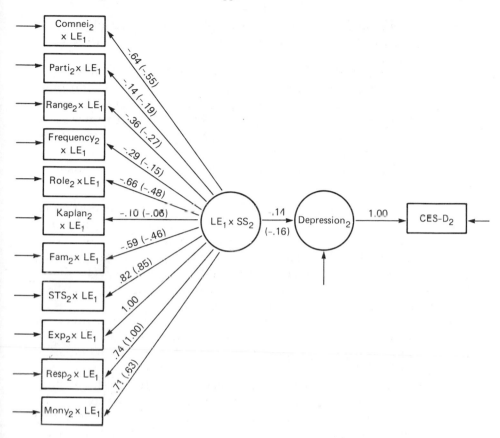

Figure 10.9 Effect of Interactions of life events at Time 1 and social support at Time 2 on depression at Time 2 (Model C1). (Figures in parentheses are estimates for a model with 10 indicators of $LE_1 \times SS_2$ by elimination of $Exp_2 \times LE_1$.) $df = 48$ (35), $\chi^2 = 682$ (316.05), and Goodness-of-fit index = .87.

ity/Demand factor (Resp), the instrumental Money factor (Mony), and the Medalie–Goldbourt scale of family support (Fam). As can be seen in the additive models (Figures 10.4, 10.5, and 10.6), they were consistently the best indicators of social support at both T1 and T2.

2. Two psychological-resources variables (self-esteem and personal competence) will be incorporated in the model to assess if (a) these personal-resources variables have any significant effects on depression and (b) their incorporation affects the effects of social support and life events on depression. The validity and reliability of these two variables have been discussed in Chapter 6. We rule out the incorporation of the subfactors associated with these variables, as they would add to the

complexity of modeling. Using these variables as indicators of personal resources (PR) is consistent with the general discussions in the literature (see Chapter 6).

3. Each model will incorporate all the additive variables (Life Events$_1$, Social Support$_1$, Personal Resources$_1$, Depression$_1$ and their change scores, LE$_c$, SS$_c$, PR$_c$, and Depression$_c$), plus one interactive latent variable (SS$_1$ × LE$_2$, SS$_1$ × LE$_1$, or LE$_1$ × SS$_2$). An interactive term will be retained in the model only when it remains significant. This strategy keeps the number of indicators and latent variables down to a manageable size, while still allowing for a systematic investigation of all possible effects.

After this trimming, each model still incorporates 20 indicators and 9 latent variables, making the chi-square statistic meaninglessly high and the goodness-of-fit indices substantially lower than those of earlier models. Nevertheless, this analysis is essential to provide the necessary information to examine both additive and interactive effects simultaneously, the absence of which has been singled out as the most serious shortcoming of most studies on this subject.

Such an approach can be said to favor additive components over interactive ones, because interactive terms are merely added on in the presence of additive components. However, it is clear that comparing previous results of the additive models to those of interactive models shows that additive components have decisively greater significance than interactive components. Unless the interactive terms remain significant in conjunction with the additive terms, it must be concluded that the interactive terms do not contribute significantly beyond the contribution of the additive terms to explaining the dependent variable—the changes in depression over time. Further, parsimony of explanation suggests preferring additive over interactive phenomena, as the latter are much more complicated to explain and analyze. This approach, however, is in no way biased against the interactive terms, as the significant ones will be retained in any event.

The incorporation of the psychological-resource (PR) variables (self-esteem and personal competence) adds to the credibility of the model, because these variables represent the other substantial body of findings in the literature, concerning the psychosocial factors in the etiology of depression and mental health in general. Their presence in the model allows a test of their explanation of changes in depression, in conjunction with the additive and interactive effects of social support and undesirable life events. Thus, the model addresses the three most dominant variables discussed in the psychosocial literature on mental health: life events, social support, and personal-coping resources. Such an examination will help us design further analyses that go beyond these basic variables.

Model of Changes with the Suppressant Interactive Factor ($SS_1 \times LE_2$)

We begin with a model that examines the additive effects of undesirable life events and social support at T1 and their changes between T1 and T2 ($SS_2 - SS_1$ and $LE_2 - LE_1$) as well as the Suppressant Interactive factor of SS_1 and LE_2 on change in depression (Depression$_2$ − Depression$_1$). It incorporates measures of psychological resources at T1 (as indicated by Self Esteem$_1$ and Personal Competence$_1$) as well as their change scores (SE_c and PC_c) between T1 and T2. Finally, it incorporates depression (CES-D) measured at T1. The model and resulting estimates of relationships are presented in Figure 10.10. Only coefficients greater than .10 are retained in the graph, and no correlations are assumed between the error terms among any of the indicators.

The model and results are quite complex. We may summarize the salient and relevant findings as follows:

1. Undesirable life events, social support, and depression show significant stability over time, as these variables measured at T1 are strongly correlated with their respective change scores. Psychological-resource variables, on the other hand, did not show substantial stability over the 1-year period. Its change score can hardly be predicted from the score at T1. (All the stability coefficients are negative because of the regression toward the mean, as mentioned earlier.)

2. Social support shows significant direct effects (from both the T1 measure and the change score, SS_c) on change in depression and as a mediating factor for undesirable life events (note the path from LE_1 to SS_c). Thus, social support affects depression contemporaneously and over time, and as well as mediating the potential effect of undesirable life events on depression. These conclusions can be drawn about depression as well as change in depression because the model takes into account the initial state of depression at T1.

3. Undesirable life events also exert a significant direct effect (both from this variable's T1 and from its change score, LE_c) on change in depression, but to a much lesser degree than does social support. It also mediates the effect of social support (note the path from SS_1 to LE_c), but again the effect is very modest.

4. Psychological resources have little effect, either direct or indirect,

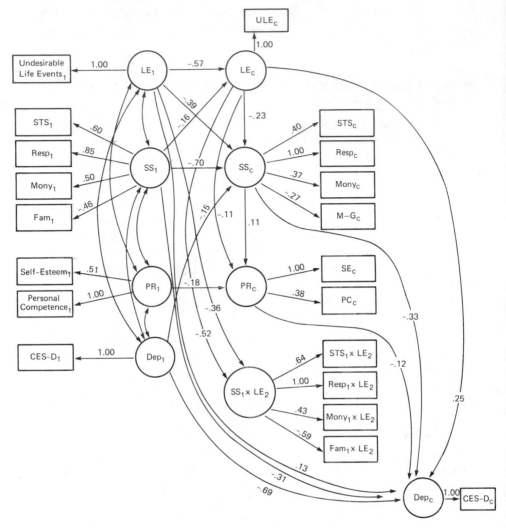

Figure 10.10 Models of changes with the Suppressant Interactive factor ($SS_1 \times LE_2$). Goodness-of-fit index = .80.

on change in depression. This variable has a slight contemporaneous effect on change in depression, but it has no mediating role to the impacts of undesirable life events or social support.

5. The Suppressant Interactive factor ($SS_1 \times LE_2$) has no effect on change in depression.

Thus, the results affirm the additive effects, both direct and indirect, of social support and, to a much lesser extent, of undesirable life events. The Suppressive Interactive factor, when considered jointly with these additive effects, makes no further contribution to the explanation of depression and its change.

The finding that personal-coping resources show slight stability over time and make little additional contribution to those made by social support and undesirable life events may be due, in part, to its overlap with depression symptoms. This result challenges the view that self-esteem and personal competence can be treated as measures of psychological traits and as factors independent of measures of psychiatric distress such as depression. The scope and purpose of this book do not allow us to further explore the consequences of these implications. Nevertheless, future research needs to take note of this possible conceptual and measurement issue.

Model of Changes with the Contemporaneous Interactive Factor ($SS_1 \times LE_1$)

In the next model, all the additive components from the previous model were retained. The Suppressant Interactive factor ($SS_1 \times LE_2$), because it did not make any significant contribution, was dropped and replaced by the Contemporaneous Interactive factor ($SS_1 \times LE_1$). Again, to keep the model simple, the assumption of no correlation between any error terms among the indicators was made. The results (appearing in Figure 10.11) are similar to those found in the previous model. Social support and undesirable life events retain their respective direct and indirect effects on change in depression. The Contemporaneous Interactive factor shows no direct effects and few indirect ones through change in personal resources. Psychological resources have only a slight contemporaneous effect on change in depression (as shown by the path from PR_c to Dep_c).

Model of Changes with the Mediating Interactive Factor ($LE_1 \times SS_2$)

The last model incorporates all the additive components plus the Mediating Interactive factor ($LE_1 \times SS_2$). Again, the interactive factor failed to show any significant relationship with change in depression (see Figure 10.12). The maximal likelihood estimates and their standard errors are presented in Table 10.3.

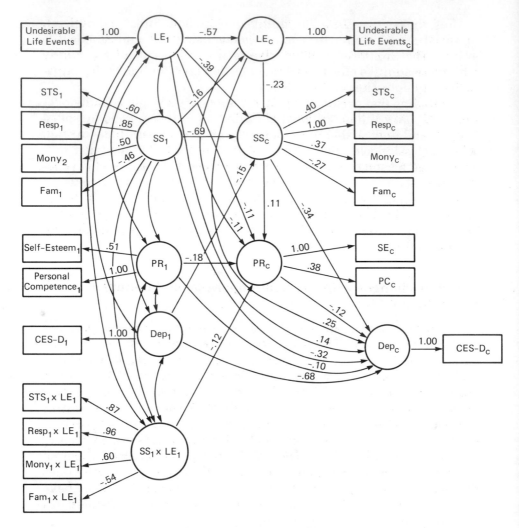

Figure 10.11 Models of changes with the Contemporaneous Interactive factor ($SS_1 \times LE_1$). Goodness-of-fit index = .81.

CONCLUSIONS

This chapter began by proposing 12 models to examine plausible causal relationships among social support, life events, and depression. These models specified additive and interactive contributions as well as time-lagged and contemporaneous effects. A review of previous

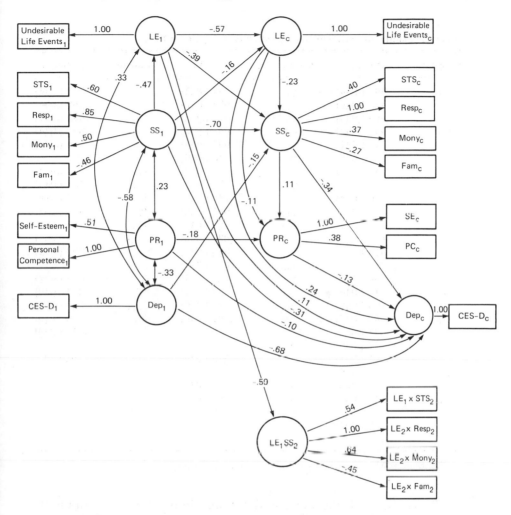

Figure 10.12 Model of changes with the Mediating Interactive factor ($LE_1 \times SS_2$)

studies pointed to confirmation of the independent or compensating effect of social support and to probable confirmation of the moderating (mediating) effect. Most confirming evidence was provided by cross-sectional rather than panel data.

We then examined these plausible models with the Albany data (T1 and T2). These models consider both additive and interactive components while controlling for depressive symptoms at T1 and for personal coping resources and their changes over time. The major findings are as follows:

TABLE 10.3
Maximum Likelihood Estimates for the Models in Figure 10.12

Parameter	Estimate	Parameter	Estimate	Parameter	Estimate
λ_{y1}	.397 (.034)[a]	γ_3	−.057 (.033)[a]	ψ_1	.725 (.038)[a]
λ_{y2}	.366 (.034)	γ_4	−.059 (.042)	ψ_2	.686 (.043)
λ_{y3}	−.273 (.035)	γ_5	−.386 (.046)	ψ_3	.952 (.049)
λ_{y4}	.384 (.034)	γ_6	−.697 (.057)	ψ_4	.655 (.034)
λ_{y5}	.544 (.031)	γ_7	.093 (.035)	ψ_5	.516 (.028)
λ_{y6}	.637 (.028)	γ_8	−.146 (.046)		
λ_{y7}	−.447 (.033)	γ_9	−.048 (.053)	$\theta_{\varepsilon22}$	.843 (.044)
		γ_{10}	.079 (.072)	$\theta_{\varepsilon44}$	.866 (.045)
λ_{x1}	.596 (.035)	γ_{11}	−.182 (.038)	$\theta_{\varepsilon55}$	.926 (.048)
λ_{x2}	.850 (.032)	γ_{12}	.021 (.049)	$\theta_{\varepsilon77}$	.852 (.044)
λ_{x3}	.498 (.037)	γ_{13}	−.590 (.044)	$\theta_{\varepsilon88}$	.704 (.036)
λ_{x4}	−.460 (.037)	γ_{14}	.092 (.060)	$\theta_{\varepsilon10,10}$	.594 (.031)
λ_{x5}	.513 (.031)	γ_{15}	−.018 (.032)	$\theta_{\varepsilon11,11}$	.800 (.041)
		γ_{16}	.038 (.041)		
β_1	−.234 (.039)	γ_{17}	.105 (.045)	$\theta_{\delta22}$	.645 (.037)
β_2	−.110 (.044)	γ_{18}	−.308 (.057)	$\theta_{\delta33}$	.277 (.030)
β_3	.108 (.047)	γ_{19}	−.099 (.029)	$\theta_{\delta44}$	.752 (.041)
β_4	−.082 (.037)	γ_{20}	−.682 (.038)	$\theta_{\delta55}$	.789 (.043)
β_5	.037 (.039)			$\theta_{\delta56}$	.737 (.038)
β_6	−.052 (.030)	ϕ_{21}	−.465 (.032)		
β_7	.244 (.033)	ϕ_{31}	−.076 (.036)	χ^2	1988.49
β_8	−.335 (.036)	ϕ_{32}	.227 (.038)	df	145
β_9	−.125 (.028)	ϕ_{41}	.329 (.031)		
β_{10}	−.013 (.033)	ϕ_{42}	−.581 (.028)		
		ϕ_{43}	−.326 (.031)		
γ_1	−.565 (.037)				
γ_2	−.163 (.050)				

[a]The standard errors of the estimates are given in parentheses.

1. Social support has a strong direct and independent (compensating) effect on depression and its change (regression coefficients in the .30s), both contemporaneously and over time. It also serves, to a lesser extent, as a mediating factor between prior undesirable life events and change in depression (with a coefficient of about .13, or −.39 × −.33). Further, it has a moderate suppressant effect on change in undesirable life events (−.16).

2. Strong-Tie (confidant) Support and Instrumental–Expressive Supports are optimal indicators of social support. Community and network supports do not exert a direct impact on depression but seem to provide the context within which effective Strong-Tie (confidant) Support and Instrumental–Expressive Supports are formed.

3. Undesirable life events have a somewhat less but still significant direct effect, both contemporaneously and over time, on change in depression (with coefficients of about .24 and .13, respectively). Some of the indirect effect is mediated through changes in social support.

4. No evidence was found of any effect exerted by the interactions between social support and undesirable life events beyond what these variables have contributed additively toward the explanation of depression and its change.

5. Psychological resources (self-esteem and personal competence) show only slight effects on change in depression (with coefficients of about $-.13$ and $\subseteq.10$ for contemporaneous and over-time effects, respectively). The effect is not mediated by other factors. Also, as far as our measures are concerned, theories concerning psychological resources as mediators are not supported.

Therefore, in the remaining chapters of this book, we focus on the additive effects of social support and life events and examine their varying effects on depression due to other factors (e.g., age, gender, marital status, social class, health history, etc.). Psychological resources and interactive effects are not further pursued. We realize that it is possible that these factors may have some effects in certain subgroups of respondents. But their overall effects are so minimal as not to justify the complexity of retaining them in further analysis. It is also clear that confidant strong-tie support and instrumental–expressive supports are optimal indicators of social support and will be used as such in subsequent analyses.

Part V

EXPLORING BASIC MODELS

Following the comprehensive examination of the basic models involving social support, life events, psychological resources, and depression in Part IV, Part V proceeds to examine the reduced basic model in terms of a number of factors, such as age, sex, marital status, social class, and history of prior illness. The fundamental question to be addressed is whether and to what extent the estimated relations among social support, life events, and depression are affected or conditioned by these factors.

Each of these factors has been offered as a major predictor of mental health and several have been considered as explanatory factors in their own right. We do not view variables in the basic model as being in competition with these factors as explanations. Rather, our position is that specification of these factors further elaborates and thus clarifies the relationships among social support, life events, and depression.

For each of these factors, a brief introduction to their usage in the literature as an independent variable in the prediction of mental health is provided. The basic model is then examined with regard to identifiable categories of the factors. Attention is given to similarities and differences in the relationships among social support, life events, and depression across the categories. This research strategy allows us to further specify the dynamics of the basic model under different conditions and to bring the contributions of the factors into the analysis and interpretation.

We do not claim that the analytic strategies used are the only methods available or appropriate. The substantive issues and nature of the measures involved dictate the selection of analytical strategies. Critical issues are addressed with the analytic strategies that are deemed appropriate. At all times, the major focus is to describe how the basic model varies across different conditions and situations.

11

The Age Structure and the
Stress Process

NAN LIN

WALTER M. ENSEL

ALFRED DEAN

There is increasing recognition that studies of the relationship between stressors, social supports, and depression need to take the factor
of age into consideration. Though it is obvious that the nature of social
supports varies over the life course, this has not been a matter of much
investigation. Thus Kahn (1979a) has called for the study of the *convoy
of social support* over the life course. Cobb (1976, 1979) has noted that
there are various orders of evidence that various types or elements of
social support have health consequences virtually from birth. Because
most of the epidemiological studies of stressors and supports are quite
recent, it is not surprising that studies that take the age factor into
consideration are even more recent and more limited. Early in our own
work we began to find clues that age was influencing our epidemiologic
models. We began progressively to attempt to clarify and to specify
both conceptually and empirically the nature and implications of the
age factor.

The present chapter explores two fundamental issues: (1) How age
should be conceived of in the analysis of our model of social support,

213

SOCIAL SUPPORT,
LIFE EVENTS, AND DEPRESSION

life events, and depression, and (2) what effects social support and life events have on depression in the context of age.

Given the lack of panel data over long periods, age can be considered as a surrogate indicator of the aging process or of life stages. This indicator is crude, because age cannot by itself tease out the period effect (e.g., the Great Depression or the Second World War). However, it does reflect the developmental and social phases of life. When it is used as a continuous variable, one can examine its relationship (both linear and nonlinear) to depression. Because the life-course literature informs us that life stages are segmented rather than transitional, our expectation is that the simple relationship between age and depression will not be significant or meaningful.

If this is indeed the case, it is then necessary to identify the life stages. Rather than setting up the age categories according to conventions (e.g., 18–24, 25–34, 35–44, 45–54, etc., or 18–24, 25–40, 41–64, etc.), we choose to conduct some empirical analysis to determine groupings. In this chapter we explore the relationship between age and certain basic sociodemographic variables (e.g., education, occupational prestige, family income, employment status), history of illness, life events, and social support. The purpose of this exploration is to ascertain if there are consistent age-related patterns across these variables. For example, if the educational level increases linearly between ages 18 and 24 but decreases or stabilizes beyond 24, the household size also increases during the period, and distribution of other variables show distinctive trends (increasing or decreasing), then the ages 18–24 can be said to constitute a significant age category reflecting a life stage. These analyses should help to identify a series of age categories reflecting life stages relevant to social, demographic, and physical health characteristics.

The empirical delineation of life stages and transitions is a prerequisite to the second major objective of this chapter: namely, an examination of the effects of life events and social supports in the context of different life stages. This is an area that is long on speculation or assumption and short on empirical evidence. Emerging findings are beginning to challenge conventional wisdom. For example, there has been a wide professional as well as popular conviction that the elderly have high rates of depression and low levels of social support. On the other hand, a number of studies, including our own, indicate that the highest rates of depression are in young adults, that the social support of the elderly is generally both objectively and subjectively favorable, and that life events contribute more to the expression of depression among the young than among the elderly. Similarly, there is growing evidence that retirement per se is not a significant stressor. In general, if we expect that the nature of life events and social supports vary significantly in the age structure, we would expect to observe significant variations in the epidemiologic functions of these variables in different life stages. Given the present state of knowledge in this area, it is not possible to offer systematic hypotheses about such variations. Thus the main objective of this inquiry is to examine empirical data, formulate hypotheses, and propose theoretical formulations. Subsequently, as we describe our approaches and findings, we also cite some of the relevant work by others in this area.

The delineation of age categories employs the panel data at Time 1. The analysis of effects of social support and life events on depression will use both the Time 1 (T1) and Time 2 (T2) data, so that time-lagged effects as well as contemporaneous effects can be assessed.

RELATIONSHIP BETWEEN AGE AND DEPRESSION

The first task is to determine the extent to which there is a discernible linear trend between depression and age. A zero-order correlation was computed between age and the CES-D (the Center for Epidemiological Studies Depression Scale) for the T1 data. The coefficient, $-.13$, statistically significant, suggested a negative trend in depression from the younger toward older age. In general, then, the younger respondents rather than the older respondents were more likely to report higher levels of depression. However, the trend was not substantial. To further explore this trend, we dichotomized the depression scores into two groups: (1) those scoring 16 or more on the Center for Epidemiological Studies Depression Scale, usually considered to differentiate those possibly clinically depressed (Myers et al., 1979), and (2) those scoring 15 or less. This dichotomized variable correlated only $-.06$ with age. Thus, there is no significant evidence by this measure that the incidence of possible clinical depression is related to age.

In order to detect any nonlinear trends of depression over age, we plotted the mean depression scores for all ages. This is shown in Figure 11.1. A visual examination indicated that there was a slight negative tendency between age and depression from 18 years of age to about 50 years of age. Then there was a slight positive trend toward depression from age 50 on. The mean level of depression, however, remained lower for this older category than for the young. These data were too scattered to provide any definitive conclusions about the relationship between age and depression. However, the distributions of sociodemo-

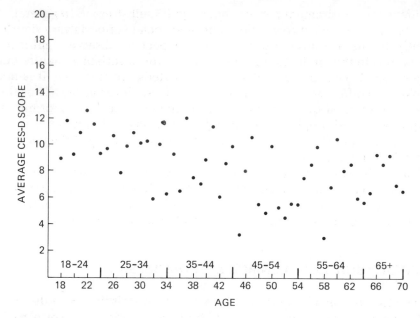

Figure 11.1   Mean depression (CES-D) score by age, Albany Area Health Study.

graphic variables, life events, social support, and prior illness over age were further examined for potential cutoff points in age.

CONSTRUCTION OF AGE CATEGORIES

The purpose of plotting the distribution of these variables over age is to determine whether they can collectively shed light on how age is segmented—that is, whether distinct age categories can be identified because of their distinct patterns along these variables. If such age segments or categories can be identified, then we may examine whether or not there are different causal patterns for depression in each age category.

The variables selected for examination include (1) sociodemographic variables—education, family income, occupational prestige, being employed, being married, household size; (2) total illnesses; (3) total life events; and (4) social support. The purpose, as mentioned earlier, is to identify socially and physically relevant life stages. Therefore, the basic sociodemographic variables along with the physical health variable (total illnesses) are used.

Also included are the two independent variables in the basic model: life events and social support. It would be useful to uncover age segments that reveal the point when life events or social support increases or decreases. Past research suggests that young adults experience many life events and little social support, whereas older adults experience relatively few life events and substantial social support. Whether these trends change smoothly or abruptly over age is the focus of the current work. Further, the degree to which these patterns exist in similar or different age categories, as identified in the distributions of the sociodemographic and health characteristics, needs to be ascertained. A finding that the same age categories are meaningful across sociodemographic, health, life event, and social support variables would add credence to the identification of age categories or groupings.

Figure 11.2 presents the distributions as plotted against age of marital status (percentage married), number of persons in household, family income, average education level, percentage employed, occupational prestige (Siegel's NORC scale), and illnesses in the past 2 years. A psychological variable, self-esteem (Rosenberg, 1965), was also plotted against age, but it showed no significant relationships either linearly ($r = .09$) or nonlinearly (the mean scale scores ranged from 20.5 to 23.4, with no visible patterns for any category of age).

Two visible inflection points were determined, at age 24–25 and at age 49–50. For example, percentage married reached its high plateau around age 25–26 and started decreasing only after the mid-fifties. The number of people in the household started increasing around age 25, peaked at age 50, and then continuously decreased from 50 on. There was a significant trend of increasing family income from age 18 to 24, then a less steep increase from age 25 to 49, and a decreasing trend from 50 on. Education increased from age 18 to 24, slightly decreased from age 25 to 49, and decreased more significantly from age 50 on. This educational distribution no doubt reflected the historical cohort effect, because more and more people have stayed longer in the educational system over the years. However, as this linear cohort trend continued, its effect on age categories became, in fact, part of the aging effect. Employment status and occupational prestige for those employed showed a significant increasing trend from age 18 to the mid-twenties, a slower increase, and then a decrease to the mid-fifties. The trend became erratic from the mid-fifties on. This last segment reflected, in part, divergent career developments: for some, gradual disengagement from the labor force and for others, further acceleration in occupational status as they continued to climb toward the upper echelons of the occupational structure. Prior illness (in the last two years) showed a

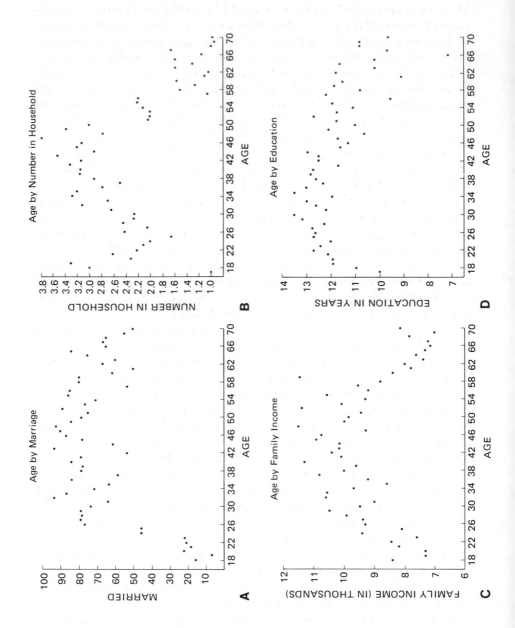

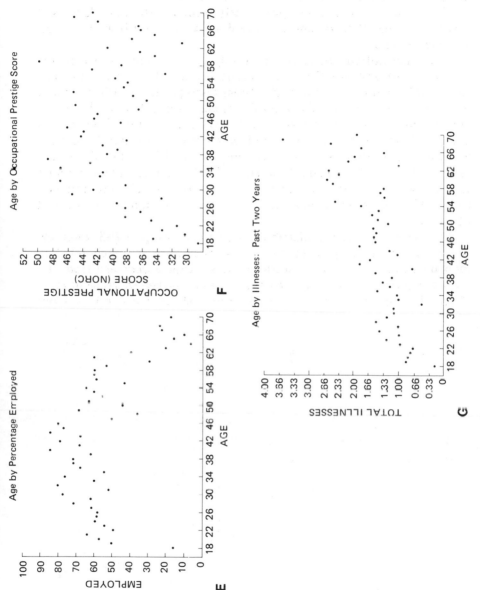

Figure 11.2 Distribution of demographics, prior illness, and stressful life events by age, Albany Area Health Study.

continuous but slow increase from age 19 to the late forties, and dras-
tically increased from then on (see Figure 11.2).

Life events (LE) increased significantly from age 18 to 24, decreased
slowly from age 25 to 49, and remained a low constant from age 50 on
(see Figure 11.3).

These distributions led us to tentatively identify three age segments:
18–24, 25–49, and 50+. These age categories seem to experience differential socioeconomic and health–illness changes. In the 18–24 group,
increasing educational and occupational achievement, as well as family formation and expansion, are coupled with increasing life events. In
the 25–49 group, occupational and economic status slowly reach a
peak, and the family structure reaches its maturity. The life events
begin to decrease in number. Finally, in the 50+ group, socioeconomic
status slowly declines and the family structure is significantly reduced
in size. The last age group experiences a significant increase in physical
illnesses.

We next examined the distribution of social support (SS) over age
(shown in Figure 11.4). Level of social support showed somewhat of an
increase from age 18 to the mid-twenties. After a decrease from the
mid-twenties to the early thirties, there was a marked increase in level
of social support. Those age 50 and older showed a continued but

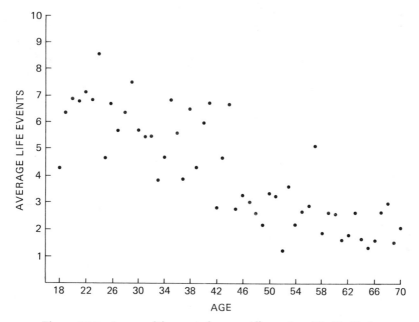

Figure 11.3 Average life events by age, Albany Area Health Study.

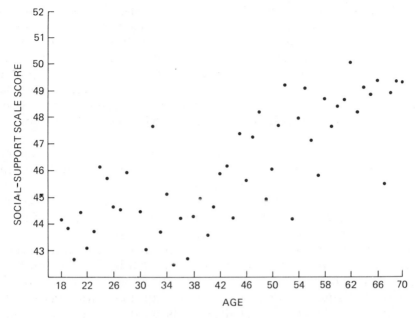

Figure 11.4   Mean social support (SS) scores by age, Albany Area Health Study.

slower rate (the slope) of increase in level of social support, which then peaked in the late sixties. This reflects, in part, the growth and maturity of support systems over the years, which appear to stabilize in the late twenties and to show a rapid increase until the early fifties.

Thus, the socioeconomic variables, life events, and social support all showed differential distribution across three age categories: 18–24, 25–49, and 50 and over. Again, we must interpret these results with caution, as they might reflect cohort as well as aging processes. It is clear, nevertheless, that they combine to reflect different life segments or passages in life. As shown, these are very much dictated by one's socioeconomic role and by the status expectations and requirements of our society. It is, therefore, important and meaningful that analysis of relationships between social support and depression be conducted separately for the different age groups.

AGE-RELATED EFFECTS OF LIFE EVENTS AND SOCIAL SUPPORT ON DEPRESSION

In determining the age-related role of life events and social support in the epidemiology of depression, the three causal sequences presented in Chapter 10 are tested: (1) contemporaneous effects of social support and life events, (2) social support following life events, and (3) social support preceding life events. Table 11.1 shows the results of the analysis for the three age groups. For this analysis, the dependent variable is depression (CES-D) at T2. The measure of social support is Strong-Tie Support (STS), and the indicator of life events is the total number of undesirable life events (ULE). These measures are discussed elsewhere in the book (CES-D in Chapter 4; STS in Chapter 8; and ULE in Chapters 5 and 10).

For the contemporaneous model, both life events and social support in T1 exert a direct effect on depression in T2. There are no significant age-related differences in the magnitude of the effect of life events and social support on depression except in the 25–49-year-old group, where life events explain significantly more of the variation in depression than for either of the other groups.

In examining the second model, in which undesirable life events preceded social support, social support exerts a large direct effect on depression across the age groups, accounting for the majority of the variance explained in depression. Two additional findings can be noted: (1) The direct effect of life events on depression in the 50+ group is somewhat less than for the other age groups, and (2) the two variables explain less variance in depression after age 50 than they do for the younger ages (16% compared to 25%). In this model, subsequent social support is found to mediate the effects of life events on depression in all age groups (the correlations between ULE_1 and SS_2 are $-.11$, $-.23$, and $-.14$ for the three age groups, respectively).

Finally, in the model where social support precedes life events, social support also performs the function of suppressing the occurrence of undesirable life events in all age groups. The correlations between STS_1 and ULE_2 are $-.07$, $-.10$, and $-.14$ for the three age groups, respectively. However, life events maintain a strong direct effect on depressive symptoms regardless of age. Life events and social support explain significantly less of the variation in depression in the older group (50+) than they do in the two younger groups (18–24 and 25–49).

In summary, we find significant direct effects of social support and undesirable life events on depression; these effects are stronger when the two factors are measured closer in time to the measure of depression. Further, social support mediates the effects of previous undesirable life events as well as suppressing the likelihood of subsequent undesirable life events. Finally, these effects of social support and life events on depression are stronger for the 18–49-year-old respondents than for those age 50 and older.

TABLE 11.1

Regression of Depression (CES-D) at Time 2 on Life Events and Social Support for Three Age Groups in the Albany Area Health Study: A Test of the Three Models[a]

	Age Groups								
	13–24			25–49			50+		
Model	Unstandardized B	Unstandardized SE	Standardized beta	Unstandardized B	Unstandardized SE	Standardized beta	Unstandardized B	Unstandardized SE	Standardized beta
Contemporaneous effects of STS and ULE									
ULE_1	.576	.326	.158	.907	.203	.214	.869	.395	.130
STS_1	−.988	.611	−.146	−1.39	.431	−.155	−1.14	.503	−.133
Constant	14.35			18.43			15.63		
Error of estimate	8.27			9.54			8.99		
R^2	.059			.088			.042		
STS following ULE									
ULE_1	.538	.589	.148	.658	.184	.155	.689	.365	.103
STS_2	−3.62	.279	−.471	−3.30	.330	−.433	−3.20	−.374	−.466
Constant	34.01			32.47			31.28		
Error of estimate	7.34			8.69			8.41		
R^2	.259			.234			.162		
STS preceding ULE									
STS_1	−1.14	.560	−.167	−1.49	.376	−.166	−1.06	.487	−.124
ULE_2	1.18	.296	.327	1.90	.172	.464	1.46	.340	.244
Constant	14.47			17.51			14.34		
Error of estimate	7.89			8.60			8.79		
R^2	.142			.258			.084		

[a]CES-D = Center for Epidemiological Studies Depression Scale. ULE = Total undesirable life events. STS = Strong-tie support (two-item scale).

FURTHER AGE-GROUP REFINEMENTS

One potential criticism of this analysis is that the older age category
fails to distinguish a critical phase in the life course: retirement. Therefore, the oldest age group (50–71) is separated into two groups: the
preretirement (50–64 years of age) and postretirement (65+) groups.
Justification for this particular cutoff point can be found in the existing
literature (Blazer, 1980; Linn, Hunter, and Harris, 1980; Fenwick and
Barresi, 1981; Mutran and Reitzes, 1981).

Table 11.2 shows the results of the analysis of the two older age
groupings, 50–64 and 65+. For the 50–64 category, the direct effect of
social support on depression is significant for two of the three models
and nearly significant for the third one. Thus, social support shows a
contemporaneous effect (Model 1), a mediating effect (Model 2; the
correlation between ULE_1 and STS_2 was $-.15$), and, to a lesser extent, a
suppressing effect (Model 3; the correlation between STS_1 and ULE_2 is
$-.21$) on undesirable life events for this group of respondents. However, for the 65+ group, social support only shows a mediating effect
(Model 2; the correlation between ULE_1 and STS_2 is $-.11$).

Undesirable life events show a lagged effect (Model 2) and contemporaneous effects (Models 1 and 3) on depression in the 50–64 group, but
no direct effect on depression for the 65+ group. Thus, it is clear that
the effects of both social support and life events decrease significantly
after 64 years of age. For the 65+ group, life events show no direct
impact on depression, although an indirect effect mediated by social
support can be seen.

SUMMARY AND IMPLICATIONS

This chapter explores age as a conditioning variable in examining the
effects of social support and life events on depression. As a first step,
we used a number of sociodemographic characteristics as well as life
events and social support to determine if there were age segments within which linear trends could be detected regarding the relationship of
these variables to age. Results showed consistent trends for three age
segments, 18–24, 25–49, and 50+; that is, trends within each age segment seemed to be in a clear and linear direction. For example, life
events increased between 18 and 24 years of age, decreased between 25
and 49, and remained low for individuals over 50.

Analysis of the effects of social support and life events on depression
for each age group ascertained which of the three models specified in
Chapter 10 was valid. In early adulthood, the transitional nature of

TABLE 11.2

Regression of Depression at Time 2 (CES-D) on Life Events and Social Support for Those Age 50–64 and 65 and Over, Albany Area Health Study[a]

Model	Age groups					
	50–64			65+		
	Unstandardized B	Unstandardized SE	Standardized beta	Unstandardized B	Unstandardized SE	Standardized beta
Contemporaneous effects of STS and ULE						
ULE_1	1.00	.484	.152	.210	.751	.029
STS_1	−1.25	.664	−.138	−.718	.763	−.098
Constant	16.38			12.77		
Error of estimate	9.54			7.82		
R^2	.054			.010		
STS following ULE						
ULE_1	.911	.436	.139	−.162	.696	−.023
STS_2	−3.17	.573	−.367	−3.30	.801	−.397
Constant	30.78			52.79		
Error of estimate	8.94			7.22		
R^2	.169			.156		
STS preceding ULE						
STS_1	−1.12	.629	−.124	−.688	.754	−.094
ULE_2	1.84	.455	.284	.682	.493	.142
Constant	14.53			12.06		
Error of estimate	9.26			7.74		
R^2	.109			.029		

[a]CES-D = Center for Epidemiological Studies Depression Scale. ULE = Total undesirable life events. STS = Strong-tie support (two-item scale).

TABLE 11.3

Relationship of Depression (CES-D) at Time 2 to Life Events and Instrumental Social Support (Excess Responsibilities/Demands) for Four Age Categories in the Albany Area Health Study: A Test of the Three Models

Model[a]	Age groups											
	18–24			25–49			50–64			65+		
	B	SE	Beta	B	SE	Beta	B	SE	Beta	B	SE	Beta
Contemporaneous model												
ULE¹	.591	.329	.162	.670	.205	.158	.989	.498	.150	.001	.001	.001
IE¹F¹	-.245	.181	-.122	-.643	.113	-.275	-.332	.215	-.117	-.486	.305	-.163
Constant	12.90			23.62			15.39			20.29		
Error of estimate	8.29			9.31			9.57			7.71		
R²	.053			.132			.049			.027		
Buffering model												
ULE¹	.097	.269	.027	.328	.188	-.077	-.858	.465	.130	-.267	.691	-.037
IE²F¹	-1.26	.156	-.594	-1.08	.098	-.488	-.645	.184	-.248	-1.11	.253	-.420
Constant	37.78			34.06			23.25			36.62		
Error of estimate	6.81			8.52			9.34			7.15		
R²	.363			.271			.095			.173		
Suppressing Model												
IE¹F¹	-.267	.166	-.133	-.509	.100	-.218	-.246		-.086	-.394	.319	-.132
ULE²	1.165	.299	.323	1.727	.176	.422	1.84		.281	.502	.514	.105
Constant	12.49			18.72			12.26			17.42		
Error of estimate	7.94			8.50			9.30			17.71		
R²	.132			.275			.101			.037		

[a]ULE¹ = Total undesirable life events (T1). ULE² = Total undesirable life events (T2). IE¹F¹ = Excess of responsibilities/demands (T1). IE²F¹ = Excess of responsibilities/demands (T2).

social statuses, roles, and life styles is highlighted. Individuals experience many life events (some of which are undesirable), and they have to rely on social support either to suppress the likelihood of such events, or, when they occur, to mediate their potentially stressful consequences. As adults age, the stabilization of socioeconomic characteristics and social roles reduces the occurrence of life events while social support remains strong and effective. Finally, when work and family roles go through further transitions and closures, life events are again reduced, and social support (especially strong-tie support) undergoes changes, becoming a less critical factor in the maintenance of one's mental health.

The causal model emerging from this analysis suggests age as an indicator of social passages creating different levels of life changes, which in turn have differential effects on social support as it relates to depression. An analysis of other measures of social support (instrumental and expressive) that documents the same age-related patterns appears in Tables 11.3, 11.4, and 11.5.

Although these findings are interesting and interpretable, caveats must be made as to their generalizability. The present chapter focuses its attention on different and simultaneous age categories rather than on cohort or life-course effects. An examination of the latter requires data that are as yet unavailable. For example, such data would allow us to examine whether or not the high rate of life events associated with young adults reflects changes in statuses inherent in this period of life. It may be that this is a life stage in which completely new forms of social ties are being developed and old ones are changing. The high rates of depression in this age group may be results of these changes. By the same token, the high levels of depression in this age group today may be caused by the newly problematic character of intimate and/or family relationships in contemporary society. This would be a potential cohort effect.

It should be noted that the analysis in this chapter is limited to ages 18 to 70. This is a function of the data collected. It remains an important issue as to whether and to what extent the contemporaneous buffering and suppressing models operate for individuals over age 70. It has been documented by others (Atchley, 1980; Bengston and Treas, 1980; Brubaker, 1983) that after age 65 significant social changes do take place. For example, in the age 55–64 group, approximately the same proportions of men and women are married (80% and 70%, respectively). But for those between age 65 and 74, 83% of the males are married, compared to only 50% of the women. More than 40% of the women in this age category are widowed. Finally, after reaching 75,

TABLE 11.4
Relationship of Depression (CES-D) at Time 2 to Life Events and Instrumental Social Support (Lack of Money) for Four Age Categories in the Albany Area Health Study: A Test of the Three Models

	Age groups											
	18–24			25–49			50–64			65+		
Model[a]	B	SE	Beta	B	SE	Beta	B	SE	Beta	B	SE	Beta
Contemporaneous model												
ULE^1	.653	.325	.179	.825	.208	.195	.849	.481	.129	.001	.001	.001
IE^1F^2	-.253	.276	-.082	-.684	.185	-.181	-.806	.293	-.202	-.243	.348	-.072
Constant	9.21			14.29			15.25			10.00		
Error of estimate	8.33			9.50			9.44			7.80		
R^2	.046			.094			.074			.005		
Buffering model												
ULE^1	.529	.311	.145	.781	.196	.184	.677	.475	.103	.100	.743	.014
IE^2F^2	-.779	.253	-.263	-.989	.616	-.285	-1.03	.274	-.272	-.545	.335	-.167
Constant	14.05			16.10			17.50			13.04		
Error of estimate	8.06			9.25			9.29			7.75		
R^2	.106			.142			.103			.028		
Suppressing Model												
IE^1F^2	-.377	.256	-.122	-.578	.162	-.153	-.715	.278	-.179	-.246	.347	-.073
ULE^2	1.22	.298	.337	1.837	.176	.448	1.73	.454	.265	.690	.494	.144
Constant	9.34			11.67			13.39			9.41		
Error of estimate	7.95			8.63			9.18			7.76		
R^2	.130			.253			.125			.026		

[a] ULE^1 = Undesirable life events (T1). ULE^2 = Undesirable life events (T2). IE^1F^2 = Lack of money (T1). IE^2F^2 = Lack of money (T2).

TABLE 11.5

Relationship of Depression (CES-D) at Time 2 to Life Events and Expressive Social Support (Unsatisfactory Intimate Relations) for Four Age Categories in the Albany Area Health Study: A Test of the Three Models

| | Age groups | | | | | | | | | | | |
| | 18–24 | | | 25–49 | | | 50–64 | | | 65+ | | |
Model[a]	B	SE	Beta	B	SE	Beta	B	SE	Beta	B	SE	Beta
Contemporaneous model												
ULE^1	.656	.323	.180	.667	.204	.157	.927	.515	.141	.104	.740	.014
IE^1F^3	−.396	.359	−.098	−1.34	.229	−.282	−.660	.395	−.131	−.835	.368	−.233
Constant	12.83			28.38			17.02			20.03		
Error of estimate	8.31			9.39			9.56			7.64		
R^2	.049			.135			.052			.054		
Buffering model												
ULE^1	.405	.278	.111	.385	.176	.091	1.06	.448	.162	.001	.001	.001
IE^2F^3	−2.01	.306	−.502	−2.26	.174	−.540	−1.52	.337	−.306	−1.56	.386	−.386
Constant	37.06			41.94			29.80			31.21		
Error of estimate	7.21			8.17			9.15			7.21		
R^2	.284			.330			.130			.149		
Suppressing Model												
IE^1F^3	−.413	.339	−.102	−1.19	.199	−.249	−.625	.360	−.124	.575	.491	.120
ULE^2	1.19	.302	.329	1.76	.171	.429	1.83	.466	.280	−.790	.367	−.220
Constant	12.21			24.26			15.52			18.91		
Error of estimate	7.98			8.41			9.26			7.59		
R^2	.125			.250			.109			.068		

[a] ULE^1 = Undesirable life events (T1). ULE^2 = Undesirable life events (T2). IE^1F^3 = Unsatisfactory intimate relations (T1). IE^2F^3 = Unsatisfactory intimate relations (T2).

although 70% of the men are married, less than 25% of the women are. In this age category, 25% of the males are widowed, compared to 70% of the women. Clearly, the death of a spouse is an important and devastating event that occurs more in the older age categories than in the younger ones. By definition, these losses present a potential disruption and/or change in the type and nature of social support available to these individuals. According to these census figures, the potential impact appears to be greater for elderly women (70% of whom are widowed) than for elderly men.

12

Sex, Marital Status, and Depression: The Role of Life Events and Social Support

WALTER M. ENSEL

GENDER, MARITAL STATUS, AND DEPRESSION: A REVIEW

Perhaps the most consistently documented finding in epidemiological research over the past several decades is the fact that females are more depressed than males (Gove, 1972; Gove and Tudor, 1973; Pearlin, 1974; Weissman and Klerman, 1977; G. W. Brown and Harris, 1978; Gove, 1978; Steele, 1978). This finding is consistent regardless of whether we are examining depressive symptomatology in a community sample, help-seeking for emotional problems in psychiatric outpatient clinics, or mental illness in mental hospitals.

Recent literature on sex differences in depression has focused on the nature of roles experienced by individuals. This approach is tied to the sex-role perspective first proposed by Gove (1972). According to Gove, men generally have multiple major roles (e.g., worker, breadwinner, household head), whereas married women generally occupy only one major role, that of housewife. Further, whereas men find their roles

231

satisfying, women find their major role frustrating and demanding. The combination of the monotony and low prestige of these women's status is not, according to Gove, consonant with the educational attainments of women in our society. As a result of the unstructured role of the housewife, Gove sees a tendency for women to brood over their troubles. Other researchers have followed upon this approach and have attempted to explain sex differences in depression among the married in terms of role strain (Fox, 1980) and more recently in terms of traditional and nontraditional sex-role relationships (Rosenfield, 1980) and family roles (Aneshensel, Frerichs, and Clark, 1981).

Rosenfield (1980) found that females had higher rates of depression than males only in traditional sex-role marriages. Among nontraditional couples, males were found to be more depressed. However, the generalizability of this finding has been questioned by Roberts and O'Keefe (1981), who are replicating Rosenfield's study with a community sample that failed to confirm Rosenfield's results for males and females in nontraditional marriages. Aneshensel and her associates (1981) found male–female differences in depression among the married only for those with children in the household; in such cases, married females (both working and nonworking) tended to be more depressed than males. Meile, Johnson, and St. Peter (1976) have cast some doubts on these strict sex-role explanations of depression, asserting that socioeconomic differences in marital roles may be a factor in explaining differences in depression between the married and unmarried.

More recently, research on sex differences in depression has focused on the role played by stressful life events. Dohrenwend (1973) has found that although there are no gender differences in the number of life events experienced by males and females, the impact of life events on emotional distress is significantly greater for females than for males. This has been further documented by Radloff and Rae (1981) and elaborated upon by Belle (1982) and Dean and Ensel (1983). Others (Kessler and McLeod, 1984; Stroebe and Stroebe, 1983) have attempted to show that this general finding cannot be applied universally to all life events. That is, according to Stroebe and Stroebe (1983), women are better able to deal with the loss of a spouse than are their male counterparts. Coupled with the suggestion (Dohrenwend, 1977) that certain life events may be sex-typed (i.e., females are more likely than males to report events dealing with their social network), it may well be the case that the relationship between sex, life events, and depression is conditioned by the type (rather than the quantity) of life events experienced. Nevertheless, life events have been consistently documented as affecting the sex–depression relationship.

Less definitive than the findings about sex differences in depression is the current debate in the literature regarding the role marital status plays in the sex–depression relationship. Generally speaking, nonmarried individuals have higher rates of depression than do married individuals. This finding has been consistently reported in epidemiological literature for the past 25 years (Gurin et al., 1960; Blumenthal, 1970; Gove and Tudor, 1973; Briscoe and Smith, 1974; Radloff, 1975; Pearlin and Johnson, 1977; Warheit, Holzer, Bell, and Arey, 1976; Ensel, 1982). What has not been consistent during the last 25 years are the explanations for the lower levels of depression among the married compared to the single, separated, divorced, or widowed. Earlier research (Gurin et al., 1960) posited that marriage is the expected norm for individuals. That is, socialization in early life is designed to prepare individuals for the institution of marriage. Marriage is seen as the most emotionally stable state of adult life. Single individuals, by this definition, are seen as going against the norm. These "deviants" are therefore constantly subjected to normative pressure to conform. The failure to do so is seen as contributing to a less than desirable psychological state. Gove (1972), on the other hand, although replicating Gurin's finding that women have higher rates of mental illness than males, found that when unmarried (single, divorced, widowed) males are compared to their female counterparts, women do not show higher rates of mental illness.

More recently, research on the relationship of marital status to depression has focused on two themes: (1) the role of life events in the relationship between marital status and depression, and (2) marital disruption as a stressor. The first perspective is best evidenced in the work of Pearlin and Johnson (1977). The approach taken here is to examine the relationships among marital status, life strains, and depression. Arguing that contemporary research on marital status and depression has ignored the stressful life events that occur in everyday life, Pearlin and Johnson examine the consequences of various stressful conditions of life to which married and unmarried individuals are exposed. Two types of life strains (economic hardship and social isolation) are found to differentially affect levels of depression for married and unmarried individuals. Generally the unmarried, when faced with these strains, are more likely to be depressed than are their married counterparts. They are also found to be more vulnerable to these strains.

The second theme, marital disruption as a stressor, links separation and divorce to a higher rate of depression and emotional disorder. According to this perspective, the change from one status to another (i.e., being married and becoming separated or divorced) is viewed as resulting in depression. According to this perspective, divorce and separation are viewed as the stressful life events leading to depression. In a review of the literature on this topic, Bloom, Asher, and White (1978) critically examine studies of individuals who have undergone marital changes and the various hypotheses that have been tested by various researchers. One of the major problems in this literature, according to them, is the fact that few researchers have focused on marital history, settling instead for current marital status. Thus the individual who is identified as being currently married may have just undergone a traumatic divorce from a former spouse. Although we might expect that the status of being married would be associated with a low level of depressive symptomatology, this case might very well prove to be an exception. By the same token, a divorce or separation does not necessarily have to be a stressor. Consider the male or female experiencing severe marital problems such as constant fighting between spouses. A separation or divorce may very well serve to improve the psychological well-being of either member of the marriage unit. In short, the marital history of a person as well as an assessment of the desirability of the particular marital status under study are two important factors that must be taken into account when marital disruption is theorized to be a stressor.

Finally, there has been some research on the relationship between sex, marital status, life events, and depression. This is best typified and summarized in the work of Cleary and Mechanic (1983). Examining the part played by a variety of role-satisfaction variables and stressors, Cleary and Mechanic found that (1) females in general were more depressed than males; (2) married women who were not working were slightly more depressed than working women but significantly more depressed than working married males; (3) married women who were employed were significantly more depressed than were their male counterparts; and (4) the stress associated with working and being responsible for raising children were dominant factors in the higher rate of depression among married women. Although the study does provide limited support for the sex-role perspective as well as for the importance of the role played by stress in the relationship between sex, marital status, and depression, it is somewhat limited in that it excludes a large percentage of individuals (i.e., males and females who are divorced, widowed, or have never married). The failure to take unmarried males and females into account leaves many questions to be answered.

Although research on sex and marital-status differences in depression has proliferated, it should be obvious from the above review that each of the perspectives currently holding attention in the literature has its weaknesses. The life-strain approach fails to account for why married individuals experience high life stress do not manifest as high a level of depressive symptomatology as do their unmarried counterparts. The marital-disruption-as-a-stressor perspective fails to acknowledge the potential positive effects of marital disruption. Finally, the sex-role perspective assumes that the majority of married women are housewives and that the singularity of this role is the cause of depression. Other researchers (Fox, 1980; Ensel, 1982) have not found this to be the case. In fact, according to recent census reports, more than 60% of women between the ages of 18 to 64 are currently in the work force. Additionally, it has been documented (Ensel, 1982) that it is the loss of (e.g., becoming unemployed) and the addition of (e.g., going to school) roles among women rather than the singularity of a role (being a housewife) that leads to higher rates of depressive symptomatology among females.

All of the weaknesses in the current approaches to examining sex and marital-status differences in depression share a common theme: the confounding of marital status as a stressor and/or as a social support.

THE CONFOUNDING ISSUE: MARITAL STATUS AS A STRESSOR OR AS A SOCIAL SUPPORT

The fact that marital disruption is often a stressor cannot be disputed. However, the use of marital disruption as a single indicator of stress overlooks a wide variety of potential stressors (economic conditions, school events, personal events, community crises, family problems, etc.). It generally fails to specify the factors leading to disruptions in existing role relationships within a family unit. A more severe criticism of this approach, however, is the implied assumption that separation or divorce are without exception negative events. As Bloom et al. (1978) point out, this need not be the case. Consider the example of two individuals married for a substantial period of time (e.g., 10 years). Assume further that the last 5 years of marriage were typified by a series of role strains and incompatability (arguing, fighting, etc.). It is highly plausible that the decision to separate and/or get a divorce is a situation desirable to one or both partners. Although we do not question that there are stresses and strains attending this decision and the initial period of becoming separated, it may be that the separation from a bad situation results in the alleviation of, or at least the reduction of, the level of depression. This issue is the subject of further discussion in a subsequent section of this chapter.

The role of marital status in depression is also confounded in another manner. The proponents of this approach use marital status (married or not married) as an indicator of social support (G. W. Brown and Harris, 1978; Kessler and Essex, 1982; Thoits, 1982). Apparently, this is done based on the assumption that the married possess more emotional support than do their unmarried counterparts. By definition, this assumes that the unmarried have no support. This would seem to indicate that two people who are not married but share a close (possibly confiding) relationship are placed in a category of having no support. Thus, it would appear that this approach has a weakness.

This is not to say that the married do not usually have more social support than do the unmarried. This may very well be the case. However, we cannot assume the functional equivalence of being married and having social support. Also, it may very well be the case that levels of support differ for males and females. A logical, and as yet untested, approach would be to control for sex and examine the relationship of some measure of emotional support and depression within each category of marital status. The findings that would result from such an analysis not only would measure the level of support available to males and females of different marital statuses, but would reveal the effectiveness of social support in reducing the impact of stressors on depression.

A MODEL OF SEX, MARITAL STATUS, LIFE EVENTS, SOCIAL SUPPORT, AND DEPRESSION

In this chapter, we examine the relationship of life events and social support to depression in the context of sex and marital status. Specifically, five marital-status groupings are defined: married, divorced, separated, widowed, and single. The advantages of this approach are threefold: (1) it allows us to separate the group of individuals in the not-married category into its component parts and to examine the model for each sex–marital-status combination; (2) it avoids the confounding issue by specifying distinct measures of life events and social support; and (3) it allows for the use of multiple measures of social support.

Life events are measured via a total summated scale of the number of undesirable life events experienced by an individual during the past 6 months. The measure of support used here is strong-tie support (see Chapter 5 for a discussion of this variable).

Given the pervasiveness of marriage as a source of support, it appears appropriate to test whether or not there is something inherent in the relationship between spouses that adds to (or detracts from) the level of support maintained by an individual. Therefore, in addition to utilizing a measure of support that applies to individuals, regardless of marital status (i.e., strong-tie support—see Chapter 8), we will also examine a measure of support unique to married individuals. The measure of marital support used here is commonly referred to as the Medalie–Goldbourt Family Problem Scale (Medalie and Goldbourt, 1976). As mentioned in Chapter 7, this scale consists of four items tapping the degree of problems, conflicts, and perceived spousal love in a marital setting. (See Chapter 7 for more details on the reliability, validity, and use of this measure). Life events, social support, and depression are examined for the two time periods in our data-collection process.

The analysis begins below with an examination of sex and marital-status differences in depression. Findings are compared to those documented in the literature. The mean level of life events, social support, and depression are then examined for males and females in the various marital-status groupings. Next, the independent effects of life events and social support on depression for males and females are examined for each category of marital status. Finally, the mediating role (see Chapter 10 for details) of social support in the life-event–depression relationship are tested for all sex–marital-status groupings.

SEX, MARITAL STATUS, AND DEPRESSION

As can be seen in Table 12.1, the major findings in the literature regarding sex and marital-status differences in depression have been confirmed in our Albany area study. Specifically: (1) females are significantly more depressed than are males, (2) married persons are significantly less depressed than are never-married or formerly married people, and (3) married females are significantly more depressed than are married males. Table 12.1 also presents mean levels of depression for males and females for each nonmarried status category. Although there are no significant differences between males and females when each category is compared, it should be pointed out that this is due to the rather small number of cases in each category. However, the pattern of relationship is quite clear. With the exception of separated individuals, females have higher levels of depression than do males.

Figures 12.1 and 12.2 show the mean levels of life events, social support, and depression over time for the five marital-status groupings: married, divorced, separated, widowed, and never married. As can be

TABLE 12.1
Mean Levels of Depression for Males and Females,
Controlling for Marital Status

	$\bar{X}$	SD	N
Sex[a]			
Males	7.88	8.74	423
Females	9.48	10.21	421
Marital Status[b]			
Married	7.74	8.53	552
Divorced	9.59	8.14	61
Separated	14.09	15.26	44
Widowed	11.19	11.86	47
Never married	9.44	9.96	140
Males[c]			
Married	6.99	7.72	271
Divorced	8.04	7.70	28
Separated	15.11	15.65	19
Widowed	9.88	9.73	8
Never married	8.74	9.21	97
Females[c]			
Married	8.46	9.21	281
Divorced	10.91	8.38	33
Separated	13.32	15.25	25
Widowed	11.46	12.35	39
Never married	11.00	11.42	43

[a] $t_{M-F} = t = 2.48$ *p < .01.

[b] $t_{married-divorced} = 1.61$. $t_{married-separated} = 4.41$ * p < .01. $t_{married-widowed} = 2.57$ * p < .01. $t_{married-never} = 2.93$ * p < .05.

[c] $t_{married} = 2.01$ * p < .05. $t_{divorced} = 1.36$. $t_{separated} = .37$. $t_{widowed} = .33$. $t_{single} = 1.23$.

seen, with the exception of widowed males, there are no significant differences over time for any of these factors across the marital-status groupings. However, there are some interesting sex/marital-status differences.

SEX, MARITAL STATUS, LIFE EVENTS, AND SOCIAL SUPPORT

For males, being divorced or never having married results in the largest number of undesirable life events. For females, on the other hand, being separated or never married result in the largest number of undesirable life events. Married males and females in the sample, on the other hand, experience an average number of life events, when

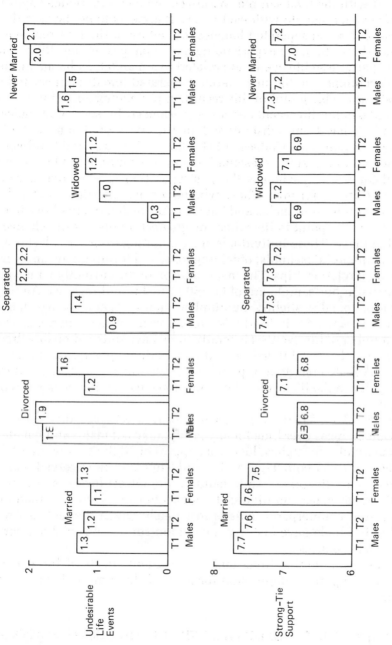

Figure 12.1 Mean levels of life events and social support at Time 1 (T1) and Time 2 (T2), controlling for sex and marital status.

compared with the total sample. Widowed females experience slightly more life events than do widowed males. It appears to be the case that divorced males and separated females, by nature of their current state of marital disruption, are experiencing more changes in their lives. For the most part, these life events are related to a mandated change in life style to accommodate the new status. Separated females appear to be the most vulnerable group in this regard, experiencing almost twice as many undesirable life events as are experienced by separated males. This finding has been substantiated in the work of Bloom and his associates (Bloom and Hodges, 1981; Bloom, Hodges, and Caldwell, 1982), who found that the presentation and separation period are more stressful for women, whereas the postseparation (predivorce) period was more difficult for men. Those who have never married are, for the most part, young adult males and females. As we documented in Chapter 11, this is the point in life when the greatest number of life changes are taking place. These individuals are graduating from school, setting up independent households, obtaining jobs, and forming new and varied personal relationships. The major portion of the currently widowed individuals in our sample are older (50+) males and females. Among this group, females slightly outnumber males. Again, as we documented in Chapter 11, individuals over 50 years of age experience the fewest number of life events. Generally, they have finished raising their families, they have stabilized in their occupational positions, and they are least likely to engage in or plan for further education. In short, they are at a point in the life cycle where they have passed the peak years of life events.

With regard to social support, we note that whereas there are no significant changes over time for any group, married males and females tend to maintain the highest levels of support of all the sex and marital-status groupings at both Time 1 (T1) and Time 2 (T2). Divorced males and females, on the other hand, maintain the lowest levels of support. Both divorced males and divorced females have less support than do their married counterparts. This is reasonable, given the fact that divorced individuals have just lost a common source of social support, namely their spouses.

We now examine the direct and independent effects of life events and social support on depression for each of three marital-status/sex groupings.

INDEPENDENT EFFECTS OF LIFE EVENTS AND SOCIAL SUPPORT

Figure 12.2 presents the mean levels of depression, controlling for levels of life events at T1 and for social support at T2. The selection of

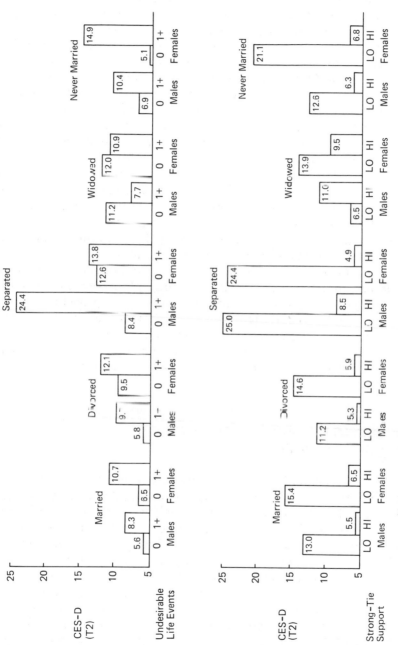

Figure 12.2 Sex and marital-status differences at Time 2 (T2), controlling for independent effects, undesirable life events, and social support.

each variable in a separate time period was dictated by the model to be tested (life events→social support→depression). For purposes of parsimony, life events and social support were collapsed into two categories. The cutoff points were based on the means for each variable. Therefore, for undesirable life events, two categories resulted: (1) no events and (2) one or more event. For strong-tie support, a score of 1 to 7 was scored as low, and a score of 8+ was scored as high.

The independent effects of life events and social support are clearly documented. For all sex and marital-status groupings, we note the following patterns: (1) With the exception of widowed males and females, those individuals experiencing one or more undesirable life events are more depressed than those experiencing no undesirable life events; and and (2) males and females with low social support are more depressed than are individuals with high support. In addition, we note that (1) separated males, separated females, and single females experiencing high life events are more depressed than are their counterparts in other marital-status groupings; and (2) separated males, separated females, and single females with low support are more depressed than are their counterparts in other marital-status groupings. Furthermore, the mean level of depression for these subgroups is at or approaching that of possible clinical caseness (16+ on the CES-D scale; see Myers and Weissman, 1980). The question becomes, given these significant independent effects of a high level of life events and a low level of support, what effect does a simultaneous consideration of both factors have on the prediction of depession?

JOINT EFFECTS, MEDIATING EFFECTS, AND INTERACTION EFFECTS

As should be evident by now, a central concern of the current monograph is the role played by social support in the life-event–depression relationship. In Chapter 10 we distinguished between a set of terms commonly used in the literature to connote joint mediating effects and terms connoting interacting effects of social support. Overall, we find a significant mediating effect for social support and no interactive effect.

Implicit in these discussions is the issue of causality. For present purposes, we examine the role played by social support in the stressor–depression model for different marital-status and sex categories. First, we examine the joint effect of life events and social support on depression. If social support and life events are having a joint effect on depression, resulting in the causal structure LE→SS→CES-D, we should note that the mean level of depression under conditions of high social support and low stress is significantly less than the level of depression given high stress and low support. The research question posed here is: "Are there any differences among the various sex and marital-status groupings with regard to the joint effect of life events and social support on depression?"

Figure 12.3 reports the results of the analysis. Mean levels of depression are reported for males and females in each of the marital-status groups, controlling for life events at T1 and social support at T2. For the majority of the marital-status and sex groupings, life events and social support are found to have a significant effect on depression. That is, with the exception of widowed males and females we find that males and females with high stress and low social support are significantly more depressed than their counterparts with low stress and high social support.

In regard to sex and marital-status differences, we find that the joint consideration of life events and social support eliminates male–female differences in depression for various marital-status groupings. Recall that married females were found to be significantly more depressed than were their male counterparts (8.5 and 7.0, respectively). However, under conditions of low life events and high support, not only does the mean level of depression fall below the average, but there are no significant male–female differences in this group $\bar{X}$ = 4.8 for males, 5.5 for females). The same is true for the never-married individuals in the sample ($\bar{X}$ = 5.1 and 4.0, respectively). However, if we examine males and females with high life events and low social support, we find that married and never-married females in this group are above the cutoff point for being possibly clinically depressed (16+) and are approaching the level of being probably clinically depressed (21+). In these two cases, females are 35% and 73%, respectively, more depressed than are their male counterparts.

Earlier analysis had documented that the separated individuals in the formerly married category had the highest mean depression score in T2 ($\bar{X}$ = 15.1 for males and 13.3 for females). When we control for high events and low social support, this increases to 29.8 for males and 23.7 for females. Not only does this exceed the cutoff point for possible clinical depression, it exceeds (by more than 5 points) the cutoff point for probable clinical depression. Indeed, an examination of frequency distributions shows that 64% of currently separated individuals with high events and low social support were probably clinically depressed (75% for males and 57% for females). However, it appears that the major portion of this increase for females is due to low social support,

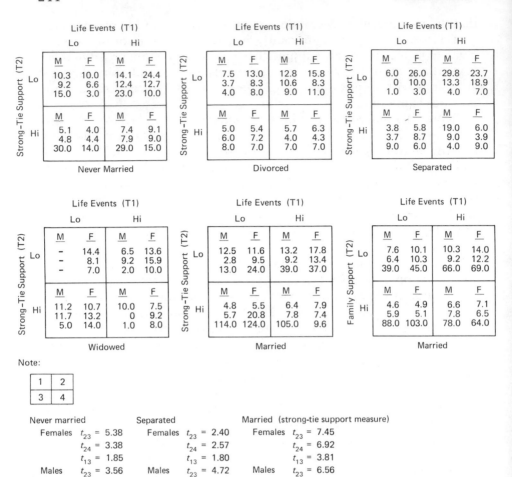

Figure 12.3 Mean depression scores by levels of social support at Time 2 (T2) and life events at Time 1 (T1), controlling for sex and marital status.

whereas for separated males, it is due to high life events. That is, when we compare separated females with low life events and low support with their counterparts (females with low support and high life events), we find no significant differences. For males, on the other hand, these differences are significant.

Although it is tempting to speculate as to reasons for this dramatic increase in depression for separated individuals, it must be noted that the number of cases involved is extremely small ($N = 11$). Consequently, further analysis is hampered by the small cell size. Nevertheless, the implications for the study of marital disruption are quite clear. Specifically, it appears that it is the ambiguity of this marital-status category (finding oneself with one foot in the married category and one foot in the not-married category) that is accounting for a large amount of the overall depression score for formerly married individuals. This issue is addressed in more detail in Chapter 15.

The next step is to determine whether social support is playing a mediating or interacting role in the relationship of life events to depression among the sex/marital-status groupings. For social support to play a mediating role in the relationship of life events to depression, the following must be true: (1) The mean level of depression for individuals under conditions of high stress and low social support (Cell 2 in Figure 12.3) must be significantly greater than the mean level of depression for individuals with high stress and high social support (Cell 4 in Figure 12.3), and (2) the mean level of depression for individuals with low stress and low social support (Cell 1 in Figure 12.3) should be significantly greater than the mean level of depression for individuals with low stress and high social support (Cell 3 in Figure 12.3). For an interaction effect to have taken place, Condition 1 should be met and Condition 2 should not be met.

An analysis of the data produced the following findings:

1. For both married and never-married males and females, social support mediated the effect of life events on depression.
2. For divorced and separated females, social support mediated the effect of life events on depression.
3. For divorced males, life events and social support exerted an interaction effect on depression.
4. For separated males, there is neither a mediating nor an interaction effect. Rather, it appears that life events are exerting a primarily independent effect on depression.

For the widowed category, the number of cases per cell was too small for a test of significance.

SUMMARY AND IMPLICATIONS

Given the above findings, we may address the issue of marital status as a stressor or as a social support with a more logical approach. That is, although marital disruption may be considered a type of stressor, it cannot, by itself, be considered as the factor accounting for the higher level of depression found in the formerly married group. Rather, it is the frequency of life events experienced by those who have undergone marital disruption in conjunction with low support that results in the higher level of depression. In fact, when we compare the mean level of depression for the married, formerly married (excluding separated), and never married, we find that under conditions of high events and high social support, the difference in depression between the married and not-married disappears. However, significant differences still remain with regard to sex. That is, never-married females, separated females, and separated males having low support and high events are the most depressed of all groups.

By the same token, being married cannot universally be considered a social-support asset. That is, according to the analysis presented in Figure 12.3, married individuals with high events and low social support are more than twice as depressed as those with high events and high support or low events and high support. Any analysis that assumes that marriage is an indication of a high level of social support ignores the dynamics that take place in and around the marital setting. However, one could legitimately raise the criticism that the measure of social support used here (i.e., strong-tie support) does not necessarily tap the type of support provided by a spouse and/or an individual's family. Although this measure does tap the adequacy of companions and close friends, it makes no specific reference to the individuals involved in the marriage and/or family. Therefore, to further test the assertion that marital status can be used as a proxy for social support (Thoits, 1981), we examined the role of family support (using the Medalie–Goldbourt scale; see Chapter 7) for married individuals as an intervening factor in the stressor–depression relationship. The findings are identical to finding a joint effect, we found that social support had a mediating effect in the life event–illness relationship, both for males and for females.

In sum, gender and marital status have been found to be crucial conditioning factors in modeling the role played by social support in the stressor–illness model. Married and not-married males and females differ with regard to the mean levels of stress, support, and depression experienced. Further, the relationships of stress and support to depression differ across sex and marital-status groupings. With the exception of divorce or separated males, social support was found to mediate the effects of life events on depression.

In Chapter 15, an alternative approach to the study of sex and marital-status differences in depression is presented. Specifically, it uses the gender of the confidant (named by an individual as the one he or she is most likely to talk to about his or her problems) as the measure of social support and attempts to further explain sex and marital-status differences in depression. In this manner, the nature of social relations between an individual and his or her confidant is explored.

13

Social Class and Depressive Symptomatology

WALTER M. ENSEL

INTRODUCTION

One of the most consistently documented finding in epidemiological research deals with the inverse relationship between socioeconomic status and mental health. Simply stated, individuals in the lower end of the status spectrum have been found to experience significantly more psychological distress than do individuals higher up on the socioeconomic ladder (Hollingshead and Redlich, 1958; Srole et al., 1962; Langner and Michael, 1963; Dohrenwend and Dohrenwend, 1969; Myers, Lindenthal, and Pepper, 1974).

Researchers over the past 10 years have argued that this relationship is in large part conditioned by life events. That is, in addition to finding the class–distress relationship, researchers have further noted that (1) higher class, status, or position is inversely related to the magnitude of life events experienced, and (2) life events are negatively related to mental health (Kohn, 1972; Dohrenwend, 1973b; Myers et al., 1974; Dohrenwend and Dohrenwend, 1974a; Kessler, 1979; G. W. Brown and Harris, 1978; Kessler and Cleary, 1980). Kessler (1979) has further refined the class–distress relationship by showing that not only is there different exposure to stress in the lower classes, but there is in addition

249

a differential impact of comparable life events across various class and occupational groupings.

The present chapter is an attempt to contribute to the growing literature on the class–distress relationship by examining the role of life events and social support in the epidemiology of depression for various occupational and class groupings. Inherent in this analysis will be an examination of (1) the relationship among social class, life events, and depression; (2) class-related effects of life events and social support on depression; and (3) the mediating and suppressing role of social support in the life-event–distress relationship.

MALE–FEMALE CLASS DIFFERENCE IN VULNERABILITY

With the growing number of women in the employed civilian labor market, it becomes relevant to control for gender in an examination of the class–distress relationship. Although some have demonstrated a gender–occupation effect on depressive symptomatology (Weissman et al., 1977; Radloff, 1975), little research has been done comparing males and females with regard to the effect of social environment on the class–distress relationship.

Turner and Noh (1983) examined the role of life events and social support in explaining class–distress relationships. In a sample of Canadian women who had recently given birth, they demonstrated that when stress and social support are taken into account, the relationship of class to depression becomes insignificant. However, when they examined the relationship of life stress and social support to depression across class categories, some interesting findings emerged. Although support made a significant and independent contribution to decreased depression in the middle and upper classes, support was more highly related to life events among lower-class women ($r = .49$). Thus, a significant portion of the effect of social support on depression in this category may be conditioned by the magnitude of life stress experienced. Indeed, as Turner and Noh point out, under conditions of high stress, social support makes a significant difference in explaining variations in depressive symptomatology among lower-class women.

Although these findings are significant in their own right, they have several shortcomings. First and foremost in these studies, a woman's social class is based on her husband's occupation according to the Hollingshead occupational prestige index (Hollingshead, 1957). In this classification scheme, the social-class distribution of married females is identical to that of married males. Given the widespread documentation of the fact that females are segregated into certain occupational categories (e.g., secretarial, clerical, nursing) and that they earn only 60% as much as do their male counterparts, any class-based inferences regarding depression differences discovered using this classification scheme must be viewed as misleading, because women, regardless of their own occupations, are classified according to their husbands' positions. The validity of these findings for employed married females remains highly tentative and questionable. In addition, there is still a large proportion of females who are not currently employed. The Hollingshead index also assigns these females to classes according to their husbands' positions.

In this chapter, we take a somewhat different approach in examining the relationship of social factors and depression in the context of the occupational structure. Specifically, we examine the relationship of life events and social support to depression among currently working males and females. In addition, we examine the specifically work-related types of life events experienced by each.

SOCIOECONOMIC CHARACTERISTICS OF MALES AND FEMALES

Table 13.1 presents the socioeconomic characteristics of males and females in the Albany Area Health Study sample. As can be seen, 68.4% of all males are employed, 20% are retired, and almost all of the remainder are unemployed or in school. Significantly fewer females are currently employed (46.2%), with a large percentage of the remainder occupying a housewife role (43.3%). The remainder, for the most part, are retired or unemployed. The mean educational level of males and females is comparable (12 years of schooling, on the average), as is the occupational status of those currently working. There is a significant discrepancy in workers' median income, however, females on the average earning 60% of their male counterparts' incomes.

Figure 13.1 presents the occupational distributions of males and females in the sample. The figure shows striking differences in males' and females' locations in the occupational structure. There are significantly more males than females working as managers and administrators, craftsmen, transport operatives, and unskilled manual laborers. Females tend to cluster in the clerical and service-worker occupations, with 60% of all working women in the sample employed in these kinds of jobs. There is little gender difference in proportions working in the professional, sales, or machine-operative positions.

Collapsing the occupational groupings into four classes, we find that

TABLE 13.1
Male and Female Employment Characteristics, Albany Area Health Study

Employment characteristics	Males		Females	
	N	%	N	%
Employment status				
Employed, full time	266	61.7	128	30.0
Self-employed	16	3.7	6	1.4
Employed, part time	13	3.0	63	14.8
Unemployed, laid off	31	7.2	11	2.6
Retired	85	19.7	30	7.0
Keeping house	5	1.2	185	43.3
In school	15	3.5	4	.9
	431	100.0	427	100.0
Average education, in years		12.0		11.8
Working individual's median annual income		$10,000–15,000		$7,000–7,999
Mean occupational status		40.9		38.6

the upper-white-collar and upper-blue-collar positions are clearly male-dominated, whereas the lower-white-collar positions are clearly female-dominated. The lower-blue-collar positions tend to be equally shared by males and females, although males have a slightly higher representation.

Thus, two findings in the literature on gender differences in socioeconomic position are validated: (1) Occupations are, for the most part, sex-stereotyped, and (2) working females earn substantially less than do their working male counterparts. Given these striking differences in male–female employment characteristics, it is quite clear that any consideration of the relationship between social class and mental health must control for male–female differences. Traditionally, females have been assigned the class position of their spouses. However, given the vast difference between males' and females' locations in the occupational structure, it does not seem appropriate to utilize the husband's position as the universal indicator of class. This is particularly true in the case of working women who have established themselves in their own occupations. By assigning class on the basis of the spouse's position, we totally obscure the potential effect of a female's work environment in the relationship between class and mental health. The same obfuscation would hold if male class positions were assigned on the basis of their spouses' occupations. This confusion is accentuated when we consider the case of single working women who, by

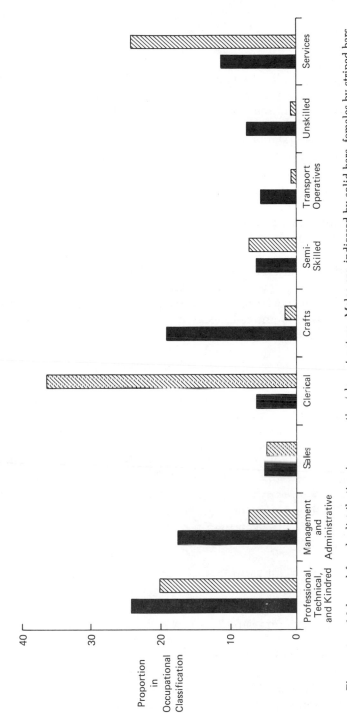

Figure 13.1 Male and female distribution in occupation/class structure. Males are indicated by solid bars, females by striped bars.

virtue of their unmarried status, can only be classified on the basis of their own occupations.

By assigning individual occupational categories for males and females separately and by basing class position on the individual's occupations, we eliminate the potential bias caused by placing females in inappropriate classes. Furthermore, as mentioned above, we allow differential work-related effects to show up in the analysis.

In our present study, social class is measured according to the Bureau of the Census Index of Occupations (1971). This index segments occupations into 10 classes or socioeconomic groups on which data on education and income were initially considered as indicators of social and economic status, respectively. Each class of workers represent a group of individuals with distinct economic, social, and intellectual standards. The scale has been found to distinguish middle-class (white-collar) individuals from working-class (blue-collar) persons (Haug, 1977). Some researchers (e.g., Mueller and Johnson, 1976) have re-grouped the major occupational categories into a four-level class hierarchy: (1) unskilled and semiskilled (lower working class), (2) skilled (upper working class), (3) clerical and sales (lower middle class), and (4) professional and managerial (upper middle class). Given the fact that occupations are considered by many to provide the best indicator of relative standing in a society (Haug, 1977), we utilize a four-category classification system that distinguishes upper and lower levels of both the working and the middle class.

The other major variables used in this chapter are total undesirable life events, strong-tie support, and depression (measured by the CES-D) at Time 1 (T1) and Time 2 (T2) of the panel study. In the following section, the means and standard deviations of these variables are broken down by class position for employed males and females, and the traditional relationships between class and life events and between class and distress are examined.

SOCIAL CLASS, LIFE EVENTS, SOCIAL SUPPORT, AND DEPRESSION

The frequency of undesirable life events in our study does not appear to vary for males, with the exception of lower white-collar workers, who on the average experience one more undesirable life event than do their counterparts in other occupational categories (Table 13.2). The correlation between class and life events for males is very low ($r = .010$). A similar pattern exists with respect to undesirable work-

TABLE 13.2
Average Number of Undesirable Life Events, Social Support, and Depression for Employed Males and Females by Class

	Class position															
	Lower working				Upper working				Lower middle				Upper middle			
	Male		Female		Male		Female		Male		Female		Male		Female	
Variable	X̄	SD	X̄	SD	X̄	SD	X̄	SD	X̄	SD	X̄	SD	X̄	SD	X̄	SD
Undesirable life events																
Time 1	1.36	1.77	1.07	1.41	1.51	2.51	a	a	2.23	2.69	1.22	1.82	1.39	2.32	1.81	2.30
Time 2	1.25	1.95	1.25	1.87	1.38	1.58			1.60	1.79	1.82	2.53	1.36	2.30	2.08	2.80
Undesirable work events																
Time 1	.45	.88	.33	.89	.69	1.51	a		.73	1.41	.32	.87	.41	1.04	.62	1.08
Time 2	.38	.91	.31	.72	.27	.71			.50	.86	.39	.84	.36	.98	.57	1.17
Strong-tie support																
Time 1	7.49	1.11	7.39	1.28	7.69	.79	a		7.47	.82	7.40	1.22	7.37	1.17	7.32	1.31
Time 2	7.41	1.35	7.56	.89	7.31	1.27			7.27	1.17	7.19	1.32	7.44	1.06	7.30	1.15
Depression (CES-D)																
Time 2	7.06	7.39	9.58	9.71	7.94	8.52	a		7.97	7.02	9.19	9.68	7.74	7.74	9.79	10.40
Number of cases	85		61		55		3		30		79		123		43	

aToo few cases for analysis.

related events. For females, on the other hand, the frequency of undesirable life events, including work-related events, increases as we move up the class structure. The correlation between class and life events generally is significant for females ($r = .134$). One may ask, at this juncture, to what degree undesirable work-related life events affect this pattern of difference between men and women. An examination of the percentage of all specifically work-related undesirable life events shows no significant differences across all classes for either females or males. Approximately one-third (30%) of the undesirable events are work-related across all class positions. Therefore, in the remainder of the analysis, undesirable life events are used as the indicator of stressors.

Social support, on the other hand, remains consistent across the class and sex structure. That is, there is no significant difference in mean level of support between males and females or across the class structure. This is reflected in the zero-order correlations of class and support for males and females ($r = .02$ and $-.11$, respectively).

Furthermore, the correlation between class and depression is negligible for both males and females ($r = .02$ and $.01$, respectively). However, females are found to be consistently more depressed than are their male counterparts.

The absence of an inverse class–life-event relationship in the current analysis can be explained by a variety of factors. First, it must be remembered that we are concerned here with undesirable life events as opposed to total life events. By focusing only on undesirable life events, we not only reduce the average number of events experienced by approximately 60%, we decrease the potential variation in the frequency of their occurrence. In addition, by focusing on the employed individuals, we exclude a substantial proportion of respondents who are more likely to experience undesirable life events.

It has been argued that an employed individual avoids a vast array of life events associated with economic instability. For example, unemployed individuals experience a significantly greater number of undesirable finance-related life events than do their employed counterparts (Catalano and Dooley, 1977). Recently retired individuals have been found to experience a change in life style often accompanied by a variety of life events (e.g., change in residence, change in living conditions, change in recreational and social activities). In our study, we find that the unemployed experience, on the average, almost twice as many undesirable life events as do their employed counterparts (2.2, compared to 1.2). In addition, the average depression score (CES-D) for the unemployed is almost 50% higher than that found for the employed ($\bar{X} = 12.2$, compared to 8.3).

It should be noted, at this point, that the absence of inverse relationships between class and distress and between class and life events does not necessarily preclude some potential class-conditioned life-event–depression relationships. It may very well be the case that certain life events differentially affect depression depending on one's position in the occupational structure.

CLASS-ORIENTED EFFECTS OF LIFE EVENTS AND SOCIAL SUPPORT ON DEPRESSION

In a review of findings on the relationships among social class, life events, and mental illness, Liem and Liem (1980) cite research that has shown that a portion of the effect of social class on mental health is mediated by differential exposure to life events. However, they go on to suggest that this finding may be secondary to the role social class plays in conditioning the effect of life events on depression. That is, although higher symptom scores for lower-class persons can be attributed to class differences in exposure to stressors, these higher scores were more likely a result of lower-class respondents' responding with greater stress than would upper-class respondents (holding exposure to stressors constant). In this vein, Dohrenwend (1973b) and Kessler (1979) found that the life-event–symptomatology relationship was significant only for lower-class individuals. Upper-class respondents, regardless of the number of life events experienced, showed low levels of symptomatology. However, neither of these studies controlled for sex of the respondent.

This section examines the relationship of life events to depression, controlling for class position and gender. In addition, the relationships of life events to social support and of social support to depression are also examined with the same controls. In this manner the role played by social class in mediating the relationships among the model variables can be empirically specified for males and females, and the viability of Liem and Liem's hypothesis examined.

Figure 13.2A shows the relationship between undesirable life events at T1 and depression at T2 in the Albany Area Health Study. In this analysis we control for both social class and gender. For males, the life-event–depression relationship is significantly greater in the lower segments of both the blue- and white-collar classes than in the upper counterparts of both these classes ($r = .32$ for lower-blue-collar males, compared to .06 for upper-blue-collar males; $r = .43$ for lower-white-collar males, compared to .15 for upper-white-collar males). However, there is no variation in the life-event–depression relationship across

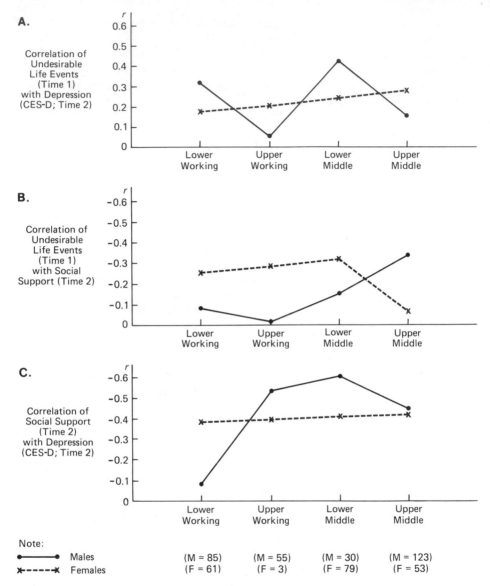

Figure 13.2A–C Correlations of life events, social support, and depression (CES-D) across class structure by gender.

classes for females. Life events have a significant impact on depression for lower-working-class and for lower- and upper-middle-class females ($r = .18$, $.24$, and $.27$, respectively).

The total effect of social support at T2 on depression, as seen in

Figure 13.2C, indicates significant class variations only for males in the sample. Although there is no variation in the support–depression relationship across classes for females, we note a significant increase in this relationship for males as we move up the status hierarchy. The most striking difference for males lies between the lower working class, where social support is virtually unrelated to depression, and the other classes, where it is strongly correlated. That is, although social support has the potential to explain from 20% to 36% of the variation in depression in the other three classes, it can explain, at best, only 1% of the variation in depression for the lower working class.

Figure 13.2B, which presents the relationship between undesirable life events and social support, shows that the greatest class–gender variation occurs among upper-middle-class workers. In addition, the pattern of the relationship between undesirable life events and social support for males and females reverses itself in this group. That is, whereas the relationship between life events and social support is significantly greater for females than for males in the other classes, the opposite is true in the upper middle class.

In fact, for males we find that the potential for an indirect effect of life events through social support exists only in the upper middle class. For females, on the other hand, the potential is primarily in the lower working and lower middle classes. It would appear, therefore, that stressors have a more deleterious effect on support for males as class position rises. For females, this relationship is most pronounced in the lower middle class and decreases significantly in the upper middle class. It may be the case that the nature of employment status for females (part time versus full time), marital status (married versus not married), and the presence of children all play a role in the relationship between life events and social support. Indeed, when we control for potential role-strain factors (being married, presence of children) we find that married females who have children and are working full time on the average experience more undesirable life events than do their single employed counterparts. This finding, couples with the fact that almost 45% of working females are clustered in the lower middle class, may account for the greater relationship between life events and social support for females in this group. Unfortunately, a control for these various role-strain factors results in subgroups too small for statistical analysis. Further examination of this explanation requires a much larger set of females.

Thus, we find that social class does condition the relationship between undesirable life events and depression. However, the relationship of life events to depression is not greatest in the lower class as was posited by Liem and Liem (1980). Moreover, social class condi-

tions the effect of social support on depression. The correlation between support and depression varies from $-.10$ to $-.61$, depending on
class position. Finally, the relationship between undesirable life events
and social support varies significantly as a function of class position.

Equally important are the gender differences in class position. Clearly, males and females differ in the class-related impact of these epidemiological factors on their levels of depression. Moreover, it should
be noted that, generally speaking, these relationships are independent
of the average amount of stress or support experienced by individuals.
For example, Table 13.2 shows that the mean level of support pos-
sessed by individuals does not vary significantly by gender or class.
However, the effect of support on depression does vary significantly.
The same thing can be said for undesirable life events. Thus it appears
that the differential-exposure argument may indeed be secondary to the
class-conditioning hypothesis (Liem and Liem, 1980). In any event, the
class-conditioning argument merits further investigation. Given these
class and gender variations in the relationships among life events, social support, and depression, we may ask to what degree social class
conditions the buffering effect of social support in the traditional
stressor–depression relationship.

CLASS AND THE MEDIATING ROLE OF SOCIAL SUPPORT

A major concern of this chapter is to reveal whether or not the two
viable causal models of the relationship among undesirable life events,
social support, and depression (i.e., the mediating model and the suppressing model) presented in Chapter 10 vary with the class position of
males and females. Figure 13.3 presents the results of the analysis
designed to address this issue with regard to Model 1, the mediating
model.

In testing Model 1, we note the following general findings:

(1) The direct effect of undesirable life events on depression increases for females as we move up the occupational hierarchy. For
males, on the other hand, life events have a significant impact only at
the lower sections of both the working and middle classes.

(2) The direct effect of social support on depression is the same
across occupational classes for females. For males, on the other hand,
support does not affect depression in the lower working class.

(3) Social support mediates the effects of undesirable life events on

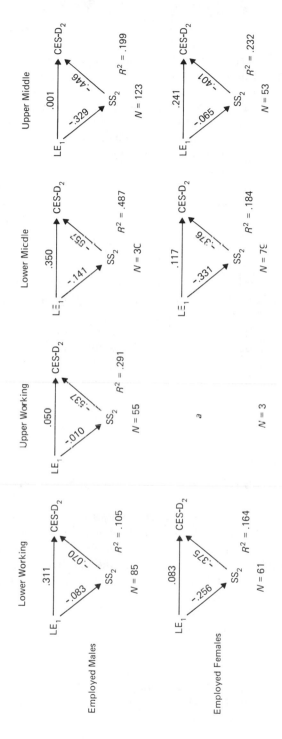

a Too few cases for analysis.

Figure 13.3 Path model of class and the mediating role of social support in the life-event–depression relationship for males and females.

depression under all but three class–gender conditions: lower- and upper-working-class males and upper-middle-class females.

With regard to the lower working class, the mediating effect is significantly different for females than for males. That is, whereas social support mediates 54% of the total effect of undesirable life events on depression for females in this class, it mediates less than 2% of the total effect for males. This pattern differs for males in the lower middle class, where social support is much stronger in its mediating role (18% of the total effect), whereas the lower-middle–class pattern remains approximately the same for females (52%). In the upper middle class, the male–female difference is the reverse. Here, social support mediates virtually all of the effect of life events experienced by males, while mediating only 10% of the total effect of life events for females.

It is important to keep in mind, however, that the ability of social support to reduce the effect of undesirable life events on depression is separated here from the direct effect of social support on depression. For it is quite clear that in all but one of the class–gender groupings, social support is most responsible in accounting for variance in depressive symptomatology. The most vivid example of this is among lower-middle-class males. Here, social support independently accounts for more than 35% of the variation in depression. In fact, with the inclusion of undesirable life events, this model accounts for almost 50% of the total variation in depression among lower-middle-class males.

CLASS AND THE SUPPRESSING ROLE OF SOCIAL SUPPORT

The second viable model of the relationship of undesirable life events, social support, and depression is concerned with the prior conditioning role of social support in the stressor-illness paradigm; it focuses on the social-support system before the occurrence of undesirable life events and depression. In this framework, social support is seen as suppressing or reducing the likelihood of undesirable life events occurring.

In testing Model 2 (Figure 13.4), we note the following general findings:

(1) For males, the direct effect of prior social support on depression is greatest in the lower working class. For females, on the other hand, the effect of prior social support is greatest among upper-middle-class workers.

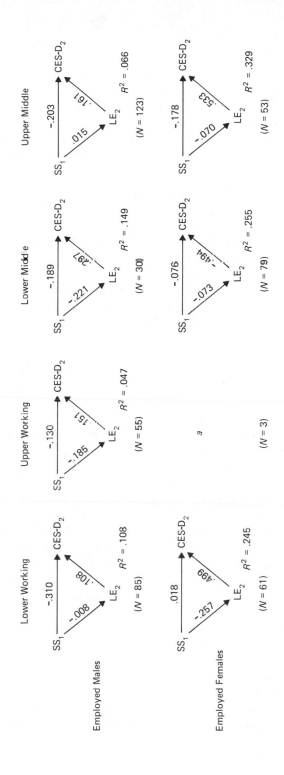

Figure 13.4 Path model of class and the suppressing role of social support.

^{a} Too few cases for analysis.

(2) The direct effect of undesirable life events is consistently and significantly high for females regardless of class position. For males, on the other hand, life events exert a significant direct effect on depression only among lower-middle-class workers.

(3) Social support suppresses the occurrence of undesirable life events for lower-working-class females and for upper-working-class and lower-middle-class males.

Generally speaking, Model 2 increases the explanation of depression among females in all class groupings. Among middle-class females, this is due primarily to the high relationship between life events and depression. For lower-working-class females, it is a combination of this relationship and the significant suppressant effect of social support on life events. For males, on the other hand, social support is most effective in suppressing depression among lower-middle-class workers. However, as far as explaining variations in depression among males across occupational class groupings, the mediating model is much more effective.

SUMMARY

The findings presented in this chapter have failed to discern any clear-cut linear relationship between social class and depression. It has further failed to determine a differential exposure to life events (total undesirable and work-related) for individuals in the lower class. However, this analysis differs from those done in the past in that it focuses only on employed individuals. Past operationalizations of the concept of social class have often failed to take employment into account. Given the facts that (1) unemployment is higher among unskilled and semi-skilled workers, and (2) unemployed individuals are significantly more depressed than are their employed counterparts, it is conceivable that the class–distress relationship documented in the literature is affected by the inclusion of unemployed individuals in the sample.

We have documented clear-cut differences in the relationship between life events and depression across social-class categories. However, the relationship was not greatest in the lower class, as was suggested by Liem and Liem. Rather, the relationship is high in the lower-middle and lower-working classes and low in the upper-working and upper-middle classes for males. For females, it is consistent across classes. We have further extended the conditioning formulation by indicating variations in the role played by social support in the interclass comparison of the effects of life events on depression. In addition to its strong independent effect, social support has been shown to differentially mediate the effect of life events on depression when controlling for class. Furthermore, evidence that prior social support has a suppressant effect on life events has been demonstrated.

Perhaps the unique contribution of the current analysis is that it demonstrates that any examination of class-conditioned relationships among epidemiological factors must take into account gender differences. This should not be surprising given the extensive documentation in the literature of male–female differences in depression. Coupled with the growing number of women in the employed civilian labor market, any classification strategy that categorizes working females based on their husbands' (or fathers', in the case of single women) occupations must be questioned.

Some caveats need to be mentioned at this point. It should be made clear that no attempt was made using data from this study to separate part-time from full-time employed women. Unfortunately, the numbers of individuals in data-classification cells using this additional control result in subgroups too small for rigorous analysis. It remains for future research to determine what, if any, effect the amount of time worked per week has on the class-conditioned relationships examined here. An examination of this issue should also take into account an examination of gender roles.

Second, the operationalization of social class utilized here focuses on location in the occupational structure as the primary determinant of class position. Although this approach has been justified elsewhere (Haug, 1977), it still has its shortcomings. That is, it may very well be the case that females (or males, for that matter) in working-class occupations have spouses in upper-middle-class jobs. The failure to take into account a spouse's occupation may result in an inaccurate ascription of a particular life style or status rank to a given individual. There is currently some work being done on this problem. Rossi and his associates, for example, have attempted to devise what they refer to as an *index of household social standing* (Rossi Sampson, and Bose, 1974; Knoke and Rossi, 1974). This is a measure of socioeconomic position that takes into account the occupation and education of both working husband and wife. Unfortunately, this index has not, as yet, been perfected. Both of these factors should be considerations in future research exploring social class and mental health.

14

Prior History of Illness in the Basic Model

MARK TAUSIG

PRIOR HISTORY OF ILLNESS

The current stress–illness model has its origins in the work of Adolf Meyer (Lief, 1948). Meyer drew up a life-history chart on which a physician could record both physiological and psychological events of importance in a patient's life course. Meyer's view that illness and life events that have occurred to individuals (sometimes in the remote past) can affect current illness provided part of the impetus for subsequent theories about the relationship between stress and illness. Beginning with Holmes and Rahe (1967), however, Meyer's methodology for recording both prior illness and prior life events was modified to emphasize the role of recent life events in producing subsequent illness (Holmes and Masuda, 1974). Although a medical history is a standard preliminary diagnostic process today, the role of prior illness as a predictor of life events and subsequent illness has been largely ignored by social epidemiologists.

The association of somatic and psychological distress is, of course, well documented as the basis of psychosomatic medicine (Hinkle and Wolff, 1957; Sheperd, Cooper, and Brown, 1966; Eastwood, 1975; Lipowski, 1975). Generally, however, when this association is in-

267

terpreted causally, stressful life events are said to precede illness. Several authors have noted the importance of examining the alternative causal ordering: illness preceding stress (Hinkle, 1974; Garrity, Marx, and Somes, 1977; Tennant and Andrews, 1978; Dohrenwend and Dohrenwend, 1981b; McFarlane et al., 1983). Dohrenwend and Dohrenwend (1981) have suggested an *event-proneness hypothesis* that proposes that prior illness may increase the likelihood of subsequent stressors[1] and then exacerbate illness or adverse health symptoms.

This chapter evaluates the event-proneness hypothesis in which prior history of illness is used to predict both subsequent life events and illness. Using our basic model as a starting point, alternative models probing the relationship between prior illness (or symptoms) and depression are also examined.

THE EVENT-PRONENESS MODEL

Dohrenwend and Dohrenwend (1981b) have argued that one of the hypothetical relationships that must be examined in order to understand life-event–illness models is one that considers life events as mediators rather than as independent causal agents of subsequent illness. This model is termed the "event-proneness model." In this formulation, adverse health leads to an increase in subsequent life events, which in turn intensify adverse health symptoms. This reciprocal relationship is diagramed in Figure 14.1.

According to this hypothesis, stressful life events are a direct consequence of prior illness or symptoms, which in turn are related to higher levels of subsequent adverse health. Several authors have demonstrated, however, that when prior history of illness is controlled, the relationship between significant life events and present health is greatly reduced (Tennant and Andrews, 1978; Kobasa et al., 1981; William, Ware, and Donald, 1981; Billings and Moos, 1982; McFarlane et al., 1983). In other words, adverse health changes have a direct effect on subsequent illness, but no effect on the number of life events. McFarlane et al. (1983) also tested the event-proneness model and found evidence that prior symptoms of illness do predict subsequent life events, but they did not find evidence of an effect from life events on subsequent symptoms.

---

[1]In this chapter, *stress* and *stressors* are used interchangeably so that the terminology will be consistent with the earlier literature. In a stricter sense, all discussion of stress here refers to stressors (see Chapter 5).

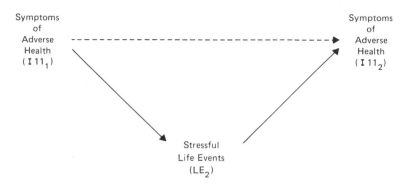

Figure 14.1   The event-proneness model. The direct relationship between symptoms in Time 1 and Time 2 is not specified in the Dohrenwend and Dohrenwend (1981) model.

Theorell and Rahe (1975), on the other hand, supply data in support of the proneness hypothesis. They followed a group of patients who had experienced a myocardial infarction (prior illness), recording evidence of their subsequent life events and health. They found that those men experiencing more significant life events were most likely to have more subsequent heart problems and were more likely to have died. Bieliauskas (1982) has proposed that the effect of life events on illness is indeed interactive, with illness causing stressful life events and vice versa. In particular, he suggests that life events provoke illness only when the incidence of preexisting illness or symptoms is high. This position is consistent with that taken by Hinkle (1974), who argues that when people have pre-existing illness patterns or susceptibility, the frequency of illness increases with changes in social and interpersonal relations, changes that are defined as significant life events. If this interaction hypothesis is true, then it would explain why Theorell and Rahe found an effect from life events in their patient sample: the patients had been ill before, whereas studies using broader community-based samples do not show any evidence for the proneness relationship because they include fewer cases of prior illness. The proneness relationship may hold only in the condition where there is high incidence of both prior symptoms and significant life events.

Figure 14.2 provides a description of this particular relationship between prior, or Time 1 (T1), and subsequent, or Time 2 (T2), illness that illustrates the interactive role of life events.

The effect of life events in this illustration is seen at the intersection of high incidences of prior illness and life events. Note that high incidence of life events shows only a small or moderate effect on T2 illness

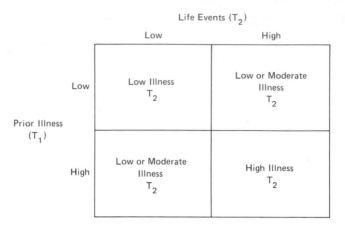

Figure 14.2 Hypothetical interactive role of life events for subsequent illness.

if prior illness is low, and that high prior symptoms have an effect on subsequent illness even in the absence of many significant life events.

PHYSICAL ILLNESS AND PSYCHOLOGICAL DISTRESS

The variables in the event-proneness model can be elaborated in various ways. Of particular interest for this volume is the question of what the effect of prior illness might be on the development of depression symptoms. To address this issue we must briefly discuss the relationship between physical and emotional distress. A strong association between physical and emotional distress has been well documented (Hinkle and Wolff, 1957; Shephard et al., 1966; Eastwood, 1975; and Lipowski, 1975). Emotional distress has been linked to indicators of adverse health (Eastwood, 1975), as well as to specific diagnosed illnesses (Shepherd et al., 1966). Hinkle and Wolff (1957) as well as others have documented a higher-than-expected frequency of physical disorders in psychiatric populations.

The association has been demonstrated, but not the causal sequence, if any. Does physical distress cause emotional distress, or vice versa? Or might the two forms of distress be aspects of a single syndrome? After all, the Center for Epidemiologic Studies Depression (CES-D) Scale, for instance, has a somatic-depression component. Although it would be helpful to determine the precise sequences here, we will confine ourselves to examining a particular order of effects, that of prior physical distress on subsequent psychological distress.

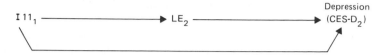

Figure 14.3   The modified event-proneness model for depression.

The event-proneness model can also be elaborated to examine the role of social support as it may affect the relationship between adverse physical and psychological health. The basic model of the relationship between life events, social support, and depression that we have been developing clearly indicates the strong direct and indirect effects of social support on depression. The absence of social support is associated with higher levels of depression symptoms. The question here is, how does social support affect any observed relationship between a history of adverse physical health and the subsequent development of depression?

MODELS TO BE EXAMINED

We therefore test three models that incorporate prior history of adverse physical health into the basic stress–illness model. First, we examine the original proneness model with its focus on the relationship of life events to physical illness (see Figure 14.1). Second, we examine a variant that substitutes psychological distress (depression) as the dependent variable, exploring its relationship to prior physical distress and life events (Figure 14.3). Finally, we examine a modified basic model that relates life events, social support, and depression to each other and to prior adverse health (Figure 14.4).

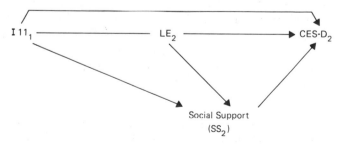

Figure 14.4   The basic model of life events, social support, and depression with prior history of illness factor.

THE MEASURE OF ADVERSE PHYSICAL HEALTH

The event-proneness hypothesis is stated in terms of adverse health symptoms rather than of specific diagnosed illness. Elliot and Eisendorfer (1982) have reviewed and summarized the cumulative evidence for a relationship between stress and specific illness. The evidence they bring together indicates that the link between stress and *specific diagnosed illnesses* can always be made, but that a relationship between stress and illness *symptoms* is regularly found. This suggests that the stress may disrupt physical systems without necessarily leading to sets of symptoms specific to a particular diagnosed illness. Such a finding supports the event-proneness hypothesis, because it focuses on the general adaptation syndrome or stress reaction, which does not specify that identifiable illness will be an outcome, but instead predicts merely a general adverse biological reaction.

Our measure of adverse physical health is thus symptom-based. It is a 40-item modification of the Cornell Medical Index (CMI) of physical symptoms (Brodman, Erdmann, Lorge, and Wolff, 1953). The symptom scale has been validated on community samples and has been used by others to document symptoms in the stress–illness model (Abramson, Terespolsky, Brook, and Kark, 1965; Abramson, 1966; Seymour, 1976; Levau, Arnon, and Portnoy, 1977; Ensel, forthcoming). Respondents were asked to report the frequency of each symptom during the last month prior to the T1 and T2 interviews. Each symptom was scored on a 4-point scale with the following values: 1 = often, 2 = sometimes, 3 = hardly ever, and 4 = never. Therefore, the higher the total score, the lower the level of physical symptoms.

The life-event measure used here is the sum of all subjectively reported undesirable life events (118 items) at T2 minus 13 event categories that are specifically related to physical illness.[2] In this way, we avoid the possible confounding of measures of stress with those for illness that Thoits (1981) warns against. Because we are testing a hypothesis in which physical health symptoms are the dependent variable, it seems prudent to remove references to physical illness and symptoms from the life-events scale in this instance, even though we did not find that health-related items in the total scale were confounded with health outcomes (Chapter 5).

---

[2]The excluded events were serious physical injury or accident, serious physical illness, change in health of family member, wanted pregnancy, unwanted pregnancy, menopause, miscarriage, stillbirth, frequent minor illness, major dental work, mental illness, abortion, and sexual difficulties.

As the measure of social support, we used the two-item strong-tie-support scale described in Chapter 8. The scale consists of two items: not having close companions and not having enough close friends.

In order to test the various relationships described, particularly those in the event-proneness model, the independent measures are also dichotomized as follows: life-events scores 0–1 = low events, 2+ events = high events; CMI scores below the mean (146) = high symptoms, above the mean = low symptoms; social support scores 1–7 = low support, 8 = high support.

MODEL 1: THE EVENT-PRONENESS HYPOTHESIS (PHYSICAL ILLNESS AND LIFE EVENTS)

Figure 14.5 permits us to examine the support provided by our data for the event-proneness hypothesis. The first value in each cell is the CMI_2 score, the second is the standard deviation, and the third is the number of cases in the cell. The cells represent combinations of dichotomized (high and low) CMI_1 and T2 life-events scores.[3] The regression results using undichotomized forms of the variables are also given.

The event-proneness hypothesis is supported, albeit weakly, by both the comparison and the regression analyses. In the regression analysis, life events show a small but significant contribution to the total explained variation in CMI_2 symptoms. These results are similar to those reported by Kobasa et al. (1981); Williams et al. (1981); Billings and Moos (1982); and McFarlane et al. (1983). There is a weak but significant tendency for prior symptoms to generate increased life events and for life events, in turn, to have an effect on subsequent illness. Most of the explained variance in the model, however, is a function of previous physical symptoms.

In the cross-tabulation presentation, the proneness hypothesis would be supported if the high-life-event cells both showed significant increases in CMI_2 symptoms compared to the respective low-life-events cells. The pattern observed suggests, rather, that the effect of life events on subsequent symptoms is more pronounced when prior symptoms are high *and* life events are high (Cell 2, Figure 14.5). These results must be considered suggestive only, because of our use of dichotomous variables for symptoms and life events (see the critique of such treat-

---

[3]The analyses reported in the following sections were also performed using all life events, regardless of desirability. The same pattern of results were observed, although undesirable events were more strongly related to the dependent measures.

CMI$_2$ Scores by Life Events and CMI$_1$[a]

Life Events

	Low	High
	$\overline{CMI}_2$ = 151.54	$\overline{CMI}_2$ = 148.34
Low	SD = 11.18	SD = 14.01
	N = 427	N = 73
	①	②
High	$\overline{CMI}_2$ = 139.76	$\overline{CMI}_2$ = 125.88
	SD = 16.13	SD = 21.24
	N = 234	N = 83
	③	④

T$_1$ Symptoms (CMI$_1$)

Comparison	t[a]	p
3–4	2.20	.05
1–2	0.79	ns[c]
1–3	3.14	.005
2–3	1.49	ns
1–4	5.54	.000
2–4	3.12	.001

Regression on CMI$_2$

	β	R^2	F	p
CMI$_1$ (Score)	.49	28.5%	288.93	.000
Life Events (Score)	−.22	4.7%	57.82	.000

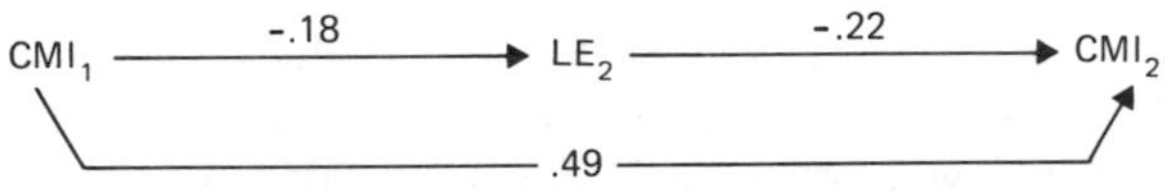

CMI$_1$ — −.18 → LE$_2$ — −.22 → CMI$_2$
     ⌄———————— .49 ————————⌃

Figure 14.5 Model 1: The event-proneness hypothesis—physical symptoms. [a]CMI = Cornell Medical Index; t = Computed from the formula provided by Blalock (1976), p. 229; and ns = Not significant.

ment of variables in Cleary and Kessler, 1982).[4] Nevertheless, both results show that prior illness symptoms have a more important effect on subsequent illness than do life events. This finding, again, is consistent with those by other investigators cited above. The results also support the arguments proposed by Theorell and Rahe (1975), Hinkle (1974), and Bieliauskas (1982)—that the life-event–illness relationship operates only in situations of high prior symptoms.

[4]This could be followed up in the regression equations by creating an interaction term for (life events × CMI$_1$). However, the main concern of this chapter is with the prediction of depression scores, and the pattern of cell means does not suggest the need to create an interaction term. A t-test comparing CMI$_2$ scores for low-life-event respondents versus high-life-event respondents without respect to CMI$_1$ scores is significant, whereas for CESD$_2$ scores it is not.

Thus the proneness hypothesis as specified by Dohrenwend and Dohrenwend (1981) has received only modest and conditional support. Where prior symptoms are high, elevated rates of life events (even excluding events that are health-related) contribute to higher subsequent symptom levels. Where prior symptoms are low, life events do not appear to make a substantial contribution to the appearance of subsequent symptoms, although they do affect the relationship somewhat.

MODEL 2: THE MODIFIED EVENT-PRONENESS HYPOTHESIS: PRIOR PHYSICAL ILLNESS, LIFE EVENTS, AND SUBSEQUENT PSYCHOLOGICAL SYMPTOMS

The previous findings suggest that it is largely incorrect to expect significant life events alone to cause physical illness symptoms. That is, events do not make one prone to illness except when physical symptoms are initially high. This relationship should hold true as well for predicting subsequent depressive symptoms instead of physical symptoms. However, whereas the previous data suggest that controlling for prior physical illness reduces the contribution made by life events to subsequent physical symptoms, the findings in Figure 14.6 indicate that prior illness does not have the same strong effect in reducing the role of life events when predicting depressive symptoms rather than physical distress. It is clear that life events retain a strong independent role in the prediction of depression.

This result clears up previous conflicting findings on the role of prior illness in the life-event–distress relationship. McFarlane et al. (1983) and Kobasa et al. (1981) used indicators of physical distress as their dependent measure: They found that the role of life events is reduced by including a measure of prior illness. Williams et al. (1981) used a mental-health index as a dependent variable: They showed a significant effect for life events, consistent with the findings obtained here, and with the event-proneness hypothesis as modified.

Whereas in Model 1 prior physical symptoms are much the better predictor of current physical symptoms, and show few or no indirect effects through life events, Model 2, predicting depressive symptoms from prior physical symptoms and stressful life events, shows independent effects for both physical symptoms and life events. In the regression analysis of neither model is there really strong substantiation for the event-proneness hypothesis. However, we have indicated that some support for this hypothesis can be found in the high-symptom–high-

CES-D$_2$ Scores by Life Events and CMI$_1$[a]

Life Events

	Low	High
Low	CES-D$_2$ = 5.66 SD = 6.63 N = 432 ①	CES-D$_2$ = 10.18 SD = 11.65 N = 72 ②
High	CES-D$_2$ = 10.00 SD = 8.91 N = 238 ③	CES-D$_2$ = 18.68 SD = 13.46 N = 84 ④

T$_1$ Symptoms

Comparison	t[a]	p
3-4	2.36	.01
1-3	2.03	.05
1-2	1.67	ns[c]
2-3	0.05	ns
1-4	4.63	.000
2-4	1.67	ns

Regression on CES-D$_2$

	ß	R^2	F	p
CMI$_1$ (Score)	-.29	7.7%	80.28	.000
Life Events (Score)	.31	13.0%	97.13	.000

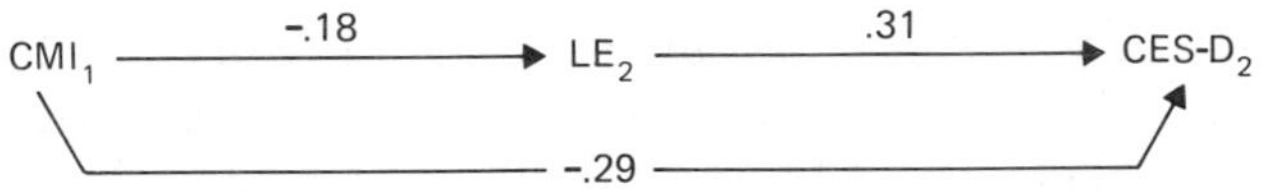

CMI$_1$ —— -.18 —→ LE$_2$ —— .31 —→ CES-D$_2$
\\—————— -.29 ——————/

Figure 14.6 Model 2: The modified event-proneness hypothesis—psychological symptoms. [a]CMI = Cornell Medical Index; t = Computed from the formula provided by Blalock (1976), p. 229.; and ns = Not significant.

life-event cell in both models. Particularly in Model 2, there seems to be some evidence for the proneness hypothesis. Prior physical symptoms are shown to have an effect on subsequent psychological symptoms; however, this relationship does not appear to be at the cost of reducing the effect of life events on repression. The collective result from testing Models 1 and 2 suggests that the proneness hypothesis is not supported.

MODEL 3: THE BASIC MODEL (LIFE EVENTS, SOCIAL SUPPORT, AND DEPRESSION) WITH PRIOR ILLNESS

The third and final model to be tested adds the variable of prior physical symptoms to the basic life-events–social-support–depression model that develop throughout this book. We have already seen in the test of Model 2 that prior physical symptoms have a direct effect on depressive symptoms and a small effect on the experience of life events. In effect, Model 3 adds a term for social support to the previous model, Model 2.

An argument similar to that concerning the possible effects of prior illness on life events can be made for the effect of prior illness on social support. In this instance we might argue that a history of illness reduces the individual's ability and interest in making or maintaining personal relationships or that a history of illness would cause others to be less interested in maintaining a relationship with the ill person. Further, from a social resource perspective, we could argue that prior illness will cause the individual to use up previously acquired social support. All of these arguments implicitly make the same prediction about the relationship between prior illness and social support—that illness will erode the level of social support. If this relationship holds, then we might also expect that the relationship between support and depression would be reduced when controlling for the effect of prior physical illness on support.

We test this argument in two phases. First, we retest the basic model with strong-tie support, depression, and the modified life-events measure that deletes the 13 health-related items. Then we add an antecedent term for T1 symptoms to examine their effects on the relationship among life events, social support, and depression.

Part A of Figure 14.7 shows the basic model using the abbreviated version of the life-events scale. The results are essentially identical to those reported earlier (Chapter 10) for the model at T2. Our measure of social support, strong-tie support, explains 20.4% of the variance in depression, whereas life events explain 6% of the variance.

Part B of Figure 14.7 shows the path coefficients derived from adding a term for T1 symptoms of physical distress. The results indicate that the addition of prior symptoms makes a significant contribution to the total explained variance. The contribution, however, is largely direct. That is, prior symptoms have little or no indirect effects on depression through either life events or social support. The first part of the path model predicts levels of social support from prior illness and life events. Prior symptoms have a significant but modest effect on social support. In fact, the effect is less than that for life events. The full model indicates that prior symptoms have very little indirect effect on depression via their relationship to either life events or social support.

High prior illness symptoms do lead to a small loss of social support (the coefficient is positive because high scores on the symptom scale indicate low symptoms). However, this effect does not significantly

A. The Basic Model

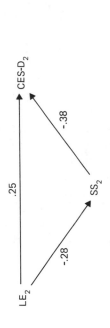

R^2 CES-D$_2$	
Social Support	20.4%
Life Events	6.0%
	26.4%

B. The Basic Model with Prior Physical Symptoms

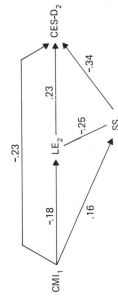

R_2 SS$_2$	
CMI$_1$	2.5%
Life Events$_2$	7.7%
	10.2%

R^2 CES-D$_2$	
CMI$_1$	6.3%
Life Events$_2$	4.6%
Social Support	20.4%
	31.3%

Figure 14.7 Model 3: The basic model—life events, social support, and depression—with prior physical symptoms. Means appear on the first line, SD on the second line, and the number of cases on the third line within each box; t = tests.

alter the relationship of support to depression (contrasting the coefficient in this model with that in the basic model). It is clear that prior illness has its principal effect on subsequent depression in a direct fashion. Higher levels of prior physical symptoms lead to higher subsequent levels of depression. Thus, the prior illness variable can be added to the model with the expectation that more of the variance in depression scores will be explained, but that the relationship between life events and social support will not be affected.

CONCLUSIONS

The event-proneness model was suggested by Dohrenwend and Dohrenwend (1981b) as one logical specification of the general life-event–illness relationship. According to the model, prior illness symptoms are generative of life events that in turn cause higher levels of physical symptoms. Previous tests of this model have found mixed support for this set of relationships. In our data, prior symptoms do not appear to reduce the causal relationship between life events and current symptoms. The exception to this finding is the condition in which prior symptoms are high. In this case, the proneness hypothesis receives some limited support.

When prior symptoms are used to predict psychological distress rather than physical distress, both symptoms and life events appear to have direct effects on depression. Thus, the role of prior illness is different for the prediction of current physical distress than it is for the prediction of current psychological distress. It has become common in the stress–illness literature to say that life events explain from 1% to 9% of the variation in illness outcomes (Rabkin and Struening, 1976; Tausig, 1982). The results obtained here suggest that part of the reason why this relationship is so small is that life events are a poor substitute measure of prior physical symptoms when predicting physical distress outcomes. When prior physical illness is explicitly incorporated into the model, the role of life events remains modest but the total explained variation is increased.

At the same time, life events retain a role in the prediction of depressive symptoms. The vulnerability of mood indicators to life events appears to be more general than are indicators of physical distress. If we take life events to represent changes in social relationships, then the results obtained here seem to indicate that their principal consequences are on mood and not on physical illness.

The final model that we explored indicates that the effect of prior symptoms on depression is largely a direct one. Only small effects through either life events or social support were observed. This finding leads to the speculation that the impact of illness symptoms on individuals is felt as much or more through the likelihood of more illness as through sociological factors (e.g., life events, social support). When life events and social support are taken into account, all these variables are seen to act independently.

The role of prior symptoms of adverse physical health on the stress–illness relationship has been the subject of some discussion and of recent empirical investigation. The findings reported here suggest that more theoretical work needs to be done to explain why prior symptoms have differential effects on subsequent physical and psychological distress.

Part VI

EXAMINING ALTERNATIVE
APPROACHES TO THE BASIC
MODELS

In this final section, we discuss several specific issues regarding the dynamics of social support. Chapter 15 examines the gender of the confidant as a factor in social support. Specifying the positive effect on one's mental health of having an opposite-sex confidant provides one example of how the concept of social support can be fine-tuned. Chapter 16 takes a direct approach to examining the buffering issue. It traces the support a person receives subsequent to the experience of an important (undesirable) life event and identifies the components of such support, which in fact buffers the expected effect of the life event on mental health.

These chapters are offered as illustrations of the ways by which the global concepts and theories of social support can be unfrozen and selectively analyzed so that a more detailed view of the functioning of social support in the mental-health process is obtained. Such analyses add to our understanding of the functioning of the basic model and offer further insights into ways in which social support can be examined as a viable concept.

15

Gender of the Confidant and Depression

NAN LIN

MARY WOELFEL

MARY Y. DUMIN

GENDER DIFFERENCES IN WELL-BEING

The epidemiological finding that women tend to be worse off than men in psychological well-being has stimulated research to provide explanations for this difference (Gove, 1972; Gove and Tudor, 1973; Radloff, 1975; Dohrenwend and Dohrenwend, 1976; Weissman and Klerman, 1977; Fox, 1980). This chapter examines the role of social support in explaining gender differences in mental health. More specifically, the role of the confidant's gender is examined as a critical component in social support for explaining gender differences in depression.

Attempts to explain gender differences have centered principally around three themes: (1) artifactual, (2) biological, and (3) sociological explanations. The artifactual explanation states that the gender difference reflects response bias rather than actual differences between men and women. In other words, the difference is more apparent than real; the overestimation of female depression is due to such factors as

283

response set. Women may simply report more symptoms than men because they are more interested in health (Feldman, 1964); and men may be reluctant to define themselves as sick or to report symptoms (Gove, 1978; Verbrugge, 1981). Empirical research does suggest that women tend to report or acknowledge symptoms and to seek help more readily than men do (Gove and Hughes, 1979). For example, Dohrenwend and Dohrenwend (1976, 1977) assert that women typically score higher on self-report inventories of symptoms. Yet women do not score higher in symptoms when reports from key informants are used.

Most investigators, however, assert that the observed gender difference is real, and they contend that these differences remain after response bias is controlled (Clancy and Gove, 1974; Gove and Geerkin, 1977). The biological or physiological explanation asserts that the differential rates are due to genetic or endocrine differences between males and females. The basic claim is that women inherently have a greater predisposition to mental disorders. For example, Golup (1973) suggests that hormonal imbalances cause women to be more susceptible to mental problems. Weissman and Klerman (1977), however, in reviewing the literature conclude there is little evidence that hormonal differences account for anything more than a negligible portion of the depression rates for females, and therefore cannot explain the observed gender differences.

A third view, which has received the most attention, explains gender differences in sex-role terms. Researchers have found that marital status and mental health are related. Married individuals of both sexes tend to have lower rates of mental distress than do unmarried individuals (Gove, 1972, 1979; Glenn, 1975). However, comparing rates of mental problems for single women with those of single men, divorced women versus divorced men, and widowed women versus widowed men, Gove (1972) found that men had higher rates of mental distress than did women in all these categories. Only among the married were women's rates of mental distress higher.

In general, these findings were interpreted to mean that males and females had different predispositions to depression and mental distress because of the way they are socialized (Gove, 1972; Dohrenwend and Dohrenwend, 1974b, 1976; Gove and Geerkin, 1977; Gove and Tudor, 1973, 1977). The traditional feminine sex role is viewed as more stressful than the masculine sex role. Gove and Tudor, in particular, assert that the female sex role is more problematic psychologically, and they show evidence that females in general have higher rates of mental distress in studies of both treated and untreated populations. They further contend that the overall sex difference in mental health can be attributed to the relatively higher rates of mental distress among married women due to their social roles. Most women, they argue, are restricted to a role consisting of raising children and keeping house. Their only source of gratification is a role that is unstructured, invisible, and of low status. Men, by contrast, occupy both work and family roles. If one role ceases to be gratifying men can shift roles. Women have no such option. Gove and Tudor suggest that sex differences in depression may shift over time as roles change.

An extension of the sex-role thesis distinguishes between traditional (nonworking) and nontraditional (working) wives, and finds that husbands in a nontraditional (working-wife) relationship have higher rates rates of depressive symptoms than do wives (Rosenfield, 1980). Cafferata, Kasper, and Berstein (1983) report that a lower percentage of men than women in a traditional family structure obtain psychotrophic drugs. In general, men do much better than women in a traditional family setting. Kessler and McRae's study (1982) also supports these findings and shows further that nontraditional (working) wives are slightly healthier psychologically than are traditional (nonworking) wives. Welch and Booth (1977), too, found that women who work are in better mental health than are nonworking wives. Gore and Mangione (1983) confirmed the positive effects of employment status and marital status on married women's mental health (less depressed mood scores) in their Boston study. This set of findings supports Gove's sex-role thesis: Women who occupy a traditional role are likely to be more depressed than are women who occupy a nontraditional role.

However, several other studies do not support Gove's sex-role interpretation. Haynes and Feinleib (1980), for example, show that under some conditions, women's working negatively affects their mental-health status. Likewise, married women seem mentally healthier than do unmarried women. Ensel (1982; 1985), investigating the relationship of age to gender and marital-status differences in depression, finds that it is not married women but rather unmarried women between the ages of 18 and 24 who account for the higher rates of depression among women. In addition, based on the Albany sample and using the 16+ cutoff method on the CES-D scale (see Chapter 12) as a clinically oriented caseness measure, Ensel reports that almost 30% of the unmarried females can be considered "possibly" clinically depressed. This is 9 percentage points higher than that for married females, and more than 16 percentage points higher than that for married males.

Other studies negate the sex-role interpretation as well. Some find that single mothers rather than married women have the highest rates of anxiety and depression among marital-status groups (Bachrach, 1975; Radloff and Rae, 1979; Guttentag, Salasin, and Belle, 1980). In addition, utilization studies show that single mothers are proportionately the highest consumers of mental-health services (Guttentag et al., 1980). This set of findings may be consistent with the view that depression is a function of recent historical changes in women's roles (see Gove, 1979, p. 41). Young unmarried women faced with critical life choices are at the same time faced with conflicting, confusing, and changing information on appropriate role behaviors.

Though not explaining sex differences explicitly, Rosenfield (1982) finds that deviations from expected role behavior affects both males and females. She finds that both females and males experience a more severe societal reaction (psychiatric hospitalization) when behavior is inconsistent with traditional norms (men for neurosis and depression, and women for personality disorders and substance abuse). Thus, it is not sex-role socialization per se but rather deviations from expected role behavior that accounts for commitment to hospitalization. If this is true, then one might expect an increase in rates of mental distress among women as women's roles undergo change, at least until the newer role becomes expected behavior.

In sum, women appear to have higher rates of depression than do men. However, this is not true across all marital-status categories, nor are women depressed to the same degree in all studies. This variation in female depression across marital-status categories and between studies calls into question the sufficiency of the artifactual, sex-role, and biological explanations in their present form, and suggests to us that an alternative explanation needs to be explored.

Gender and Social Support

Findings of different patterns for men and women across various statuses may be consistent with recent evidence pointing to the role of social support as an important factor for mental health. This evidence suggests that social support may be a key element accounting for gender and marital-status differences in mental health.

Numerous studies have addressed themselves to the relationship between marital status, social support, and mental health. For example, in the examination of support networks, the spouse is often viewed as a key resource for most adults, providing a large share of the emotional and instrumental support received (Brown et al., 1975). The marital relationship is viewed as constituting a primary resource for mitigating the effects of stressful life events, providing emotional support, and affirming one's identity (Rosen, Goldsmith, and Redick, 1979; Campbell, 1980). Research evidence indicates that, in general, being married is better for one's mental health (Vanfossen, 1981). The mental well-being of married persons may in part be attributable to the social support provided by an ongoing primary relationship with a spouse. The presence of a spouse presumably provides the opportunity to engage in an intimate and trusting relationship in which problems and daily experiences can be shared, anxieties reduced, and emotional assurance and self-validation gained (Burke and Weir, 1977; Campbell, 1980; Hughes and Gove, 1981; Vanfossen, 1981). However, research on friendship among nonmarried persons shows that friendships of a close, caring, and trusting nature can offer an alternative source for the intimacy, caring, and social support found in marriage (Nelson, 1966; Stein, 1981). For females, during certain phases of their life, friendships with other females have been found to be just as supportive and intimate as relationships with husbands or male friends (McLanahan, Wedemeyer, and Adelberg, 1981). Furthermore, these relationships can be of therapeutic value (Candy, 1981; Davidson and Packard, 1981).

Another important reason for considering social support as a factor in explaining gender and marital-status differences in mental health comes from its success in predicting mental-health status in general. Lin, Woelfel, and Light (see Chapter 16), for example, found that strong ties have a significant effect in reducing the potential impact of important and undesirable events on depression. A healthy mental state requires sharing and confiding with intimates who can empathize with the problems involved. Depression is a problem requiring expressive action, which is most successfully accomplished through access to and use of strong social ties. Social-resources theory predicts, therefore, that depression is a function of the strength of tie between ego and alter. The stronger the social tie used for expressive problems, the lower the depression.

Many investigators have directed their attention toward the confidant as an indicator of social support. Evidence from these studies indicates that having a confidant significantly affects an individual's mental health (Lowenthal and Havens, 1968; Cassel, 1974a; Brown et al., 1975; Kaplan et al., 1977). The presence of a person whom one can confide in and relate to in an intimate manner seems to protect one's mental health and buffer potential adverse effects of stressful life events.

In this chapter we examine the gender of the confidant and the role relationship between the confidant and the respondent. The support of a confidant may be crucial for maintaining a sense of mental well-being. Relationships that provide face-to-face interaction of an intimate and trusting nature are fundamental to the continuing legitimation of an individual's identity and self-worth (Cooley, 1902; Mead, 1934; McLanahan et al., 1981).

Gender of the Confidant and the Respondent's Well-Being

Although social support provided by social-network relationships has become a topic of increasing interest among mental-health researchers, few have investigated whether or not characteristics of confidant relations influence the nature and quality of social support and, in turn, mental health. Although the presence of a confidant has been shown to relate to mental health and well-being, it is not known whether or not the sex of one's confidant makes a difference.

From the previous discussion, we can posit that the sex of the confidant should indeed make a difference. Two major themes can be derived from the literature. On the one hand, women are viewed as society's primary confidants for both sexes. On the other hand, each gender is viewed as serving the other in a mutually comforting capacity.

The predominant argument states that a female confidant is better than a male confidant in providing emotional support for both sexes. This argument is based on the theory that *expressive roles* are assumed by women. Parsons and Bales (1955) and Zelditch (1955), for example, maintain that women are more likely than men to be socialized into expressive roles emphasizing nurturance and emotional sustenance, whereas men are more likely to be socialized into *instrumental roles* emphasizing achievement and accomplishment. Parsons and Bales (1955) argue that it is functional for society that men perform the instrumental role and that women perform the expressive role. Others support variations of this theme (McClelland, 1964; Erikson, 1968). Bernard (1971) has more recently argued that the expressive function, which she calls the stroking function, is the all-pervading task of women. An expressive person is said to show solidarity, to raise the status of others, to give help, reward, agree, concur, comply, understand, and passively accept (Vanfossen, 1981).

The traditional stereotype of men, on the other hand, consists of a cluster of the traits that are instrumental in nature. Being masculine means being assertive; strong; analytical; interested in things, not people; and dominant. Men are supposed to be unexpressive and unemotional at least to the extent that it is not considered masculine to cry, be sad, or appear vulnerable (see Forisha, 1978).

Empirical evidence reveals that females perceive themselves as more expressive than do males. In a study of college students' self-ratings, M. M. Johnson (1975) found that women see themselves as "more positively expressive (sweeter and kinder)" and "not as negatively expressive (quarrelsome and unfriendly)" as men see themselves.

The research literature has extensively linked women to a nurturing role. According to Shields (1975), many functional psychologists hold that women evolved with an inborn tendency to nurture others. Oakley (1981) reports on studies that show that boys choose toys that symbolize physical and mechanical activities, whereas girls choose toys that symbolize nurturing and adornment. In a study by Rosenthal, Archer, DiMatteo, Kowumaki, and Rogers (1974), women were shown to be more accurate in identifying various emotions than were men.

Empirical studies investigating sex differences in the quality of marital interaction report differential effects on the mental health of spouses. For example, Blood and Wolfe (1968) report that on the average husbands do not carry out the "mental hygiene functions" of marriages. Almost a third of the husbands of 731 respondents were reported to respond to their wives' stress problems with criticism, rejection, passive listening, or dismissal. The idea that wives perform the expressive function more than do husbands received further support in Vanfossen's (1981) study of the mental-health effects of spousal support. Husbands consistently reported greater support from spouses, and expressive support by the spouse was negatively associated with depression.

Women's expressive–accommodative behavior is important not only in marital relationships but in primary relationships in general. In a study of friendship dyads, Booth (1972) found that males had more friends of the opposite sex than did females. In fact, women had a greater propensity for same-sex close friendships. He suggests that socialization is a factor in explaining his findings, arguing that men are encouraged early to make contact with females, whereas women are socialized to be more passive in cross-sex contact. In examining the quality of friendships, he reports that female friendship ties are richer in spontaneity and confidences than are males', which he attributes to women's early training in socioemotional roles. Further corroboration comes from Weiss's (1973) study of members of Parents Without Partners. Although both men and women tended to seek new emotional cross-sex attachments, women were likely to form close friendships with members of the same sex whereas men exhibited little interest in forming such relationships.

However, an alternative argument that males should be more effective as confidants for women also appears in the literature. R. P. Bell

(1981) states that many women find that their adult status or prestige depends on their attachment to a male. This is not surprising because women not only have lower social status than do men in our society, but both sexes tend to value male characteristics and activities more highly than they do those of women (Brown, 1956; Goode, 1965; Goldberg and Lewis, 1969; Skolnick and Skolnick, 1974). In addition, the family serves as the major paradigm of social relations in our society. Whereas women are seen as serving a supportive function for males, males are seen as the basis of economic support for women. In exchange for her supportive role, woman is provided with a sense of security and comfort based on the male's status and money. In this sense, man can be viewed as woman's *protector*, in addition to being an important source of her status or prestige. Therefore, to the extent that males serve these functions, or more precisely, to the extent that a woman perceives this to be the case, a woman who has a confidant-type relationship with a male would be less depressed.

There is some tangential support for this line of reasoning. Forisha (1978) notes that women's friendships with other women lack staying power when men are involved. Women are seen as abandoning women's friendships to get access to approval from men, perhaps because women receive status and security from men and not from other women. However, Almquist (1979) posits that there is cultural pressure for women to be attached to males. She also argues that the need for approval from men arises from the fact that a woman's self-esteem rests, in part, upon affirmation of her femininity, and femininity includes the ability to attract men. As Kagan (1964) has noted, the definition of a woman's femininity requires reaction from other people. Hence, women cannot assess whether they are attractive, nurturing, or helpful without continual interaction and feedback from others. Consequently, women have a greater need for the approval of men as well as a greater fear of rejection than men have (Bardwick, Douvan, Horner, and Gutman, 1970). Arguments that men seek out women and women seek out men can also be derived from the general fear in our society that seeking out a same-sex confidant is associated with homosexuality. In this case, having a same-sex confidant would be uncomfortable. This set of arguments leads one to conclude that having a cross-sex confidant may be associated with lower levels of depression.

We have thus far presented arguments suggesting on the one hand that women are society's foremost nurturers and, on the other hand, that each sex serves the other in a mutually beneficial, albeit different, capacity. Although the preponderance of evidence and conjecture does lend itself to the view that women are the preferred confidants, there are plausible arguments that cross-sex confidants are most valuable.

Thus, in view of the significant role social support has played in explanations of mental health in general, and in light of evidence that having a confidant is a significant factor for an individual's mental health, we propose to examine the gender of the confidant as a critical component of social support in explaining both gender and marital differences in mental health, as revealed in our data from the Albany Area Health Study. We investigate (1) the extent to which each gender is elected as confidants, (2) whether the gender of the respondent's confidant makes a difference in the level of depression, and (3) whether this difference can account for the gender and marital-status differences in mental health.

DATA AND MEASUREMENT

The major variables include gender of the respondent and of the confidant, marital change, age, role relationship between respondent and confidant, and respondent's employment status.

Measurement of gender of the respondent was straightforward, with males assigned the value of 1 and females the value of 2. Prior to determining the gender of the confidant, and the role relationship between respondent and confidant, we first operationalized the confidant concept as proposed by Lowenthal and Havens (1968) and Kaplan et al. (1977), which focused on the individuals to whom one can confide problems (see Chapter 7). In both the first wave in 1979 at Time 1 (T1) and the second wave in 1980 at Time 2 (T2), respondents were asked if, during the past 6 months, there had been anyone in particular they could trust and talk to (T1) or confide in or talk to about themselves or their problems (T2). The wording change between T1 and T2 was made to more specifically focus on a respondent's own problems (see Chapter 9). As will be seen later, this change did elicit clearer responses in that more respondents named confidants at T2, and the effects of such confidants were also more significant at T2. The reader should keep this in mind as we proceed.

If respondents responded yes to this confidant question, they were asked a series of questions that elicited information permitting us to determine the number and characteristics of confidants. For the most important confidant named, we ascertained the confidant's gender. The gender of the confidant was assessed at both T1 and T2.

It should be noted that of the 866 respondents who provided responses on the confidant questions, 574 specified characteristics of confidants for both the T1 and T2 surveys. These 574 individuals constituted the respondents for analysis in this chapter. Another 265 respondents did not provide confidant information on one of the two surveys, and 27 others did not furnish the information on either survey.

As our depression measure we used the Center for Epidemiologic Studies Depression (CES-D) Scale (Radloff, 1975; 1977). The respondent's score is based on a simple summated score from 20 items reported for the week prior to the survey. Its reliability in community studies is well documented (see Chapter 4).

Gender Differences in Depression and the Naming of Confidants

We first verified the basic assumption that females are more depressed than are males. Our data are consistent with previous studies that show females scoring higher on CES-D than males. At T1, the mean CES-D score was 9.67 for females and 8.13 for males. At T2, the mean CES-D score was 10.08 for females and 8.38 for males. These differences are statistically significant at the .05 level. The zero-order correlation between gender and CES-D was .09 at T1 and .08 at T2, both statistically significant although low in magnitude.

We next examined the gender of those selected as confidants by the gender of the respondent. At T1, 63% of the male respondents chose female confidants, whereas only 47% of the female respondents chose male confidants. At T2, 78% of the male respondents chose female confidants and 55% of female respondents chose male confidants. The results thus show a gender difference in choice of confidants. At both T1 and T2, more male respondents than female respondents chose opposite-sex confidants. These percentages appear in Figure 15.1.

Note that both male and female respondents named more opposite-sex confidants at T2 as compared to T1. This may have been due in part to the differences in the wording of the confidant question. Nevertheless, within-time-period analysis (comparing the difference between male and female respondents at each time period) showed a significant difference between the males and females in naming opposite-sex confidants ($p < .05$ at T1).

We next investigated whether the differences in naming opposite-sex confidants could explain the difference in depression between males and females. In other words, we wished to test the extent to which the gender–depression relationship was in fact due to fewer opposite-sex confidants among the females.

The panel data not only allowed us to examine these effects for T1 and T2 separately; they also provided the opportunity to explore whether change of confidants between T1 and T2 affected mental health. To assess these effects, we examined the four categories of male

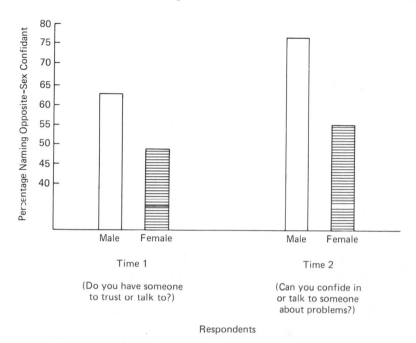

Figure 15.1   Percentage of male and female respondents choosing opposite-sex confidants at Time 1 and Time 2, Albany Area Health Study.

and female respondents: (1) those who named same-sex confidants at T1 and T2, (2) those who named opposite-sex confidants at T1 but same-sex confidants at T2, (3) those who named same-sex confidants at T1 but opposite-sex confidants at T2, and (4) those who named opposite-sex confidants at both T1 and T2.

If an opposite-sex confidant lowers a person's depression, then we would expect the depression scores to be highest among Group 1 above (having same-sex confidants at both T1 and T2) and lowest among Group 4 (having opposite-sex confidants at both T1 and T2). Furthermore, when a person changes from a same-sex to an opposite-sex confidant, the person's depression score should be lower than that for the person who made the change the other way around (changing from an opposite-sex to a same-sex confidant). Data for these comparisons are presented in Figure 15.2.[1]

As can be seen, the highest mean CES-D scores were registered by

---

[1]When a person named an opposite-sex or a same-sex confidant at both T1 and T2, that confidant may have been either the same individual or different individuals. This finer distinction is not made here.

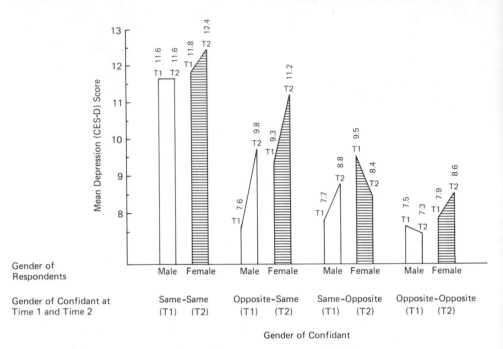

Figure 15.2 Depression (mean CES-D scores) for male and female respondents with same-sex and/or opposite-sex confidants at Time 1 and Time 2, Albany Area Health Study.

both males and females who had had same-sex confidants at both T1 and T2. Furthermore, there was no significant difference in these depression scores between males and females. The lowest average CES-D scores were obtained for both males and females who had had opposite-sex confidants at both T1 and T2. Again, there was no significant difference in the scores between the males and females.

The average CES-D scores of respondents switching confidants between T1 and T2 fall between the two no-change categories—lower than those with same-sex confidants at both T1 and T2, and higher than those with opposite-sex confidants. There is an increase in CES-D scores from T1 to T2 for those who switched from an opposite-sex confidant in T1 to a same-sex confidant in T2. However, part of the increase may be due to the wording change in the confidant question.

Similar caution must be exercised in interpreting a slight (and insignificant) increase in CES-D scores for those males who switched from a same-sex confidant in T1 to an opposite-sex confidant in T2. Among those females who switched from a same-sex confidant to an opposite-sex confidant, CES-D scores show the expected decrease from T1 to T2.

These patterns, therefore, clearly link opposite-sex confidants to lower depression scores. Having an opposite-sex confidant negatively affects depression for both males and females. The data strongly suggest that when the gender of the confidant is taken into account, much of the difference in depression between males and females disappears. To further demonstrate the effect of the confidant's gender, we recall that the zero-correlation between the gender and the CES-D of the respondent at T2 was .09. We now construct a variable called CONFSEX (confidant's sex), which carries four value categories: 1 = naming a same-sex confidant at T1 and T2; 2 = naming an opposite-sex confidant at T1 and a same-sex confidant at T2; 3 = naming a same-sex confidant at T1 and an opposite-sex confidant at T2; and 4 = naming an opposite-sex confidant at both T1 and T2. Thus, the variable assumes a greater value when it represents a higher probability of having an opposite-sex confidant. Regressing CES-D$_2$ on the sex of the respondent and on CONFSEX resulted in two standardized coefficients of .04 and −.17, respectively. This, again, shows that when the gender of the confidant is taken into account, the low but significant effect on depression of gender of the respondent alone is reduced to insignificance.

Thus, the results of our research support the view that the gender of the confidant is an important predictor of mental-health status. Most important, gender differences in our measure of mental health substantially disappear with the inclusion of the gender of the confidant as a control variable. Depression levels are similarly low for both sexes when each has an opposite-sex confidant; switching from a same-sex confidant to an opposite-sex confidant also reduces the depression score.

These results bring into focus other marital-status and marital-change variables. One plausible confounding factor, for example, might be that most married respondents name their spouses as confidants, whereas most unmarried respondents (especially women) name same-sex confidants. The effect of the opposite-sex confidant might simply be a surrogate effect of marital status. Further, what happens to the social ties and therefore the confidants of individuals who have experienced marital change or disruption (especially those separated, divorced, or widowed)? We now turn to these issues.

MARITAL CHANGE AND CONFIDANTS

A marital-change variable was created from our measurement of marital status over both time periods. Marital-status categories include married, divorced, separated, widowed, and single. Because recency of marital disruption is associated with high levels of depression and because it may necessitate a change in the respondent's social network, a marital-disruption variable was added to this typology (see Chapter 16). From the responses the following marital-status and disruption typology was constructed: (1) married, (2) divorced (both in the past year and for more than a year), (3) stably separated (a year or more), (4) stably widowed, (5) recently separated or widowed (within a year), and (6) never married. A stable status means that the status has not changed over a period of at least 1 year, whereas a "recently" changed status refers to a status change within the prior 12-month period.

We expect that access to social-network resources is affected not only by marital status itself but by the changes brought about by any recent shift in marital status, because being married provides the maximum opportunity to gain access to an opposite-sex confidant. Furthermore, change in marital status may have a differential effect by gender on access to opposite-sex confidants.

Each respondent was asked to identify his/her relationship to the confidant from among 12 categories: (1) spouse/lover, (2) son/daughter, (3) mother/father, (4) brother/sister, (5) in-law, (6) other relative, (7) close friend, (8) other acquaintance, (9) neighbor, (10) co-worker, (11) boss/superior, and (12) helping professional.

The gender of confidants over the two time periods for each marital-change category are presented in Table 15.1.

Note that the proportion of females and males in each marital category is approximately the same, with the exception of the never-married category and those widowed more than a year. Consistent with census data, widowed females far outnumber widowed male respondents. By contrast, in our data more males are single than are females.

Of great interest is the fact that in all marital categories males chose females as confidants at one time or another far more often than females chose males. For example, 58% of the married males had female confidants in both time periods, whereas 43% of the married females chose male confidants in both periods. In addition, 50% of divorced males consistently chose females in both time periods, whereas only 19% of divorced females consistently chose males; 39% of never-married males consistently chose females, but only 6% never-married females chose males in both periods; 57% of the men separated more than a year consistently chose females as confidants, whereas only 17% of such females chose males; and 50% of the males widowed more than a year consistently chose females, whereas 11% stably widowed females chose males. Thus, men tended to choose females as confidants across all marital categories, whereas females tended to choose males over

TABLE 15.1

Percentage Distribution of Gender of Confidant at Time 1 and Time 2 by Marital Category and Gender of Respondents[a,b]

Gender of confidant at Time 1 and Time 2	Marital category					
	Married	Divorced	Never married	Stably separated[c]	Stably widowed[d]	Recently separated/ widowed[d]
Male respondents						
	(N = 169)	(N = 18)	(N = 56)	(N = 7)	(N = 2)	(N = 1)
Male–male	8.3%	16.7%	19.6%	28.6%	—	100.0%
Male–female	26.6	27.8	19.6	(14.3)	(50.0%)	—
Female–male	7.1	(5.6)	21.4	—	—	—
Female–female	58.0	50.0	39.3	57.1	(50.0)	—
	100.0	100.1	100.1	100.0	100.0	100.0
Female respondents						
	(N = 195)	(N = 21)	(N = 56)	(N = 7)	(N = 18)	(N = 1)
Male–male	42.6%	19.1%	5.6%	(16.7%)	11.1%	(100.0%)
Male–female	13.9	9.5	16.7	(16.7)	11.1	—
Female–male	21.0	28.6	30.6	(16.7)	22.2	—
Female–female	22.6	42.9	47.2	50.0	55.6	—
	100.1	100.1	100.1	100.1	100.0	100.0

[a]Some percentages total more than 100% due to roundings.
[b]All single-case cells are in parentheses.
[c]For more than a year.
[d]For less than a year.

females as confidants only when they were married. The conclusion is clear. Men choose women as confidants far more often than women choose men, regardless of marital-change categories.

We then examined the effect of the gender of the confidant on depression itself for each marital-status category. Because of the large number of cells and the limited number of respondents, the mean CES-D scores can only be considered suggestive. Nevertheless, the pattern of results is persistent and clear (see Table 15.2).

Among the married female and male respondents, high levels of depression (CES-D) are found among those who chose same-sex confidants in both time periods and low levels among those who chose opposite-sex confidants in both time periods. Our analysis shows, therefore, that among the married, choosing an opposite-sex confidant results in a better state of mental health. Second, high levels of CES-D are associated with divorced women independent of the sex of the

TABLE 15.2
Depression (CES-D) by Marital Category and Gender of Respondents and Confidants[a]

	Married	Divorced	Never married	Stably separated[b]	Stably widowed[b]	Recently separated/widowed[c]
Male respondents						
Depression (CES-D) at Time 2	(N = 165)	(N = 18)	(N = 56)	(N = 7)	(N = 1)	—
	7.33	8.33	10.09	20.43	(13.00)	—
Gender of confidants at Time 1 and Time 2						
Male–male	9.8	8.7	13.8	23.0	—	—
Male–female	8.3	8.6	8.1	(9.0)	(13.0)	—
Female–male	9.5	(12.0)	10.1	—	—	—
Female–female	6.2	7.7	9.0	22.0	—	—
Female respondents						
Depression (CES-D) at Time 2	(N = 192)	(N = 20)	(N = 35)	(N = 6)	(N = 17)	—
	9.33	13.00	10.63	4.17	9.06	(31.0)
Gender of confidants at Time 1 and 2						
Male–male	8.0	13.5	14.0	(5.0)	(6.0)	(31.0)
Male–female	8.6	20.5	17.0	(4.0)	6.0	—
Female–male	8.3	14.0	6.9	(5.0)	7.8	—
Female–female	13.2	10.1	10.3	3.7	10.5	—

[a]All single-case cells are in parentheses.
[b]For more than a year.
[c]For less than a year.

confidant. Third, high levels of CES-D are associated with never-married women independent of the sex of the confidant, except for those women who had switched from a female confidant at T1 to a male confidant at T2. And high levels of CES-D can be observed also for never-married men, especially those who chose same-sex confidants over both time periods.

In general, then, men benefited more from opposite-sex confidants than from same-sex confidants in any marital category. On the other hand, women benefited more from opposite-sex confidants only when they were married. When they were single or divorced, opposite-sex confidants didn't seem to help. The effects for the separated and widowed were less clear, because there were too few cases for analysis.

We wondered whether these differences could be accounted for by the specific role relationship between respondent and confidant. Were all or most opposite-sex confidants of the married respondents their spouses? Who were the opposite-sex confidants for the never-married and divorced women who seem to have provided ineffective support? The number of possible categories and sample sizes do not permit detailed analysis. However, we explored these issues by focusing on the confidants of the married, divorced, and never-married respondents at T2.

We found that the overwhelming majority of the married respondents, both males and females, chose spouses/lovers as opposite-sex confidants (131 of the 137 males and 85 of the 89 females who named opposite-sex confidants chose their spouses/lovers). Most of the married females who named same-sex confidants chose relatives (30) or friends (35), and only one named a lover. On the other hand, married males when naming same-sex confidants chose friends (10), lovers (7), relatives (5) acquaintances (4), and a helping professional (1). Most of the married respondents who chose spouses/lovers scored low on the CES-D (in the range of 4 to 9) as compared to those who chose other opposite-sex or same-sex confidants.

For the divorced, both males and females tended to name spouses/lovers, relatives, or friends as their confidants. Divorced males who chose opposite-sex confidants showed low CES-D scores regardless of whether the confidant was a lover, relative, or friend. Divorced females who named relatives fared much better than did those who named a friend, acquaintance, or even a lover. For example, one divorced female respondent who named a male spouse/lover at T1 and a female acquaintance at T2 as confidants, scored a high 32 and 23 on the CES-D scale at T1 and T2, respectively. Another who named a male spouse/lover as confidant at T1 and a male friend at T2 scored 25 and

29, respectively, on the CES-D. The only type of confidant who seemed to provide adequate and consistent support for the divorced females was a relative. But there were too few cases to permit any definitive conclusions.

Most never-married males and females named lovers, relatives, and friends as confidants. For the never-married males, the strength of the role tie with the confidant was consistently the clear predictor of CES-D scores—the stronger the tie (lovers, relatives), the lower the CES-D score. This held true for both opposite-sex and same-sex confidants. For the never-married females, the pattern was much more mixed. Many ($N = 9$) seemed to benefit from having opposite-sex lovers as confidants (with CES-D scores less than 10), but two suffered as a result (CES-D scores of 14 and 26). Female-friend confidants (5) mostly did not help female respondents (with CES-D scores between 13 and 23), although a few (3) seemed to be doing fine (CES-D scores from 0 to 3). Female relatives were not particularly effective, either (CES-D scores from 8 to 14).

These observations do not permit any definitive generalizations, but they seem to suggest that (1) married respondents benefited from their spouses, (2) opposite-sex ties benefited divorced men, (3) divorced females drew support most effectively from relatives, and (4) married males benefited from strong-role ties, but never-married females showed varying effects on their mental health from confidants with different degrees of role ties.

MULTIVARIATE ANALYSIS

Because these findings are representative only of mean differences between categories, we now present the hypotheses within the context of a multivariate design. At this point the model is made slightly more complicated by the inclusion of several additional control variables. Age and depression level at T1 (CES-D_1) are included, because there is evidence that both are related to marital status and depression at T2 (CES-D_2). In addition, two previous categorical variables have been reconstructed as continuous variables for this analysis. A marital-change variable was constructed: (1) married at T2, independent of T1 marital status, (2) separated or widowed for more than a year or non-married at T2, and (3) separated or widowed within the year at T2. The strength-of-role-tie variable was constructed from the respondent's role relationship with the confidant, with the following values: 0 = acquaintance or helping professional was named at T2, regardless of who was named at T1; 1 = friend was named at T2, regardless of who was named at T1; 2 = relative was named at T2, regardless of who was named at T1; 3 = spouse was named at T1 but not at T2; and 4 = spouse was named at both T1 and T2. Again, these represent an ordered set that is consistent with our theory. We also included employment status to assess the effects of traditional versus nontraditional status on CES-D (1 = employment, 0 = no employment). The basic statistics and the zero-order correlations of these variables appear in Table 15.3.

For the first equation, we regressed marital change at T2 on CES-D at T1, gender, age, and employment status at T1 and T2. As presented in Table 15.4, the results show a positive relationship between CES-D$_1$ and marital change, no relationship between gender and marital change, and a negative relationship between age and marital change. A negative but very small association is shown between marital change and employment at T1, and a positive but very small association is shown between marital change and employment at T2. Thus, the higher the CES-D$_1$ score and the younger the age, the more likely it is that the respondent will have undergone marital change.

In the second equation, the gender of the respondent in relation to that of the confidant (CONFSEX) was regressed on these same variables. Table 15.4 shows that male gender and marital change of the respondent were negatively related to CONFSEX; that is, females were more likely than males to name a same-sex confidant, and marital change was likely to result in a switch to a same-sex confidant. CES-D$_1$, age, employment status at T1, and employment status at T2 had no direct relationship to gender of the confidant.

Strength of the role tie between confidant and respondent, the third equation, as expected was best predicted by the gender of the confidant in relation to that of the respondent. The only other variable exerting direct influence on strength of tie was marital change. CES-D$_1$ and gender of the respondent had only indirect influence on the strength of tie between confidant and respondent, mainly mediated through marital change and gender of the confidant, respectively, as already indicated in earlier discussions. As with the other dependent variables, no relationship appeared between strength of role tie and employment status.

Finally, the results of the fourth equation reveal that the best predictors of CES-D$_2$ are CES-D$_1$ and the strength of tie between confidant and respondent. The remaining variables have significant, although indirect, effects on CES-D$_2$. These findings are summarized in a path model presented in Figure 15.3.

TABLE 15.3
Correlations among Model Variables with Means and Standard Deviations[a]

Variable	Depression at T1 (CES-D$_1$)	Gender	Age	Marital change	CONFSEX	Strength of tie	Depression at T2 (CES-D$_2$)	Employment status at T$_1$	Employment status at T$_2$
Depression (CES-D), Time 1	560	560	560	552	534	536	553	556	557
Gender (1 = male, 2 = female)	.09	574	574	566	547	549	567	570	570
Age, Time 1	-.10	-.03	574	566	547	549	567	570	570
Marital change	.21	-.01	-.21	566	539	541	559	562	562
CONFSEX (confidant's gender)	-.16	-.26	.08	-.22	547	545	541	545	544
Strength of role tie	-.19	-.12	.08	-.44	.68	549	543	547	546
Depression (CES-D), Time 2	.43	.08	-.08	.18	-.18	-.22	567	563	563
Employment status, Time 1 (0 = not working, 1 = working)	-.12	-.26	-.19	.01	.14	.04	-.10	570	567
Employment status, Time 2 (0 = not working, 1 = working)	-.05	-.26	-.26	.08	.08	-.01	-.07	.68	570
Mean	8.94	1.53	39.40	1.36	2.87	2.60	9.45	.58	.61
SD	8.90	.50	15.20	.51	1.19	1.28	10.07	.49	.49

[a]Correlation coefficients are in the lower off-diagonals. The sample sizes are in the diagonals and upper off-diagonals.

TABLE 15.4
Correlations among Model Variables for Those with Confidants at Time 1 and Time 2

	Equations							
	Marital change		CONFSEX (gender of confidant)		Strength of role tie		Depression, T2 (CES-D2)	
Variable	Standardized	Metric (standard error)	Standardized	Metric (standard error)	Standardized	Metric (standard error)	Standardized	Metric (standard error)
Depression (CES-D), T1	.19	.01 (.00)	-.03	-.01 (.01)	-.04	-.01 (.00)	-.39	.44 (.05)
Gender	-.03	-.03 (.05)	-.24	-.57 (.10)	.03	.07 (.08)	.01	.26 (.84)
Age	-.18	-.01 (.00)	.04	.00 (.00)	-.05	-.00 (.00)	-.04	-.02 (.03)
Marital change	—	—	-.20	-.44 (.09)	-.30	-.70 (.07)	.04	.80 (.83)
CONFSEX	—	—	—	—	.62	.67 (.03)	-.02	-.15 (.47)
Strength of role tie	—	—	—	—	—	—	-.11	-.88 (.45)
Employment status, T1	-.06	-.07 (.06)	-.09	.22 (.14)	-.04	-.10 (.11)	-.02	-.42 (1.10)
Employment status, T2	.08	.09 (.06)	-.03	-.06 (.14)	-.02	-.05 (.11)	-.05	-.97 (1.12)
Intercept		1.55		4.22		1.85		8.56
R² (%)	.08		.13		.55		.21	

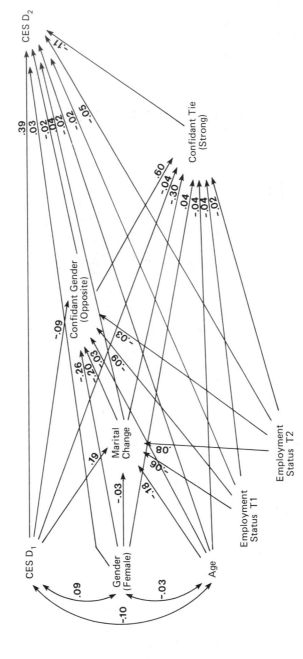

Figure 15.3 Path analysis for model variables.

SUMMARY AND DISCUSSION

Depression differences between men and women constitute an important problem for researchers. In this chapter we have argued that the difference may be due in large part to the nature of social relations between intimates. In particular, we suggest that intimate association with those of the opposite sex promotes mental health.

The Albany Area Health Study data confirmed this expectation. Both men and women exhibited lower scores on the CES-D scale when they reported having opposite-sex rather than same-sex confidants. Indeed, when the gender of the confidant was held constant, the difference in depression between men and women largely disappeared, because women had more same-sex confidants than men did. The panel data further confirmed that those switching from a same-sex confidant to an opposite-sex confidant over a 1-year period had improved mental health.

Further analysis showed that the effect of the opposite-sex confidant held true for both married and unmarried men. It also held true among married women. But for unmarried women (especially for the never-married and the divorced), the opposite-sex confidants did not show an appreciably more positive effect than did same-sex confidants. These women showed uniformly high depressed mood, regardless of the gender of their confidants. These differences were related to the role relationship between the respondent and the confidant. For married respondents, there was a strong tendency to select the spouse as the confidant, although such a tendency was stronger among men than among women. For unmarried men (except those recently separated), association with a lover or a relative reduced depression. For unmarried women, depression was uniformly high, especially among the divorced. Gender of the confidant made little difference.

In our multivariate analysis, there was a strong direct positive impact of gender of the confidant in relation to that of the respondent on the strength of role tie between the respondent and the confidant, and an indirect negative effect of the confidant's gender on depression (mediated by the strength-of-role tie), even when other control variables ($CESD_1$, gender, and age) and other causal factors (marital change and employment status) were taken into consideration.

The present theory and data do not explain why females are less likely to name opposite-sex ties as confidants. This question deserves further research attention. We suspect that it is related to the socially normative roles assigned to females, as well as to hierarchical status differentiation between the sexes. In our society, males are expected to actively initiate intimate relations, whereas females tend to be reactive. Such expected social roles place the female in a situation in which distrust of confiding relations persists and is costly to mental health. And men and women occupy different positions in the status hierarchy. Furthermore, the inferior economic position usually occupied by women also makes it uncomfortable for a woman to initiate intimate relations. Efforts by women to overcome role and status inequalities with men may generate antagonistic, and consequently uncomfortable, feelings for both sexes. Further investigation is warranted.

These social-structural and normative factors may also account for the lack of positive mental-health effects from opposite-sex confidants for unmarried and divorced women. Our limited data suggest that these women's relationships with opposite-sex confidants (especially male friends) were less stable, suggesting that reluctance or inability to construct intimate and confiding relationships with persons of the opposite sex outside the family deprives them of positive social support. How to overcome such role and status expectations and behavior constitutes an important topic for future research and advocacy.

16

Buffering the Impact of the Most Important Life Event

NAN LIN
MARY WOELFEL
STEPHEN C. LIGHT

INTRODUCTION

Since the mid-1970s, when social support began to be examined in the context of the psychosocial dynamics of physical and mental health, and conceptually integrated into the stressor–illness model (Cassel, 1974; Cobb, 1976; Kaplan et al., 1977; Dean and Lin, 1977; Henderson, 1977), much effort has been devoted to examining the independent as well as the buffering effects of social support. Recent reviews tend to show that social support does exert a direct effect on a number of mental-health measures, but research examining the buffering hypothesis has yielded inconsistent results. Whereas some investigations failed to support the hypothesis (S. R. Pinneau, 1975; Andrews et al., 1978; Lin et al., 1979; Henderson, Byrne, Jones, Scott, and Adcock, 1980; Williams et al., 1981), others found evidence supporting it (R. D. Caplan, 1972; Nuckolls et al., 1972; Brown et al., 1975; Eaton, 1978; Gore, 1978; House and Wells, 1978; LaRocco et al., 1980; Turner, 1981).

SOCIAL SUPPORT,
LIFE EVENTS, AND DEPRESSION

Although the evidence for the buffering effect of social support is mixed, the idea that social support may serve as a buffer against the potential harmful effects of life events remains theoretically intriguing and practically inviting. This chapter represents an attempt at resolving some of the theoretical and empirical issues involved.

Social support for our purpose is defined as the access to and use of strong and homophilous ties (see Chapter 2). The primary research question to be addressed is whether the access to and use of strong and homophilous ties can buffer the potentially harmful effect of an important yet undesirable life event. We begin with specifications of the buffering model.

PREREQUISITES AND ELEMENTS OF THE BUFFERING MODEL

Causal inferences from social-survey data must be made with caution. All research designs, including experimental ones, impose sets of assumptions and biases on any causal inference. With respect to the buffering issue, further complications arise because there is no consensus as to what constitutes evidence of the buffering effect. We consider three possible interpretations (see Chapter 10 for elaborations), propose a set of elements that must be present to test the buffering models, and discuss a possible design that incorporates these elements.

In the narrowest interpretation, buffering is equated with interaction. Social support is said to reduce mental-health problems only in the presence of stressors (i.e., important life events). In this model, social support should not make any difference if important life events are absent. Social support is seen to exert an effect only in conjunction with an adverse condition. This is probably the most popular interpretation. The effect is demonstrated by a negative association between a product term (LE $\times$ SS, a life-events measure multiplied by a social-support measure or their deviation scores) and a mental-health measure.

A second interpretation argues that social support buffers either through its interaction with life events or when it counteracts life events directly. In the counteracting situation, social support becomes mobilized as a result of the occurrence of an adverse condition (creating a positive association between life events and social support). Lin and his associates (1979) and Wheaton (1983a) seem to espouse this interpretation, which proposes that the buffering effect is present either (1) as an interactive effect when the interaction between stressors and social support is significant or (2) as a counteractive effect when stressors and social support are positively associated (LE $\times$ SS), and when each of the two variables also directly affects mental health. Statistically, buffering is said to have occurred if the total effect of stressors on mental problems is reduced in the presence of social support.

Still a third interpretation, and the most liberal one, states that if the direct effect of stressors on mental-health problems varies because of variation in social support, then social support serves as a buffer. This interpretation sees buffering as a global term describing any intervening effect of social support between stressors and mental health. Kessler and McLeod (1984b) and Lin and Dean (1984) seem to prefer this interpretation. This interpretation of the buffering effect encompasses (1) the interaction effect, (2) the counteractive effect, and (3) the mediating effect, when the stressors and social support are negatively related and each exerts a direct effect on mental health. A more detailed discussion of these models can be found in Chapter 10.

The position we adopt here is the last, most liberal interpretation— that buffering occurs when the direct relationship between stressors and illness varies as social support varies. Specifically, we demonstrate the buffering effect by way of a mediating model that shows (1) stressors that are related to mental health and (2) reduction in this relationship in situations where help is provided by strong and/or homophilous ties.

A causal demonstration of the buffering effect further requires the following design conditions: For each case, (1) the design must identify the presence or absence of a set of life events (or a life event considered most important) that is followed by (2) the presence or absence of social support during and subsequent to the events and (3) an indicator of mental health. Conditions (1) and (3) are necessary to demonstrate that poorer mental health is associated with the presence of a set of life events or a single most important life event. Condition (2) is necessary to test whether or not social support alleviates the stress of the event for mental health. Unless these three pieces of information are collected in a clear time-order sequence, the role of social support as an ameliorative agent between stressors and mental health cannot be properly assessed.

There are at least two research strategies one might adopt to meet these conditions, each with its virtues and limitations. One design increasingly used is the panel analysis. Although this design has as its advantage a specific clear-cut time sequence, it is difficult to determine meaningful time lags, and estimations tend to be complicated by problems of autocorrelations among repeated measures of the same variables and by measurement errors. Several studies are currently underway to resolve these problems by using change scores or regression residual scores as dependent variables (Lin and Dean 1984; Lin and Ensel, 1984).

The second design, the one adopted here, traces an individual's experience of a most important life event and ascertains what particular person the individual interacts with during and subsequent to the event. The advantage of this approach is the clear linkage between a particular event and the nature of the social relationship evoked (Dohrenwend, 1982). It therefore becomes possible to compare the depressive symptoms of those who experienced the important life event with those of the individuals who did not. Then, focusing on whether the event experienced was desirable or not, it is possible to identify the exact type of social relationship evoked and the extent to which such a relationship ameliorates the effect of the event on depressive symptoms.[1]

DESIGN AND HYPOTHESES

The theory outlined in the above discussion led to a research design in which the data were collected in the following sequence: Each individual respondent was asked to identify life events experienced during the past 6 months. From the list of life events, each respondent was asked to single out one event that she or he considered most important. Then a series of questions was asked to determine if she or he interacted with any one concerning the event during or after it. If so, information regarding their relationship (strength of the tie and homophily of characteristics) was requested. (See Chapter 9 for more details on this measure.) Finally, the respondent's present depressive symptoms (during the previous week) were asked for.

Further considerations led to the inclusion of several additional variables in the design:

1. *Desirability of an event:* Previous research has suggested that this is a critical variable. Undesirable events seem to exert a greater effect

---

[1]This model can be thought of as an additive model. One disadvantage of this design is its reliance on the respondent's recall of life events and the social support experienced subsequent to the event. However, recall problems are not unique to this particular type of design; all paper-and-pencil or personal surveys confront such risk. Because this design does focus on a particular event, the recall problems are minimized. The ideal design of this kind calls for diary-keeping by each respondent. Eventually the buffering hypothesis should be examined in both its additive and multiplicative forms as well as in panel and tracing designs. Multimethod approaches will add to the credibility of the hypothesis.

than do desirable events on mental-health measures (Myers et al., 1971; Gersten et al., 1974; Paykel, 1974; Vinokur and Selzer, 1975; Ross and Mirowsky, 1979; Tausig, 1982). Thus, it is important to assess the desirability of the important event to the individual.

2. *Most important life event:* The basic research design focuses on the single most important event; it assumes that the depressive impact of this event on those experiencing it is similar to or greater than the impact of the totality of events on those respondents not reporting a single most important one. This assumption needs to be verified, for unless the single most important event can be shown to exert such impact, any further information on social interactions and social support in conjunction with this event would not be worth pursuing. Hypothesis 2 below addresses this issue.

Utilizing all our variables, we now examine a series of hypotheses (depicted in Figure 16.1). Three of the hypotheses (1, 2, and 3) test the effects of the most important life event relative to the totality of life events; the remaining hypotheses (4 and 5) examine the buffering effect of social support.

Hypothesis 1: The mean level of depressive symptoms is positively related to the total number of significant life events. (The initial hypothesis establishes the overall impact of life events on depressive symptoms).

Hypothesis 2: Among those experiencing significant life events, the mean level of depressive symptoms is higher for those experiencing an event they consider most important than for those who did not report experiencing such an important event. (The hypothesis establishes the relative significance of the most important life event. In other words, it tests the assumption that the impact of life events can be best represented by the single most important life event experienced.)

Hypothesis 3: Among those who experienced a most important life event, an undesirable event rather than a desirable one is positively associated with the depressive symptoms. (This hypothesis verifies the effect of desirability of the event as a conditional variable.)

Hypothesis 4: Interaction with others with whom the respondent has stronger ties, during and subsequent to the most important and undesirable life event, will be associated with a lower level of depressive symptoms. (This hypothesis tests the buffering effect of the strength of social ties.)

Hypothesis 5: Interaction with those with whom the respondent has more homophilous ties, during and subsequent to the most important and undesirable life event, will be associated with a lower level of

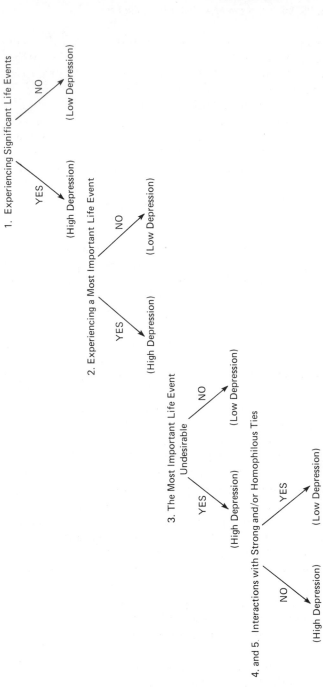

Figure 16.1 Hypotheses (numbered) and predicted outcomes (in parentheses).

depressive symptoms. (This hypothesis examines the buffering effect of the homophily of the ties.)

At this point some notes about measurement are in order. Although this design focuses mainly on a perceived single most important life event that occurred to the respondent in the prior 6-month period, along with the social support received during and after the event, it also examines the effects of the total of life events summated in a score.[2] This allows a comparison between the effect of the total number of significant life events on depressive symptoms and the effect of the single most important life event on the symptoms. Unless there is evidence that the presence of a most important life event has an impact on depression that is greater than or equal to the total events score, we will not proceed to examine the buffering effect. Furthermore, because recent discussion and empirical evidence have pointed to the importance of the degree of desirability of a life event as a qualifying variable, attention will be given to this variable as well.

THE MEASURES

The stressful-life-events variables and the desirability of the event were measured by the interviewer's presenting the respondent with a list of 118 life events and asking: "Have any of these events happened to you in the past six months?" For any event that had happened, the respondent was asked if the event was considered good or bad. Good was assigned a value of 1, and bad, a value of 3. If the respondent was uncertain, the desirability of the event was assigned a value of 2. To measure the important life event, each respondent was asked to name one of the events listed as most important.[3]

[2] The 6-month cutoff period was selected for two reasons. First, Myers et al., (1975) demonstrated that the effects of life events occurring in the past 6 months were more significantly stressful than the effects of life events longer ago. Secondly, Jenkins et al. (1979) demonstrated that recall of events diminishes over time at an approximate rate of 5% per month.

[3] The question reads, "Of all these events occurring to you, which one would you say was the most important?" That is, which one, for better or worse, changed or affected your life the most?" Although it may be the case that the respondents will designate a most important life event from among the set of events experienced simply to oblige the interviewer, while still others are unable to designate a most important life event from among the set of events, either case would bias our results against rather than in support of our hypotheses. We expect high depression levels among those who experience a most important life event and low depression levels among those who do not. Those who

The strength of ties was measured in terms of both the role relationships involved and the dimensions of the interactions. Following
the identification of the most important event, the respondent was
asked whether anyone had helped during or after the event, and what
the role relationship was between the helper and the respondent
(spouse, close friends, etc.). The strength of the tie was represented by
the following categories: 4—spouse/lover, 3—other relative(s), 2—
close friend(s), and 1—weak ties (acquaintances and helping professionals). The higher the category value, the stronger the tie. This classification is consistent with common usage in the literature. The dimensions of interactions were captured with the following series of questions on the frequency and intensity of interactions: (1) number of years
known, (2) frequency of contact during the past 6 months, (3) frequency
of the respondent talking to this person about his/her problems, (4)
frequency of this person talking about his/her problems to the respondent, (5) ease with which to get in contact with the person, (6)
talking freely to the person, and (7) importance of the person to the
respondent (Kaplan, 1975). One additional dimension was added to
assess (8) how much the person helped during the most important life
event (see Chapter 9 for details). These items were scored such that the
lower the score, the more (or longer) the relationship or the greater its
ease, freedom, or importance. To avoid confusion in analysis, the score
was reversed so that the higher the score, the stronger the tie.

To measure homophily of characteristics, a set of questions was
asked about the helper's characteristics, including age, gender, occupation, education, and marital status. An occupational prestige score (Siegel, 1971) was computerized. For the homophily variable, the absolute
difference in scores between the respondent and the helper was calculated for each of these characteristics. The absolute score difference
was then reversed so that the higher its value, the greater homophily
(similarity) there was between the respondent and the helper on that
characteristic.

The dependent variable in the analysis was the Center for Epidemiologic Studies Depression (CES-D) Scale (Markush and Favero,
1974; Radloff, 1977), which was a simple summated score of 20 items

---

designate a most important life event not actually experienced would be included among
those who have experienced a most important life event, thereby artifically lowering the
mean levels of depression for that group according to our hypothesis. Likewise, those
who did not designate a most important life event but who actually did experience it will
be included among those who did not experience the event, artifically inflating the mean
level of depression among those not reporting a most important life event.

related to depression reported for the week prior to the survey (see Chapter 4). The higher the score, the greater the depressive symptoms or the depressed mood. The mean CES-D for the entire sample was 8.63.

EFFECT OF THE MOST IMPORTANT LIFE EVENT

The analyses began with an examination of Hypotheses 1, 2, and 3, concerning the effects on depression of the total sum of life events, the most important life event, and the desirability of the most important life event.

When we compared the low mean CES-D levels for those who did not experience any life events ($\bar{X} = 6.88$) with the high scores for those who did ($\bar{X} = 8.90$), the difference was significant ($p < .05$). Thus, Hypothesis 1 was confirmed. However, as suggested in Hypothesis 2, this association might be due to the most important life event experienced rather than to the total number of life events.

Figure 16.2 presents the mean CES-D scores for three categories of

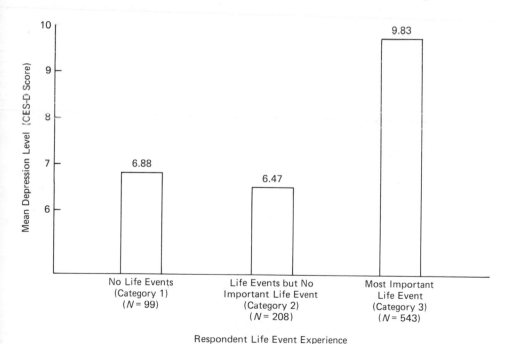

Figure 16.2   Effect of life-events experience on depressive symptoms (CES-D scores).

respondents (excluding missing data): (1) those who did not name any life event(s) during the prior 6 months, (2) those who mentioned life event(s) but did not single out any one as most important, and (3) those who identified a most important life event.

As expected, the mean level of CES-D is highest for those persons who mentioned a most important life event. Based on *t*-tests of significance, the mean difference is significantly high between those who experienced a most important life event and those who did not ($p < .01$ between Category 1 and Category 3, $p < .001$ between Category 2 and Category 3). Furthermore, the mean CES-D scores for those who did not experience any life events and those who experienced life events but did not consider any of them important are both low ($p \leq .10$ between Category 1 and Category 2). Hypothesis 2 is therefore confirmed; that is, although experiencing life events (Categories 2 and 3 combined) is associated with higher depressive symptoms, the association is entirely accounted for by the experience of a most important life event.

We next examine the effect of the desirability of the most important life event (Hypothesis 3). As shown in Figure 16.3, 61% (256) of the respondents (excluding missing data) who mentioned a most important life event perceived the event as *good*, 30% (127) perceived it as *bad*, and the remaining 9% (36) perceived it as of uncertain desirability. And *t*-tests of significance show a significant difference ($p \leq .001$) in the mean CES-D scores between the good and the bad event categories. Those perceiving the event as undesirable score much higher on CES-D ($\bar{X} = 13.25$) than do those perceiving it as desirable ($\bar{X} = 8.55$). Thus, the data show perceived desirability of the important event to be a significant factor in predicting depressive symptoms, a confirmation of the third hypothesis.

To summarize our results thus far, we find that experiencing a most important event during the prior 6 months is decisive in predicting depressed mood. Experiencing an event perceived as bad exacerbates the level of depressive mood. From this point on, we focus only on those who experienced a most important event. It has become clear that those merely experiencing life events, but with no reported important life events, did not show greater depressive symptoms than did those who experienced no life events (see Figure 16.2). The undesirability of the most important event significantly increased the CES-D level and should, therefore, be taken into account.[4]

---

[4]It should be noted that the most important reported events pertained to family and marriage, work and finance, illness and death, and injuries and accidents. No personal habits concerning changes in events (e.g., in sleeping and eating) were mentioned, thus avoiding the problem of confounding such events with depressive symptoms (see Tausig, 1982).

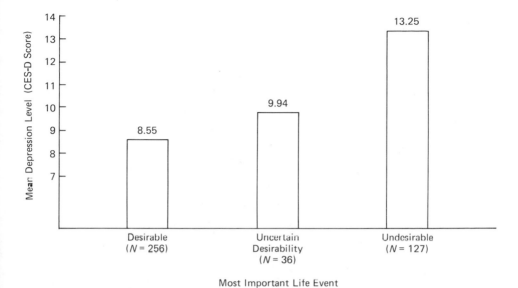

Figure 16.3   Effects of the desirability of the most important life event on depression (CES-D scores).

BUFFERING EFFECTS OF STRONG TIES

Role Relationship with the Helper

As we have proposed, one dimension of social support is the extent to which help is provided by strong and homophilous ties. The results already presented demonstrate that those who experience a most important and undesirable life event show a significantly higher level of depression than do others. If strong and homophilous ties buffer such an event, then respondents experiencing a most important and undesirable event who receive help from strong ties should show lower CES-D scores than do those with similarly stressful experiences but without help from such ties. These hypotheses (4 and 5) will now be examined. We first explore the hypothesis on the effect of the strength of ties (Hypothesis 4).

Figure 16.4 shows mean CES-D scores by the desirability of the event and by the role relationship with the helper for those respondents who received help with a most important life event. As expected, help from stronger ties is generally associated with lower levels of depressed mood. For each level of event desirability, help from a spouse/lover is related to a lower level of depressed mood than is help from any other type of tie. Furthermore, when an event is considered desirable and is

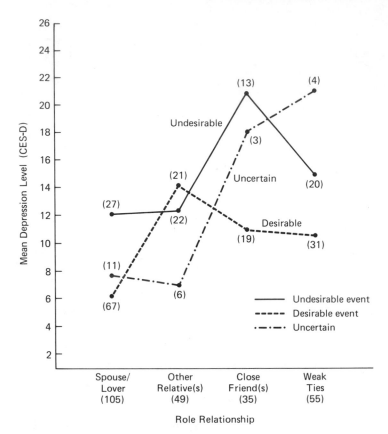

Figure 16.4 Effects of strength of helper's role relationship and the desirability of the most important life event on depression (CES-D scores). (Number of respondents are in parentheses.)

accompanied by help from a spouse/lover, the level of depression is lower than would be expected had the event not occurred (see Figure 16.2). And when an event is considered bad or uncertain and is accompanied by help from a spouse or relative, the mean CES-D level is substantially lower than it is when the event is accompanied by help from a close friend or an acquaintance or helping professional (weak tie). Thus, this is evidence for the buffering effect of social support as indexed by the strength of role relationship of the respondent to the person providing help. There are, however, several anomalies. For bad events, close friends are less effective than are weak ties in reducing depression; and for good events, relatives are less effective than are close friends and weak ties.

The Effect of Marital Status

Because evidence exists that marital disruption is accompanied by high levels of mental disorder, we wondered if it also disrupts other normative social support: In time of marital crisis, such ties as those with close friends or relatives might be rendered ineffective in resolving the tension due to significant life events. Therefore, we conducted separate analyses for those currently married and for those not married. The latter category consists of the single, separated, divorced, and widowed. Among those experiencing an important life event (excluding missing data), 63% (155) were married and 37% (89) were unmarried.

Figure 16.5 shows that for the married, the strength of social ties, as indexed by the role relationship of the helper to ego, is negatively related to the level of depression (CES-D scores) when events are uncertain or undesirable. For the undesirable or uncertain event, those who received help from the strongest ties (spouse/lover) showed lower mean CES-D scores than did those receiving help from weaker ties

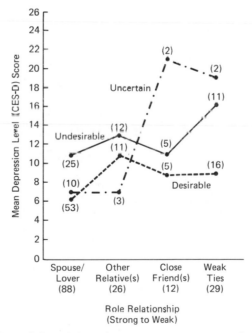

Figure 16.5 Effect of desirability of most important event and strength of helper's role relationship for married respondents on depression (CES-D scores). (Number of respondents in parentheses.)

(other relatives and weak ties). For events considered good, the strength of the tie makes less difference on CES-D scores.

For the unmarried, as shown in Figure 16.6, the hypothesis on the effect of strength of ties on depression does not hold. For undesirable and uncertain events, for example, help from a spouse/lover was associated with a higher rather than a lower level of depressive symptoms. On the other hand, weak ties were associated with a lower level of CES-D in the case of an undesirable event. Thus, anomalies in the initial analysis were found to be due to the responses of the unmarried. This led to further exploration of the possible effects of marital disruption.

Because data on marital status were collected in both the first (1979) and second (1980) surveys, it was possible to examine changes in marital status over the 1-year period. From these data, we constructed nine types of marital engagement and disengagement categories: (1) recently married—those married during the 1-year period, (2) already married—those who had been married before 1979, (3) recently widowed—those who were widowed during the 1-year period, (4) recently

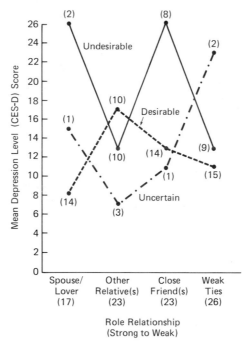

Figure 16.6 Effects of desirability of most important event and strength of helper's role relationship for unmarried respondents on depression (CES-D scores). (Number of respondents in parentheses.)

separated—those who became separated during the 1-year period, (5) already separated—those who had been separated before 1979, (6) recently divorced—those who became divorced during the 1-year period, (7) already divorced—those who had been divorced before 1979, (8) already widowed—those who had been widowed before 1979, and (9) already single—those who had been single since before 1979. These categories were constructed to reflect marital status as a process—from entering into marriage to disruptions of marriage and the return of single status. We then analyzed the depression (CES-D) levels as well as the role relationships with the helpers for each of these categories of respondents. Again, analysis was conducted only for those who had experienced an important life event. Because of the relative sample sizes, it was not feasible to divide the categories further into those experiencing desirable and undesirable events. The results appear in Table 16.1.

As can be seen, CES-D levels were lowest for the recently married and already married, and highest for the recently disrupted (recently widowed and already separated). The disengaged (already separated, recently divorced, already divorced, and already widowed) had moderate CES-D levels, in most cases not showing significantly higher levels than did the married. Thus, if the married–disrupted–disengaged–single are approximate phases in the marital engagement–disengagement process, their expected mental-health statuses can be differentiated.

The role relationships with the helper for these phases also showed differences. For the married, it was the spouse/lover and other relative(s) that accounted for the overwhelming percentage of the helpers with the most important life event. For the disrupted (recently widowed and recently separated), help was mostly provided by other relatives and close friends. For the disengaged (already separated, recently divorced, already divorced, and already widowed), the spouse/lover (probably mostly lovers), other relatives, and close friends were all used as helpers. There was also a trend toward less use of spouse/lover and more use of close friends, acquaintances, and helping professionals (weak ties) further along in the disengagement process (from the already separated and recently divorced to the already divorced and widowed). The single tended to use weaker ties, as compared to the other groups.

The limitations of the sample size do not allow us to control for the desirability of the event or to assess the different depression levels (CES-D) for each combination of marital status and role relationship. However, the marital engagement–disengagement process shows that it affects the type of social ties used as helpers with the most important

TABLE 16.1
Marital Engagement–Disengagement, Proportional Strength of Ties, and Depressive Symptoms (CES-D Scores) for Those Experiencing an Important Life Event

	Marital engagement–disengagement								
Relationship of helper	Recently married (N = 10)	Already married (N = 169)	Recently widowed (N = 2)	Already widowed (N = 14)	Recently separated (N = 12)	Already separated (N = 5)	Recently divorced (N = 6)	Already divorced (N = 15)	Single (N = 49)
Spouse/lover	60.0%	52.7%	0%	7.1%	8.3%	40.0%	33.3%	13.3%	18.8%
Other relative(s)	30.0	16.6	100.0	50.0	16.7	20.0	50.0	6.7	22.9
Close friend(s)	0	8.9	0	7.1	58.3	40.0	0	46.7	20.8
Weak ties	10.0	21.9	0	35.7	16.7	0	16.7	33.3	37.5
Average depression level (CES-D score)	7.4	9.1	26.6	10.6	21.1	12.5	8.1	11.2	9.9

life events, with apparent differential consequences for depressive symptoms. As a person's marital status is disrupted, there is less tendency to use stronger ties and evidence of greater distress.

In the conclusion, the hypothesis on the strength of ties seems to apply only to individuals in a stable marital status (married, divorced, or single). For those who are experiencing marital disruption (recently separated or widowed), the social network is also disrupted in that those who otherwise perform their normative buffering roles can no longer operate effectively.

Interactions with the Helper

Next we examined dimensions of interactions between the respondent and the helper as indicators of the strength of their ties. Correlations were computed between each dimension of interaction and depressive symptoms (CES-D) for three categories: all respondents, married respondents, and unmarried respondents who experienced a most important life event (see Table 16.2). When the effect of the desirability of the event is factored out, results show significant negative relationships between CES-D and most of these interaction dimensions for the married but not for the unmarried. For the married, frequency of contact, reciprocal relations, accessibility, importance of the relationship, and amount of help are significantly and negatively correlated with CES-D. Only durability (years known) and talking freely with the helper do not have any effect on depression. None of the correlations are significant for the unmarried. Again, further analysis of the unmarried is unwarranted because of the categorical nature of the marital engagement–disengagement process and the small sample size. Nevertheless, we speculate that the same interaction processes also affect their interactions with helpers.

Buffering Effects of Homophily of Ties

The theory presented here predicts that the interaction with others who share homophilous characteristics is most effective in promoting mental health (Hypothesis 5). To test this hypothesis, separate analyses were again done for the married and the unmarried. Because the use of a spouse as helper is associated with a lower mean CES-D for the married, gender homophily was not considered for the married. Nor is homophily of occupational prestige included either, because many wives do not work. Because of the small sample size for the homophily

TABLE 16.2

Correlations between Depression (CES-D) and Dimensions of Interaction between Respondent and Helper

Interaction dimensions[b]	Depression (CES-D)[a]					
	Total sample (N)		Married (N)		Not married (N)	
Years helper known	−.04	(274)	−.06	(175)	.06	(99)
	−.08	(241)	−.11	(152)	.009	(86)
Frequency of contact with helper	−.12*	(280)	−.21**	(178)	.02	(102)
	−.12*	(243)	−.20**	(153)	−.003	(87)
Helper talked with about problem	−.06	(279)	−.13*	(178)	.05	(101)
	−.04	(243)	−.11	(153)	−.07	(87)
Helper talking about own problem	−.16**	(278)	−.21**	(178)	−.06	(100)
	−.14*	(242)	−.21**	(153)	−.04	(86)
Helper easy to get in touch with	−.18**	(279)	−.19**	(178)	−.10	(101)
	−.17**	(243)	−.19**	(153)	−.10	(87)
Helper easy to talk freely with	−.04	(277)	−.10	(177)	.02	(100)
	−.04	(241)	−.12	(152)	.04	(86)
Importance of helper	−.10*	(278)	−.19**	(175)	.05	(101)
	−.11	(242)	−.23**	(153)	.04	(87)
Amount of help by helper	−.08	(275)	−.19**	(171)	.11	(100)
	−.08	(239)	−.22**	(150)	.14	(86)

*$p < .05$.

**$p < .01$.

[a]The first coefficient for each item is the zero-order correlation with CES-D, and the second coefficient is the partial correlation, controlling for desirability of event.

[b]For "frequency of contact" through "amount of help," the signs have been changed so that the higher the score, the more of the particular interaction.

variable, results for the unmarried must be read with caution. The results of these analyses appear in Table 16.3.

Negative correlations were expected between the homophily variables and the CES-D scores. That is, the greater the similarity (the higher the score) between the respondent and the helper, the lower the depression score. As predicted for the married, age homophily is negatively related to CES-D as is education, although the latter relationship is not statistically significant. In other words, the greater the dissimilarity in age and, to a lesser extent, education between the respondent and the helper, the more the depressive symptoms. For the unmarried, a stronger negative relationship than expected exists between occupational homophily and CES-D between the ego and the helper. The more dissimilar the occupational prestige between ego and

TABLE 16.3

Correlations between Depression (CES-D) and Homophily of Respondent and Helper Characteristics by Marital Status

| Characteristic | Depression (CES-D)[a] | | | |
	Married (N)[b]		Not married (N)	
Age similarity	−.13*	(169)	.12	(90)
	(−.09)	(148)	(.15)	(90)
Sex similarity	n.a.		.11	(100)
			(.08)	(87)
Education similarity	−.12	(158)	.09	(86)
	(−.09)	(138)	(.17)	(77)
Occupational-status similarity (Seigel scale)	n.a.		−.23*	(73)
			(−.24*)	(62)

*$p < .05$.

[a]The first coefficient for each item is the zero-order correlation, and the second coefficient (within parentheses) is the partial correlation, controlling for desirability of event.

[b]na = No answer.

the helper, the greater the depression. For the unmarried, none of the remaining homophily variables was significantly related to depression.

DISCUSSION

This study examined the buffering effect of social support by identifying the most important life event experienced by an individual and by tracing the characteristics of the person who helped during, and, or after the event. Using the social-resources theory, which links social actions with resources embedded in one's social network, we operationalized social support in terms of the strength of social ties and homophily of characteristics between ego and the helper. Hypotheses were also constructed to test whether one life event considered most important and undesirable by the individual could adequately represent the relationship between stressors and illness (between total life events and depressive symptomatology). We found that individuals did show a greater level of depressive symptoms if they experienced a most important and undesirable event. This effect was reduced if help came from strong rather than weak ties. This was not true, however, for those who had just experienced marital disruption (recently separated or widowed). Similarities in age and education between respondent and

326

helper lowered the married respondents' depressive symptoms, and similarity of occupational status affected the unmarried in the same way.

These findings suggest that social-resources theory may provide a viable theoretical perspective in resolving previous conceptual confusion regarding the relationship between social support and illness. Although the study calls attention to the limiting conditions (e.g., marital ties) within which the theory was shown to operate, it has the potential to bring about a unified perspective on social support and to provide specific hypotheses for testing.

An important serendipitous finding from this study is that marital disengagement may have a substantial disruptive impact on a person's social environment so as to render it, although apparently only temporarily, incapable of providing the necessary support. Such disruption may be due to the transition from old support resources to new ones. Analysis of the unmarried suggests that disruption in marital relations erodes the effectiveness of support provided by those in close social circles. Strong ties are associated with intense and frequent interaction with others who share similar attitudes, values, and lifestyles. Severance of a strong tie may require readjustment on the part of other members of the shared social network, and time may be required to permit reassembly of the same network or construction of a new one.

These variations convinced us that in examining the effects of social support on depression, two dimensions of marital status should be taken into account: (1) current marital status and (2) stability of recent changes in marital status. We conceptualize a *cyclical process of marital engagement and disengagement*. Marital engagement begins with the event of marriage, followed by a period of being married. The marital disengagement begins by two routes: separation and/or divorce or death of the spouse. For those who are separating or divorcing, it takes time to disengage and to reassemble one's old social ties and/or reestablish new ties. For this group, social ties and social resources should resemble somewhat those of the single person. For some, the marital engagement process starts anew. This cyclical process is shown in Figure 16.7.

In this conceptualization, we are guided by the data on how the various groups fared in terms of the depressed mood. This inductive exercise seems informative and meaningful in that the process shows that the stably married (including the recently married) experience low levels of depression (the upper-right-hand quadrangle), whereas the unstable and unmarried (the lower-left-hand quadrangle) experience high levels of depression, especially those recently disengaged from

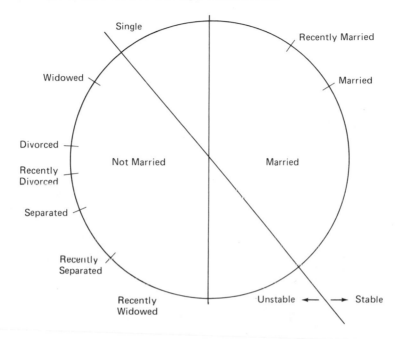

Figure 16.7   The marital engagement–disengagement process.

marriage (the recently separated or widowed). If this conceptualization is meaningful, we should be further informed about how social ties and social resources affect this process. We now turn to these data.

Tables 16.4 and 16.5 present descriptive data on the measures of the strength of ties for the various groups. Because the group sizes are small in most cases, these can only provide heuristic information. In terms of the relationship between helper and respondent relative to the important life event, the recently separated showed a tendency to use close friends and weak ties rather than spouse/lover or other relatives. The use of weak ties continued to be pervasive among the unmarried, especially the divorced, the widowed, and the single. These ties include professionals as well as co-workers.

Recent disengagement from marriage also is linked to the use of ties of less durability. With the exception of the widowed, marital disengagement seems to be associated with ties of more recent acquaintance (see the recently separated, widowed, and divorced). The recently divorced relied on ties of longer duration, mainly because of some use of siblings. Other measures of strength of ties seem to support the general finding that marital disengagement results in the use of ties of less

TABLE 16.4
Strength and Dimensions of Ties by Marital Engagement–Disengagement

Variables	Recently married (N = 10)	Married (N = 169)	Recently widowed (N = 2)	Recently separated (N = 12)	Separated (N = 5)	Recently divorced (N = 6)	Divorced (N = 15)	Widowed (N = 14)	Single (N = 49)
$\bar{X}$ CES-D	7.4	9.05	26.6	21.1	12.5	8.1	11.2	10.6	9.9
$\bar{X}$ years known helper	6.9	17.1	42.5	10.1	7.8	12.5	4.9	21.6	10.6
Relationship of helper									
Spouse/lover	60.0%	52.7%	0%	8.3%	40.0%	33.3%	13.3%	7.1%	18.8%
Other relatives	30.0	16.6	100.0	16.7	20.0	50.0	6.7	50.0	22.9
Close friends	0	8.9	0	58.3	40.0	0	46.7	7.1	20.8
Weak ties	10.0	21.9	0	16.7	0	16.7	33.3	35.7	37.5
Frequency of contact (most or all time)	90.0	76.9	50.0	75.0	100.0	83.3	46.7	71.4	65.3
Talked with helper (most or all time)	70.0	66.9	50.0	75.0	80.0	66.7	33.3	64.3	62.5
Helper talked to respondent (most or all time)	70.0	60.4	50.0	50.0	60.0	83.3	33.3	42.3	55.3
Very easy to get helper	90.0	82.2	50.0	83.3	100.0	83.3	40.0	71.4	70.8
Talked very freely	80.0	70.8	100.0	91.7	100.0	66.7	66.7	57.1	70.2
Helper very important	80.0	82.7	100.0	91.7	60.0	83.3	53.3	71.4	70.8
Helper helped very much	77.8	82.5	100.0	100.0	75.0	100.0	66.7	85.7	72.9

TABLE 16.5
Strength and Homophily of Social Ties by Marital Engagement–Disengagement

	Stable					Unstable			
Variable	Married (N = 169)	Divorced (N = 15)	Separated (N = 5)	Widowed (N = 14)	Single (N = 49)	Married (N = 10)	Divorced (N = 6)	Separated (N = 12)	Widowed (N = 2)
X̄ CES-D	9.05	11.2	12.5	10.6	9.9	7.4	8.1	21.1	26.6
X̄ years known helper	17.1	4.9	7.8	21.6	10.6	6.9	12.5	10.1	42.5
Relationship of helper									
Spouse/lover	52.7%	13.3%	40.0%	7.1%	18.8%	60.0%	33.3%	8.3%	0%
Other relatives	16.6	6.7	20.0	50.0	22.9	30.0	50.0	16.7	100.0
Close friends	8.9	46.7	40.0	7.1	20.8	0	0	58.3	0
Weak ties	21.9	33.3	0	35.7	37.5	10.0	16.7	16.7	0
Contact most or all time	76.9	46.7	100.0	71.4	65.3	90.0	83.3	75.0	50.0
Talked with helper most or all time	66.9	33.3	80.0	64.3	62.5	70.0	66.7	75.0	50.0
Helper talked to most or all time	60.4	33.3	60.0	42.9	55.3	70.0	83.3	50.0	50.0
Very easy to get helper	82.2	40.0	100	71.4	70.8	90.0	83.3	83.3	50.0
Talked very freely	70.8	66.7	100	57.1	70.2	80.0	66.7	91.7	100.0
Helper very important	82.7	53.3	60.0	71.4	70.8	80.0	83.3	91.7	100.0
Helper helped very much	82.5	66.7	75.0	85.7	72.9	77.8	100.0	100.0	100.0

329

duration. However, this trend is not clear-cut because of the variations due to group sizes and the difference in the use of ties by the recently disengaged (especially the recently separated), who seem to engage in an attempt to reverse the process of disengagement. Note the significant differences in the ties used by the recently separated and the stably separated.

As to the homophily of characteristics between the helper and the respondent, Table 16.6 shows that the recently disengaged tended to use ties that were homophilous in age and sex but hetrerophilous in education and occupational prestige. These differences were mainly due to their greater use of weak ties, including professional helpers. These results seem to contradict our predictions, as we expected that the use of homophilous ties would be more beneficial. The data are too sketchy and need further verification. However, it is clear that the theory of social resources needs further specification relative to the marital disengagement process. It seems to do well at predicting for those maritally engaged. For those few who are in the process of marital disengagement, we need to take into account their mixed use of old and new ties in their effort to resolve the crisis. These ties possess an as yet unknown ability to buffer the effect of the important event (mostly related to the marital disengagement itself). Only when the crisis is gradually resolved are these individuals able to firm up new ties and establish a stable social-support system (see the contrast between those recently separated and those stably separated and divorced).

The effects of social support on mental health are complex. Although this chapter focused on the buffering effect (and one particular sub-model, the mediating effects of buffering), other models need to be examined. It would be interesting if future research showed that propositions derivable from social-resources theory also hold up for the independent relationship between social support and mental health; that is, access to and use of strong and homophilous ties promote mental health, regardless of whether or not significant and undesirable events occur, in contrast to the merely interactive model's assumption that these ties do not have an independent effect.

The study also demonstrates the need to improve measurements of variables. Recent studies suggest that intimacy or quality of relationship is a better measure of the strength of ties than is the particular role relationship (Marsden and Campbell, 1984). In this study, both measures were employed and the results seem to be consistent. The role-relationship measure clarifies the social network in conjunction with marital status. Therefore, we propose that a variety of strength-of-tie measures be used until their specific properties (especially relative to the social structure) are clarified.

TABLE 16.6
Homophily of Characteristics by Marital Engagement–Disengagement

Variable	Recently married	Married	Recently widowed	Recently separated	Separated	Recently divorced	Divorced	Widowed	Single
$\bar{X}$ age difference	11.9	8.3	17.0	3.8	16.0	9.2	5.0	20.4	12.9
$\bar{X}$ sex difference	0.6	0.6	0.0	0.3	0.4	0.7	0.5	0.8	0.4
$\bar{X}$ occupation prestige difference	11.0	18.2	49.0	30.4	13.0	21.0	23.0	28.9	19.3
$\bar{X}$ education difference	1.2	1.6	2.5	0.8	1.6	1.8	1.9	1.7	1.3

Finally, it is perhaps less important to determine what is or is not a buffering effect than to learn what the effects are of one variable on another, tested using clearly conceptualized and designed research. The study reported here is a preliminary attempt at demonstrating such an approach. With all its limitations and defects, we hope it has identified some benchmarks and advanced some questions for future research on the important relationships between social support and mental health.

17

Epilogue: In Retrospect and Prospect

NAN LIN

This volume represents an attempt to explore the relationships between two social factors (social support and life events) and depressive symptoms (the CES-D scale). Three fundamental issues are addressed: (1) How should social support be conceptualized? (2) How should it be measured? and (3) How is it related to depressive symptoms, either directly or jointly with life events and other factors? With the help of a two-wave panel data set from a community sample, we try to explore as many facets of these issues as the data and techniques allow. We consider our effort to be one more step in the long process of attempting to understand social influences on mental health. The contributions and limitations of this effort should be made explicit so as to shed light on some current research questions and to help formulate future research questions and study designs.

SUMMARY OF MAJOR FINDINGS

Although the findings are too numerous to be discussed in detail here, certain major conclusions can be stated as follows:

333

1. Intimate and confiding relations and instrumental–expressive functions are important components of social support. It is clear that among the different sources of social support (intimate and confiding partners, network relations, and community participation), intimate and confiding relationships provide the most important effective support, whereas community and network support have only marginal direct effects. A relationship with a confidant is critical. For example, we found that opposite-sex confidants are more effective than same-sex confidants in buttressing against depressive symptoms. This, to a large extent, reflects the intimate and confiding nature of the relationship between marital partners.

Further, social support serves expressive and instrumental functions. Intimate and confiding ties provide both expressive and instrumental support. An individual in an emotional crisis (e.g., separation or divorce) needs not only someone to confide in but also someone who can provide realistic and practical consultations on how to change and modify his or her social environment so as to reduce or eliminate the source of the emotional strain. Likewise, an individual confronted with an instrumental problem (i.e., not getting proper monetary reward or a promotion in a job) needs not only support in the resolution of the problem but someone to whom he or she can air legitimate grievances.

2. Social support both directly affects depressive symptoms and significantly mediates the effect of undesirable life events. Such effects remain strong and significant when other factors such as psychological resources (e.g., self-esteem and personal competence) are taken into account. This mediating effect is also clear when the most important undesirable life event is examined. The adverse effect of such an event is greatly reduced when an intimate and strong tie provides support during or after the event.

After the mediating effect is accounted for, there is little evidence of an interaction effect (e.g., social support is important only when there is a high-stressor condition—the presence or high frequency of undesirable life events). This further confirms the cumulating evidence in the literature that the interaction effect, if significant, becomes relatively small or insignificant when the main effects of social support and undesirable life events are accounted for.

3. Psychological resources (self-esteem and personal competence) show a slight but significant direct effect on depressive symptoms but do not mediate the effects of undesirable life events and social support. Thus, our data do not provide confirmation for recent proposals concerning the mediating function of psychological coping in the social-support-and-distress relationship or for the appraisal hypothesis (e.g., lack of mastery of the situation conditions stress).

4. The basic relationships among undesirable life events, social support, and depressive symptoms remain significant when other factors usually considered to be associated with mental health are taken into account. These factors include age, gender, marital status, social class, and history of illness (physical health). Some of these factors have direct effects on depressive symptoms, whereas others interact with social support and undesirable life events in exerting an effect.

5. Females tend to show more depressive symptoms than do males, and the unmarried show more depressive symptoms than do the married. Direct and mediating effects of social support are present in most sex–marital status categories. There is evidence that females are less likely than males to have opposite-sex confidants, and the presence of an opposite-sex confidant is negatively related to depressive symptoms. When the gender of the confidant is controlled for, sex differences in depressive symptoms for the most part disappear.

6. Marital disruption (separation, divorce, or death of a spouse) has a substantial effect on depressive symptoms. Marital disruption not only constitutes an adverse life event but also causes the disintegration of one's previous network of intimate and confiding ties. The effect is all the more severe for women, because their intimate and confiding ties are often either restricted to their spouses or persons associated with their spouses. This double jeopardy results in longer and more severe depressive symptoms for women.

7. Social support and undesirable life events affect depressive symptoms in all age groups we have studied. However, the direct effect of undesirable life events on depressive symptoms becomes insignificant for those over age 65. There is also a slight decrease in the direct effect of social support on depressive symptoms for those over 65. However, because all of the respondents were 70 or younger, the data do not shed light on the stress process for a significant portion of the aged population.

8. There is no direct effect of social class on depressive symptoms, and we are not able to confirm the class–vulnerability hypothesis. Specifically, there is no clear-cut evidence that working-class respondents are more vulnerable than are middle-class respondents (e.g., that undesirable life events have a greater effect on depressive symptoms among the working class). On the other hand, the negative effect of social support on depressive symptoms is not as strong among the lower working class as it is among higher-class respondents, according to our data.

9. History of illness (symptoms and diagnoses) shows an effect on depressive symptoms, independent of undesirable life events and social support. However, there is no confirmation in our data that history

of illness increases the likelihood of experiencing undesirable life events. Thus, the data do not support the event-proneness hypothesis, which suggests that physical conditions affect the subsequent likelihood of stressful life events.

FUTURE RESEARCH AGENDA

These findings and our research experience with this study, although answering several crucial questions, highlight the need for future examinations of several critical issues. We now propose several topics that seem to us to constitute the critical next steps in studying the social process of mental health. In the discussion that follows, we also discuss our current thinking regarding these issues.

1. There is a need to further clarify the components of social support. Our data indicate the importance of differentiating support sources (intimate and confiding relations, network relations, and community participation) and functions (instrumental and expressive), but these are not the only conceptually interesting components. In our analysis, we also examined support in reaction to a crisis situation (a most important and undesirable life event). This can be contrasted with support for routine, day-to-day activities. There has also been a discussion of the distinction between actual (or received) and perceived (or cognitive) support. Efforts must be continued to refine these components and to specify their relationships. We will return to one such example shortly.

2. Life-events research should focus on types of life events, the degree of undesirability of the events, and the consequences of specific events. Global scales (both unweighed and weighed) have had a substantial and steady influence for the past 2 decades. Cumulating evidence suggests that an examination of the specificity of events and an in-depth probing of a specifically significant and adverse event would be useful next steps. We found, for example, that the effect of a single important undesirable life event is an adequate reflection of the adverse consequence of aggregated events. However, we also see a need for specifications of strains that are more routine and chronic in a person's life. These routine strains, in conjunction with crisis events, should more appropriately represent stressors in the social environment.

3. Other measures of mental health and physical health should be systematically explored. Much confusion exists as to the extent to which the results of a particular study can be generalized. Even in the

case of depression, recent developments in measuring depressive disorders, such as the depression portion (major depressive episodes) of the Diagnostic Interview Schedule (DIS-3), have raised the issue of the extent to which various research results concerning social support, life events, psychological resources, and distress can be generalized across various diagnostically undifferentiated symptom measures and diagnostically designed disorder measures used in community surveys and conducted by lay interviewers. Different criterion variables may offer insights into different processes of mental health.

Likewise, measures of dependent variables other than depression should be examined. Such analyses should again broaden our understanding of the various processes involving different aspects of mental and physical health.

4. There are a number of issues unresolved in this study that need further verification. For example, the role of social class in the social etiology of mental health remains unclear. Our data support neither its direct effect on depressive symptoms nor the vulnerability-to-stressors hypothesis. Nor do we find support for the event-proness hypothesis, concerning the impact of physical health on life events and its relationship to distress. It may well be that alternative measures should be used to indicate social class, stressors, and physical health. Or it may be the case that different designs and approaches are required to tease out their hypothesized relationships.

We likewise do not find that psychological resources mediated the effects of social support and undesirable life events on depressive symptoms in our study. Again, perhaps, the problem lies in the measures. We used self-esteem and personal-competence scales that show significant associations with depressive symptoms in cross-sectional analysis. When these measures are incorporated over time, much of the effect disappears in lagged paths. Delineation of the conceptual and measurement overlaps between psychological resources and measures of mental health remains a critical topic for further research.

5. The age-structure and life-course issues deserve further research attention. As many communities experience substantial increases in their aged populations, the way in which the older residents maintain and promote social support and mental health will increase in its research significance. There is little knowledge regarding which social-support components are significant for the aged, how the elderly mobilize social support to counter adverse stressors and strains, and the extent to which professional services can effectively substitute for natural support elements. We predict these issues will be salient topics for research in the next decade.

6. The whole issue of marital disruption and confidant relationships needs intensive examination. Marital relations are provide significant and positive support for most individuals. By the same token, marital disruption is also devastating for most. It not only breaks the most important binding relationship, it also snaps the link to many significant others. The process by which such intimate ties are reconstituted and mental health regained is seldom examined and little understood. We see it as the pivotal issue in understanding the observed sex difference in mental health as well as the health and mental-health implications of the cyclical process of marital change.

7. The confounding of measures for different variables will always need research attention. In our study, we attempt to examine confounding between life events and depressive symptoms, social support and depressive symptoms, psychological resources and depressive symptoms, and physical health and depressive symptoms. We conclude, within the confines of the design, data, and analysis, that confounding has no substantial effects on our findings. Nevertheless, these are serious issues requiring continuous conceptual and methodological attention.

8. Better panel data are needed. Our study employed two waves of data. Because there were three critical variables (social support, life events, and depressive symptoms), the temporal sequence of the variables cannot be completely represented. For example, although the causal sequence between life events and social support can be temporally separated with the Time 1 (T1) and Time 2 (T2) data sets (e.g., life events during the 6 months preceding the T1 interview and social support in the 6 months preceding the T2 interview), the ultimate dependent variable, depressive symptoms, overlaps one week with either of the other two variables (the week preceding the T2 interviews). In the future, multiple waves of data (at least as many waves as the number of variables in the basic model) should be employed to assure that all causal relationships are mapped over time. However, temporal data are not a substitute for a conceptual causal sequence. It is difficult to identify the meaningful time-lags in a multiwave design. Further, a specific time-lag may be meaningful for one relationship but not for another. Unless the causal relationships make sense conceptually, empirical cross-lagged relationships may pose serious interpretative problems, just as they do in cross-sectional data. All these issues are in need of further research attention.

9. Measurement of the key variables requires continued critical design and assessment. There are several issues involved. To begin with,

it is important that measurements be designed for theoretically derived variables. That is, attention must first be given to the theoretical development of the concepts involved. Taking social support as an example, our conceptualization led us to design particular measures of social support. In our analysis we found that there was a substantial empirical overlap between support functions (instrumental and expressive) and sources of support (intimate and confidant support). However, we felt we should maintain a conceptual distinction between the two. Future research design and measurement may further resolve the question as to whether these are independent or related dimensions.

There is also a clear need for improved measures. Some of our social-support measures were less successful than others. For example, the network-support measures were generally lacking in either validity or reliability. However, one must not hasten to the conclusion that network support is therefore inconsequential. Our conceptualization suggests that both community support (representing belongingness) and network support (representing bonding) both provide the more global relations within which more intimate and binding relations are molded. Better measures of these types of relations and support will allow a more adequate examination of the hypothesized relationships among the three types of support relationships. Liekwise, integration of support sources and other aspects (e.g., support processes and support content, discussed in the last section of this chapter) in the measures is important. It would be very useful, for example, to construct an inventory of social support in which the sources, content, and processes are all integrated

10. Finally, prevention and/or intervention experiments concerning social support should proceed. We believe that both basic and applied research are essential in understanding the social process of distress. Our research (Lin and Ensel, 1984) suggests that monitoring prior mental state, changes in social support, and undesirable life events can make feasible the prediction of the subsequent mental state. The next steps involve both refinement in the prediction methods and actual field experiments in which individuals in natural settings (e.g., members of a health-maintenance organization) are randomly assigned to different conditions exposing them to information regarding various prevention or intervention strategies (e.g., training on improving cognitive support and on mobilizing actual support). Evaluations of such experiments are important transitional steps to move basic knowledge into practice. They also provide feedback to researchers regarding which specific elements of social support may in reality be effective.

TOWARD A THEORY OF THE INTERNAL STRUCTURE
OF SOCIAL SUPPORT

As the social-support research field moves forward, one dominant issue will be the conceptualization and integration of the various elements of social support. A clear conceptual framework for the internal structure of social support is a prerequisite for a comprehensive theory concerning the relationship of social support to other variables. Let us examine one such internal structure.

We begin by focusing on two major components of social support: support resources and support processes. This conception breaks the concept of social support into two global components: the social (structural) component and the support (processing) component. Support resources include social relations for which the structural or social components are specified, and we tentatively identify community relations, network relations, and intimate relations as such possible resources.

Support processes describe how the various support resources impinge on ego. Two types of such processes can be differentiated: (1) actual (received) versus perceived (cognitive) support and (2) routine versus crisis support. In the first category, actual support describes the process by which support (regardless of its content) is transmitted from the support resources to ego, and perceived support indicates the cognitive process (or the outcome of this process) by which ego deems such support accessible. In the second category, routine support is the process by which support is received or perceived relative to routine, day-to-day activities (e.g., child care, car-pooling, grocery shopping), whereas crisis support reflects the process by which support is received or perceived when ego is confronted with a crisis situation or event (e.g., a divorce or a car accident). The two categories jointly identify four processes: perceived routine support, actual routine support, perceived crisis support, and actual crisis support.

These categories allow the postulation of a structure of social support by linking support resources and support processes. As indicated in Figure 17.1, the structure proposes how the various sources are linked and how they impinge upon the support processes.

It proposes first of all that community and network relations promote and enhance intimate relations. This proposition can be argued from two theoretical perspectives. From the structural perspective, it can be argued that having diverse social contacts and ties increases the likelihood of finding and forging intimate ties. From the social-psychological perspective, we may argue that persons capable of establishing di-

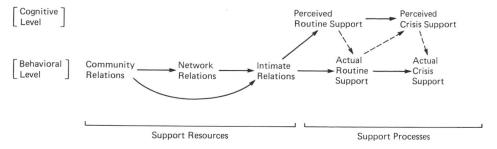

Figure 17.1   Proposed structure of social support.

verse social contacts and ties are also capable of finding intimate ties, for either cognitive or psychological (personality) reasons. Further, intimate relations have a direct impact on the support processes, whereas community and network relations do not. This is in line with our findings and consistent with the discussions in the literature.

Next, the structure proposes linkages between support resources and support processes. Support processes are identified in two levels: the cognitive level and the behavioral level. It is postulated that intimate relations are linked to both perceived and actual routine supports. We may also postulate (not shown in Figure 17.1) that intimate relations affect perceived and actual crisis supports. Further, perceived routine and perceived crisis supports are linked. Likewise, actual routine and actual crisis supports are linked. However, perceived supports and actual supports may or may not be related; these uncertain relations are represented with dotted lines in the figure.

We see this proposed structure as an example of a way in which various current concerns regarding the components of social support (cognitive versus behavioral, sources versus content versus processes) can be integrated. Other conceptual developments should also be explored. For example, the issue of active versus reactive support constitutes another component. It may be argued that reactive support may apply to both routine and crisis processes. However, the way in which active support relates to the crisis process is unclear.

Such a structure not only identifies the components of social support but also stipulates the internal relations among the components. Empirical data can be obtained to estimate the actual relationships and to modify the proposed structure. Further elaborations can also be made. For example, the content of the support process may consist of instrumental, expressive, and other elements. The sources, content, and processes may interact to produce effects on mental health.

There is a long list of items on the research agenda ahead. The tasks will be both exciting and difficult. Hopefully, stimulation, encouragement, and challenges provided by our colleagues in the research community, and by the users of the research literature constitute the essential social support for those choosing to undertake these tasks.

References

Abramson, J. H. The Cornell Medical Index as an epidemiological tool. *American Journal of Public Health*, 1966, 56, 287–298.

Abramson, J. H., Terespolsky, L., Brook, J. G., and Kark, S. L. Cornell Medical Index as a health measure in eqidemiological studies: A test of the validity of a health question naire. *British Journal of Preventive Sociological Medicine*, 1965, 19, 103–110.

Adler, A. *A study of organ inferiority and its physical compensation*. New York: Nervous and Mental Diseases Publishing, 1917.

Allport, G. W. *Becoming*. New Haven: Yale University Press, 1955.

Almquist, E. Black women and the pursuit of equality. In J. Freeman (Ed.). *Women: A feminist perspective* (2nd ed.). Palo Alto, CA: Mayfield, 1979.

Alwin, D. F., and Jackson, J. The statistical analysis of Kohn's measures of parental values. In H. O. A. Wold and K. G. Joreskog (Eds.). *Systems under indirect observation: Causality, structure, and prediction*. New York: Elsevier North Holland, 1980.

Andrews, G., Tennant, C., Hewson, D., and Valliant, G. W. Life event stress, social support, coping style, and risk of psychological impairment. *Journal of Nervous and Mental Disease*, 1978, 166,(5) 307–316.

Aneshensel, C. S., and Frerichs, R. R. Stress, support and depression; A longitudinal causal model. *Journal of Community Psychology*, 1982, 10(4), 363–376.

Aneshensel, C. S., Frerichs, R. R., and Clark, V. A. Family roles and sex differences in depression. *Journal of Health and Social Behavior*, 1981, 22(4), 379–393.

Aneshensel, C. S., and Stone, J. D. Stress and depression: A test of the buffering model of social support. *Archives of General Psychiatry*, 1982, 39, 1393–1396.

Atchley, R. C. *Social forces in later life* (3rd ed.). Belmont, CA: Wadsworth, 1980.

Bachrach, L. L. *Marital status and mental disorder: An analytical review* (DHEW Publication No. ADM 75–217). Washington, DC: U.S. Government Printing Office, 1975.

Backstrom, C. H., and Hursh–Cesar, G. *Survey research* (2nd ed.). New York: John Wiley, 1981.

Bardwick, Judity M., Douvan, E., Horner, M. S., and Gutman, D. *Feminine personality and conflict*. Belmont, CA: Brooks/Cole, 1970.

343

Barrera, M., Jr. Social support in the adjustment of pregnant adolescents: Assessment issues. In B. H. Gottlieb (Ed.), *Social networks and social support.* Beverly Hills, CA: Sage, 1981.

Barron, F. An ego-strength scale which predicts response to psychotherapy. *Journal of Consulting Psychology,* 1953, *17,* 327–333.

Beck, A. T. *Depression: Clinical, experimental and theoretical aspects.* New York: Harper and Row, 1967.

Beck, A. T., Ward, C. H., Mendelson, M., Mock, J., and Erbaugh, J. An inventory for measuring depression. *Archives of General Psychiatry,* 1961, *4,* 561–571.

Bell, R. A., LeRoy, J. B., and Stephenson, J. Evaluating the mediating effects of social support upon life events and depression symptoms. *Journal of Community Psychology,* 1982, *10*(4), 325–340.

Bell, R. P. Women and friendship. In Robert R. Bell (Ed.), *Worlds of friendship* (pp. 55–93). Beverly Hills, CA.: Sage, 1981.

Belle, D. The stress of caring: Women as providers of social support. In Leo Goldberger and Shlomo Breznitz (Eds.), *Handbook of stress: Theoretical and clinical aspects* (pp. 495–504). New York: Free Press, 1982.

Bengston, V. L., and Treas, J. The changing family context of mental health and aging. In J. E. Birren and R. B. Sloane (Eds.), *Handbook of mental health and aging.* New Jersey: Prentice–Hall, 1980.

Berkman, L. F., Syme, S. L. Social networks, host resistance, and mortality: A nine year followup study of Alameda County residents. *American Journal of Epidemiology,* 1979, *109,* 186–204.

Berkowitz, S. D. *An introduction to structural analysis.* Toronto: Butterworths, 1982.

Bernard, H. R., Killworth, P. D., and Sailer, L. A note on inference regarding network subgroups: Response to Burt and Bittner. *Social Networks,* 1981, *3,* 89–92.

Bernard, H. R., Killworth, P. D., and Sailer, L. Informant accuracy in social network data: A comparison of clique-level structure in behavioral and cognitive network data. *Social Networks,* 1980, *2,* 191–218.

Bernard, J. *Remarriage: A study of marriage.* New York: Russell and Russell, 1971.

Bieliauskas, L. A. *Stress and its relationship to health and illness.* Boulder, CO: Westview Press, 1982.

Billings, A. C., and Moos, R. H. Stressful life events and symptoms: A longitudinal model. *Health Psychology,* 1982, *1,* 99–117.

Blalock, H. M., Jr. *Social statistics* (2nd ed.). New York: McGraw Hill, 1979.

Blau, Peter M. *Inequality and heterogeneity.* New York: Free Press, 1977.

Blazer, D. Life events, mental health functioning and the use of health care services by the elderly. *American Journal of Public Health,* 1980, *70,* 1174–1179.

Blood, P., and Wolfe, D. *Husbands and wives.* New York: Free Press, 1960.

Bloom, B., Asher, S. S., and White, S. W. Marital disruption as a stressor: A review and analysis. *Psychological Bulletin,* 1978, *85,* 867–894.

Bloom, B. L., and Hodges, W. F. The predicament of the newly separated. *Community Mental Health Journal,* 1981, *17,* 277–293.

Bloom, B. L., Hodges, W. F., and Caldwell, R. A. Marital separation: The first eight months. In E. J. Callahan and K. A. McKluskey (Eds.), *Life span developmental psychology* (pp. 217–239). New York: Academic Press, 1982.

Blumenthal, R. Measuring depressive symptomatology in a general population. *Archives of General Psychiatry,* 1975, *32,* 971–978.

Booth, Alan. Sex and social participation. *American Sociological Review,* 1972, *37,* 183–187.

Bott, E. *Family and social network.* New York: Free Press, 1957.

Bowlby, R. *Attachment and loss: Volume 1. Attachment.* London: Hogarth Press, 1969.

Bowlby, R. *Attachment and loss: Volume 2. Separation, anxiety and anger.* London: Hogarth Press, 1973.

Boyd, J. H., Weissman, M. M., Thompson, W. D., and Myers, J. K. Screening for depression in a community sample: Understanding the discrepancies between depression symptoms and diagnostic scales. *Archives of General Psychiatry,* 1982, *39,* 1195–1200.

Brenner, M. H. *Mental illness and the economy.* Cambridge, MA: Harvard University Press, 1973.

Briscoe, B. W., and Smith, J. Depression and marital turmoil. *Archives of General Psychiatry,* 1974, *29,* 811–817.

Brock, A. J. *Greek medicine* (trans. and ann.). London: J. M. Dent, 1929.

Brodman, K., Erdmann, A. J., Lorge, I., and Wolff, H. G. The Cornell Medical Index: The relation of patients complaints to age, sex, race, and education. *Journal of Gerontology,* 1953, *8,* 339–342.

Brown, D. G. Sex role preference in young children. *Psychological Monographs,* 1956, *70*(14), 1–19.

Brown, G. W., Bhrolchain, M. N., and Harris, T. Social class and psychiatric disturbance among women in an urban population. *Sociology,* 1975, *9,* 225–254.

Brown, G. W., and Harris, T. *Social origins of depression: A study of psychiatric disorder in women.* New York: Free Press, 1978.

Brubaker, T. H. (Ed.). *Family relationships in later life.* Beverly Hills, CA: Sage Publications, 1983.

Burke, R. J., and Weir, T. Marital helping relationships: The moderator between stress and well-being. *The Journal of Psychology,* 1977, *95,* 121–130.

Burt, R. S. Studying status/role sets as ersatz network positions in mass surveys. *Sociological Methods and Research,* 1981, *9,* 313–337.

Burt, R. S. *Toward a structural theory of action: Network models of social structure, perception, and action.* New York: Academic Press, 1982.

Burt, R. S., and Bittner, W. M. A note on inferences regarding network subgroups. *Social Networks,* 1981, *3,* 71–83.

Burt, R. S., and Minor, M. J. (Eds.). *Applied network analysis.* Beverly Hills, CA: Sage, 1982.

Cafferata, G., Kasper, J., and Berstein, A. Family Roles, Structures, and Stressors, *Journal of Health and Social Behavior,* 1983, *24,* 132–143.

Campbell, A. *The sense of well-being in America.* New York: McGraw Hill, 1980.

Campbell, A., Converse, P. E., Miller, W. E., and Srokes, D. E. *The American voter.* New York: Wiley, 1960.

Campbell, A., Converse, P. E., and Rodgers, W. *The quality of American life: Perceptions, evaluations, and satisfactions.* New York: Russell Sage Foundation, 1976.

Candy, S. G. A developmental exploration of friendship functions in women. *Psychology of Women Quarterly,* 1981, *5*(2), 456–472.

Caplan, G. Support systems. In G. Caplan (Ed.), *Support systems and community mental health.* New York: Basic Books, 1974.

Caplan, G., and Killilea, M. (Eds.). *Support systems and mutual help: Multidisciplinary explorations.* Grune and Stratton, New York, 1976.

Caplan, R. D. Organizational stress and individual strain: A socio-psychological study of risk factors in coronary heart disease among administration, engineers and scientists. *Dissertation Abstracts International,* 1972, *32,* 6706B–6707B.

Caplan, R. D. Social support, person–environment fit, and coping. In L. A Ferman and J. P. Gordus (Eds.), *Mental health and the economy* (pp. 89–138). Michigan: W. E. Upjohn Institute for Employment Research, 1979.

Caplan, R. D., Cobb, S., French, J., VanHarrison, R., and Pinneau, S. R. *Job demands and worker health.* (DHEW NIOSH Publication No. 75–160. Washington, DC: U.S. Department of Health, Education, and Welfare, 1975.

Carveth, W. B., and Gottlieb, B. H. The measurement of social support and its relation to stress. *Canadian Journal of Behavioural Science*, 1979, 11, 179–187.

Cassel, J. Psychosocial processes and "stress": Theoretical formulations. *International Journal of Health Services*, 1974a, 4, 471–482.

Cassel, J. An epidemiological perspective of psychosocial factors in disease etiology. *American Journal of Public Health.* 1974b, 64, 1040–1043.

Cassel, J. The contribution of the social environment to host resistance. *American Journal of Epidemiology*, 1976, 104, 107–123.

Catalano, R., and Dooley, D. Economic predictors of depressed mood and stressful life events in a community. *Journal of Health and Social Behavior*, 1977, 18, 292–307.

Clancy, K., and Gove, W. Sex differences in respondents' reports of psychiatric symptoms: an analysis of response bias. *American Journal of Sociology*, 1974, 80, 205–216.

Cleary, P. D., and Kessler, R. C. The estimation and interpretation of modifier effects. *Journal of Health and Social Behavior*, 1982, 23, 159–169.

Cleary, P. D., and Mechanic, D. Sex differences in psychological distress among married women. *Journal of Health and Social Behavior*, 1983, 24, 111–121.

Cobb, S. Physiologic changes in men whose jobs were abolished. *Journal of Psychosomatic Research*, 1974, 18, 245–258.

Cobb, S. Social support as a moderator of life stress. *Psychosomatic Medicine*, 1976, 38, 300–314.

Cobb, S. Social support and health through the life course. In Matilda White Riley (Ed.), *Aging from birth to death: Interdisciplinary perspectives* (pp. 93–106). Washington, D.C.: American Association for the Advancement of Science, 1979.

Cobb, S., and Kasl, S. V. *Termination: the consequence of job loss* (Report No. 76–1261). Cincinnati, OH: National Institute for Occupational Safety and Health, Behavior, and Motivational Factors Research, 1977.

Coleman, J. S., and MacRae, D., Jr. Electronic processing of sociometric data for groups up to a thousand in size. *American Sociological Review*, 1960, 25, 722–726.

Community Support Systems Task Force of the President's Commission on Mental Health, 1978.

Comstock, G. W., and Helsing, K. J. Symptoms of depression in two communities. *Psychological Medicine*, 1976, 6, 551–563.

Cooley, C. H. *Human nature and the social order.* New York: Scribner, 1902.

Craig, T. J., and VanNatta, P. A. Influence of demographic characteristics on two measures of depressive symptoms. *Archives of General Psychiatry*, 1979, 36, 149–154.

Craig, T. J., and VanNatta, P. Recognition of depressed affect in hospitalized psychiatric patients: Staff and patient perceptions. *Diseases of the Nervous System*, 1976, 37, 561–566.

Dahlstrom, W. G., and Welsh, G. S. *An MMPI handbook.* Minneapolis: University of Minnesota Press, 1960.

Davidson, S., and Packard, T. The therapeutic value of friendship between women. *Psychology of Women Quarterly*, 1981, 5(3), 495–510.

Dean, Alfred, and Ensel, Walter M. Modelling social support, life events, competence, and depression in the context of age and sex. *Journal of Community Psychology*, 1982, *10*, 392–408.

Dean, Alfred, and Ensel, Walter M. Socially structured depression in men and women. In James R. Greenley (Ed.), *Research in community and mental health, Volume 3* (pp. 113–139). Greenwich, CT: JAI Press, 1983.

Dean, Alfred, and Lin, Nan. The stress buffering role of social support. *Journal of Nervous and Mental Disease*, 1977, *165*(2), 403–413.

Dean, Alfred, Lin, Nan, and Ensel, Walter M. The epidemiological significance of social support systems in depression. In Roberta G. Simmons (Ed.), *Research in community and mental health* (pp. 77–109). Greenwich, CT: JAI Press, 1981.

deCharms, R. *Personal causation*. New York: Academic Press, 1968.

Dohrenwend, B. P. *Alternative social and psychological models of relations between life stress and illness*. Paper presented at the National Conference on Social Stress Research, University of New Hampshire, Durham, NH, October 11, 1982.

Dohrenwend, B. P. Problems in defining and sampling the relevant population of stressful life events. In B. S. Dohrenwend and B. P. Dohrenwend (Eds.), *Stressful life events: Their nature and effects* pp. 275–312). New York: Wiley, 1974.

Dohrenwend, B. P., and Dohrenwend, B. S. Reply to Gove and Tudor's comment on 'Sex differences in psychiatric disorders.' *American Journal of Sociology*, 1977, *82*, 1336–1345.

Dohrenwend, B. P., and Dohrenwend, B. S. *Social status and psychological disorder: A causal inquiry*. New York: John Wiley, 1969.

Dohrenwend, B. P., Shrout, P. E., Egri, G., and Mendelsohn, F. C. Nonspecific psychological distress and other dimensions of psychopathology: Measures for use in the general population. *Archives of General Psychology*, 1980, *37*, 1229–1236.

Dohrenwend, B. S. Sex differences in psychiatric disorders. *American Journal of Sociology*, 1973a, *81*, 1447–1454.

Dohrenwend, B. S. Social status and stressful life events. *Journal of Personality and Social Psychology*, 1973b, *28*, 225–235.

Dohrenwend, B. S., and Dohrenwend, B. P. A brief historical introduction to research on stressful life events. In B. S. Dohrenwend and B. P. Dohrenwend (Eds.), *Stressful life events: Their nature and effects* (pp. 1–30). New York: John Wiley, 1974b.

Dohrenwend, B. S., and Dohrenwend, B. P. Class and race as status related sources of stress. In S. Levine and N. A. Scotch (Eds.), *Social stress*. Chicago: Aldine, 1970.

Dohrenwend, B. S., and Dohrenwend, B. P. Life stress and illness: Formulation of the issues. In B. S. Dohrenwend and B. P. Dohrenwend (Eds.), *Stressful life events and their contexts* (pp. 1–28). New York: Prodist, 1981.

Dohrenwend, B. S., and Dohrenwend, B. P. Some issues in research on stressful life events. *Journal of Nervous and Mental Disease*, 1978, *166*(1), 7–15.

Dohrensend, B. S., and Dohrenwend, B. P. *Stressful life events: Their nature and effects*. New York: Wiley–Interscience, 1974a.

Dohrenwend, B. S., Dohrenwend, B. P., Dodson, M., and Shrout, P. E. Symptoms, hassles, social supports, and life events: Problems and confounded measures. *Journal of Abnormal Psychology*, 1984, *93*(2), 222–230.

Dohrenwend, B. S., Krasnoff, L., Ashehasy, A., and Dohrenwend, B. P. Exemplification of a method for scaling life events: The PERI life events scale. *Journal of Health and Social Behavior*, 1978, *19*, 205–229.

Douvan, E., and Walker, A. M. The sense of effectiveness in public affairs. *Psychological Monographs*, 1956, *70*(22), Whole #429, 1–19.

DSM-3 (*Diagnostic and Statistical Manual of Mental Disorders, 3rd Edition*). Washington, DC: American Psychiatric Association, 1980.

Durkheim, E. *Suicide.* Glencoe, IL: Free Press, 1951.

Eastwood, M. R. *The relation between physical and mental illness.* Toronto: University of Toronto Press, 1975.

Eaton, W. W. Life events, social supports, and psychiatric symptoms: A reanalysis of the New Haven data. *Journal of Health and Social Behavior,* 1978, *19,* 230–234.

Eaton, W. W., and Kessler, L. G. Rates of depression in a national sample. *American Journal of Epidemiology,* 1981, *114,* 528–538.

Ensel, Walter M. The role of age in the relationship of gender and marital status to depression. *Journal of Nervous and Mental Disease,* 1982, *170*(9), 536–543.

Ensel, Walter M. Sex differences in the epidemiology of depression and physical illness: A sociological perspective. In A. Dean (Ed.), *Depression in multidisciplinary perspective.* New York: Brunner/Mazel Press, (forthcoming).

Ensel, Walter M., and Lin, Nan. *Gender differences with the use of social resources in occupational status attainment.* Paper presented at the annual meetings of the American Sociological Association, Toronto, August 1981.

Ensel, Walter M., and Tausig, Mark. *The social context of undesirable life events.* Paper presented at the National Conference on Social Stress Research, University of New Hampshire, Durham, October 1982.

Erikson, E. H. Identity and the life cycle: Selected papers. *Psychological Issues,* 1959, *1,* 1–174.

Erikson, E. H. *Identity, youth and crisis.* New York: Norton, 1968.

Fairbank, D. T., and Hough, R. L. Life event classifications and the event–illness relationship. *Journal of Human Stress,* 1979, *5,* 41–47.

Faris, R. E. L., and Dunham, H. W. *Mental disorders in urban areas.* Chicago: University of Chicago Press, 1939.

Feldman, H. *Development of the husband–wife relationship: A research report.* New York: Cornell University Press, 1964.

Fenwich, R., and Barresi, C. M. Health consequences of marital-status change among the elderly. *Journal of Health and Social Behavior,* 1981, *22,* 106–116.

Festinger, L. The analysis of sociograms using matrix algebra. *Human Relations,* 1949, *2,* 153–158.

Festinger, L. S., Schachter, S. and Back, K. W. *Social pressures in informal groups.* Stanford, CA: Stanford University Press, 1950.

Fischer, C. S. *To dwell among friends: Personal networks in town and city.* Chicago: University of Chicago Press, 1982.

Fischer, C. S. et al. *Networks and places: Social relations in the urban setting.* New York: Free Press, 1977.

Folkman, S., and Lazarus, R. S. An analysis of coping in a middle-aged community sample. *Journal of Health and Social Behavior,* 1980, *21,* 219–239.

Forisha, B. L. *Sex roles and personal awareness.* New York: Silver Burdett, 1978.

Fox, J. W. Gove's specific sex-role theory of mental illness: A research note. *Journal of Health and Social Behavior,* 1980, *21,* 260–267.

Frerichs, R. R., Aneshensel, C. S., and Clark, V. A. Prevalence of depression in Los Angeles County. *American Journal of Epidemiology,* 1981a, *113,* 691–699.

Frerichs, R. R., Aneshensel, C. S., Clark, V. A., and Yokopenic, P. Smoking and depression: A community survey. *American Journal of Public Health,* 1981b, *71,* 637–640.

Fried, M. Social differences in mental health. In J. Kosa and I. K. Zola (Eds.), *Poverty and health: A sociological analysis.* Cambridge, MA: Harvard University Press, 1975.

Gardner, E. A. *Development of a symptom checklist for the measurement of depression in a population.* Unpublished manuscript, 1968.

Garrity, T. F., Marx, M. B., and Somes, G. W. The influence of illness severity and time since life change on the size of the life change–health change relationship. *Journal of Psychosomatic Research,* 1977, *21,* 377–382.

Gersten, J. C., Langner, T. S., Eisenberg, J. G., and Orzek, L. Child behavior and life events: Undesirable changes or change per se. In B. S. Dohrenwend and B. P. Dohrenwend (Eds.), *Stressful life events: Their nature and effects* (pp. 159–170). New York: Willey Press, 1974.

Glenn, N. D. The contribution of marriage to the psychological well-being of males and females. *Journal of Marriage and the Family,* 1975, *34,* 21–32.

Goldberg, S., and Lewis, M. Play behavior in the year-old infant: Early sex differences. *Child Development,* 1969, *40,* 21–30.

Golup, S. The effect of premenstrual depression and anxiety on personality and cognitive function. Unpublished doctoral dissertation, Fordham University, New York, NY, 1973.

Goode, W. J. *The family.* Englewood Cliffs, NJ: Prentice Hall, 1965.

Gore, S. The effect of social support in moderating the health consequences of unemployment. *Journal of Health and Social Behavior,* 1978, *19,* 157–165.

Gore, S. Stress-buffering functions of social supports: An appraisal and clarification of research models. In B. S. Dohrenwend and B. P. Dohrenwend (Eds.), *Stressful life events and their contexts.* (pp. 202–222). New York: Prodist, 1981.

Gore, S., and Mangione, T. W. Social roles, sex roles, and psychological distress: Additive and interactive effects. *Journal of Health and Social Behavior,* 1983, *24,* 300–313.

Gottlieb, B. H. The development and application of a classification scheme of informal helping behaviors. *Canadian Journal of Behavioral Science,* 1978, *10,* 105–115.

Gottlieb, B. H. (Ed.), *Social networks and social support.* Beverly Hills, CA: Sage Press, 1981.

Gottlieb, B. H. *Social support strategies.* Beverly Hills, CA: Sage Press, 1983.

Gove, W. The relationship between sex roles, marital status, and mental illness. *Social Forces,* 1972, *51,* 34–44.

Gove, W. Sex differences in the epidemiology of mental disorder: Evidence and explanations. In Edity S. Somberg and Violet Franks (Eds.), *Gender and disordered behavior* (pp. 23–68). New York: Brunner/Mazel Press, 1979.

Gove, W. Sex differences in mental illness among adult men and women: An evaluation of four questions raised regarding the evidence on the higher rates of women. *Social Science and Medicine,* 1978, *128,* 187–198.

Gove, W., and Geerkin, M. R. Response bias in surveys of mental health: An empirical investigation. *American Journal of Sociology,* 1977, *82,* 1287–1317.

Gove, W., and Hughes, M. Possible causes of the apparent sex differences in physical health: An empirical investigation. American Sociological Review, 1979, 44, 126–146.

Gove, W., Hughes, M., and Style, C. B. Does marriage have positive effects on the psychological well-being of the individual? *Journal of Health and Social Behavior,* 1983, *24,* 122–131.

Gove, W., and Tudor, J. F. Adult sex roles and mental illness. *American Journal of Sociology,* 1973, *78,* 812–835.

Gove, W., and Tudor, J. F. Sex differences in mental illness: A comment on Dohrenwend and Dohrenwend. *American Journal of Sociology,* 1977, *82,* 1327–1336.

Granovetter, M. _Getting a job._ Cambridge, MA: Harvard University Press, 1974.

Granovetter, M. The strength of weak ties. _American Journal of Sociology,_ 1973, _78,_ 1360–1380.

Granovetter, M. The strength of weak ties: A network theory revisited. In Peter V. Marsden and Nan Lin (Eds.), _Social structure and network analysis_ (pp. 105–130). Beverly Hills, CA: Sage Press, 1982.

Grant, I., Sweetwook, H., Gerst, M. S., and Yager, J. Scaling procedures in life events research. _Journal of Psychosomatic Research,_ 1978, _22,_ 525–530.

Gunderson, E., and Rahe, R. H. _Life stress and illness._ Springfield, IL: Charles C. Thomas, 1974.

Gurin, G., Veroff, J., and Feld, S. _Americans view their mental health._ New York: Basic Books, 1960.

Guttentag, M., Salasin, S., and Belle, D. _The mental health of women._ New York: Academic Press, 1980.

Hammer, M. Social networks and the long term patient. In S. Budson and M. Barofsky (Eds.), _The chronic psychiatric patient in the community: Principles of treatment._ New York: Spectrum Press, 1981.

Hankin, J. R., and Locke, B. Z. The persistence of depressive symptomatology among prepaid group practice enrollees: An exploratory study. _American Journal of Public Health,_ 1982, _72,_ 1000–1007.

Haug, M. R. Measurement in social stratification. _Annual Review of Sociology,_ 1977, _3,_ 51–77.

Henderson, S. The social network, support, and neurosis: The function of attachment in adult life. _British Journal of Psychiatry,_ 1977, _131,_ 185–191.

Henderson, S. Social relationships, adversity, and neurosis: An analysis of prospective observations. _British Journal of Psychiatry,_ 1981, _138,_ 391–398.

Henderson, S., Byrne, D. G., and Duncan–Jones, P. _Neurosis and the social environment._ Australia: Academic Press, 1981.

Henderson, S., Byrne, D. G., Duncan-Jones, P., Scott, R., and Adcock, S. Social relationships, adversity and neurosis: A study of associations in a general population sample. _British Journal of Psychiatry,_ 1980, _136,_ 574–583.

Henderson, S., Duncan–Jones, P., Byrne, D. G., and Scott, R. Measuring social relationships: The interview schedule for social interaction. _Psychological Medicine,_ 1980, _10,_ 723–734.

Hinkle, L. E. The effect of exposure to culture change, social change, and changes in interpersonal relationships on health. In B. S. Dohrenwend and B. P. Dohrenwend (Eds.), _Stressful life events: Their nature and effects._ New York: Wiley, 1974.

Hinkle, L. E., and Wolff, H. G. Health and social environment. In A. H. Leighton, H. A. Clausen, and R. N. Wilson (Eds.), _Explorations in social psychiatry._ New York: Basic Books, 1957.

Holland, P. W., and Leinhardt, S. Structural sociometry. In S. Leinhardt and P. W. Holland (Eds.), _Perspectives in Social Network Analysis._ New York: Academic Press, 1979.

Hollingshead, A. B. _Two factor index of social position._ New Haven, CT: Mimeo, 1957.

Hollingshead, A., and Redlich, F. _Social class and mental illness._ New York: John Wiley, 1958.

Holmes, T. H., and Masuda, M. Life change and illness susceptibility. In B. S. Dohrenwend and B. S. Dohrenwend (Eds.), _Stressful life events: Their nature and effects_ (pp. 45–78). New York: John Wiley, 1974.

Holmes, T., and Rahe, R. The social readjustment rating scale. *Journal of Psychosomatic Research*, 1967, *11*, 213–218.

Homans, G. C. *The human group*. New York: Harcourt, 1950.

Hornstrata, R. K., and Klassen, D. The course of depression. *Comprehensive Psychiatry*, 1977, *18*, 119–125.

House, J. S. *Work stress and social support*. Reading, MA: Addison–Wesley, 1981.

House, J. S., and McMichael, A. J., Wells, J. A., Kaplan, B. H., and Landerman, L. R. Occupational stress and health among factory workers. *Journal of Health and Social Behavior*, 1979, *20*, 139–160.

House, J. S., and Wells, J. A. Occupational stress, social support and health. In Alan McLean, G. Black, and M. Colligen (Eds.), *Reducing occupational stress: Proceedings of a conference* (HEW NIOSH Publication No. 78–140. Washington, DC: U.S. Department of Health, Education and Welfare, 1978.

Hudgens, R. W. Personal catastrophe and depression. A consideration of the subject with respect to medically ill adolescents, and a requiem for retrospective life event studies. In B. P. Dohrenwend and B. S. Dohrenwend (Eds.), *Stressful life events: Their nature and effects* (pp. 190–134). New York: John Wiley, 1974.

Hudgens, R. W., Robins, E., and Delong, W. B. The reporting of recent stress in the lives of psychiatric patients. *British Journal of Psychiatry*, 1970, *117*, 635–643.

Huessy, H. R. Stress, social support, and schizophrenia: A discussion. *Schizophrenia*, 1981, *7*(1), 173–178.

Hughes, C. C., Tremblay, M. A., et al. *People of Cove and Woodlot* (Vol. 2 of the Stirling County Study). New York: Basic Books, 1960.

Hughes, M., and Gove, W. R. Living along, social integration, and mental health. *American Journal of Sociology*, 1981, *87*, 48–74.

Husaini, B., and Neff, J. Social class and depressive symptomatology: The role of life change events and locus of control. *The Journal of Nervous and Mental Disease*, 1981, *169*(10), 638–647.

Husaini, B. A., and Neff, J. A. The stress buffering role of social support and personal competence among the rural married. *Journal of Community Psychology*, 1982, *10*, 409–426.

Husaini, B. A., Neff, J. A., and Harrington, J. B. *Depression in rural communities: Establishing CES-D cutting points*. (Tennessee State University Health Research Project, Nashville, Final Report for NIMH Contract 278–77–0044.) Bethesda, MD: NIMH, 1979.

Ilfeld, F. W. Methodological issues in relating psychiatric symptoms to social stressors. *Psychological Reports*, 1976, *39*(3), 1251–1258.

James, W. *The principles of psychology*. New York: Henry Holt, 1890.

Jenkins, D. C., Hurst, M. W., and Rose, R. M. Life changes: Do people really remember? *Archives of General Psychiatry*, 1979, *36*(4), 379–384.

Johnson, J. H., and Sarason, I. G. Life stress, depression, and anxiety: Internal–external control as a moderator variable. *Journal of Psychosomatic Research*, 1978, *22*, 205–208.

Johnson, M. M. Fathers, mothers, and sex-typing. *Sociological Inquiry*, 1975, *45*, 15–26.

Joreskog, K. G., and Sorbom, D. *Advances in factor analysis and structural equation models*. Cambridge, MA: ABT Books, 1979.

Joreskog, K. G., and Sorbom, D. *LISREL: Analysis of linear structural relationships by the method of maximum likelihood*. Chicago, IL: National Educational Resources, 1981.

Joreskog, K. G., and Sorbom, D. *LISREL VI: Analysis of linear structural relationships by maximum likelihood, instrumental variable, and least squares methods.* Gary, Indiana: Scientific Software, 1984.

Kahn, R. L. Aging and social support. In M. W. Riley (Ed.), *Aging from birth to death: Interdisciplinary perspectives* (pp. 77–91). Boulder, CO: Westview Press, 1979a.

Kahn, R. L. Aging and social support. *Medical Care,* 1979(b), *15,* 47–58.

Kahn, R. L., and Antonucci, T. Convoys over the life course: Attachment, roles, and social support. In P. B. Bales and O. Brim (Eds.), *Life span development and behavior,* Vol. 3. Boston: Lexington Press, 1980.

Kapferer, B. Norms and the manipulation of relationships in a work context. In H. C. Mitchell (Ed.), *Social networks in urban situations.* Manchester, UK: Manchester University Press, 1969.

Kaplan, B. Toward further research on family and health. In B. Kaplan and J. Cassel (Eds.), *Family and health: An epidemiological approach* (pp. 89–106). Chapel Hill, NC: Institute for Research in Social Science, University of North Carolina, 1975.

Kaplan, B. H., Cassel, J. C., and Gore, S. Social support and health. *Medical Care,* 1977, *15,* 47–58.

Kessler, R. Stress, social status, and psychological distress. *Journal of Health and Social Behavior,* 1979, *20,* 259–273.

Kessler, B. Methodological issues in the study of psychosocial stress. In H. B. Kaplan (Ed.), *Psychosocial Stress* (pp. 267–342). N.Y.: Academic Press, 1983.

Kessler, R. C., and Cleary, P. D. Social class and psychological distress. *American Sociological Review,* 1980, *45,* 463–478.

Kessler, R. C., and Essex, M. Marital status and depression: The role played by coping resources. *Social Forces,* 1982, *61,* 484–507.

Kessler, R. C., and Greenberg, D. F. *Linear panel analysis: Models of quantitative change.* New York: Academic Press., 1981.

Kessler, R. C., and McLeod, J. Sex differences in vulnerability to undesirable life events. *American Sociological Review,* 1984a, *49*(5), 620–631.

Kessler, R. C., and McLeod, J. Social support and mental health in community samples. In S. Cohen and L. Syme (Eds.), *Social support and health.* New York: Academic Press., 1984b.

Kessler, R. C., and McRae, J. A. The effects of wives' employment on the mental health of married men and women. *American Sociological Review,* 1982, *47,* 216–227.

Kobasa, S. C. Stressful life events, personality, and health: An inquiry into hardiness. *Journal of Personality and Social Psychology,* 1979, *37*(1), 1–11.

Kobasa, S. C., Maddi, S. R., and Coddington, S. Personality and constitution as mediators in the stress–illness relationship. *Journal of Health and Social Behavior,* 1981, *22,* 368–378.

Kohn, M. L. Class, family and schizophrenia. *Social Forces,* 1972, *50,* 295–302.

Kohn, M. L. Reassessment. In M. Kohn, (Ed.), *Class and conformity: A study in values* (2nd ed.) (pp. 25–60). Chicago: University of Chicago Press, 1977.

Kohn, M. L., and Schooler, C. The reciprocal effects of the substantive complexity of work and intellectual flexibility: A longitudinal assessment. *American Journal of Sociology,* 1978, *84,* 24–52.

Langner, T. S. A twenty-two item screening score of psychiatric symptoms indicating impairment. *Journal of Health and Human Behavior,* 1962, *3,* 269–276.

Langner, T. S., and Michael, S. T. *Life Stress and Mental Health.* New York: Free Press, 1963.

LaRocco, James M., House, J. S., and French, J. Social support, occupational stress and health. *Journal of Health and Social Behavior,* 1980, *21,* 202–218.

Laumann, E. O. *Prestige and association in an urban community.* Indianapolis: Bobbs Merrill, 1966.

Lazarsfeld, P. F., and Merton, R. K. Friendship as social process: A substantive and methodological analysis. In M. Berger, et. al., (Eds.), *Freedom and Control in Modern Society.* New York: Octagon, 1964.

Lefcourt, H. M. Locus of control and stressful life events. In B. S. Dohrenwend and B. P. Dohrenwend (Eds.), *Stressful life events and their contexts* (pp. 157–166). New York: Prodist, 1981.

Lei, H., and Skinner, H. A. A psychometric study of life events and social readjustment. *Journal of Psychosomatic Research,* 1980, *24,* 57–66.

Leighton, A. H. My name is legion. New York: Basic Books, 1959.

Leighton, D. C., Harding, J. S., Macklin, D. G., MacMillan, A. M., and Leighton, A. H. *The character of danger.* New York: Basic Books, 1963.

Leinhardt, S. (Ed.). *Social networks: A developing paradigm.* New York: Academic Press, 1977.

Levau, I., Arnon, A., and Portnoy, A. Two shortened versions of the Cornell Medical Index: A new test of their validity. *International Journal of Psychosomatic Research,* 1977, *6,* 135–141.

Lief, A. (Ed.). *The commonsense psychiatry of Dr. Adolf Meyer: Fifty-two selected papers* (1st ed.). New York: McGraw Hill, 1948.

Liem, R., and Liem, J. H. Relations among social class, life events, and mental illness: A comment on findings and methods. In B. S. Dohrenwend and B. P. Dohrenwend (Eds.), *Stressful life events: Their nature and contexts.* New York: Prodist, 1980.

Lin, Nan. *Foundations of social research.* New York: McGraw Hill, 1976.

Lin, Nan. Social resources and instrumantal action. In P. Marsden and N. Lin (Eds.), *Social structure and network analysis* (pp. 131–146). Beverly Hills, CA: Sage, 1982.

Lin, Nan. Social resources and social actions: A progress report. *Connections,* 1983, 6(2), 10–16.

Lin, Nan. *Social ties and social resources: A theory of instrumental action.* Paper presented at the Seminar on Communication Theory from Eastern and Western Perspectives, the East West Communication Institute, Honolulu, Hawaii, December 1980.

Lin, Nan, Dayton, P., and Greenwald, P, Analyzing the instrumental use of social relations in the context of social structure. *Sociological Methods and Research,* 1978, *7,* 149–166.

Lin, Nan, and Dean, Alfred. Social support and depression: A panel study. *Social Psychiatry,* 1984, *19,* 83–91.

Lin, Nan, Dean, A., and Ensel, Walter M. Development of social support scales. *Proceedings of the Third Biennial Conference on Health Survey Methods* (pp. 201–211). Washington, DC: National Center for Health Services Research, 1981a.

Lin, Nan, Dean, A., and Ensel, Walter M. Social support scales: A methodological note. *Schizophrenia Bulletin,* 1981b, *7*(1), 73–90.

Lin, Nan, Dean, Alfred, and Ensel, Walter M. Support methodology from the sociological perspective. Schizophrenia Bulletin, 1981c, 7, 73–90.

Lin, Nan, Dean, Alfred, Ensel, Walter M., and Tausig, Mark. *Social support and depression in the age structure.* Paper presented at the 75th annual meeting of the American Sociological Association, New York, 1980.

Lin, Nan, and Dumin, Mary. *Access to occupational resources in ecological analysis.* Paper presented at the Tenth World Congress of Sociology, Mexico City, August 1982a.

Lin, Nan, and Dumin, Mary. *Access to occupations through social ties.* Paper presented at the American Sociological Association Meetings, San Francisco, 1982b.

Lin, Nan, and Ensel, Walter M. Causal interpretation of interaction effects. Reply to W. Thomas Boyce. *Journal of Health and Social Behavior*, 1981a, *22*, 2–4.

Lin, Nan, and Ensel, Walter M. Depression mobility and its social etiology: The role of life events and social support. *Journal of Health and Social Behavior*, 1984, *25*(2), 176–189.

Lin, Nan, and Ensel, Walter M. *Structural equation modelling of the social support, life events, and depression.* Paper presented at the Association for the Social Sciences in Health at the American Public Health Association, Los Angeles, November 1981b.

Lin, Nan, Ensel, Walter M., and Vaughn, J. C. Social resources and strength of ties: Structural factors in occupational status attainment. *American Sociological Review*, 1981, *46*(4), 393–405.

Lin, Nan, Light, S., and Woelfel, Mary. *The buffering effects of social support: A theoretical framework and an empirical investigation.* Paper presented at the National Conference on Social Stress Research, University of New Hampshire, October 1982.

Lin, Nan, Simeone, Ron, Ensel, Walter M., and Kuo, Wen. Social support, stressful life events, and illness: A model and an empirical test. *Journal of Health and Social Behavior*, 1979, *20*(1), 108–119.

Lin, Nan, Vaughn, John C., and Ensel, Walter M. Social resources and occupational status attainment. *Social Forces*, 1981, *59*, 1163–1181.

Linn, M. W., Hunter, K., and Harris, R. Symptoms of depression and recent life events in the community elderly. *Journal of Clinical Psychology*, 1980, *36*, 675–682.

Lipowski, Z. J. Psychiatry of somatic diseases: Epidemiology, pathogenesis, and classification. *Comprehensive Psychiatry*, 1975, *16*, 105–124.

Lips, H. M., and Colwill, N. L. *The psychology of sex differences.* New York: Prentice Hall, 1978.

Locke, B. Z., Eaton, W., Reigier, D. A., and Taube, C. A. *The epidemiologic catchment area program of the National Institute of Mental Health.* Paper presented at the Third National Conference of Need Assessment in Health and Human Service Systems, University of Louisville, Kentucky, 1981.

Lowenthal, M. F., and Haven, C. Interaction and adaptation: Intimacy as a critical variable. *American Sociological Review*, 1968, *33*, 20–30.

Markush, R. E., and Favero, R. V. Epidemiologic assessment of stressful life events, depressed mood, and psycho-physiological symptoms: A preliminary report. In B. S. Dohrenwend and B. P. Dohrenwend (Eds.), *Stressful life events: Their nature and effects* (pp. 171–190). New York: John Wiley, 1974.

Marsden, P. V., and Lin, Nan. (Eds.). *Social structure and network analysis.* Beverly Hills, CA: Sage, 1982.

Marshall, J. R., Funch, D. P., and Feather, J. N. *The temporal distribution of the effects of stress on mental health.* Paper presented at the National Conference on Social Stress Research, University of New Hampshire, Durham, October 1982.

Maslow, A. H. *Motivation and personality.* New York: Harper, 1954.

Masuda, M., and Holmes, T. H. Magnitude estimations of social readjustments. *Journal of Psychosomatic Research*, 1967, *11*, 219–225.

McClelland, D. *The achieving society.* New York: Free Press, 1964.

McFarlane, A. H., Norman, G. R., Streiner, D. L., and Roy, R. G. The process of social stress: Stable, reciprocal and mediating relationships. *Journal of Health and Social Behavior*, 1983, *24*, 160–173.

McGuire, W. J., and Padawer–Singer, A. Trait salience in the spontaneous self-concept. *Journal of Personality and Social Psychology*, 1976, *33*, 743–754.

McKinlay, J. B. Social networks, lay consultation, and help seeking behavior. *Social Forces*, 1973, *51*, 275–292.

McLanahan, S. S., Wedemeyer, N. V., and Adelberg, T. Network structure, social support, and psychological well-being in the single-parent family. *Journal of Marriage and the Family*, 1981, *3*, 601–612.

Marsden, P., and Campbell, K. E. Measuring tie strength, *Social Forces*, 1984, *63*, 482–501.

Mead, G. H. *Mind, self, and society*. Chicago: University of Chicago Press, 1934.

Medalie, J. H., and Goldbourt, U. Angina pectoris among 10,000 men. II: Psychosocial and other risk factors as evidenced by a multivariate analysis of a five-year incidence study. *American Journal of Medicine*, 1976, *60*, 910–921.

Meile, R., Johnson, D., and St. Peter, L. Marital role, education, and mental disorder among women: Test of an interaction hypothesis. *Journal of Health and Social Behavior*, 1976, *7*, 279–305.

Mitchell, J. C. The concept and use of social networks. In J. C. Mitchell (Ed.), *Social networks in urban situations*. Manchester, UK: Manchester University Press, 1969.

Moreno, J. L. *Who shall survive?* Washington, DC: Nervous and Mental Disease Publishing Company, 1934.

Moriwaki, S. Y. Self disclosure, signficant others, and psychological well-being in old age. *Journal of Health and Social Behavior*, 1973, 14(3), 226–232.

Morrison, J. R., Hudgens, R. W., and Barcha, R. G. Life events and psychiatric illness: A study of 100 patients and 100 controls. *British Journal of Psychiatry*, 1968, *114*, 423–432.

Mueller, C. W., and Hohnson, W. T. Socioeconomic status and religious participation. *American Sociological Review*, 1976, *40*, 785–800.

Mueller, D. P. Social networks: A promising direction for research on the relationship of social environment to psychiatric disorder. *Social Science and Medicine*, 1980, *14a*, 147–161.

Mueller, D. P., Edwards, D. W., and Yarvis, R. M. Stressful life events and psychiatric symptomatology: Change or undesirability? *Journal of Health and Social Behavior*, 1977, *18*, 307–317.

Murphy, G. *Personality*. New York: Harper, 1947.

Mutran, E., and Reitzes, D. C. Retirement, identity, and well-being: Realignment of role relationships. *Journal of Gerontology*, 1981, 36(6), 733–740.

Myers, J. K., and associates. *The prevalence of psychiatric disorders (DSM III): Report from the epidemiological catchment area studies*. Paper presented at the annual meeting of the American Public Health Association, Montreal, 1982.

Myers, J. K., Lindenthal, J. J., and Pepper, M. P. Life events and psychiatric impairment. *Journal of Nervous and Mental Disease*, 1971, *152*, 149–157.

Myers, J. K., Lindenthal, J. J., and Pepper, M. P. Life events, social integration, and psychiatric symptomatology. *Journal of Health and Social Behavior*, 1975, *16*, 421–429.

Myers, J. K., Lindenthal, J., and Pepper, M. Social class, life events, and psychiatric symptoms: A longitudinal study. In B. S. Dohrenwend and B. P. Dohrenwend (Eds.), *Stressful life events: Their nature and effects* (pp. 191–205). New York: John Wiley, 1974.

Myers, J. K., and Pepper, M. P. Life events and mental status: A longitudinal study. *Journal of Health and Social Behavior*, 1972, *13*, 398–406.

Myers, J. K., and Weissman, M. M. Use of a self-report symptoms scale to detect depression in a community sample. *American Journal of Psychiatry*, 1980, *137*(9), 1081–1084.

Myers, J. K., Weissman, M., and Thompson, D. *Screening for depression in a community sample: The use of a symptom scale to detect the depressive syndrome.* Paper presented at the annual meetings of the Society for Epidemiological Research, Yale University, 1979.

National Center for Health Statistics. *Basic data on depressive symptomatology, United States, 1974–1975.* (Vital and Health Statistics Series 11, No. 26, DHEW Publication No. PHS 80–1666). Hyattsville, MD: Author, 1980.

Nelson, Joel. Clique contact and family orientations. *American Sociological Review,* 1966, *31*, 663–672.

Nuckolls, C. G., Cassel, J., and Kaplan, B. H. Psycho-social assets, life crises and the prognosis of pregnancy. *American Journal of Epidemiology,* 1972, *95*, 431–441.

Oakley, A. *Subject women.* New York: Pantheon Books, 1981.

Ostrow, E. Review of 'The self-concept. Vol. 2: Theory and research on selected topics,' revised edition, by Ruth C. Wylie. *American Journal of Sociology*, 1982, *87*, 1443–1446.

Parsons, T., and Bales, R. F. *Family socialization and interaction process.* Glencoe, IL: Free Press, 1955.

Paykel, E. S. Life stress and psychiatric disorder: Applications of the clinical approach. In B. S. Dohrenwend and B. P. Dohrenwend (Eds.), *Stressful life events: Their nature and effects* (pp. 135–149). New York: John Wiley, 1974.

Paykel, E. S., and Dienelt, M. N. Suicide attempts following acute depression. *Journal of Nervous and Mental Disease*, 1971, *153*, 234–243.

Paykel, E. S., Myers, J. K., Dienelt, M. N., et al. Life events and depression. *Archives of General Psychiatry*, 1969, *21*, 753–760.

Paykel, E. S., Prusoff, B. A., and Tanner, J. Temporal stability of symptom patterns in depression. *British Journal of Psychiatry*, 1976, *128*, 369–374.

Pearlin, L. Sex roles and depression. In *Life span developmental psychology: Normative life crisis.* New York: Academic Press, 1974.

Pearlin, L. I. Social structure and social supports. In Sheldon Cohen and Leonard Syme (Eds.), *Social support and health.* New York: Academic Press, 1984.

Pearlin, L., and Johnson, J. S. Marital status, life strains, and depression. *American Sociological Review,* 1977, *42*, 704–715.

Pearlin, L. I., and Lieberman, M. A. Social sources of emotional distress. In Roberta Simmons (Ed.), *Research in community and mental health, Vol. 1* (pp. 217–248). Greenwich, CT: JAI Press, 1979.

Pearlin, L. I., Lieberman, M. A.,., Menaghan, E. G., and Mullan, J. T. The stress process. *Journal of Health and Social Behavior,* 1981, *22*, 337–356.

Pearlin, L. I., and Schooler, C. The structure of coping. *Journal of Health and Social Behavior,* 1978, *19*(1), 2–21.

Phares, E. J. *Locus of control in personality.* Morristown, NJ: General Learning, 1976.

Phillips, D. L., and Segal, B. F. Sexual status and psychiatric symptoms. *American Sociological Review,* 1969, *34*, 56–72.

Pinneau, S. R. *Effects of social support on occupational stresses and strains.* Paper presented at the meeting of the American Psychological Association, Washington, DC, 1976.

Pinneau, S. R. *Effects of social support on psychological and physiological stress.* Unpublished doctoral dissertation, University of Michigan, Ann Arbor, 1975.

Pugh, W. M., Erickson, J., Rubin, R. T., Gunderson, E. K., and Rahe, R. H. Cluster analyses of life changes. *Archives of General Psychiatry*, 1971, *25*, 333–339.

Rabkin, J. G., and Struening, E. L. Life events, stress, and illness. *Science*, 1976, *194*, 1013–1020.

Radloff, L. S. The CES-D scale: A self-report depression scale for research in the general population. *Applied Psychological Measurement*, 1977, *1*, 385–401.

Radloff, L. S. Sex differences in depression: The effects of occupation and marital status. *Sex Roles*, 1975, *1*(3), 249–265.

Radloff, L. S., and Rae, D. S. Components of the sex differences in depression. In R. G. Simmons (Ed.), *Research in Community and Mental Health* (pp. 111–138). CT: JAI Press, 1981.

Radloff, L. S., and Rae, D. S. Susceptibility and precipitating factors in depression: Sex differences and similarities. *Journal of Abnormal Psychology*, 1979, *88*, 174–181.

Rahe, R. H. *Update to life change research.* Unpublished manuscript, 1975.

Raho, R. H., Pugh, W., Erickson, J., Gunderson, E., and Rubin, R. T. Cluster analyses of life changes. *Archives of General Psychiatry*, 1971, *25*, 330–332.

Raskin, A., Chulterbrandt, J. S., Reating, N., and McKeon, J. Replication of factors in psychopathology in interview, ward behavior and self report ratings of hospital depressives. *Journal of Nervous and Mental Disease*, 1970, *198*, 87–96.

Regier, D. A., et al. *The NIMH epidemiological catchment area (ECA) program: Historical context, major objectives, and study population characteristics.* Paper presented at the annual meeting of the American Public Health Association, Montreal, 1982.

Roberts, Robert E., and O'Keefe, S. J. Sex differences in depression re-examined. *Journal of Health and Social Behavior*, 1981, *22*(4), 394–399.

Roberts, R. E., and Vernon, S. W. The Center for Epidemiological Studies Depression Scale: Its use in a community sample. *American Journal of Psychiatry*, 1983, *140*(1), 41–46.

Robins, L. N., Helzer, J. E., Croughan, J., and Ratcliff, K. S. National Institute of Mental Health Diagnostic Interview Schedule. *Archives of General Psychiatry*, 1981, *38*, 381–389.

Robins, L. N., Helzer, J. E., Croughan, J., and Ratcliff, K. S. The NIMH Diagnostic Interview Schedule: Its history, characteristics, and validity. In J. K. Wing, P. Bebbington, and L. N. Robins (Eds.), *The concept of a case: Theory and method in community psychiatric surveys.* London: Grant McIntyre, 1980.

Robinson, J. P., Rusk, J. G., and Head, K. B. Measures of political attitudes, In *Measures of social psychological attitudes* (pp. 649–660). Ann Arbor, MI: Survey Research Center, Institute for Social Research, 1968.

Robinson, J. P., and Shaver, P. R. (Eds.), *Measures of social psychological attitudes.* Ann Arbor, MI: Institute for Social Research, 1975.

Rogers, C. R. *On becoming a person.* Boston: Houghton Mifflin, 1961.

Rogers, E. M., and Kincaid, D. L. *Communication networks: Toward a new paradigm for research.* New York: Free Press, 1981.

Rosen, B., Goldsmith, H. F., and Redick, R. W. Demographic and social indicators: Uses in mental health planning in small areas. *World Health Statistics Quarterly Report*, *32*(1), Geneva: World Health Organization, 1979.

Rosenberg, M. *Society and the adolescent self-image.* Princeton, NJ: Princeton University Press, 1965.

Rosenfield, S. Sex differences in depression: Do women always have higher rates? *Journal of Health and Social Behavior*, 1980, *21*, 33–43.

Rosenfield, S. Sex roles and societal reaction to mental illness: The labelling of 'deviant' deviance. *Journal of Health and Social Behavior*, 1982, *73*, 18–24.

Rosenthal, R., Archer, D., DiMatteo, M., Kowumaki, J. H., and Rogers, P. O. Body talk and tone of voice: The language without words. *Psychology Today*, 1974, *8*, 64–68.

Ross, C., and Mirowsky, J. A comparison of life event weighting schemes: Change, undesirability, and effect-proportional indices. *Journal of Health and Social Behavior*, 1979, *20*, 166–177.

Ross, C. E., and Mirowsky, J. Components of depressed mood in married men and women. *American Journal of Epidemiology*, 1984, *119*, 997–1004.

Rossi, P. H., Sampson, W. A., and Boss, C. E. Measuring household social standing. *Social Science Research*, 1974, *3*, 169–190.

Rotter, J. Generalized expectancies for internal versus external control of reinforcement, *Psychological Monographs*, 1966, *80*(1), Whole #609, 1–28.

Ruch, L. O. A multidimensional analysis of the concept of life change. *Journal of Health and Social Behavior*, 1977, *18*, 71–83.

Ruch, L. O., and Holmes, T. H. Scaling of life change. Comparison of direct and indirect methods. *Journal of Psychosomatic Research*, 1971, *15*, 221–227.

Sarason, I. G., Levine, H. M., Basham, R. B., and Sarason, B. R. Assessing social support: The social support questionnaire. *Journal of Personality and Social Psychology*, 1983, 44(1), 127–139.

Sarason, I. B., Smith, R. E., and Deiner, E. Personality research: Components of variance attributable to the person and the situation. *Journal of Personality and Social Psychology*, 1975, *32*, 199–204.

Schaefer, C., Coyne, J. C., and Lazarus, R. S. The health-related functions of social support. *Journal of Behavioral Medicine*, 1981, *4*, 381–406.

Schroenbach, V. J., Kaplan, B. H., Grimson, R. C. et al. Use of a symptom scale to study the prevalence of a depressive syndrome in young adolescents. *American Journal of Epidemiology*, 1982, *116*, 791–800.

Schwab, J. J., and Schwab, M. E. *Sociocultural roots of mental illness: An epidemiological survey.* New York: Plenum Press, 1978.

Schweder, R. A. How relevant is an individual difference theory of personality? *Journal of Personality*, 1975, *43*, 455–484.

Seeman, M., and Seeman, T. E. Health behavior and personal autonomy: A longitudinal study of the sense of control in illness. *Journal of Health and Social Behavior*, 1983, *24*, 144–160.

Seligman, M. E. P. *Helplessness.* San Francisco: W. H. Freeman, 1975.

Selye, Hans. History and present status of the stress concept. In L. Goldberger and S. Breznitz (Eds.), *Handbook of stress: Theoretical and clinical aspects* (pp. 7–17). New York: Free Press, 1982.

Selye, H. *The stress of life.* New York: McGraw Hill, 1956.

Seymour, G. E. The structure and predictive ability of the Cornell Medical Index for a normal sample. *Journal of Psychosomatic Research*, 1976, *20*, 469–478.

Sheperd, M., Cooper, B., and Brown, A. C. *Psychiatric illness in general practice.* London: Oxford University Press.

Shields, S. Functionalism, Darwinism, and the psychology of women: A study in social myth. *American Psychologist*, 1975, *30*, 39–54.

Shils, E. A., and Janowitz, M. Primary groups in the German army (abridged and adapted from 'Cohesion and disintegration in the Wehrmacht in World War II,' *Public Opinion Quarterly*, 1948). In L. Broom and P. Selznick (Eds.), *Sociology* (5th ed.). New York: Harper and Row, 1955.

Shryock, H. S., Siegel, J. S., and associates. *The methods and materials of demography.* (U.S. Census Bureau, condensed edition by Edward G. Stockwell). New York: Academic Press, 1971.

Siegel, P. *Prestige in the American occupation structure.* Unpublished doctoral dissertation, University of Chicago, 1971.

Skinner, H. A., and Lei, H. The multi-dimensional assessment of stressful life events. *The Journal of Nervous and Mental Disease,* 1980, *168,* 535–541.

Skolnick, A., and Skolnick, J. H. *Intimacy, family, and society.* Boston: Little, Brown, 1974.

Smith, K. W., and Sasaki, M. S. Decreasing multicollinearity: A method for models with multiplicative functions. *Sociological Methods and Research,* 1979, 8(1), 35–56.

Srole, L. Measurements and classifications in socio-psychiatric epidemiology: Midtown Manhattan Study I (1954) and Midtown Manhattan Restudy II (1974). *Journal of Health and Social Behavior,* 1975, 16, 347 364.

Srole, L. Social integration and certain corollaries. *American Sociological Review,* 1956, 21, 709–716.

Srole, L., Langner, T. S., Michael, S. T., et al., *The Midtown Manhattan Study.* New York: McGraw Hill, 1962.

Steele, R. Relationship of race, sex, social class, and social mobility to depression in normal adults. *Journal of Social Psychology,* 1978, 104, 37–47.

Stein, P. J. A developmental exploration of friendship functions in women. *Psychology of Women Quarterly,* 1981, 5(3), 456–472.

Stochard, J., and Johnson, M. M. *Sex roles, sex inequality and sex role development.* New York: Prentice Hall, 1980.

Stroebe, M. S. and Stroebe, W. Who suffers more? Sex differences in health risks of the widowed. *Psychological Bulletin,* 1983, 93, 279–301.

Sullivan, H. S. *Conceptions of modern psychiatry: The first William Alanson White memorial lectures.* Washington, DC: The William Alanson White Psychiatric Foundation, 1947.

Swank, R. L. Combat exhaustion. *Journal of Nervous and Mental Disease,* 1949, 109, 475–508.

Tausig Mark. Measuring life events. *Journal of Health and Social Behavior,* 1982, 23, 52 64.

Tennant, C., and Andrews, G. The pathogenic quality of life event stress in neurotic impairment. *Archives of General Psychiatry,* 1978, 35, 859–863.

Theorell, T., and Rahe, R. H. Life change events, ballistocardiography, and coronary death. *Journal of Human Stress,* 1975, 1, 18–24.

Thoits, P. A. Conceptual, methodological and theoretical problems in studying social support as a buffer against life stress. *Journal of Health and Social Behavior,* 1982, 23, 145–159.

Thoits, P. A. Undesirable life events and psychophysiological distress: A problem of operational confounding. *American Sociological Review,* 1981, 46(1), 97–109.

Titmuss, R. M. Problems of Social Policy. His Majesty's Stationery Office, London, 1950. Quoted by E. W. Bovard in 'The effects of social stimuli on the response to stress.' *Psychological Review,* 1959, 66, 267–277.

Turner, R. J. Social support as a contingency in psychological well-being. *Journal of Health and Social Behavior,* 1981, 22, 357–367.

Turner, R. J., and Noh, S. Class and psychological vulnerability among women: The significance of social support and personal control. *Journal of Health and Social Behavior,* 1983, 24, 2–15.

U.S. Bureau of the Census. *1970 Census of Population: Alphabetical index of industries and occupations* (366 pp.). Washington, DC: U.S. Government Printing Office, 1971.

Vanfossen, B. E. Sex differences in the mental health effects of spouse support and equity. *Journal of Health and Social Behavior*, 1981, *72*(2), 130–143.

Verbrugge, L. Female illness rates and illness behavior: Testing hypotheses about sex differences in health. *Women and Health*, 1979, *4*(1), 61–79.

Verbrugge, L. Sex differentials in health and mortality. In A. H. Stromberg (Ed.), *Women, Health, and Medicine*, Palo Alto, CA: Mayfield, 1981.

Vinokur, A., and Selzer, M. L. Desirable versus undesirable life events: Their relationship to stress and mental disease. *Journal of Personality and Social Psychology*, 1975, *32*(2), 329–339.

Wan, T. *Stressful life events, social support networks, and gerontological health.* Lexington, MA: Lexington Books, 1982.

Warheit, G. J., Holzer, C. E., Bell, R. A., and Arey, S. A. Sex, marital status, and mental health: A reappraisal. *Social Forces*, 1976, *55*, 459–470.

Warheit, G. J., Holzer, C. E., and Schwab, J. J. An analysis of social class and racial differences in depressive symptomatology: A community study. *Journal of Health and Social Behaviors*, 1978, *14*, 291–299.

Warheit, G. J., Vega, W., Shimizu, D., and Meinhardt, K. Interpersonal coping networks and mental health problems among four race–ethnic groups. *Journal of Community Psychology*, 1982, *10*, 293–311.

Weiss, R. The contributions of an organization of single parents to the well-being of its members. *The Family Coordinator*, 1973, *2*, 321–326.

Weiss, R. S. The provisions of social relations. In Z. Ruben (Ed.), *Doing unto others.* Englewood Cliffs, NJ: Prentice Hall, 1974.

Weissman, M. M., and Klerman, G. L. Sex differences and the epidemiology of depression. *Archives of General Psychiatry*, 1977, *34*, 93–111.

Weissman, M. M., and Locke, B. Z. Comparison of a self report symptom rating scale (CES-D) with standardized depression rating scales in psychiatric populations. *American Journal of Epidemiology*, 1975, *102*, 430–441.

Weissman, M. M., and Myers, J. K. Affective disorders in a U.S. Community: The use of research diagnostic criteria in an epidemiological survey. *Archives of General Psychiatry*, 1978, *35*, 1304–1311.

Weissman, M. M., Myers, J. K., and Harding, P. S. Psychiatric disorders in a U.S. urban community: 1975–1976. *American Journal of Psychiatry*, 1978, *135*, 4.

Weissman, M. M., Prusoff, B., and Newberry, P. *Comparison of the CES-D with standardized depression rating scales at three points in time.* (Tech. Rep., Yale University, Combrad ASH 74–1666). Washington, DC: NIMH, 1975.

Weissman, M. M., Scholomskes, P. S., Pollenger, M., Prusoff, R., and Locke, B. Z. Assessing depressive symptoms in five psychiatric populations: A validation study. *American Journal of Epidemiology*, 1977, *106*, 203–214.

Welch, S., and Booth, A. Employment and health among married women. *Sex Roles*, 1977, *3*, 385–397.

Wellman, B. Applying network analysis to the study of support. In B. H. Gottlieb (Ed.), *Social networks and social support.* Beverly Hills, CA: Sage, 1981.

Wheaton, B. *Models for the stress-buffering functions of coping resources.* Paper presented at the annual meeting of the American Sociological Association, Detroit, 1983a.

Wheaton, B. Stress, personal coping resources, and psychiatric symptoms: An investigation of interactive models. *Journal of Health and Social Behavior*, 1983b, *24*, 208–229.

Wheaton, B., Muthen, B., Alwin, D. F., and Summers, G. F. Assessing reliability and stability in panel models. In D. R. Heise (Ed.), *Sociological Methodology* (pp. 84–136). San Francisco: Jossey–Bass, 1977.

Wilcox, B. L. Social support in adjusting to marital disruption: A network analysis. In B. H. Gottlieb (Ed.), *Social networks and social support*. Beverly Hills, CA: Sage, 1981a.

Wilcox, B. L. Social support, life stress and psychological adjustment: A test of the buffering hypothesis. *American Journal of Community Psychology*, 1981b, *9*, 371–386.

Williams, A. W., Ware, J. E., and Donald, C. A. A model of mental health, life events, and social supports applicable to general populations. *Journal of Health and Social Behavior*, 1981, *22*(4), 324–336.

Wolfe, A. W. Stress, social support, and schizophrenia: A discussion. *Schizophrenia*, 1981, *7*(1), 178–180.

Zegans, L. S. Stress and the development of somatic disorders. In L. Goldberger and S. Breznitz (Eds.), *Handbook of stress: Theoretical and clinical aspects*. (pp. 134–152). New York: Free Press, 1982.

Zelditch, M., Jr. Role differences in the nuclear family. In T. Parsons and R. F. Bales (Eds.), *Family socialization and interaction process* (pp. 307–351). Glencoe, IL: Free Press, 1955.

Zung, W. W. K. A self rating depression scale. *Archives of General Psychiatry*, 1965, *12*, 63–70.

Author Index

Numbers in italics refer to pages on which complete references are found.

A

Abramson, J. H., 272, *343*
Adcock, S., 24, 307, *350*
Adelberg, T., 287, 288, *354*
Adler, A., 102, *343*
Allport, G. W., 102, *343*
Almquist, E., 290, *343*
Alwin, D. F., 98, 141, 145, *343, 360*
Andrews, G., 23, 25, 183, 184, 186, 268,
    307, *343, 359*
Aneshensel, C. S., 13, 53, 56, 182, 183,
    184, 186, 232, *343, 348*
Antonucci, T., 23, 24, *352*
Archer, D., 289, *357*
Arey, S. A., 233, *360*
Arnon, A., 272, *353*
Ashehasy, A., 73, 75, 86, *347*
Asher, S. S., 234, 235, *344*
Atchley, R. C., 227, *343*

B

Bachrach, L. L., 286, *343*

Back, K. W., 348
Backstron, C. II., 35, *343*
Bales, R. F., 288, *356*
Barcha, R. G., 74, *355*
Bardwick, J. M., 290, *343*
Barrera, M., Jr., 21, 25, 148, 183, 184, *344*
Barresi, C. M., 224, *348*
Barron, F., 103, *344*
Basham, R. B., 23, 27, 185, *358*
Beck, A. T., 53, 103, *344*
Bell, R. A., 183, 184, 186, 283, 289, *344,
    360*
Bell, R. P., 289, *344*
Belle, D., 232, 286, *344, 350*
Bengston, V. L., 227, *344*
Berkman, L. F., 11, 18, 155, 185, *344*
Berkowitz, S. D., 159, *344*
Bernard, H. R., 153, *344*
Bernard, J., *344*
Berstein, A., 285, *345*
Bhrolchain, M. N., 22, 24, 29, 183, 286,
    287, 307, *345*
Bieliauskas, L. A., 269, 274, *344*

363

Subject Index

A

Agencies, community, 159
Age structure and stress process
  category construction, 216–221
  depression and, 215–216
  discussion, 13, 213–215, 224–230
  future research, 337
  life events and, 221–223, 225–226
  older age groupings in, 224–225
  social support and, 221–223, 225–226
Alarm reaction to stress, 5
Albany Area Health Survey
  demographic characteristics, 31–32,
    38–39
  design, 33
  geographic characteristics, 31
  interview schedules
    additions, 40–44
    deletions, 40–44
    respondent attitudes, 44–45
    variables, 39–40
  pretest
    assessments, 34
    characteristics, 33–34
    purposes, 33

  sampling design
    characteristics, 36–38
    data waves, 35–36
      comparisons, 36, 39
    drawing, 34–35
    staff, interview, 33, 47
    summary, 47–48

B

Buffering model of social support
  design, 310–311
  discussion, 13, 307–308, 325–332
  elements, 308–310
  hypotheses, 311–313
  life event, most important, and, 315–
    317
  measures, 313–315
  strong ties and
    homophily, 323–325, 331
    interactions, 323
    marital status, 319–323, 327–329,
      331
    role relationship, 317–318
Bureau of the Census Index of Occupa-
    tions, 254

371